THE OMAHA TRIBE

Volume II

VOLUME II

ALICE C. FLETCHER
AND
FRANCIS LA FLESCHE

UNIVERSITY OF NEBRASKA PRESS • LINCOLN AND LONDON

Manufactured in the United States of America

First printing of this Bison Book edition: 1992

Library of Congress Cataloging-in-Publication Data
Fletcher, Alice C. (Alice Cunningham), 1838–1923.
The Omaha tribe / Alice C. Fletcher and Francis La Flesche; introduction by Robin Ridington.—Bison book ed.
p. cm.
"A Bison book."
Includes bibliographical references and index.
ISBN 0-8032-6876-9 (v. 1).—ISBN 0-8032-6877-7 (v. 2).—
ISBN 0-8032-6878-5 (set)
1. Omaha Indians. I. La Flesche, Francis, d. 1932. II. Title.
E99.04F64 1992 91-42657
973′.04975—dc20 CIP

This Bison Book edition is reproduced from the Twenty-Seventh Annual Report of the Bureau of American Ethnology to the Secretary of the Smithsonian Institution, 1905–1906 (Washington: Government Printing Office, 1911).

CONTENTS

Page

VIII

Social life 313
  Kinship terms 313
  Courtship and marriage 318
  Care and training of children 327
  Etiquette 334
  Avocations of men 338
  Avocations of women 339
    Cooking and foods 340
    Dressing and tanning skins 342
    Quill work 345
    Weaving 347
  Personal adornment 349
  Clothing 354
    The wai^{n}′ or robe 356
      Personal significance 356
      Social significance 358
      Language of the robe 360
  Property 362
  Amusements 363

IX

Music 371
  Instruments 371
  Songs, singing, and rhythm 373
  The Wa′wa^{n} ceremony 376
    The ceremony among the Ponca 400

X

Warfare 402
  Influence on tribal development 402
    Wai^{n}′waxube 404
    Authorization of a war party 405
    Organization of a war party 408
    Dress of warriors 409

Warfare—Continued
Influence on tribal development—Continued | Page
Sacred War Pack and contents 411
Departure ceremonies of an aggressive war party 415
The we'to^n waa^n 421
Sending out scouts 423
Departure of a defensive war party 426
Return of a war party 431
The Wate'giçtu 434
Graded war honors 437
War honor decorations 438
The Ponca ceremony of conferring war honors 439
"The Crow" 441
The feather war bonnet 446
Weapons 448
Contents of the Tent of War 452
The Sacred Shell 454
The Cedar Pole 457

XI

Societies 459
Social societies 459
The Hethu'shka 459
The Pu'gtho^n 481
The Ki'kunethe 485
The T'e ga'xe 486
The Mo^{n}wa'dathi^n and the Toka'lo 486
Secret societies 486
The Mo^{n}chu' ithaethe 486
The Te' ithaethe 487
The Wano^n'xe ithaethe 489
The I^{n}gthu^n' ithaethe 490
The Ho^n'hewachi 493
The one hundred wathi^n'ethe 495
The Watha'wa (Feast of the Count) 497
The Feast of the Ho^n'hewachi 500
The tattooing 503
The Washis'ka athin (Shell society) 509
Origin 509
Organization 516
Regular meetings 520
Ceremonies on the death of a member 553
Magic ceremony for punishing offenders 554
The I^n'kugthi athi^n (Pebble society) 565
Opening ritual 568
Ritual for sweat lodge, No. 1 571
Ritual for sweat lodge, No. 2 574
Ritual for sweat lodge, No. 3 575

XII

Disease and its treatment 582
Some curative plants 584

XIII

Death and burial customs 588

CONTENTS

XIV

Page

Religion and ethics 595
- The keeper 595
- We'waçpe 596
- Wako^{n}'da 597
- Interrelation of men and animals 599
- Veneration for the Ancients 601
- Position of chiefs 601
- Totems 602
- Magic 602
- Warfare and ethics 602
- Terms for good traits and conduct 603
- Terms for bad traits and conduct 604
- Proverbs 604

XV

Language 605

XVI

Conclusions 608

APPENDIX: Recent history of the Omaha tribe 611
- Contact with the white race 611
- Early traders 612
  - Introduction of metal implements 613
  - Decline of old avocations and the effect on the people 614
  - Changes in ornaments and decoration 615
  - Introduction of cloth 616
  - Introduction of guns 617
  - Introduction of money; pelt values 617
  - Introduction of intoxicants 618
    - Drunkenness and its punishment 618
  - Government control of traders 619
- Introduction of new foods, games, and diseases 620
- Introduction of new words 620
- Treaties with the United States 622
- Work of missionaries 625
  - The Mission 627
- New reservation and agency 629
  - Agency buildings 630
- Pressure of traders on tribal affairs 630
- Joseph La Flesche 631
  - "The village of the 'make-believe' white men" 633
- Survey of the reservation 634
- Extermination of the buffalo 634
- Establishment of "the Council" 635
- The Ponca tragedy 635
- Appeal for land patents 636
- Present condition 641

PHONETIC GUIDE

All vowels have the continental values.

Superior *n* (^{n}) gives a nasal modification to the vowel immediately preceding.

x represents the rough sound of *h* in the German *hoch*.

th has the sound of *th* in *the*.

ç has the sound of *th* in *thin*.

Every syllable ends in a vowel or in nasal *n* (^{n}).

VIII

SOCIAL LIFE

Kinship Terms

Kinship terms played an important part in all social intercourse. They not only designated the actual relationship between persons but the custom of never addressing anyone—man, woman, or child—by his personal name or of using a person's name when speaking of him, if he chanced to be present, made the use of kinship terms a practical necessity. These terms were also applied to what may be called potential relationships, that is, relationships that would be established through marriage made in accordance with tribal custom. If the wife had sisters, these women held a potential relationship to her husband, as they might become his wives either during his wife's lifetime or at her death. According to tribal usage a man had the potential right to marry his wife's sisters and also her nieces and her aunts. On the other hand, a man was under obligation to marry his brother's widow. Should he fail in this respect, he was liable to suffer in person or property, either by the act of the woman herself or by that of her near of kin, in order to force him to recognize or make good her rights. Because of these potential relationships the children of the wife called all those whom their father might marry "mother" and all their father's brothers "father." Moreover, all the children of such relationships called one another "brother" and "sister." There was no cousinship. All the brothers of the mother were called "uncle" by her children, and the father's sisters were called "aunt."

The regulation of marriage implied in these potential relationships was explained to be for the purpose of "holding the family intact, for should the children be bereft of their own mother they would come under the care of her close kindred and not fall into the hands of a stranger." This interpretation seems borne out by the approval still expressed when a woman weds the brother of her late husband or a man marries the sister of his dead wife or the widow of his brother; even when there is a marked disparity in the ages of the parties, it is said, "The marriage does not make a break in the family and it shows respect for the dead." The interweaving of actual and potential relationships greatly extended the family connection and supplied the proper terms for familiar and ceremonial address. Mention is made of the custom of speaking of the women of the tribe as "sisters" (p. 474). At meetings of the Council of Seven duty to the tribe was ceremonially recognized by a formal mention of kinship terms between the members. The same practice obtained in several of the societies within the tribe.

In the Omaha language the term for relationship, or the accent on the word, was varied according to the sex of the speaker and according to his or her relation to the person spoken of, as (1) when a father or mother was spoken to by a son, (2) when addressed by a daughter, (3) when spoken of by a male relative, (4) when spoken of by a female relative, and (5) when spoken of by a person not a relative.

The following table sets forth these distinctions:[a]

[a] The first-born male child was called I^{n}gtho^n; the first-born female, Wihi. Both these names are old and untranslatable terms; they were strictly "baby names" and were "thrown away" at the ceremony of Turning the Child and bestowal of the *ni'kie* name (pp. 117, 136). There were no other special "baby names" in use among the Omaha.

Omaha terms of relationship

	Spoken of by one not related	Spoken of by son or daughter		Spoken to by son or daughter	
1. Father	Itha'di	I^{n}da'di		Dadi'ha (m.), Da'diha (f.)	
2. Mother	Iho^{n}'	I^{n}'no^{n}ha		No^{n}how' (m.), No^{n}ha' (f.)	
3. Grandfather	Iti'go^{n}	Witi'go^{n}		Tigo^{n}'ha (m.), Ti'go^{n}ha (f.)	
4. Father-in-law	Iti'go^{n}	Witi'go^{n}		Tigo^{n}'ha (m.), Ti'go^{n}ha (f.)	
5. Grandmother	Iko^{n}'	Wiko^{n}'		Ko^{n}how' (m.), Ko^{n}ha' (f.)	
6. Mother-in-law	Iko^{n}'	Wiko^{n}'		Ko^{n}how' (m.), Ko^{n}ha' (f.)	
		Spoken of by nephew or niece		Spoken to by nephew or niece	
7. Uncle (mother's brother)	Ine'gi	Wine'gi		Negi'ha (m.), Negiha (f.)	
8. Uncle (father's brother)	No such uncle among the Omaha, the father's brother being the same as the father				
9. Uncle by marriage	No such uncle				
10. Uncle (direct descendant of mother's brother)	The son, grandson, and great-grandson of uncle no. 7 are uncle to all the children who address aunt no. 11 as "mother"				
11. Aunt (father's sister)	Iti'mi	Witi'mi		Timi'ha (m.)	
12. Aunt (uncle's wife)	Iti'mi	Witi'mi		Timiha' (f.)	
		Spoken of by		Spoken to by	
		Uncle	Aunt	Uncle	Aunt
13. Nephew (as spoken of in relation to his uncle)	Ito^{n}'shka	Wito^{n}'shka	Witu'shka	To^{n}shka'ha	Wi'tushkeha
14. Nephew (as spoken of in relation to his aunt)	Itu'shka				
15. Niece (as spoken of in relation to her uncle)	Iti'zhu^{n}	Witi'zhu^{n}	Witu'zhu^{n}ge	Tizho^{n}'ha	Wituzhu^{n}geha
16. Niece (as spoken of in relation to her aunt)	Itu'zhu^{n}ge				

Omaha terms of relationship—Continued

	Spoken of by one not related	Spoken of by		Spoken to by	
		Father	Mother	Father	Mother
17. Son	Izhi^{n}′ge	Wini′çi	Wizhi^{n}′ge	Niçi′ha	Wi′zhi^{n}geha
18. Daughter	Izhu^{n}′ge	Wini′çi	Wizhu^{n}′ge	Niçi′ha	Wi′zhu^{n}geha
		Grandfather	Grandmother	Grandfather	Grandmother
19. Grandson	Itu′shpa	Witu′shpa	Witu′shpa	Tushpa′ha	Tu′shpaha
20. Grandaughter	Itu′shpa	Witu′shpa	Witu′shpa	Tushpa′ha	Tu′shpaha
		Younger brother	Younger sister	Younger brother	Younger sister
21. Brother, elder (as spoken of in relation to his younger brother or brothers)	Izhi^{n}′the	Wizhi^{n}′the	Witi′nu	Zhi^{n}the′ha	Tinuha′
22. Brother, elder (as spoken of in relation to his younger sister or sisters)	Iti′nu				
		Elder brother	Elder sister	Elder brother	Elder sister
23. Brother, younger (as spoken of in relation to his elder brother or brothers)	Içu^{n}′ga	Kage′	Kage′	Kage′	Kage′
24. Brother, younger (as spoken of in relation to his elder sister or sisters)	Içu^{n}′ga				
		Younger brother	Younger sister	Younger brother	Younger sister
25. Sister, elder (as spoken of in relation to her younger brother or brothers)	Ito^{n}′ge	Wito^{n}′ge	Wizhu^{n}′the	To^{n}ge′ha	Zhu^{n}theha′
26. Sister, elder (as spoken of in relation to her younger sister or sisters)	Izhu^{n}′the				
		Elder brother	Elder sister	Elder brother	Elder sister
27. Sister, younger (as spoken of in relation to her elder brother or brothers)	Ito^{n}′ge	Wihe′	Wihe′	Wihe′	Wihe′
28. Sister, younger (as spoken of in relation to her elder sister or sisters)	Ito^{n}′ge				

29. Brother-in-law (as spoken of in relation to his brother-in-law)	Ita'ho^n	Brother-in-law speaking of brother-in-law Wita'ho^n	Sister-in-law speaking of brother-in-law Wishi'e	Brother-in-law speaking to brother-in-law Taho^n'ha	Sister-in-law speaking to brother-in-law Wishie'
30. Brother-in-law (as spoken of in relation to his sister-in-law)	Ishi'e				
31. Son-in-law	Ito^n'de	Father-in-law speaking of son-in-law Wito^n'de	Mother-in-law speaking of son-in-law Wito^n'de	Father-in-law speaking to son-in-law To^{n}de'ha	Mother-in-law speaking to son-in-law To^{n}de'
32. Daughter-in-law	Iti'ni	Father-in-law speaking of daughter-in-law Witi'ni	Mother-in-law speaking of daughter-in-law Witi'ni	Father-in-law speaking to daughter-in-law Tini'ha	Mother-in-law speaking to daughter-in-law Tini'
33. Sister-in-law (as spoken of in relation to her brother-in-law)	Iho^n'ga	Brother-in-law speaking of sister-in-law Wiho^n'ga		Brother-in-law speaking to sister-in-law Wiho^{n}ga'ha	
34. Sister-in-law (as spoken of in relation to her sister-in-law)	Ishi'ko^n		Sister-in-law speaking of sister-in-law Wishi'ko^n		Sister-in-law speaking to sister-in-law Shiko^n'
35. Husband	E'gthu^{n}ge		Wife speaking of husband Wie'gthu^{n}ge		Wife speaking to husband Thano^n'
36. Wife	Igaxtho^n	Husband speaking of wife Wiga'xthu^n		Husband speaking to wife Thano^n'ha	

When the son is grown, the father generally uses the term I^{n}gtho^n' in addressing him, and the mother I^{n}gtho^n (an old term).

When the daughter is grown, the father and the mother address her as Wino^n' (my eldest).

An aunt usually uses the same term toward her nephew and niece as the mother uses toward her grown son and daughter.

All members of the mother's gens were generally spoken of or to by her children as "Uncle" or "Aunt," but this term of address was changed, if need be, to conform to the near relationship of the mother, actual or potential.

Members of gentes in cognate tribes having a similar tabu generally spoke of one another as kindred and used kinship terms.

A stranger who is making his home among the people is spoken of as U'thixe (an old term).

A bride is spoken of as Mi'wathixe (woman married).

A groom is spoken of as Migtho^n'tega (newly married).

When a man not a relative makes his home with a family, he is spoken of as Ici'nu (an old term).

The proper modes of address were difficult to master by one not born to their usage and mistakes were regarded as impolite as they were embarrassing; therefore children were carefully trained in these forms. This custom of address facilitated story telling, for the narrative was not broken by such expressions as "he says" or "she says" or by explaining the relation "he" or "she" bore to the hero of the tale, as the form or accent of the terms of relationship used made this clear.

Courtship and Marriage

Friendship played an important part in the lives of both men and women and the intimacies begun in childhood often extended

FIG. 65. Playing on the flute.

throughout life. The friendships among the women had seemingly fewer dramatic incidents than those between young men, the lives of the former being less exposed to the stirring incidents of the warpath and the chase. Nevertheless, instances have come to the writers' knowledge of enduring friendships between women under circumstances that would be apt to test the strength of affection and kindness. Friends were apt to be confidants and few secrets appear to have been withheld from one's intimate companion. A man would cleave to his friend, follow him in the face of danger, and if necessary protect him with his life. To be false to a friend in either love or war marked such an individual as without honor and especially to be shunned. Young men befriended one another in minor matters as well as in the graver affairs of life. A young man would be assisted by his friends to deck himself. Two friends would paint each other's faces, fasten each other's ornaments, and at the close of the toilet they were resplendent in their finery. Not only would a friend help to make his friend look well but he would act as a go-between and secure an interview for his friend with the chosen girl. Such meetings generally took place at the spring, in the early morning. Girls never went alone to get water for the family; two sisters, an aunt and niece, or else two intimate friends and neighbors started off together. The young men haunted these places; they lay hidden in the grass or among the bushes, so that one could suddenly seize a favorable opportunity to speak with the girl of his fancy. These encounters were sometimes accidental but generally the lover made his presence known to the girl by his love song played on the flute (fig. 65). Music was composed especially for this flute, as songs that were sung were not played on the instrument, its compass being too limited. The following is a favorite flute song:

LOVE CALL

As custom did not permit young men to visit young women in their homes, the opportunities for the young people openly to become acquainted were limited to gatherings for tribal ceremonies and during the confusion incident to breaking up or making camp when the tribe was on the annual hunt. The stream and spring were at all times the favorite trysting places. Men sometimes composed their own love songs and by the song the girl not only identified her lover but became aware of his nearness. There are pathetic as well as humorous stories told which hinge on these individual love songs. It has been stated that a true love song, one that had for its purpose the honorable wooing of a maid, did not exist among peoples living in the stage of development represented by the native tribes of America. This statement does not hold good for the Omaha and their close cognates. The following songs belong to the love-song class. The words are few; soft, breathing vocables float the voice throughout most of the melody. Where there are words, they generally refer to the morning but most of the songs have only vocables. These songs are called *biçe'waa*^{n}. The music expresses the purpose of the song. The songs are all major and generally joyous in feeling, although there are others that express considerable subjective emotion. Sometimes in singing songs of the latter class, of which no. 2 is an example, the hand is waved at a little distance from the mouth to produce a vibrating effect.

BIÇE′ WAA^{N} No. 1

There is another class of songs that have been mistaken by some writers for love songs. These songs refer to flirtatious and amorous adventures. They were not sung in the presence of women but by men when by themselves. The existence of this class of songs was withheld from the knowledge of women of the better class. These songs were called *wau'waa^{n}*, "woman songs." They were composed by men yet they always represent the woman as speaking, betraying her fondness for some one and thus violating social etiquette by speaking of her personal liking for a young man. They sometimes refer to uncongeniality in the marriage relation; the unhappy wife begs her lover to fly with her to another tribe. In most of these songs the act of the man is made to originate with the woman. The following belongs to the *wau'waa^{n}* class of songs. It reveals something of social customs and also fairly well portrays the character of this class of songs, of which few if any are what might be termed ribald.

WAU' WAA^{N}

83993°—27 ETH—11——21

ke the the......... hi! ha ha E-be-i^n-te the a-be-
da^n e-he ni-ke the the wa-ge^n-tha ma e-he
mi-ke the the! the! E-zha zhe we-btha-de the the! tha! hi

Dadu^n na ibahu^n biakithe, the
Dadu^n na ibahu^n biakithe, the
Ho^{n}adi uthagthaa thu^n izhazhe wibthade the tha
Dadu^n na ibahu^n biakithe the; hi
Ebei^{n}te the! abeda^n ehe mike the; the
Wagu^{n}tha ma ehe mike the; the
Izhazhe wibthade the, the hi

Literal translation

Dadu^n, an exclamation denoting anticipated trouble from fear of consequences; *na*, a part of *ena*, a woman's exclamation indicating surprise; *ibahu^n*, known; *biakithe*, I have made myself; *the*, vocable; *ho^{n}adi*, last night; *uthagthaa*, you sang; *thu^n*, a part of *tethu^{n}di*, when; *izhazhe*, name; *wibthade*, I spoke your; *the*, feminine ending of a sentence; *the*, vocable; *ebei^{n}te*, who is it?; *abeda^n*, when they said; *ehe mike*, I said, sitting; *Wagu^{n}tha*, her lover's name; *ma*, a suffix indicating that he was moving, passing along. The word *the* (the next to the last word in each line) is the feminine termination of a sentence; the final *the* is a vocable which serves as a sort of refrain; *hi,* a punctuation word equivalent to a period.

Free translation

Dadu^n na—I have made myself known, the!
Dadu^n na—I have made myself known, the!
Last night when you sang I uttered your name, the!
Dadu^n na—I have made myself known, the! hi.
"Who is it that sings?" the! they said, and I sitting there, the!
"Wagu^{n}tha is passing," I said, the!
It was your name I uttered, the! hi.

As with all Indian songs, both as to words and music, there is no setting or introduction. Nothing is said of the girl or her surroundings. The stanza opens with her lament addressed to her lover, who, having won her affection, has so possessed her thoughts that when he sang without the tent and the family asked "Who is it that sings?" the girl unconsciously lets drop his name. All eyes are turned on her and then she realizes what she has done. When next day she meets her lover she tells him in distress of her betrayal of their secret. The young man responds by making this song, in which he betrays the girl's confidence to his companions and scores his conquest.

The structure of the song reveals a groping after metrical form. The choice of words and their arrangement are not colloquial and indicate a desire to express the story effectively and not in a commonplace way. The use of the vocable *the* at the end of each musical phrase is of interest, and its introduction into the fifth line after *ebei^{n}te,* "Who is it that sings?," has the effect of a sigh—it adds to the dramatic expression and gives a touch of pathos to the narrative.

The opening lines present at once the theme of the song, therein resembling the chorus of a ballad, which always sets forth the central thought or feeling around which the circumstances of the story cluster. In this Omaha ballad there is no elaboration in literary form and the music is equally simple; but we find here indications that the Omaha had begun more or less consciously to desire that the rhythm of emotions should have an answering expression in measured language. It is not improbable that the nascent poetic form of this class of songs may account in a measure for their popularity. While all other songs depended largely on vocables for carrying the voice, the "woman songs" were well supplied with words that always told a story.

Men and women were socially on a moral equality. Tribal custom favored chastity and those who practised it stood higher in public esteem than those who did not. In the case of a woman who in her youth committed indiscretions and later led a moral life, while her former acts were remembered, they were not held against her or her husband or children. Both men and women were allowed to to win back by subsequent good conduct their lost position.

When a young man asked the hand of a girl in marriage he observed a certain conventional form of address. The words were not always the same but the aspect put on the proposal was practically uniform. The young man extolled the girl and her relations; he did not vaunt himself; he pleaded his constancy and asked, rather than demanded, that she become his wife, craving it as a boon. There were signals other than songs or flute calls to let a girl know her lover was near. A tent pole might fall or some other noise be made which she would know how to interpret and so be able to meet the young man if a meeting had been agreed on. Marriage was usually by elopement. The claims on a girl by men holding a potential right to marry her almost necessitated her escaping secretly if she would exercise her free choice in the matter of a husband. When a young couple during their courtship determined on taking the final step of marriage, they agreed to meet some evening. The youth generally rode to a place near the lodge of the girl and gave the proper signal; she stepped out and they galloped off to one of his relations. In a day or two the young man took the girl to his father's lodge, where, if she was received as his wife, all claims by other men as to marriage were canceled by this act, but gifts had to be made to the girl's parents and shared with her relatives, in order to ratify the marriage. To bring this about, the father of the young man made a feast and invited the relatives of the girl. When this invitation was accepted and the presents received, the marriage was considered as settled beyond all dispute. In the course of a few months the father of the bride generally presented his daughter with return gifts about equal in value to those he had received and the young husband was expected to work for a year or two for his father-in-law. This latter claim was frequently rigidly exacted and the father-in-law was sometimes a tyrant over his son-in-law's affairs.

The following story is told of a man who was highly respected, industrious, and thrifty. He never married; why, no one knew, for he was an attractive man. He had a brother who for some reason was always unsuccessful in his wooing and as he greatly desired to marry a certain girl the bachelor brother was moved to say: "I will help you to get the girl you want." To the surprise of everyone, the girl included, the bachelor was seen at the spring, where he wooed the girl and planned their elopement. At the appointed hour he signaled her, she came to him, and together they rode to the lodge of one of his near relatives where the brother was in waiting. The bachelor explained to the girl that he had been wooing her for his brother, and the girl, having compromised herself by running away with her sup-

AN ELDERLY BEAU

posed lover, concluded to accept the transfer; the marriage so strangely entered on turned out pleasantly for both parties.

The marriage ceremony as described above depended for its completion on the recognition of the girl as the son's wife by the father of the young man, but should this formal consent be denied by either parent, while this act interrupted the festivity, it did not invalidate the marriage or have any effect on the issue of such marriage; it merely made the lives of the young couple difficult and uncomfortable. There was no tribal usage or tradition which made it possible to deprive a child of its rights to or through its father; according to tribal custom all a man's children had equal claim on him and he was responsible for all his progeny.

Cohabitation constituted marriage whether the relation was of long or short duration, always provided that the woman was not the wife of another man, in which case the relation was a social and punishable offense. Prostitution, as practised in a white community, did not exist in the tribe.

It was obligatory that a man and wife should belong to different gentes and not be of close blood relation through their mothers. It was counted an honor to a man to marry a woman who had tattooed on her the "mark of honor" (fig. 105). Marriage with a man either on or about to go on the warpath was not permitted; such a union was looked on as a defiance of natural law that would bring disaster on the people for the reason, it was explained, that "War means the destruction of life, marriage its perpetuation." The same law was thought to be operative when a hunter failed to kill game; it would be said: "His wife may be giving birth to a child."

In the family the father was recognized as having the highest authority over all the members, although in most matters pertaining to the welfare of the children the mother exercised almost equal authority. In the event of the death of the mother and father, provided the father had no brothers, the uncle (mother's brother) had full control of the children and no relative of the father could dispute the right of the uncle to the children. During the lifetime of the parents the uncle was as alert as their father to defend the children or to avenge a wrong done them. The children always regarded their uncle as their friend, ever ready to help them.

When a marriage was arranged by a girl's parents, with or without her consent, it was apt to be with a man in mature life and established position. The would-be husband made large presents to the girl's parents and relatives. When the time came for the marriage the girl was well dressed, mounted on a pony, and accompanied by four old men she was taken to the lodge of her husband. Young men derided this kind of marriage, saying, "An old man can not win a girl; he can win only her parents." (Pl. 42.)

Polygamy existed, although it was not the rule; in the majority of families there was but one wife. A man rarely had more than two wives and these were generally sisters or aunt and niece. These complex families were usually harmonious and sometimes there seemed to be little difference in the feeling of the children toward the two women who were wives to their father. No special privileges were accorded to the first wife over the others. Polygamy was practised more among the prominent men than among any other class. On the former devolved the public duty of entertaining guests from within and without the tribe. This duty brought a great deal of labor on the household. There was no serving class to render help to man or woman, so that the wife could not hire anyone to assist her in any extra labor or in her daily work or her varied avocations, as in the dressing and tanning of skins, the making of tent covers and clothing, not to mention the embroidery put on garments and regalia. It will be remembered that embroidered garments, robes, pipestems, and other articles were required for gifts that went toward a man's "count," which led to his tribal honors. Looking at the duties and customs of the tribe, it seems that the question of domestic labor had a good deal to do with the practice of polygamy. "I must take another wife. My old wife is not strong enough now to do all her work alone." This remark was made not as if offering an excuse for taking another wife but as stating a condition which must be met and remedied in the only way which custom permitted.

Divorce was not uncommon, although there were many instances in the tribe in which a man and woman lived together throughout a long life in monogamous marriage. If a man abused his wife, she left him and her conduct was justified by her relations and by tribal opinion. As the tent or dwelling always belonged to the woman, the unkind husband found himself homeless. The young children generally remained with the mother, although the father's brothers would be expected to assist the woman in their support. If the woman was immoral, she was put away and sometimes punished by her husband. In that case no one interfered to protect her. These punishments were sometimes very severe. Generally speaking, the family was fairly stable; tribal sentiment did not favor the changing of the marriage relation from mere caprice.

The Omaha woman worked hard. Upon her depended much of the livelihood of the people—the preparation of food, of shelter, of clothing, and the cultivation of the garden patches. In return, she was regarded with esteem, her wishes were respected, and, while she held no public office, many of the movements and ceremonies of the tribe depended on her timely assistance. In the family she was generally the center of much affection. There were many happy Indian families in which affection bound all hearts closely together.

One can sometimes judge of the light by the depth of the shadow cast. An old Omaha man stood beside a husband whose wife lay dead. The mourner sat wailing, holding the woman's cold hand and calling her by the endearing terms that are not uttered to the living. "Where shall I go, now you are gone?" he cried. "My grandson," said the old man, "It is hard to lose one's mother, to see one's children die, but the sorest trial that can come to a man is to see his wife lie dead. My grandson, before she came to you no one was more willing to bring water for you; now that she has gone you will miss her care. If you have ever spoken harshly to her the words will come back to you and bring you tears. The old men who are gone have taught us that no one is so near, no one can ever be so dear, as a wife; when she dies her husband's joy dies with her. I am old; I have felt these things; I know the truth of what I say."

Care and Training of Children

In the Omaha family the children bore an important part; they were greatly desired and loved. Mention has been made of the belief that women who bore the "mark of honor" would become mothers of many children who would live to grow up. The baby was its mother's constant companion, although other members of the family often helped to take care of it. (Fig. 66.) More than one instance is recalled where the father took considerable care of the little ones and it was not an uncommon sight to see a father or grandfather sooth or amuse a fretful child. Soon after birth the baby was laid in its own little bed. This was a board about 12 or 14 inches wide and 3 feet long. On this was laid a pillow stuffed with feathers or the hair of the deer, over which were spread layers of soft skins. On this bed the baby was fastened by broad bands of soft skin, which in recent years were replaced by similar bands of calico or flannel. There was no headboard to the Omaha cradle-board but the skins that were laid over the pillow were so arranged as to form a shelter and protection for the top of the baby's head. While the child slept its arms were bound under the cover but as soon as it awoke they were released. The cradle-board (*u'thuhe*) was principally used in carrying the baby around and it served as a bed when the little one was asleep. A good portion of the time the baby lay on a soft skin in a safe warm place where it could kick and crow, while the mother sat by with her sewing or at some other employment. If the mother's duties took her out of doors the baby might be laced on its cradle and hung up in the shade of a tree; or, if the mother happened to be going away on horseback the baby in its cradle was hung at her saddle, where it rode safely and comfortably. When the child was old enough to cling to its mother it was thrown over her shoulder, where it hugged her tightly around the neck while she adjusted her robe or blanket. The robe worn by the women was tied by a girdle around the waist, the upper part was placed over the clinging child, and the ends were crossed in front and tucked into the girdle. Then the mother gave a gentle but decided shrug, when the child loosened its arms and settled itself into its bag-like bed, from out of which it winked and peered at the world or fell fast asleep as the mother trudged about her business.

It is a mistake to suppose that Indian babies never cry. They do cry, most lustily at times, but efforts are always made to soothe a child. No true lullaby songs have ever been heard in the tribe by the writers, but both men and women make a low murmuring that resembles somewhat the sound of the wind in the pines and sleep soon comes to the listener. There was a belief that certain persons were gifted with an understanding of the various sounds made by a baby; so when a little

FIG. 66. Omaha mother and child.

one cried persistently, as if in distress, some one of these knowing people was sent for to ascertain what troubled the child. Sometimes it was said that the baby did not like the name given it and then the name would be changed. Sometimes the difficulty was of a more practical kind, as in the case of a baby whose mother, being particularly desirous of having her son lie on the softest of beds, had put next to him the soft skin of a buffalo calf; whenever the child was laid on its bed its cries kept everyone awake. In her distress the mother sent for a person who understood the talk of a baby. This person was evidently a keen observer, for he at once saw what the trouble was—the fur tickled the child! He turned the skin and the baby was pacified.

The birth of twins was considered a sign that the mother was a kind woman. It was said, "Twins walk hand in hand around the *hu'thuga* looking for a kind woman; when they find her, she becomes their mother." When a woman desired to ascertain the sex of her coming child, she took a bow and a burden strap to the tent of a friend who had a child not yet old enough to speak and offered it the articles. If the bow was chosen the unborn would be a boy; if the burden strap, a girl. If a teething child looked at one, at the same time grinding its teeth, stretching out its arms, and clenching its hands, it meant to break friendship with that person. A child who had lost either one or both of its parents was called *waho^{n}'thi^{n}ge* ("no mother"), "orphan."

As soon as a child could walk steadily it passed through the ceremony called Turning the Child, and, if a boy, through the supplemental ceremony of cutting the lock of hair in consecration of its life to the Thunder and to the protection of the tribe as a warrior. (See p. 122.) After this experience home training began in earnest. The child had now its name, marking its *ni'kie* rites, and its gentile relationship. Careful parents, particularly those who belonged to the better class, took great pains in the training of their children. They were taught to treat their elders with respect, to be particular in the use of the proper terms of relationship, to be peaceable with one another, and to obey their parents. Whipping was uncommon and yet there were almost no quarreling and little downright disobedience. Much attention was given to inculcating a grammatical use of the language and the proper pronunciation of the words. There was no "baby talk." Politeness was early instilled. No child would think of interrupting an elder who was speaking, of pestering anyone with questions, of taking anything belonging to an older person without permission, or of staring at anyone, particularly a stranger. Yet the children were bright and had their share of curiosity but they were trained not to be aggressive.

Little girls were subject to restraints that were not put upon the boys. The mother was particular in teaching the girl how to sit and how to rise from a sitting posture. A woman sat sidewise on the left, her legs drawn round closely to the right. (Fig. 67.) No other posture was good form for a woman. Sometimes old women sat with the feet stretched out in front but that was the privilege of age. All other attitudes, as kneeling or squatting, were only for temporary purposes. Concerning this point of etiquette mothers were rigid in the training of their daughters. To rise well, one should spring up lightly, not with the help of both hands; one hand might be placed on the ground for the first movement, to get a purchase. A girl was taught to move about noiselessly as she passed in and out of the lodge. All her errands must be done silently. She must keep her hair neatly braided and her garments in order. At an early age little girls assumed the rôle of caretaker of the younger children. The boys had to help about the ponies but not much training in etiquette fell to the lot of the boy—he could jump about and sit in any manner he chose, except after the fashion of a girl. Later he had to learn to sit steadily on his heels, to rise quickly, and to be firm on his feet.

When quite small the two sexes played together but the restraints and duties put on girls soon separated them from the boys and when girls were grown there were few recreations shared in common by the

FIG. 67. Sitting posture of women.

sexes. In olden times no girl was considered marriageable until she knew how to dress skins, fashion and sew garments, embroider, and cook. Nor was a young man a desirable husband until he had proved his skill as a hunter and shown himself alert and courageous.

Politeness was observed in the family as well as in the presence of strangers. The etiquette in reference to the fire was always observed and care was taken not to interrupt a speaker, and never to accept anything from another without recognition by the use of an expression the equivalent of "thank you;" this equivalent was the mention of a term of relationship.

To elucidate further the teachings and training given to children and youths, the insistence with which industry, good manners, and consideration for others were impressed upon the young, the following notes, taken beside a camp fire one evening in early September years ago, are here given. An old man, no longer living, was on that occasion in a reminiscent mood and somewhat inclined to question the advantage of influences that were creeping in among the people. As he talked he sat playing with a little stick, tracing figures on the ground, while the firelight shed a ruddy glow on the faces of those who made the circle. In the distance the tents stood pale and specterlike, overhead the stars were brilliantly white in the clear dark sky and no sound but the snapping of the burning wood broke in on the flow of the old man's words.

The children do not receive the training that we men did from our fathers. Everything is changed. I remember some of the sayings that used to be common in my young days: sayings that were supposed to hold us young people in order and teach us to be mindful of our elders and not become self-indulgent. Write them down; I would like the Omaha to know how children were talked to in the old times—children from 10 to 15 years of age.

When a boy used a knife in cutting meat the old men said: "The knife eats more meat; you should bite it." This saying means, the use of the knife makes one lazy; a man should rely on his own resources; the one who so trains himself is ready for any emergency.

In old times kettles were scarce and the same kettle would often serve several families. It was also customary never to return a borrowed kettle entirely empty but to leave a little of the last portion that was cooked in it. If a lad should help himself to that which came home in the kettle the old men would say: "If you eat what is brought home in the kettle your arrows will twist when you shoot" [will not go straight], adding in explanation: "The youth who thinks first of himself and forgets the old will never prosper, nothing will go straight for him."

There is a part of the intestine of the buffalo, called *washna*, that is very tender, so that the old people who have no teeth, or but few, can eat it, chew and digest it. If the lads want to eat this tender bit the father would say: "You must not eat the *washna*, for if you do, and go with a war party for spoils, the dogs will bark at you." Why the dogs would bark was left a mystery, which fact would make the young people afraid to take the *washna*, and so the old people could enjoy it in peace.

When a young man attempted to drink the broth in the kettle, the old men would say: "A young man must not drink the broth; if he does, his ankles will rattle and his joints become loose."

When the marrowfat was tried out and the lad desired some of it with his meat, the old men would say: "If you eat of the marrowfat you will become quick tempered, your heart will become soft, and you will turn your back to your enemy" [be afraid].

In my day the young men were forbidden to smoke, for smoking, we were told, would make young men short winded and when they went into battle they would be quickly overcome.

The old men used to tell the young men that they must learn to make arrows. They said: "If one does not make arrows he will borrow moccasins, leggings, and robes and be disliked by the persons from whom he borrows." This meant that one must be industrious in order to have things of one's own. The old men also said: "If you don't make arrows yourself and a young man who is industrious shows you his arrows, you will be tempted to steal from him." Also: "If you are not industrious you will borrow a horse from a young man who may be insignificant [of no position in the tribe], and you may be proud that you ride a horse even if it is not your own; you will borrow a bridle, too, and you will be disliked by the men from whom you borrow." Also: "If you are not industrious, when a herd of buffalo is slaughtered you may come across a young man whom you may consider insignificant but who has killed a buffalo by his energy; you will look longingly at the best portions of the meat, but he will give to another who is known to be thrifty and generous and you will go away disappointed."

Boys used to be made to swallow a turtle's heart so as to make their hearts strong. I was an orphan, and tender hearted and when any woman talked to me I would easily weep. I did not like this, but I could not help it. I swallowed a turtle's heart and since then I can control myself. He [pointing to a man in the group about him] has swallowed three. The turtle is hard to kill; even when the heart is cut out it will still quiver and the turtle's head will be able to bite after it is severed from the body. The heart is flat and about an inch long. The boy took the heart and swallowed it by himself. Only the heart was used.

In eating the rib of the game, if the young man tried to unjoint it the old men say: "You must not do that; if you do, you will sprain your ankles."

Once when I had killed an elk I wanted to eat the marrow in the bone; so I roasted it but when I was ready to eat it some old men saw me, and they said: "If you, a young man, eat that, your leg bone will become sore."

The lad must not pick the bones of the rabbit with his teeth, but must pull off the meat with his fingers. If he used his teeth they would become cracked. He must use his fingers in order that his teeth may be sound.

If a lad desired to eat the turkey's head he was told: "If you eat that, tears will come into your eyes when you hunt. You will have watery eyes." If he should wish to play with the turkey's legs after they had been cut off, the old men said: "If you play with turkeys' legs your fingers will be cold in winter and liable to be frost-bitten; then you can not handle anything."

The fat about the heart of the buffalo was given to children that they might have strong hearts—be courageous.

The liver of the buffalo must be eaten raw. This was said to make a man courageous and to give him a clear voice.

We were taught that when a man wounded a buffalo a lad must not shoot an arrow at it. He would be justly chastised if he did, as the buffalo belonged to the man who first wounded it.

I was told: You must not be envious and maim the horse of another man if it is a fine horse to look at. You must not take another's robe or blanket, or his moccasins, or anything that belongs to another. You will be tempted to do these things if you are not industrious and if you yield to the temptation you will be shunned by all persons. A man must be energetic, industrious—*kiwa'shkoⁿ*. If you are not industrious your blanket will be ragged, your moccasins will be full of holes, you will have no arrows, no good, straight ones; you will be in poverty and finally you will go to neighboring tribes to avoid meeting the members of your tribe, who should be your friends. If you are lazy, by chance you may have a horse that is stalled and you will think that you own property. You may have a horse that is blind and you will think yourself well off. You may have a horse with a disjointed hip and you will think yourself rich. If you are lazy, your tent skin will be full of holes. You will wear leggings made out of the top of an old tent that is smoked yellow; for a robe you will wear a buffalo skin pallet pieced with the fore part of a buffalo hide—such is a lazy man's clothing. An industrious man wears leggings of well-dressed deer skin; his robe is of the finest dressed buffalo skin and he wears earrings—such is the dress of the energetic, industrious man. If a man is not industrious and energetic, he will not be able to entertain other people. A lazy man will be envious when he sees men of meaner birth invited to feasts because of their thrift and their ability to entertain other people. If you are lazy, nobody will have pleasure in speaking to you. A man in passing by will give you a word with only a side glance and never stand face to face in talking with you. You will be sullen, hardly speaking to those who address you—that is the temper of the lazy man. The energetic man is happy and pleasant to speak with; he is remembered and visited on his deathbed. But no one mourns for the lazy man; nobody knows where he is buried; he dies unattended. Even when only two or three are gathered to a feast the industrious and energetic man is invited. People in speaking of him say: He is pleasant to talk with, he is easy of approach. Such a man has many to mourn his death and is long remembered. A thrifty man is well spoken of; his generosity, his help are given to those who are weaker than he and all his actions are such as to make others happy. Such are some of the things that used to be said by the old to the young men.

Yes, girls were also talked to by the old men and all this talk to both boys and girls was to prevent their becoming thieves through envy. When they saw valuable things and desired them, they should know that if they were industrious they could have such things for themselves. And these sayings were also to prevent the young men from growing up in laziness so that they would go from house to house in order to live. Girls were required to know how to scrape and to dress skins and to tan them; to cut and make tent covers, garments of all kinds, and moccasins. There were many other things that a woman must know. She had much to do, and upon her work the people depended.

These are some of the sayings to girls: If you do not learn to do these things [mentioned above] and abide by the teachings of the elders [about thrift, honesty, etc.], you shall stop at a stranger's house and your place will be near the kettle pole, your hand shall rest on the kettle pole and without being told to go you shall go for water, and when you have brought the water you shall look wistfully into the door of the lodge, and they will tell you to open a pack so that they may do their cooking. On opening the pack you will take a bit of the dried meat, thrust it slyly into your belt, and take it away with you and eat it stealthily—but it shall not satisfy you. Food eaten in fear satisfies not the hunger.

The thrifty woman has a good tent; all of her tools are of the best; so is her clothing.

Hear what happens to the thriftless woman: She shall stop at a stranger's place; there are holes in her moccasins but she has nothing to patch them with, so she will cut a piece out of her robe to mend her moccasins with; then she will borrow her neighbor's workbag and from it take sinew stealthily and tuck it into her belt.

If you are a thrifty woman, your husband will struggle hard to bring you the best of materials for your tent and clothing and the best of tools. If you have a good tent, men and women will desire to enter it. They will be glad to talk with you and your husband.

If you are willing to remain in ignorance and not learn how to do the things a woman should know how to do, you will ask other women to cut your moccasins and fit them for you. You will go on from bad to worse; you will leave your people, go into a strange tribe, fall into trouble, and die there friendless.

If you are thrifty, build yourself a good tent or house [earth lodge], and people will like you and will assist your husband in all his undertakings.

Etiquette

In the tent and in the earth lodge the fire was always in the center and was the point from which certain lines of etiquette were drawn. The space back of the fire, opposite the entrance, was the place of honor. It was therefore the portion of the tent given to guests, to which they always directed their steps when entering a lodge; it answered to the reception room or parlor of a white man's dwelling. Skin robes were spread here to make the visitor comfortable and welcome. The guest on entering must never pass between his host and the fire. When the guest was seated no one, not even a child, would pass between him and the fire. If by any chance it became necessary to do so, notice was given to the person passed and an apology made. This etiquette applied to the members of the family as well as to guests. When a guest arrived he took his seat quietly and remained quiet for a little time, no one addressing him. This was for the purpose of giving him time to "catch his breath" and "compose his thoughts." When conversation opened it was genial, although formal, and if there was any matter of importance to be discussed it was never hastily or quickly introduced. Deliberation was a marked characteristic of Indian etiquette.

When a guest was ready to leave, he rose and, using the proper term of relationship, added, *Sho*ⁿ*pa'xe ha* ("I have finished," i. e., my visit), or he said, *te ha* ("permit me") and without further ceremony departed.

There was a peculiar courtesy practised toward the parents of a man by his wife and toward the parents of a woman by her husband. A man did not directly address his wife's father or mother, nor did any of his brothers do so. If the parents were visiting in the same tent with their son-in-law or any of his brothers, conversation could be carried on but it was generally done indirectly, not directly between these persons. A wife did not directly address her husband's father but this did not apply to his mother. This custom has been explained by old Omaha men to mean that respect was thus shown by the younger to the elder generation. This rule of conduct was not, however, rigidly practised. There are stories told in which a man and his son-in-law were very close friends, living and hunting together.

Mention has been made of the custom of never addressing an individual by his personal name; etiquette demanded also that a person's name should not be mentioned in his presence. It may be recalled that a man's name referred to the rites in charge of his gens or to some personal experience—a dream or a valorous deed. The personal name sustained therefore so intimate a relation to the individual as to render it unsuitable for common use. It is doubtful, however, whether this characteristic was the fundamental motive for the custom under discussion; it is more likely that the benefits to be derived from the daily emphasis of kinship as a means to hold the people together in peaceable relations had to do with the establishment of the custom, which was strengthened by the sanctity attached to the personal name. This interpretation seems to accord with the comment made by an aged Omaha on the custom of the white people of addressing one another by name, particularly members of the same family: "It sounds as though they do not love one another when they do not use terms of relationship."

While only kinship terms were used in social intercourse, no one, not even children, being called by a personal name, there was a term employed in making a formal address to a stranger: *kage'ha*, "friend;" this term was used also between men not closely related to each other. Its use was confined strictly to men. When a man of distinction was spoken to, etiquette demanded that he be addressed as *i*ⁿ*sha'ge*, "aged man;" the term was one of respect and implied his possession of wisdom, dignity, and position. A woman addressed another of her sex as *wihe'*, "younger sister," and when speaking to a boy or a young man she had to use the term *kage'*, "younger brother."

Under no circumstances would politeness permit a person to ask a stranger his name or what business brought him to the tribe. If one was curious he must await the development of events. It is said that men sent on an embassy from another tribe have come, transacted their business, and departed without anyone learning their personal names.

A curious reversal of these social customs is shown in the following sayings about birds:

The whip-poor-will sings its own name, *ha'kugthi* ("translucent skin").

An unidentified bird having a brown back, yellow breast, and a black ring around the neck, says, *Oki'te dada*ⁿ*?* ("Of what tribe are you?").

The meadow lark, which heralds the time for the ceremonies connected with the children (see p. 118), sings, *Çni'tethu*ⁿ*gthi tegaze* ("winter will not come back").

Generally two meals were taken, one in the morning, the other at night. When the food was cooked it was removed from the fire and the kettles were set near the mother's place in the tent. The family took their places in a circle around the fire. If there were neighbors or informal guests, they sat with the family. The mother apportioned the food into bowls, which she set on a skin spread in front of those who were to eat. In the duty of passing the food she might be assisted by her elder daughter or some near kinswoman or an intimate friend. After all had been served, including herself, the father or the principal guest made the offering of food, lifting a small portion and dropping it into the fire, in recognition that all food was the gift of Wako^{n}'da. After this ceremony everyone was at liberty to eat. If for any reason this ceremony was omitted, no one touched his food until everyone had been served. If there were many present the mother would be apt to say, "Eat; do not wait." After that, anyone who had been served would be at liberty to partake of the food. Each person was served separately except in the case of infants or very young children. When the meal was at an end the dishes were handed back to the mother. In returning his dish, each person gave thanks by mentioning a term of relationship. When a child was too young to speak for itself the father or mother offered thanks for it. Should a dish be returned with a portion of the food uneaten, an apology or explanation was made to the mother or hostess. At an informal meal at which guests were present the host and hostess ate with their visitors. When only the family were present, the thanks to the mother were not exacted from the children. The exchange of hospitalities, however, was so frequent that the little ones soon learned what was expected of them in the presence of company. If a child or a guest seemed to be confused as to the right expression of relationship to use, the host or hostess helped the embarrassment by suggesting the proper term. Children were corrected if they made noises or grimaces when eating. Silence with the lips, when eating, was not exacted except from the chiefs when they were taking their soup. This act must be done quietly. It was said there was a religious reason attached to this custom, but just what could not be definitely ascertained.

At a formal feast men served the food. The offering to Wako^{n}'da was made by the man of highest rank present. Etiquette demanded that after the food was placed before the company a prominent man should say to the servers, "Have you provided for yourselves?" On the occasion of a formal feast the host, the one who gave the feast, never partook of the food. This custom obtained whatever the feast might be; whether it was given by a man to the chiefs, or by a member to a society, or by a group, as a subdivision of the Ho^{n}'ga, on the occasion when the ceremonies in its charge took place.

It was also in accord with etiquette to eat all placed before one; if, however, it was not possible to do so, the untasted food should be carried home. This custom was made practical by the custom of guests bringing their own bowls to use; untasted food was regarded as a reproach to one's host. If a kettle was borrowed for any purpose, on being returned a little of whatever had been cooked in it must remain in the vessel. This remnant was called *the'xuxe*. Anyone disregarding this custom could never borrow again, as the owner must always know how the kettle had been used and what had been cooked in it. An incident is told of a white woman who

PE'DEGAHI AND WIFE

scoured a borrowed kettle before returning it to the owner; the well-meant act was resented as showing a lack of respect and courtesy toward the latter.

Looking into a lodge and seeing all the inmates sitting or lying on the ground, it would hardly occur to one unfamiliar with Indian life that the ground space of a lodge was almost as distinctly marked off as the different rooms in our composite dwellings; yet such was the fact. The father occupied the middle of the space to the left of the fire as one entered. The mother kept all her household belongings on the left, between the father's place and the entrance. It was thus easy for her to slip in and out of the lodge without disturbing any of the inmates when attending to the cooking and getting the wood and water. If there were young men in the family, they generally occupied the space near the door to the right, where they were in a position to protect the family should any danger arise. If there were old people, their place was on the right, opposite the father. The young girls were farther along, more toward the back part. The little ones clung about the mother but were welcome everywhere and seldom made trouble. Each member had his packs in which his fine garments and small personal treasures were kept. These packs were set against the wall back of the place belonging to the owner.

In the earth lodge the compartments were quite commodious. The willow seats were lounges by day and beds by night. There was ample space beneath them for stowing packs, although storage spaces adjoined the lounges. In cold weather skins were sometimes hung between the inner circle of posts, making an inclosed space about the fire where the family gathered—the children to play games or to listen to the stories of the old folk. It was a picturesque scene that can never be forgotten by one who has enjoyed the welcoming cheer and kindly hospitality of an Indian family circle in its earth-lodge home.

Young girls were carefully guarded; they never went to the spring or to visit friends unless accompanied by an older woman—mother, aunt, or relative. Young married women seldom if ever went anywhere alone. Custom permitted only elderly women to go about unattended.

Etiquette demanded that when husband and wife walked abroad, the man precede the woman. (Pl. 43.) This was explained by the old men and women, "The man ought always to go first; it is his duty to see that the path is safe for the woman."

Women held no official position in the tribe but under certain circumstances they were consulted during the annual buffalo hunt (see p. 277); they were respected, the value of their industry was recognized, and their influence was potent in all affairs pertaining to the home.

83993°—27 ETH—11——22

Avocations of Men

The avocations of men were chiefly those connected with their duties as providers for and protectors of the family. As hunter (p. 270) the man secured the meat and the pelts but the work of transforming these into food, clothing, and shelter did not belong to him. As warrior (p. 474) he was obliged to be on the alert and ever ready to respond at once to the cry of danger. Men made all their own weapons.[a] Bows and arrows were used for the hunt as well as for battle (for the method employed in making these see p. 449). The manufacture of stone implements was accomplished in two ways: (1) by flaking by pressure from an elk horn, or (2) by placing the piece of flint between the folds of a strip of rawhide, holding this between the teeth as in a vise and working it sideways so as to break or chip the edge of the flint within the skin without injury to the teeth, a somewhat difficult and hazardous process. Men made all the stone implements used in felling trees, as the stone ax and wedge; these were ground into shape and smoothed, a slow and tedious operation. Disks about four inches in diameter and an inch in thickness were made in the same manner. These disks (*i*ⁿ*'thapa*) were used to crush kernels of corn into meal, also wild cherries into pulp for cooking; they were mainly used for grinding corn when traveling, as the large mortar and pestle were inconvenient for transportation.

The making of wooden articles was also the task of the men. The mortar (*u'he*), which was a necessity in every household, was formed from a section of a tree-trunk a foot or so in diameter and about three feet long. One end was chipped to a point so that it could be thrust into the ground to hold the utensil steady when in use; the other end was hollowed out to form the receptacle for the corn, by the following process: Coals were placed on the surface and were kept "alive" by being fanned as they slowly burned their way into the wood, until a sufficiently large cavity had been burned out, when the mortar was smoothed with sandstone and water, inside and outside. The pestle (*we'he*) was between three and four feet long, large and heavy at one end, and smaller and tapering at the other. When in use the small end was inserted into the mortar, the weight of the large end giving added force to the pounding of the corn. Wooden bowls (*zho*ⁿ*u'xpe*) were made from the burrs of the black walnut. These were burned into shape as described and polished with sand and water; experience and skill were needed to make the bowl symmetrical. Some of these bowls were beautiful in the marking and grain of the wood as well as in form. The one shown in the illustration (fig. 68) was made in the eighteenth century and was prized as an heirloom. Each of the several societies had its ceremonial bowl or bowls. Wooden ladles

[a] The manufacture of the shield, the war club, and the spear is dealt with on p. 448.

were made with the handle so shaped that it could be hooked on the edge of the bowl so as not to drop into the contents. Smaller bowls for individual use were not uncommon. Spoons were made of wood or of buffalo horn; the latter kind were in general use although tabu to one subdivision of the Tha'tada gens (p. 162).

In clearing the ground for planting, the heavy part of the work was not infrequently done by men as were the cutting and transporting of the large posts needed for building the earth lodge (p. 97). The weaving of the slender ends of the roof poles to form the circular opening over the fireplace was always done by men.

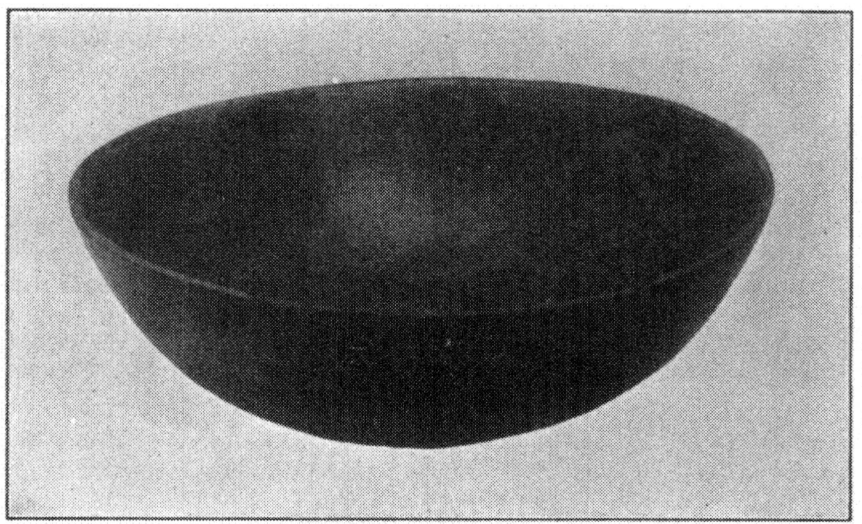

FIG. 68. Bowl made from walnut burr.

All rituals and religious rites were in charge of men; therefore the painting and tattooing of symbols devolved on them.

The life of the man was not an idle one; he could not pass his time in self indulgence, for want and danger were never far distant, and plenty and peace for the family and the tribe depended on his industry, skill, and courage.

Avocations of Women

The avocations of women all pertained to the conservation of life. She transmuted the raw material provided by the man into food, raiment, and shelter; the home was the product of her labor and all its duties belonged to her.

Bringing the wood for the fire was a part of the woman's task. For this purpose she used the burden strap; the broad band was worn across the chest and the long thongs were used to tie the wood in a bundle at her back. The illustration shows a burden strap that had been the lifelong possession of a woman who died at a great age more than twenty years ago. It is made of buffalo hide; on the side of the broad band worn next to the body the wool had been left to make it soft; the other side had been painted red. (Fig. 69; Peabody Museum no. 27578.)

The care of the garden has already been mentioned. This was the principal outdoor work of the women; not that their labors were otherwise confined to the house, for during warm weather everything that could be done out of doors was performed under a shade set up

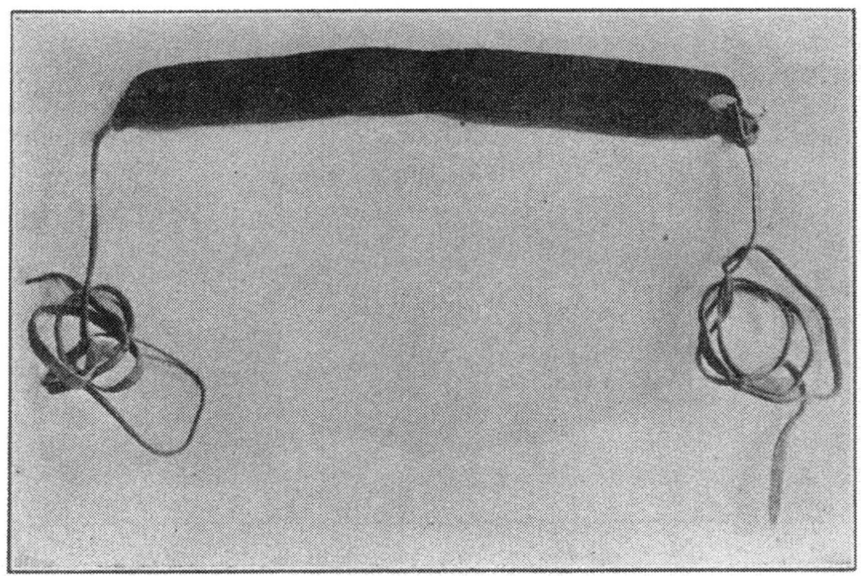

FIG. 69. Burden strap.

outside the dwelling. (Pl. 44.) Cooking, sewing, and the eating of meals all took place under this temporary structure.

COOKING AND FOODS

The appliances for cooking were simple. A pole called *uhoⁿ uthugashke* ("to tie on what is cooking") was set on the edge of the fireplace so as to slant toward the fire and from this "kettle pole" the pot (*ne'xe*) was hung. In old times the Omaha women made pottery of a rather coarse type, ornamented with incised lines. These pottery kettles could be hung or set over the fire. Horn spoons, *tehe'* (the word means "buffalo horn"), were used. The wooden spoon was called *zhoⁿ'tehe* (*zhoⁿ*, wood), "wooden buffalo horn;" later the metal spoon, *moⁿ'çetehe* (*moⁿçe*, metal), "metal buffalo horn," still kept *tehe'* as part of the name. There were no plates or forks and it is

DOMESTIC SCENE

doubtful if flint knives were ever used to cut food when eating. Bowls of pottery and of wood were used, which bore the general name *uxpe'*. Gourds sometimes served as cups. The introduction of copper or brass kettles and of steel knives made changes in domestic life and in many ways lightened the task of the women. It is said that in the olden days women had to make and keep on hand a supply of pottery vessels for visitors, and that when a great feast was to be held the kindred and friends of the women came and helped to make the necessary supply of dishes. The custom for guests at a feast, when not from a great distance, to bring their own bowls and spoons may have taken its rise in the pottery-making time.

Among the roots and plants used for food was the "pomme blanche," called *nu'gthe*. The root was dug from the time the plant first appeared until late in the fall. The line of march taken on the tribal buffalo hunt was sometimes determined by the localities where this desirable plant grew in abundance. It was eaten raw. The dark skin was peeled by the help of the teeth; the inner flesh is white and though rather tasteless it is not unpleasant. The roots were preserved by slicing, and drying them in the sun, after which they were stored in bags, like the shelled corn. They were cooked by being boiled with the meat, particularly the tripe of the buffalo.

The ground nut (*Apios tuberosa*) called *nu*, was boiled, then peeled, and eaten as a vegetable.

Artichokes (*Helianthus tuberosus L.*), called *po^{n}'xe*, were used in the early spring. They were eaten only raw and were spoken of as the food of homeless boys who had no near relative to feed them.

The root of the great yellow water lily (*Nelumbium luteum*), called *te'thawe*, and the bulb of the lily (*Sagittaria variabilis*) were gathered in the spring. The root of the latter lily was called *çi^{n}*. It was boiled and eaten as a vegetable and was said to taste like salsify. The root was never cooked with meat. It was gathered only in the spring, as later in the season the bulb became spongy and unpleasant. The root of the *Amphicarpæa monoica*, called *ho^{n}bthi^{n}'abe*, was gathered in the fall from the storehouses of the field mouse. This little animal gathers these roots in large quantities. The Indians kept the roots in skin bags during the winter. Before boiling, the outer skin was removed by rubbing the root between the palms of the hands. The flesh is whitish before cooking and reddish afterward; it is sweetish in taste and very nutritious.

Slippery-elm bark was used for flavoring. Small bunches were dropped into fat that was to be used in cooking.

A milk weed or silk weed (*Asclepias syriaca L.*), known to the Omaha as *waxtha'*, was used as a vegetable. The tender shoots were cut and boiled; sometimes corn and meat were added to give flavor.

Mushrooms (*mika'exthi,* "looks like tripe") were eaten boiled or fried in fat.

The leaves of *Ceanothus americanus,* "New Jersey tea," were made into a tea to be taken with the food; this was called *tabe'hi.*

The shoulder of game was always roasted and because it was so cooked it was called *waba'çnoⁿ.*

The thigh was cut in thin slices and jerked. This meat was always boiled even when it was fresh. The broth (*tezhe'ga*) was eaten with the meat.

The marrow (*wazhi'be*) from the fore-leg and hind-leg bones was considered a delicacy. The bones were roasted and served hot with the roasted shoulder. A brush made by pounding the end of a sprig of the wild cherry was used in serving the marrow. This cherry stick brush was called *wazhi'be ibagu'de.*

The ribs (*tethi'te*) were used only when fresh; they were roasted, never boiled.

The *tezhu',* a special cut already described, was either roasted or boiled; it was also jerked.

Birds were both boiled and roasted. All roasting was done by thrusting the bird on a stick which was then stood up before the fire. This mode of cooking was called *baçnoⁿ'.*

The methods of preparing and cooking corn have been already described.

Salt was obtained from a stream near the present city of Lincoln, Nebraska, known to the Omaha as Salt creek, the waters of which left on the grassy banks a white saline deposit. This fine salt the women brushed into piles by means of feathers and afterward it was deposited in bladder bags for future use.

DRESSING AND TANNING SKINS

Among the most important of the woman's duties were the care and preparation of the pelts, as on these the people depended for clothing and shelter. The work of dressing and tanning, which was arduous, bore the general name *watoⁿ'the.* When the tribe was on the annual hunt a certain part of the work of dressing the skins had to be done at once in order to preserve the pelts for future use and tanning.

First, the green skin was washed in order to remove all evidences of the slaughter.

Second, slits were cut along the edges, and through these slits pegs were driven so that the hide could be stretched taut on the ground, the inner side uppermost.

Third, an implement made from the leg bone of the elk, called *we'bazhabe* (fig. 70; Peabody Museum no. 40109), was used to remove any fleshy portions adhering to the green skin, which was called *taha'nuka*, literally, "wet skin." This work on a single skin, which usually occupied two or more hours, was called *waba'zhabe*. When this task was finished the skin was left to dry in the sun. When it became dry and hard it was called *waha'çage*. If the hide was to be used as a robe or to serve as bedding, it was then folded up to be packed back to the village, where the work of tanning was

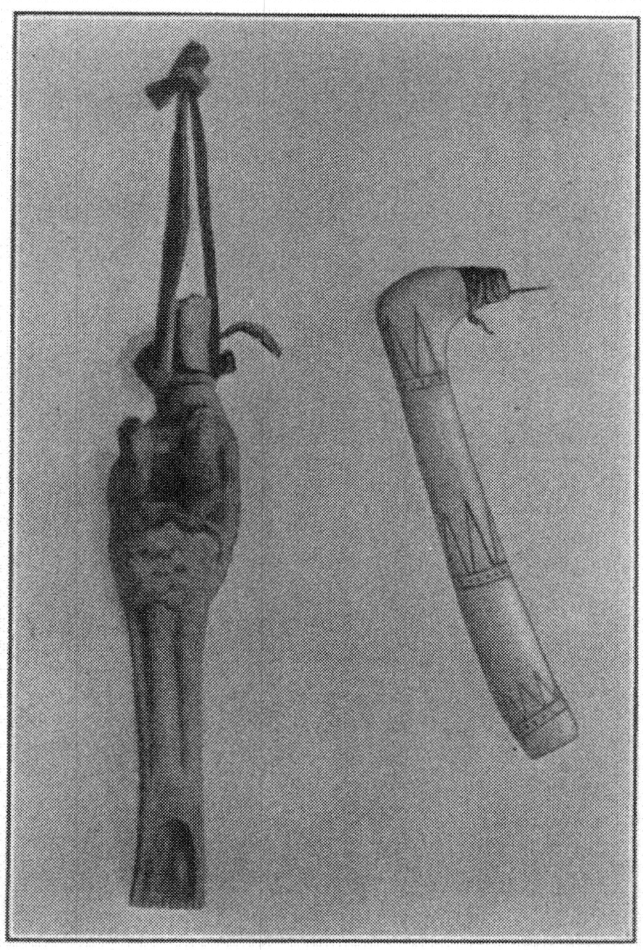

We'bazhabe *We'uhi*

FIG. 70. Implements for dressing skins.

always done. But if the skin was to be used for moccasins or a tent cover, it would have to be made ready for tanning on both sides. In that case the dried hide would be turned and the hair scraped off with an implement called *we'uhi*—a short adze, sometimes called *we'ubazhoⁿ* (really the name of the handle), figure 70 (Peabody Museum no. 27576). The process of scraping off the hair was called *wa'u*. The hide was next turned skin side up and scraped to an even thickness with the same implement; this process (fig. 71) was called by the same name as that by which the hair was removed. After this the skin was folded in an oblong shape convenient for packing and was taken home for tanning. Often a family would have a number of skins to prepare in this way when on the hunt and the women would be kept busy day and night if the hunters were successful.

FIG. 71. Scraping a skin.

Not only did the skins have to be attended to at once in order to save them but the meat had to be jerked immediately, otherwise it would spoil and be attacked by insects. Jerking (*wa'ga*) was done by cutting the flesh in very thin slices and hanging these on frames, so that the wind and sun could dry them rapidly. If a rain set in just after a hunt, quantities of meat and pelts were apt to spoil, owing to the difficulty of preserving them in a warm, moist atmosphere.

The rapidity with which the women worked was remarkable. In jerking the meat men sometimes helped if necessity required.

When the people reached home the tanning was done at the convenience of the women. For this process the brains of the slaughtered buffalo were saved in bladder bags, where they became dry and hard. These dried brains were boiled. Then the hard skin was stretched on the ground and the boiled brains were smeared over it by means of a brush made of a bunch of wild sage (artemisia). It is said that the artemisia was used to counteract the unpleasant odor of the brains. This process was called *i'thixthi*. If there were no brains available, broth from boiled meat was substituted.

Next, the skin was immersed in a stream, weighted down with stones and left there over night. This soaking was called *washpo*^{n}*'the*. The water was wrung out and the skin stretched lightly on a frame set either upright or flat; a knife-shaped implement, called *we'bamo*^{n}, was used to press out the remaining water. Dry corn meal was then rubbed on the skin to absorb any moisture yet unexpelled.

The final process was called *wathi'ki*^{n}*de*, meaning softening the skin by friction. A post was driven into the ground, a small sinew rope (*we'thiki*^{n}*de*) was fastened to it in a loop, and the skin run through the loop and pulled from side to side. This pulling was done inch by inch and was repeated three or four times, making the skin soft and pliable for use.

Skins to be used in making moccasins were browned by smoke. This process was called *wana'çithe*. The skins for tent covers were not smoked but were kept white. The same process of tanning and softening was used in preparing robes, except that the hair was left. Deer and elk skins, not being so harsh as the buffalo hide, did not require as much labor in tanning. The processes employed were similar to those above described.

QUILL WORK

Embroidery with porcupine quills was a feminine accomplishment. The Omaha women did fairly good work but it is doubtful if they were as expert as the women of some of the northern tribes. The following was the Omaha method of preparing and dyeing the quills:

The quills were plucked as soon as possible after the porcupine was killed, for if the skin became dry the quills were liable to break. The quills were sorted as to length and size and laid in bladder bags, the outer or black ends being placed together. The largest quills, those on the tail, were kept by themselves and were used in ornamenting comb cases and workbags. The long ones of medium size were reserved for fine work. The hair of the porcupine and that of the turkey's tassel were used for very fine embroidery—finer than was possible with the quills. Fine quills were used in embroidering the line on the middle of the upper part of the moccasins; the larger ones were used in decorating the flaps about the ankle. The Omaha did not often ornament garments with quill work.

It is said by some of the old women that in early times only black, red, and white were used; that red and black were the only native dyes; and that yellow, blue, and green were introduced by traders. Yet yellow and dark blue were made from roots known to some of the women, so these may have been used before the day of the trader.

The black dye was made from a yellow earth, or clay, called *waçe'-zhide nika.* This earth was put into a vessel over the fire and a piece of tallow added. The earth was stirred constantly until it was roasted black. A decoction was then made by cutting the inner bark of the maple into strips, adding leaves from the trees that had been mashed and boiling these in water until it became a dark red. The roasted earth was added to the boiling decoction. After the earth had been boiled in it, the water was very black. The mixture was then taken off the fire and the quills were put into it and left over night; in the morning they would be found dyed black.

The red dye was made from the root of a small plant that grows in the marshes or lowlands. This root was boiled in water and the quills were boiled with it for a short time until all were colored a bright red. The Omaha called this dye "feather dye." The plant has not been identified botanically. The red quills were dyed early in the morning, before the first meal was eaten, as the process was thought to succeed best at that time. It is said that but few persons were competent to dye a good red.

The yellow dye was made from the early buds of the cottonwood, "the buds out of which the leaves spring." This color was also made from the roots of a vine (not identified). After these roots had been boiled the quills were dropped into the water but were allowed to remain only a very short time.

White was the natural color of the quills; they were never bleached.

Verdigris was used for coloring green.

The quills were never split. They were held in the mouth to make them pliable, as they needed both warmth and moisture to bring about that condition. Cold water would not serve the purpose.

To flatten them for working, the black end, or tip, was held by the thumb and finger of the right hand, the nails being used to flatten the quills, which were warm and moist and pliable, being taken directly from the mouth for this flattening process. A number would be treated in this way but just before using them in sewing the same treatment would be again applied.

Quill work was called *u'thiçke,* an old, untranslatable term.

The patterns were not often traced. They were generally evolved by the worker as she proceeded. In olden times only the awl was

COSTUME AND ADORNMENT OF WOMAN

COSTUME AND ADORNMENT OF MAN

used to pierce the holes for the sinew and quills. A stitch was taken but not through the skin and the sinew was passed through and pulled tight. Then another stitch was taken in the same way but the sinew was not pulled tight. A little loop was left and through this loop the blunt ends of the quills were put. If, for example, four quills were to be used, they were placed one on the other through the loop, which was then tightened. A quarter of an inch from the first stitch of sinew a similar stitch was taken and in the loop four quills were fastened in the same way. Then the first quill was bent toward the second loop and the first quill of the second loop was bent toward the first loop, and the braiding went on, back and forth, until all four quills were in place, the last quill being doubled under and the sinew used in a stitch to hold it in place. In this way little by little the pattern progressed.

Quill work for pipestems was made as follows: Two long threads were doubled, making four threads. The free ends were wound about a stick and fastened to a stationary object. The doubled ends were made fast to the belt of the worker. A few inches of the doubled ends were left unworked for fastening to the pipestems. The quills were woven one at a time in and out over the four threads. Two threads formed one column. The ends of the quills were fastened between the two threads of a column. The new quill was fastened in the same place by the blunt end.

No trustworthy information has been obtained relative to symbolic designs being worked with quills on garments worn by the Omaha. The designs employed were generally geometric, this characteristic being due probably to the stiffness of the quills. Later these designs were reproduced by narrow ribbons hemmed on to the cloth or skin. This style was in greater favor among the Omaha women than embroidering with beads. (Pl. 45.)

WEAVING

Among the Omaha weaving was not practised on a large scale. So far as is known, cloth was not woven nor were the people acquainted with the cotton plant. One of the birds found in the honor pack belonging to the Sacred Tent of War was lined with cloth which may have been of native manufacture. If the cloth lining was strictly a native product it probably was obtained through barter or gift from some tribe which practised the art of weaving. Omaha women wove scarfs which were used as belts, being wound around the waist, by both men and women. The term applied to these scarfs suggests the material out of which they were formerly woven—*tezhi*$^{n\prime}$*hi*^{n}*de* (*tezhi*$^{n\prime}$, "little buffalo," or "calf;" *hi*^{n}*de*, "hair.") Scarfs bound about the head were worn exclusively by men. (Pl. 46.) Women used the scarf to gird the robe or blanket about their waists. They also wove bags, which were generally made from broad, short scarfs, doubled and sewed together at the sides. These bags were used by men as receptacles for ceremonial objects, as shown by the bags of different sizes found in the pack belonging to the Shell society of which the old chief Big Elk was the keeper. (See p. 554.) Women made use of these woven bags for various purposes. They had also bags of deerskin to contain their sewing materials—sinew, awl, and bladder cases containing dyed porcupine quills.

Necklaces of beads were woven, the different colored beads being arranged so as to make elaborate patterns (pl. 47; Peabody Museum no. 27551.) The short necklaces which were tied about the throat were woven on horsehair. The longer ones woven on thread were worn about the neck, being allowed to hang down in front.

FIG. 72. Hairbrushes.

The loom used by the Omaha women was a very simple device. The strands forming the warp were fastened at each end to a stick slightly longer than the width of the scarf or necklace to be woven; a thong was attached to each end of the sticks holding the warp and by these thongs one stick was fastened to a post and the other one to the woman's belt. She sat on the ground so as to stretch the threads of the warp taut and then wove the woof in accordance with the design she desired to produce. The different weaves and patterns used by the Omaha women are shown in the illustration given of the bags of their manufacture (figs. 114–116, 118, 120, 121). To weave the long necklaces required considerable counting and careful arrangement of the beads in order to produce the chosen design.

Ropes for lariats and cords were made from the nettle (*Urtica gracilis* Ait.), which was gathered in the fall when dry. The fiber was separated from the woody part by pounding between stones and was then braided. The native name for the plant was *ha'nugahi*. The fiber was called *mi'non̈zhiha*, "maiden's hair." When the hemp rope was introduced by traders it was given the same name. Lariats were also made in former times, of buffalo hair. Such ropes, usually of eight strands, were called *taha'thiçin*. Few knew how to braid them.

BEAD NECKLACES

Personal Adornment

Toilet appliances were few. The hairbrush, *mika'he*, (fig. 72; Peabody Museum no. 27561), and the paint stick (*peu'gaçoⁿibathoⁿ*, "to part the hair") were the two requisites. The paint stick, as its name

Fig. 73. Costumes of young men.

implies, served a double purpose. It was made of wood and was about 6 or 8 inches long, one end tapering to a blunt point. The case in which the stick was kept was generally ornamented and sometimes had a pointed flap which served as a cover to protect the stick and keep it from dropping out.

The brush (*mika'he*, possibly from *mi*, "woman;" *ka'he*, "to comb," although this is not a certain derivation) was made of stiff grass called by the same name. One end of the brush was tightly wound about to form a sort of handle. Both of these articles were used by both men and women. The hair was kept neatly brushed and glossy. Buffalo fat, well fried out, was sometimes used on the hair but it was more commonly employed on chapped lips, face, and hands.

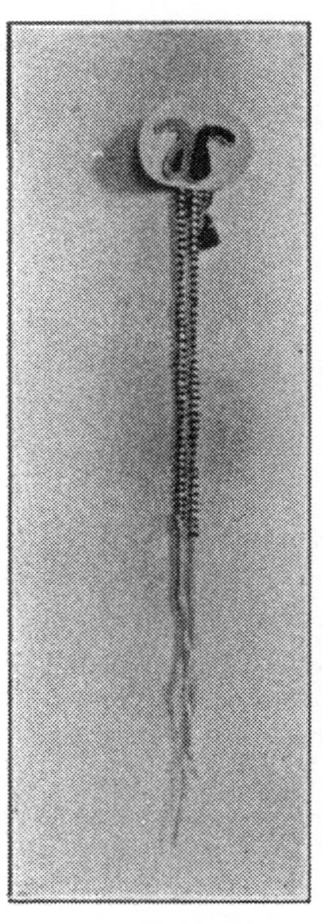

FIG. 74. Man's necklace.

The men wore the hair either flowing or cut close to the scalp, leaving only a stiff roach extending from the forehead over the top of the head to the neck. All wore the scalp lock. The sister or wife braided this lock in a fine, even braid. On this lock the eagle feather war honor was worn. A bone case was made, in which the quill of the feather was fastened securely; the feather could thus be made to stand erect or slanting, or to hang, according to the honor accorded the wearer. The bone case was fastened to the scalp lock. When the hair was worn flowing, the middle parting line was painted red and the circular line of parting around the scalp lock was generally kept painted the same color.

The word for paint varied with the use to which the paint was put. Thus, *we'uga* was paint for a tent; *waçe'zhide* meant red paint for the person (*waçe'* is part of *waçe'çoⁿ*, "clay"; *zhide*, "red"; *waçe'tu*, "blue paint," etc.).

Men generally painted their faces or bodies in accordance with dreams or in representation of some achievement or accorded honor. Young men used merely fanciful designs. Before the advent of looking-glasses a young man was painted by his friend. Men were frequently nude except for the breechcloth. When going to battle, on the surround at the tribal buffalo hunt, when taking part in the He'dewachi ceremony, at the races, at the Hethu'shka society, and the Pebble society, the painting on their faces and bodies had a serious significance, partaking of the nature of an appeal or prayer. Except with very young men, painting could hardly be called strictly an adornment. (See pls. 46, 49, 50, and fig. 73.)

The regalia worn by men indicated grades of war honors (p. 438). Earrings were worn. Piercing the ears was a costly ceremony, each hole generally representing the gift of a pony to the man who did the piercing; so the number of holes in a man's ears was an indication of the wealth of his near kindred. The necklace (*wanoⁿ'piⁿ*) (pl. 47 and fig. 74) was a part of an Omaha man's adornment, as were the beaded garters (*hi'thawiⁿ*), tied below the knee outside the legging. (Fig. 75; Peabody Museum no. 27545.) Bells were

FIG. 75. Man's garters.

sometimes fastened about the garter and their tinkle emphasized the rhythm of the dance. The belt (*i'pithage*) was worn, and to it was attached the embroidered case of the paint stick, and a little bag which contained tinder and flint for making fire. Perfumery (*i'nubthoⁿkithe*) was commonly used by the men. Braids of sweet grass were worn about the neck, under the robe. Columbine seeds were pulverized, mixed with water, and sprinkled over the robe to perfume it. A man attired for a dance often presented a gay appearance. The skin of the skunk or of the fox was sometimes bound about the leg below the knee, the tail hanging as an ornament on the outside of the leg.

Women parted the hair in the middle from the forehead to the nape of the neck (pl. 45). The hair, thus divided, was arranged in two braids, the ends of which were bound together and brought up to

FIG. 76. Mounted warriors.

the back of the neck so as to let the braids fall in a long loop behind the ears. The parting was painted red and similar treatment was bestowed on the cheeks, back to the ear. A narrow necklace was worn about the throat. Earrings also were worn, and a braid of sweet grass was often tucked in the belt.

A man frequently painted his horse to represent a valorous act in which the man had won honors, or he might paint the animal in a

CRUPPER FOR HORSE USED BY WOMAN

manner intended as a symbolic representation of a vision. (Fig. 76.) Such a decoration partook of the nature of a prayer. The bridles

FIG. 77. Painting a tent cover.

of horses were sometimes ornamented and occasionally the young men decked the manes and tails of their animals with bright ribbons or bands painted in gay colors. Women embroidered the cruppers for their horses, which were cut in such fashion as to spread over the sides of the animals, as shown in the accompanying illustration. (Pl. 48). This crupper formerly belonged to an Omaha woman by whom it was used some fifty years ago.

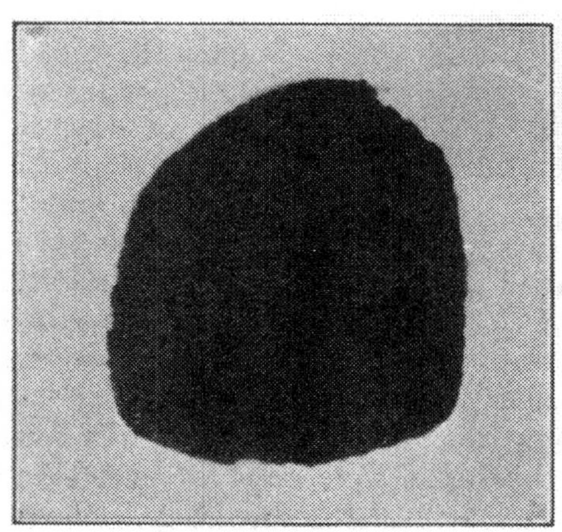

FIG. 78. Paint brush.

Men outlined designs on their tent covers. These represented symbolically their visions and so were more than a mere decoration, as they implied an invocation in behalf of the household. In the putting on of the color a man's wife or children might assist. The illustration (fig. 77) shows how the tent cover was spread on the ground, the design sketched in, and then the color applied by the assistant.

Robes were sometimes painted, this work being done in the same manner as the painting on the tents.

Paint brushes were made from the porous bone of the hip joint and shaped as shown in fig. 78. The paint was applied with the blunt edge of the bone brush.

FIG. 79. Ornamentation of chiefs' leggings.

The peculiar headgear shown in plates 36 and 49 was worn only by chiefs; it bore the name *watha'ge*, which was applied to all caps cut to fit the head. The style of headdress shown in plate 50 was called *tezhi*ⁿ*'hi*ⁿ*de*, which was the name applied to the woven scarfs, as already explained on page 347.

CLOTHING

Wa'thaha is the general term for clothing. It seems probable that in earlier days fewer garments were worn than in recent years; yet some of the articles of clothing, judging from their names, must have been long in use. To this class belong the leggings (*uto*ⁿ*'*). These varied in their cut. The simplest style consisted of a straight piece of skin folded and sewed at one side. A string at the top fastened the leggings to the belt. This style was used for little boys. A more elaborate style was that with a long pointed flap, which hung from the hip to below the knee. Other forms were the legging having a wide band of embroidery down the side and the kind called *uto*ⁿ*'to*ⁿ*ga*, "big leggings," with large flaps at the ankle; these were worn exclusively by the chiefs. The ornamentation on the big leggings, or chiefs' leggings,

COSTUME AND ADORNMENT OF MAN

COSTUME AND ADORNMENT OF MAN

was peculiar. The round dots represent hail. (Pl. 49 and fig. 79.) It will be remembered that the Nu'xe gens, the people whose rites were connected with the hail in both the Ponca and the Osage tribe, camped with the gentes which composed the division that represented the Upper World; and it will be remembered also that it was from that division of the Omaha tribe (the I^{n}shta'çu^{n}da) that the authority of the supernatural was symbolized in the rites that were employed in confirming the office of chief. The decoration put on these garments of the chief had reference to the sacred and responsible character of his office.

FIG. 80. Shirt.

The shirt, *uno^n'zhi^n* ("to stand in"), figure 80, was generally ornamented with bands of embroidery, fringe, or painted devices of various kinds.

The moccasins of the Omaha were made without soles and the embroidery was confined to a narrow band on the top of the foot and the flap about the ankle. There was no marked difference in style between the moccasins worn by men and those which belonged to women.

The tunic of the woman was called by the same name as the shirt—*uno^n'zhi^n*. It was formerly made of two skins fringed at the sides and tied together so as to hang from the shoulders and leave the arms free. The tunic fell below the knee.

The woman's leggings bore the same name as those of the men. They were shorter and were fastened by a garter at the knee and tied at the bottom with the moccasin string. In later times the tunic became shorter and was worn over a scant skirt laid in plaits at the hips and plain in front and behind. (Fig. 81.) This skirt was held in place by the belt which was bound about the waist. The skirt was called *wate'*, a term now applied to a dress. Calico has taken the place of skin as the material for a woman's clothing but her gala dress consists of a skirt of strouding, or cloth, sometimes embroidered with ribbon work on the front, and a short sack.

FIG. 81. Woman's costume.

THE WAI$^{N'}$ OR ROBE

The one article of clothing that has played an important part in the dress of the people is the *wai$^{n'}$*, or robe. The same word is now applied to the blanket. The robe is probably one of the oldest types of garment. The manner of fashioning and of wearing the robe has acquired during the centuries a ceremonial and a personal significance that does not belong to any other garment, although this is shared in a degree by the moccasin. (Pl. 51, *a*, Peabody Museum no. 51842; pl. 51, *b*, Peabody Museum no. 27579.) These two, the robe and the moccasin, may be considered primal articles of clothing and they deserve special consideration as revealing the native ideas and their expression. Looking at the significance of the garment in the light of religious observances, social usages, and individual habits of the Omaha, this significance appears to have a personal and a social aspect.

PERSONAL SIGNIFICANCE

(*a*) As distinguishing a man from the horde. In the Sacred Legend already referred to, which recounted the epochal events in the history of the people, it is said: "As the people came forth from the water they were naked and shame they knew not. But as the days passed they desired covering and took the fiber of weeds and grass and wove it about their loins." According to the interpretation of the

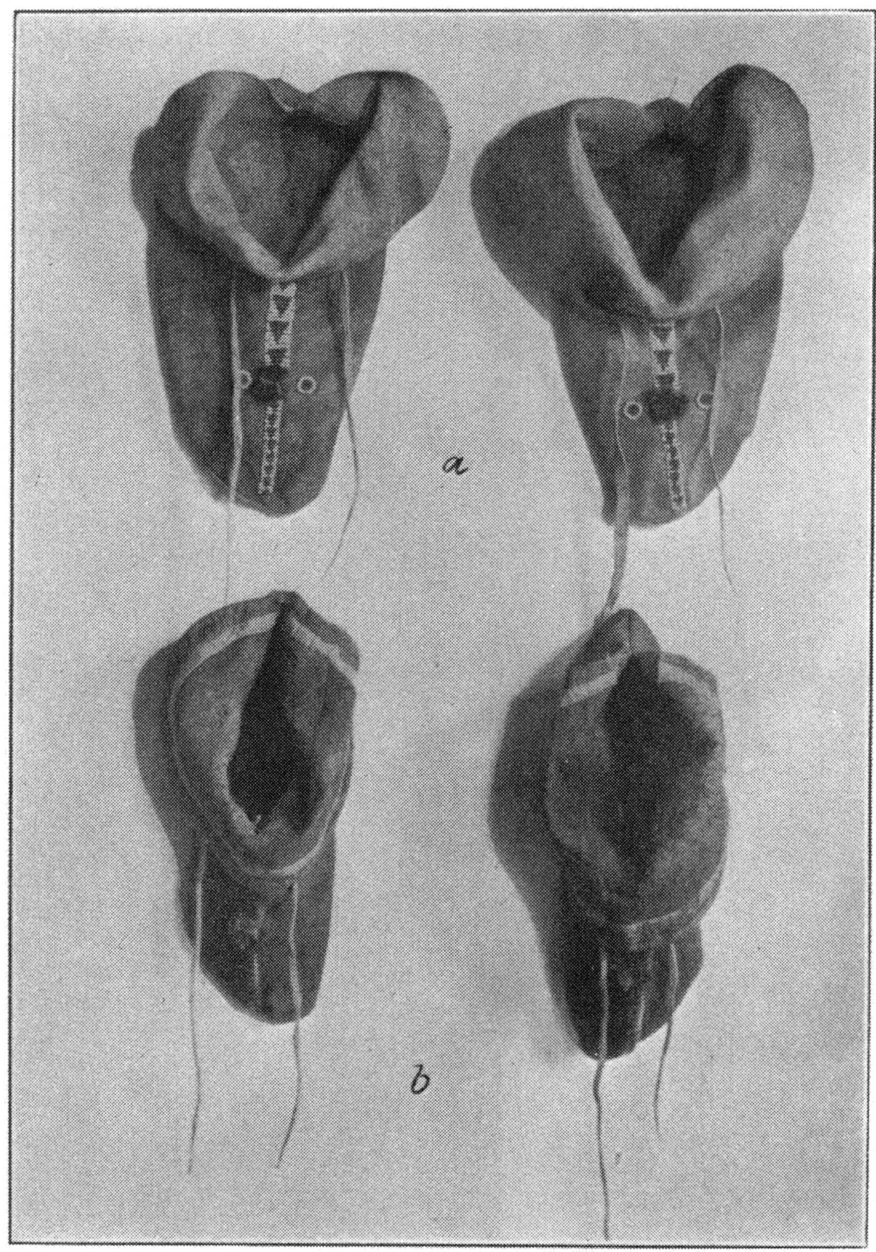

MOCCASINS WORN BY MEN (*a*) AND WOMEN (*b*)

old keeper, this passage referred to the natural birth, as well as to the development of the people, who then dwelt near "a great water," and whose "desire for covering" marked the arousing of self-consciousness. The words used in the Legend are *itha'kigtha xade*, "to cover ones' self with;" and the expression is distinct from *wa'thaha*, the word for clothing. The words used in the Legend carry the idea of something placed on the body of a person with the motive of withdrawing himself and differentiating himself from his fellows—a simple act of self-consciousness expressive of the idea fundamental to costume, decoration, and regalia.

(*b*) As symbolizing dependence on the supernatural. Nature was looked on subjectively and anthropomorphically; all life was considered as one and as related. Man's physical existence is sustained by other forms of life. Eating the products of the earth and the flesh of the animals is essential to bodily vigor. And this physical dependence on living forms was carried a step further in the idea that man's spirit (*wazhi*^{n}*'*), his will, his power to do, can be strengthened by being supplemented by the spirit or power of the bird, the animal, or the plant, since he believed, first, that all things on the earth or above in the sky are permeated by the same life or force that man is conscious of within himself; second, that this invisible life or force is continuous, not to be broken even by physical death; and, third, that the qualities or potentialities of one form can be transmitted to another form so as to augment power. Moreover, as man has to make an effort, has to perform some act in order to secure food for the nourishment of his body, the Omaha seems to have argued by analogy that he would have to go through some form of appeal if he desired to have his spirit strengthened. The visible medium of help for both body and spirit was some natural form imbued with life from Wako^{n}'da. In accordance with these beliefs, rites seem to have grown up around the quest for food and the dress worn at these ceremonies exemplifies these beliefs.

In common with other tribes the Omaha conserved in his religious ceremonies those articles which had contributed to the betterment of the people in their long, slow struggle upward. One of the earliest, if not the earliest, garment which served to protect the body from cold and storm seems to have been the unfashioned hide. This garment retained the semblance of the animal and the comfort the skin contributed to the body seems to have served to increase the native confidence in the close relation he conceived to exist between all other visible forms and himself. Although in later times his ordinary clothing ceased to exemplify this close relation, yet when the Omaha entered on sacred ceremonies with the desire of securing supernatural aid there was a return in his apparel to the primitive form. For example, in the rites preceding the tribal buffalo hunt, when the main supply of meat was to be secured, the priests and chiefs wore the uncut buffalo robe, the hair outside, so wrapped about their bodies that as they sat they presented somewhat the appearance of a group of buffalo. This manner of wearing the robe was explained as being in recognition of the transmission of life from the buffalo to man that the latter might live. Again, the warrior when going to battle might wear a wolf skin over his shoulder or put on himself the skin of some swift bird of prey. This semblance of the living creature not only indicated an appeal for help but was believed to promote the transmission of the help and to make it more direct in the hour of need.

(*c*) As proclaiming personal achievements. It will be recalled that war honors were graded and could be bestowed only at the public ceremony called Wate′giçtu, and that each grade had its peculiar decoration, so that a man's costume and regalia proclaimed the character of his deeds, his personal achievements. The decorations which appeared on the face, body, or garments of a warrior not only indicated what had been the character of deeds performed by him in battle but they asserted his right to appeal to certain powers for supernatural aid.

Social Significance

(*a*) Marking the kinship group. As the life of the people became more complex, the idea seems to have developed of making the skins of the helpful animals subservient to man under his new requirements. This idea seems to have found expression in the moccasin. To make this foot gear it was necessary so to cut the skin that when the parts were sewed together all semblance of the animal was lost and the form pertained wholly to man. The moccasin also became typical of man as a social being. In the Omaha and its cognate tribes the moccasin held an important place in rites which laid stress on the obligation of a gens and which were social in character. For example, when the ceremony took place which marked the initiation of the child into the tribe and it was given a name which belonged to its gens, moccasins were put on its feet with song and ritual as it was "turned by the winds" and sent forth "into the walk of life." Among the Ponca, a subdivision of the Ni′kapashna gens to whom the deer was tabu put on their dead moccasins made from deer skin, so that on the journey the spirit might be recognized by its own people and not lose its way. The same custom obtained in the Tapa′ gens of the Omaha tribe, which had the same tabu. The We′zhi^{n}shte gens followed a similar custom and put on the feet of their dead members moccasins made from the skin of the elk, the elk being tabu to the living.[a] Less serious in character but still related to the ideas embodied in the above rites is the following saying: "On a journey if one's

[a] Similar customs pertaining to moccasins in connection with the dead obtained among the Osage.

moccasins wear out and they are set on the trail, pointed toward home, and are told to go back and tell of the welfare of the wearer, they will do so." The moccasin was formerly the only part of personal attire which was not regarded as interchangeable between tribes, as each tribe had its peculiar cut and ornamentation and a man's tribe could be recognized by the moccasins he wore.

While the war bonnet can hardly be called a garment, yet it was a marked article of dress and was of special social significance, as it emphasized interdependence among men. While all the materials used in its construction were symbolic, its manufacture was attended with ceremonies significant of the development of social ideas. The special point of interest in connection with this article is that no man, whatever his rank or his record, could make or purchase for his own use a war bonnet. In olden days it had to be built by his fellow-tribesmen. Its feathers represented the war record of the warriors of the tribe, who thus gave their consent to place upon a fellow-tribesman this picturesque mark of distinction. In like manner the hair fringe on a war shirt represented the consent of the warriors to allow the owner so to decorate his garment.

The dress of societies served to mark their respective membership and stimulated a feeling of brotherhood independent of the ties of blood, thus promoting the social growth of the tribe.

Looking back along the pathway of progress from those early conditions wherein man's fears and needs held him in vague dread, from the time when his appeals to the supernatural were a constant duty to the time when these appeals were relegated to particular times and seasons, we note that under the regulating influence of established rites and ceremonies and the growth of social order, mental bewilderment gave way and conditions arose that were favorable to the development of a secular life, a life in which the individual could enjoy a freedom hitherto impossible for him. This personal freedom under the influence of social order and secular life was apparent in the varied manner of wearing the robe. During the long stay among the Omaha of one of the writers the different ways in which the robe was worn and shifted to meet the requirements of varying moods arrested her attention and a study of the subject ensued, the results of which are here given.

The blanket began to supersede the robe even before the extinction of the buffalo made the latter no longer possible to obtain. The well-dressed robe was almost as pliant as the blanket and it was during the period when only robes were worn that this garment seems to have become expressive of the wearer's moods and actions. The adjustment never seemed to be the arranging of a costume for effect but a free expression of a passing emotion. The picture presented by the draped figure told its story with simplicity and truthfulness.

While each man wore his robe in a manner characteristic of the individual, either gracefully or otherwise, yet there was a typical way of expressing certain purposes or feelings by the adjustment of the robe that was persistent and easily recognizable.

Language of the Robe

The Omaha had never been trammeled by his clothing; every limb had been free to answer to any impulse, to respond to any wave of emotion. His clothes were few; and the *wai*ⁿ, or robe, was never lacking and lent itself easily to the needs of the moment. There still lives in the memory of one of the writers a June day nearly thirty years ago when an Omaha girl was seen flitting among the tall prairie flowers, shifting her white blanket to suit her varying moods—now gathering it closely about her slight, swaying figure, now letting it float as she swept in ever-widening curves, or at the slightest sound hiding her glossy head and laughing face among its soft folds. All the beauty and poetry of her race were in the pretty maiden, who was as wayward and blithe as the fleecy clouds drifting above her through the deep blue sky. With the Omaha, as with other peoples, the airy pleasures of youth must give place to the prosaic duties of mature life. So the blanket of the woman was worn very practically. It was belted at the waist, thus affording a close covering and also a pouch or pocket within which she could snugly tuck her baby or carry some other burden on her back. Her figure suggested little of beauty.

The freer life of the man was manifest in his use of the robe. The accompanying illustrations show some of the ways in which the robe was worn and shifted and suggest something of the interesting language of this garment.

The first of the series shows hesitation (pl. 52, *a*). The man has not determined whether he will go forth to take an active part in the particular affair occupying the people or will sit down and become a mere spectator.

Next appears a young man walking (pl. 52, *b*). The robe is thrown loosely over the left shoulder and gathered on the left arm. The right arm is free and the limbs unincumbered. The folds of the garment add grace and dignity to the figure. Youths thus attired could often be seen walking with elastic step over the hills.

The third illustration depicts a young man about to run (pl. 52, *c*). The blanket hangs over the left shoulder, relieving the arm of its weight. In long runs, as when on the annual hunt the runners were sent out to search for a buffalo herd, the robe was gathered in a roll, passed over the left shoulder and tied beneath the right arm. In races the robe was dropped altogether.

a

b

c

d

THE LANGUAGE OF THE ROBE

a

b

c

d

THE LANGUAGE OF THE ROBE

In the picture of the old man walking (pl. 52, *d*) the adjustment of the robe indicates the weakness of age, the desire for bodily comfort, and the slow and feeble step that bears the burden of the years.

The next figure is that of a young man watching for his sweetheart (pl. 53, *a*). Courtship was by stealth and the lover when going to the trysting place guarded against recognition. He concealed himself in his blanket, one eye only being visible. In the picture

FIG. 82. Language of the robe—Anger.

he has arrived at his destination; a slight movement of the head has caused the blanket to fall back a little and leave both eyes free to watch for the maiden as she comes to the spring to draw water for the household.

In strong contrast to the observant lover is the pose of the man who stands watching some transaction of public interest (pl. 53, *b*). His attitude is quiet and firm, the robe is not definitely adjusted, and resembles somewhat the picture representing "hesitation;" but there is no indecision in the mind of the wearer—he will be ready for speech or act when the opportune moment arrives.

Now the man is addressing the tribe or council (pl. 53, *c*). The moment waited for has arrived and he steps forth to speak his thought, to impress his views upon his tribesmen.

In "The admonition" the adjustment of the drapery suggests a pause, a change of mental attitude (pl. 53, *d*). The mind of the speaker has reverted to some past experience in his long career, from which he draws a lesson and gives it as an admonition to the people.

Perhaps the most striking illustration of this expressive use of the garment was its adjustment in the case of anger (fig. 82). Stung by sudden wrong or injury, the man grasps the edges of his robe and hastily draws it up over his head, thus withdrawing from observation. The rousing of his anger has made him intensely conscious of his personality and he responds to the primitive impulse "to cover himself," to put something upon himself, that he may feel consciously separate from his fellows. The draped figure of the man hooded by the robe which he holds with tense hands not only emphasizes the impulse which the legend assigns as fundamental to the garment—that of the desire to differentiate one's self from the horde—but it suggests the steps we have traced in the use and purpose of the garment from the uncut animal skin up to the period when it could express man's personal emotions, a freedom he could have achieved only within the arena of society.

Property

Household furniture was simple. The robes used for bedding were of hide taken from the buffalo bull in the winter when the fur was the heaviest. This bedding was called *umi'zhe*. The pillows (*i'behi*ⁿ) were of soft deerskin stuffed with the long winter hair of the deer. There were no contrivances for seats in the tent. In the earth lodge were couches, already described (p. 98). The cooking and eating utensils, the mortar and pestle for grinding corn, and the packs for storing food and clothing—all those things which pertained to the household were the property of the wife. Hers, also, was the tent. All other things were individual property and belonged to the members of the family. Even the articles belonging to the children were considered as their own, and were not disposed of without their consent. In the Omaha tribe there was no communal property. The land was the bountiful "mother earth" which brought forth food for all living creatures. There was no property in land or in springs, as the country was well supplied with never-failing springs and streams. Proprietorship in garden plots was recognized as long as the plots were used but the produce belonged to the woman.

To a man belonged his regalia, clothing, weapons, and other personal property. Horses were not exclusively the property of the men. Women owned their own ponies and disposed of them as they pleased. Children owned their ponies and a parent did not assume the right to give away one of them without the child's consent.

At death, the articles that had been in immediate use by the deceased were buried with the body. Other possessions, as extra weapons and utensils, passed to the children if they were old enough to use them, otherwise to the brothers of the dead man or woman.

Hospitality was the rule and food was shared as long as it lasted but food was not communal property. No corn was raised and kept for the use of the tribe nor was any meat set apart for general use. An offering of meat was made at the ceremony of Anointing the Pole but the meat was contributed by members of the tribe.

Societies owned certain articles, as wooden bowls, packs containing regalia, and medicines (see p. 518). Songs were the property of certain subgentes, societies, or individuals (pp. 233, 249, 373). Some songs, however, were free to the people, particularly the songs belonging to the Wa′wa^n ceremony (p. 376).

Amusements

In their play the children were apt to mimic the occupations of their elders. At an early age the girls began to play "keep house." Miniature tents were set up. The mother's robe or shawl was often seized for a tent cover; the poles were frequently tall sunflower stalks. If the boys were gallant, they would cut the poles for the girls. It was a matter of delight if the tent was large enough to creep into. Generally the feet and legs would protrude but if the heads were well under cover it was easy to "make-believe." Both boys and girls liked to play "going on the hunt." The boys took two parts—they were hunters sometimes and sometimes ponies. When the latter, the girls tied the tent cover in a bundle and fastened it and the tent poles to the boy pony, who might be a docile creature or a very fractious animal and particularly troublesome when fording a stream or if the camp was attacked by enemies, as such ponies always stampeded. Sometimes men carried through life their pony reputation. Women would laughingly point out some elderly man and say: "He used to be a very bad pony" or else "a very good pony." The boys who played warrior wore war bonnets made from corn husks, which cost much labor to manufacture and were quite effective when well done. Children made many of their playthings out of clay and some of the boys and girls were very clever in modeling dishes, pipes, dolls, tents, etc. The writer once came across a miniature clay coffin with a bit of glass set in, beneath which was a clay baby. Some child had seen the funeral of a white person and had devised a new plaything. Dolls were improvised by children from corncobs. Sometimes mothers made dolls for their little girls and also small dishes for the young housekeepers. The hobby-horse of the boys was a sunflower stalk with one nodding bloom left on the end. Races were run on these "make-believe" ponies. Generally the boys rode one stalk and trailed two or three others as "fresh horses."

The game of *uhe'basho^n sho^n* (literally, "the crooked path") was the game familiarly known to us as "Follow my leader." The children sang as they ran and made their merry way through the village, each one repeating the pranks of the leader. The line was kept by each boy holding to the string about the waist of the boy in front. It is said that the song which accompanied this game had been handed down by generations of children. Certainly every Omaha seemed to know it. (Fig. 83.)

"FOLLOW MY LEADER"

The quiet games often played about the fire were "cat's cradle" (*wa'baha*, meaning "the litter") and a game resembling jackstraws, in which a bunch of joints of prairie grass was dropped from one's hand and the players strove to pull out one joint after another without disturbing the bunch. The player could use a joint to disentangle those he was trying to secure. Another game, called *dua*, was played with a long stick one side of which was notched. The person who could touch the greatest number of notches, saying *dua* at every notch without taking breath, was winner.

The boys enjoyed the game called *wahi'gaçnugithe*, "bone slide." Formerly ribs were used; sticks are now substituted. Four or five could play at this game. The sticks are about 4½ feet long, made of red willow, and ornamented by banding with bark and then holding them over a fire. The exposed part turns brown and when the bands are removed the sticks are striped brown and white. Each boy holds a number of sticks and throws one so it will skim or slide along the level ground or the ice. The boy who throws his sticks farthest wins all the sticks; the one who loses is tapped on the head by the winner. The Ponca call this game *mo^{n}i'bagi^n*, "arrow throwing."

During the annual buffalo hunt when the tribe remained in a camp for more than a day the boys, ranging from ten to fourteen years of age, would engage in a sport called *zhi^{n}ga uti^n* (*zhi^{n}ga*, "little," referring to the little birds (*wazhi^{n}ga*, "bird"); *uti^n*, "to strike"). The boys armed themselves with sticks about a yard long, to which small twigs were attached; then ranging in line through the prairie grass they scared up the little birds. As these rose, the boys threw their sticks into the air and the fledglings, mistaking them for hawks, tumbled into the grass to hide, only to be caught by the hands of the boys. One lad was chosen to carry the quarry. As soon as a bird was caught, it was killed, scalped, and thrown at the boy appointed to take charge of the game; then it was his duty to run ahead and fall into the grass as if shot. On rising, he took the bird and strung it on his bow string. This little pantomime was enacted with every bird caught. When a number of birds had been captured, the boys retired to a place where they could roast

FIG. 83. Group of Omaha boys.

the birds and enjoy a feast. Boys of the Wazhi^n'ga itazhi subgens of the Tha'tada gens could join in the sport but could not touch the birds or share in the feast, as small birds were tabu to them.

In winter the boys played whip top. They made their own tops out of wood. Sometimes a round-pointed stone served as a top, and was spun on the smooth ice.

A ball game called *tabe'gaçi* (*tabe*, "ball;" *gaçi*, "to toss by striking"), which resembles somewhat the game known as shinny, was played by two groups, or parties. This is the game before referred to (see p. 197) as sometimes played between the two divisions of the tribe, which had a cosmic significance in reference to the winds and the earth. When it was played between the two divisions of the tribe it had to be formally opened by a member of the Ko^{n}'çe gens in the manner already described. When it was played merely for pleasure between two groups of boys, if among the number there chanced to be a boy from the Ko^{n}'çe gens, he would be the one to open the game and first to toss and strike the ball. Two stakes, as goals for the two sides, were set at a considerable distance apart. The players with the ball started from the center. The aim of each player was to drive the ball to the goal of his side, while the players on the opposing side tried to prevent this and to drive the ball to their own goal. The bat used was a stick crooked at one end. When boy neighbors played together, the "sides" were chosen in the following manner: A boy was selected to choose the sticks. He took a seat on the ground and another boy stood behind him. The standing boy held his hands over the eyes of the seated boy. Then all the sticks were laid in a pile before the latter. He took two sticks, felt them, trying to recognize to what boy they belonged. Then he crossed his hands and laid one stick on one side and the other on the other side of the place where he was sitting. When all the sticks had been taken up and laid on one or the other pile, the standing boy removed his hands and the boy who had chosen the sticks indicated to which pile or side he would belong. There were no leaders in the game—the ball was tossed and the sides fell to playing. When men played this game, large stakes were often put up, as garments, robes, horses, bows and arrows, and guns. No stakes were ventured when boys were the players.

Pa'çi^{n}zhahe was a game adopted from the Pawnee some generations back. It was played with a hoop and a peculiar stick which was thrown so as to intercept the rolling hoop. (Fig. 84; Peabody Museum no. 37776.)

Lads sometimes indulged in a game called *wa'thade*. This game, which may be called "dare," consisted in lads doing ridiculous things, which required exertion to accomplish. Some of the number were detailed to see that the boys actually did the things called for. Many are the laughs the older men have over these "hazing" sports of their youth, as they recount their escapades.

Girls had a game, *tabewaba'zhnade* (*tabe*, "ball;" *waba'zhnade*, "stick"), played with two balls tied together and a stick. Two goals were set up several yards apart. The players were divided into two parties, each with its goal. They started in the middle and each side tried to prevent the other's balls from reaching the goal.

There were two games which were rarely, if ever, played except for stakes. One of these was played exclusively by women; this was called *ko^n'çi* (*ko^n*, part of the word *ko^{n}de*, the name of the plum; *çi*, "seeds"). The appliances were few and simple—a wooden bowl and five plum stones. Two played at a time. First, the number of counts that should constitute the game was determined—50 or 100 points. Sticks were used for keeping tally. The plum stones were "burned" so as to show certain forms. Two on one side had moons, two on one side had stars; there were three black sides and three white sides. The bowl containing the plum stones was tossed and the combinations of the stones as they fell had certain values. These counts were as follows:

Two moons and 3 black counted 5 if the game was 50, and 10 if the game was 100.

Two moons and 3 white, 2 stars and 3 black, and 2 stars and 3 white had the same count as the above. These counts were called *xu'be*, and whoever tossed and got any of these throws might keep on tossing so long as she could make *xu'be*.

One moon, 1 star, and 3 white counted 1.

One moon, 1 star, and 3 black counted 1 in a game of 50, and 2 in a game of 100.

One moon, 1 star, 1 black, and 2 white counted nothing.

Two moons, 1 black, and 2 white counted nothing.

Two moons or 2 stars, 1 white, and 2 black counted nothing.

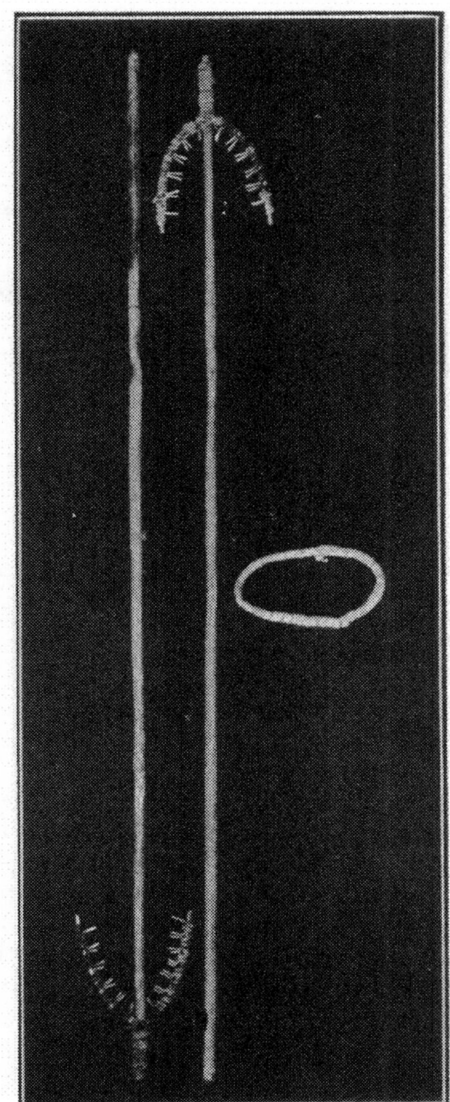

FIG. 84. Implements used in game of *pa'çi^{n}zhahe*.

The stakes put up were necklaces, moccasins, earrings, and paint.

The gambling game of the men was called *i'uti^n*, "hiding the stone." For this game there were used four moccasins and two small stones. Four persons played—two to hide the stones, two to watch and guess.

The two sides had their backers and watchers, who often contributed to the stakes, which consisted of all manner of articles—garments, weapons, horses, and other property. The number of chances to constitute a game was agreed on. Then the players sat down. Before one of the couples were laid four moccasins, the heels toward the player, two moccasins to a man. These each had a small stone which they were to hide under the moccasins before them while the men who sat opposite guessed under which of the moccasins the stones were hid. During the process of hiding, which was accompanied with many feints and movements intended to conceal the decisive act, songs were sung by the side supporting the guessers. The following belong to this class of songs:

GAME SONG No. 1.

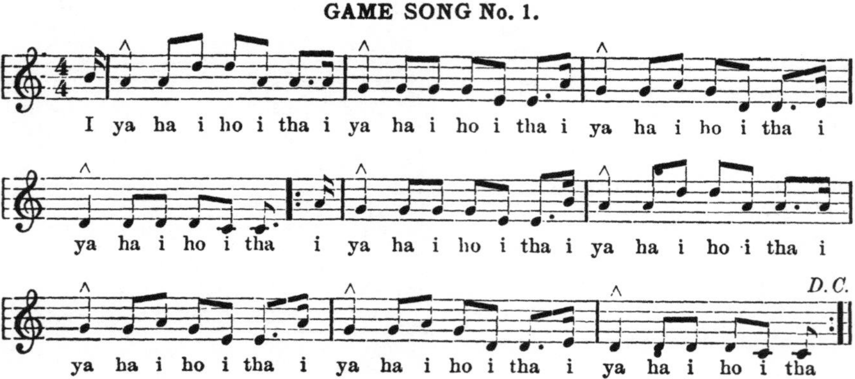
I ya ha i ho i tha i ya ha i ho i tha i ya ha i ho i tha i
ya ha i ho i tha i ya ha i ho i tha i ya ha i ho i tha i
ya ha i ho i tha i ya ha i ho i tha i ya ha i ho i tha
D. C.

The only words in song no. 2 are: *I'e zhi^n ga dada^n shkaxe,* "Little stone, what are you making?" All the rest in both songs are vocables.

Sometimes the game was played without moccasins, when the little stone or a small ball of buffalo hair was tossed between the hands. The outstretched arms were moved from side to side and the ball was dexterously passed from one hand to the other. This form of the game was very attractive, as the movements of the arms conformed to the rhythm of the song, and if the player was graceful as well as rhythmic, it was a pleasure to watch the game. The following song was a favorite for this game:

GAME SONG No. 2.

Ha a a ho e tha a Ha a a ho e tha a
Ha a a ho e tha a ho a a ho e tha I - e zhiⁿ - ga
da-daⁿ shka-xe? Ha a a ho e tha a Ha a a ho e tha

Foot racing was another pastime. Races generally took place among the Omaha, however, after a death, when gifts contributed by the family of the deceased youth or maiden were distributed among the successful competitors. At these races sharp contrasts marked the occasion. The race generally took place a short time after the burial. A feast was given by the parents, after which if the deceased was a young man his young men friends took part in the race; if a girl, her young companions competed for her possessions. The distribution of the goods was made by a personal friend, while the parents often retired to the grave, where the sound of their wailing could be heard above the noise of the contestants.

There was no ceremony in the tribe that corresponded to the drama, the acting out of a myth, a legend, or a story. There were dances and movements which were dramatic in character, as when at the meetings of the Hethu′shka society a man acted out his warlike experience (p. 466); also during the closing scenes at the ceremony of Anointing the Sacred Pole (p. 243). The dance at the Hoⁿ′hewachi was dramatic in purport and expression (p. 502); the secret societies had their dramatic acts in which both men and women took part (pp. 509, 565). The nearest approach to a drama was the He′dewachi ceremony (p. 251), but this was too fragmentary rightfully to claim to belong to the drama class. The tribal rites combined religious and social elements, and these ceremonies and the meetings of the different societies formed the principal social recreations of the people.

There was one amusement in which both sexes of all ages, except infants, took great pleasure; this was swimming. The Omaha swam by treading, moving hands and legs like a dog, or by keeping the body horizontal and throwing the arms up and out of the water alternately as the body was propelled by the legs. The people were good swimmers. The current in the Missouri is always strong, so that it requires a good swimmer to make a safe passage across the stream. During the flood season the current is too rapid for anyone to venture to cross the river. Diving was practised by boys and girls and was enjoyed by men and women also. In these water sports the sexes did not mingle; women and girls kept together and apart from the men and boys.

Story telling was the delight of everyone during the winter evenings. It was then that the old folk drew on their store of memories, and myths, fables, the adventures of the pygmies and of the *gajazhe* (the little people who play about the woods and prairies and lead people astray)—all these and also actual occurrences were recited with varying intonation and illustrative gesture, sometimes interspersed with song, which added to the effect and heightened the spell of the story or myth over the listeners clustered about the blazing fire The uncle (the mother's brother), who was always a privileged character and at whose practical jokes no nephew or niece must ever take offense, often made the evening merry with pranks of all sorts, from the casting of shadow pictures on the wall with his fingers to improvising dances and various rompings with the little ones.

In the spring, after the thunder had sounded, the boys had a festivity called *i^{n}de'gtheçe* (*inde*, "face;" *gtheçe*, "striped"), the word referring to the mask worn by the boys. A dried bladder, with holes cut for the mouth and eyes, was pulled over the head; the bladder was striped lengthwise in black and white, to represent lightning. The boys carried clubs and scattered over the village. Each boy went to the tent of his uncle (his mother's brother) and beat with his club against the tent pole at the door, while he made a growling sound in imitation of thunder. The uncle called out, "What does Striped Face want?" The boy disguised his voice, and said, "I want leggings or moccasins or some other article." Then the uncle called him in and made him a present. Should the uncle refuse to give anything the boy might punch a hole in the tent or do some other mischief. But generally the sport ended pleasantly and was greatly enjoyed by old and young.

IX

MUSIC

Instruments

The drum was the most important of Omaha musical instruments and generally accompanied most of the songs, both religious and secular. The large drum, called *ne'xegaku* (*ne'xe*, "a water vessel;" *gaku*, "to beat"), was made from a section of a tree hollowed out and partially filled with water containing charcoal. A buffalo skin, dressed or undressed, was stretched taut over the open end. A drum was always tuned before being used and if necessary during a ceremony it was tuned again. Tuning was done by tipping the drum so as to wet the skin cover from the water within and then drying it before the fire until it yielded the desired resonant tone in response to the tap of the drumstick. The tones were full and clear and could be heard at a great distance on a calm day. Drums were beaten either with a single strong stroke or with a rebounding movement—a strong stroke followed by a light one.

The small drum (*ne'xe gaku bthaçka—bthaçka*, "flat") was made by stretching a skin over a small hoop. This kind of drum was used by the "doctors" when attending the sick and in magical performances. It was beaten with a small stick, the movement being a rapid tapping—an agitated pulsation.

The whistle (*niçude*) was about 6 inches long; it was made from the wing bone of the eagle. It had but one opening and but one tone, a shrill sound, which was repeated with moderate rapidity, to simulate the call of the eagle. This instrument was used only in certain parts of the Wa'wa^{n} ceremony.

The flute or flageolet (fig. 85), *niçude tu^{n}ga* (*tu^{n}ga*, "big"), was generally made of cedar; it was about 20 inches in length and an inch in diameter. The holes—six in number—began about 4 inches from the lower end and were about an inch apart. The stop was placed 5 or 5½ inches from the mouthpiece at the end. This instrument had a flutelike tone but, being made by the "rule of thumb," lacked accuracy of pitch. To be acceptable, a flute must give forth a full, vibrating tone when blown with all the six holes closed. It was interesting to watch men, old and young, take up a flute to test it; they would readjust the stop piece, bound to the top over the opening and usually carved, and if after several trials the instrument

FIG. 85. Flute or flageolet.

could not be made to give this vibratory tone the flute would be laid aside and no words would avail to make the man take it up and play a tune on it. The compass of the *niçudetu^{n}ga* was an octave. The intervals did not correspond exactly to our diatonic scale.

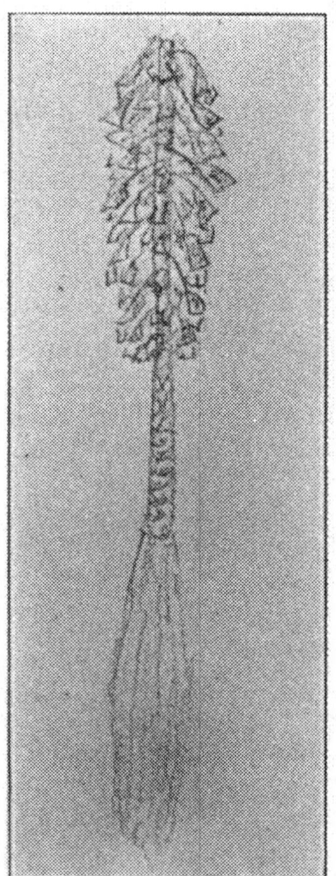

FIG. 86. Deer-hoof rattle (native drawing).

Two kinds of rattles were used: the *tasha'ge*, literally "deer hoofs" (fig. 86), and the *pe'xe*, "gourd rattle" (fig. 87, *d*). The *tasha'ge* was made by fastening the deer hoofs by thongs in a cluster to the sides of a beaded stick some 8 to 10 inches long, the handle being ornamented with a a long tassel of buckskin thongs. The *pe'xe*, as its name indicates, was made from a gourd from which the contents had been carefully removed and the interior surface of which made smooth, so that nothing should impede the contact of the fine gravel or beads with the inner side of the gourd and blur the sound. Through the holes made in both ends of the gourd, in order to remove the contents, a stick was thrust, closing them tight. One end of the stick protruded an inch or more from the top of the gourd; the other end, which formed the handle, was bound with buckskin, so adjusted as to make it firm and not to slip from the gourd. This kind of rattle was symbolically painted and used in the Wa'wa^{n} ceremony. The *pe'xe* was used also in the Wate'giçtu rite, when war honors were conferred. The Shell and Pebble societies and the "doctors" used this kind of rattle.

Songs, Singing, and Rhythm

Song was an integral part of the life of the Omaha. Through song he approached the mysterious Wakoⁿ'da; through song he voiced his emotions, both individual and social; through song he embodied feelings and aspirations that eluded expression in words. As is amply demonstrated in this volume, the Omaha did not depend on words to convey the meaning of his songs, so many have few or no words, the voice being carried by vocables only, and yet the songs were able to convey a well-understood meaning.

Songs, like the language, were transmitted from one generation to another and care was taken to preserve accurately both songs and language. No liberties were permitted with either. As to the songs, the writers have phonographic records of the same song sung by different groups of singers, the records having been taken at an interval of more than ten years, yet the songs show no variation. An interesting instance occurred some ten years ago. An old Ponca was visiting the writers, when, in a period of silence, he was heard to hum a familiar Omaha song. He was asked to sing the song into the phonograph, and did so. Then he was asked, "Where did you learn the song?" Among the Omaha," he replied. "When did you learn it?" "When I was a lad." "Have you always sung it as you sing it now?" With a look of astonishment he replied: "There is but one way to sing a song!" As he was a man then more than 70, his version of the song must have been of full fifty years' standing. On comparison of his rendition of the song with three other records of the same song from different singers in the possession of the writers, no variation was discovered. This incident, so far as it goes, indicates a fair degree of stability in the songs of this people. In many of the societies a fine was imposed if a member made mistakes in singing. As has been shown in preceding pages, a mistake in the singing of ritual songs invalidated the ceremony and made it necessary to begin again. It will be recalled that in the ceremonies connected with the Sacred Pole and the White Buffalo Hide if a mistake was made, a rite of contrition had to be performed, after which the ceremony was begun anew so far as singing the songs was concerned.

Songs were property. They belonged to a society, to a gens, or to an individual. They could generally be purchased from the last-named but the right to sing any of the songs belonging to societies or gentes could come only through membership or birth.

In singing, the Omaha was not concerned with his audience, he was not seeking to present a musical picture, his mental attitude was wholly subjective, he was completely occupied with voicing his own emotion, consequently he paid little attention, generally speaking, to any shading or what we term "expression." This statement can be fully appreciated only by those who have sympathetically watched the faces of Indian singers when they were singing with all the power of their lungs to the accompaniment of the drum. Nevertheless, beneath the noise moved the melody of which the singer was alone conscious.

Among the Omaha there was a standard of musical tones. The tuning of the drum has been spoken of and anyone who has observed the process can not deny that there was a standard of tone sought after. Among singers there were men and women who were recognized as "good singers." Their services were sought and paid for. They formed the choir or leaders on occasions when song had an important part, as in the Wa'wa^{n}, the Hethu'shka, and elsewhere.

Few Indian songs were ever sung solo. Almost all were sung by a group, many by a hundred or more men and women. The volume not only strengthened the tone but steadied the intervals. A single singer frequently wavered from pitch, but when assisted by a friend or friends the character of the tone at once changed and the pitch was steadied by the union of voices. It has been the constant experience of the writers that the Omaha objected to the presentation of their songs on a piano or reed organ as unsupported arias. As almost all their songs were sung by a number of singers, the melody moving by octaves, the overtones were often strongly brought out, and this may account for the Indian's preference for a simple harmony of implied chords, when their songs were interpreted on these instruments. "That sounds natural!" was their comment on hearing their songs so played, even when it was explained to them that they did not sing their songs in concerted parts; yet they still persisted, "It sounds natural."

The harmonic effects are more noticeable when women join in the singing. Women form part of many of the choirs, even of the warrior societies, and they join in the choral songs during religious ceremonies. The women sing in a high falsetto, consequently one often heard the melody sung in two octaves. When the song dropped too low for a natural tenor the singer took the octave above. In the same way, by octaves, the bass and contralto voices adjusted themselves in the unison singing.

The octave is seemingly the one fixed interval. The songs are not built on any defined scale. What has often been taken for a minutely divided scale is probably due to certain qualities in the native tone of voice, which is reedy and lends itself to vacillation of tone. The same song sung by a group, piano, and then sung forte is often hardly recognizable to the untrained listener. The noise of strenuous singing drowns the music to an alien audience accustomed to hear music objectively presented.

In a few instances the songs herein given have been interpreted by adding a simple harmony and in every instance the harmony given has been tested among the Omaha and been preferred by them when the song was played on the piano or organ. This manner of presentation has been chosen in order t o give some of these songs a chance to be really heard by the average person, for only the exceptional and musically gifted can discern the possibilities that lie in an unsupported aria; moreover, the single line of music stands for a song that is sung in octaves by a group of male and female voices and therefore is not a true picture of the song itself.

Rhythm is a marked characteristic of Indian music. Most songs present one or more rhythms in their rendition, for besides the rhythm of the melody with its rhythm of phrase the singers pulsate their voices, thus adding an inner rhythm, so to speak, to the general rhythm. This custom of pulsating the voice tends to produce the effect of uncertain intonation and interval. This statement is based on many experiments with different singers during a number of years. When in transcribing a song these pulsations were noted, so that when the song was played on a piano or organ the pulsations were represented by rapidly repeated notes, the rendition was always declared to be incorrect. In every instance in which a note was pulsated by a singer the tone had to be represented by a single note on the instrument and no argument would prevail to permit the pulsation to be indicated by rapidly struck notes on the piano or organ. In love songs, which frequently have long notes, the hand is sometimes waved at slight distance from the mouth so as to break the continuity of sound and give the tone a wavering character.

Frequently the aria of a song is in triple time, 3/4, 6/4, or 9/4, while the drum is played in 2/4 or 4/4 time. In these songs the two conflicting rhythms are syncopated and play against each other in a bewildering manner. The precision with which these complicated rhythms are given by the Omaha is remarkable. In the Wa′wa^{n} ceremony the movement of the pipes adds another rhythm, so that the ear and the eye are addressed simultaneously by the rhythm of the melody, of the drum, and of the swaying pipes, all forming, however, one harmonious rhythmic presentation. The rhythmic movement of a song must never be altered; to do so in even a slight degree blurs or destroys the song for the Indian.

In view of the above statements, it will be seen that the mere aria can not portray an Indian song as it really sounds when interpreted by the Indian singers, and these facts seem to justify their preference for a harmonized version of their songs when translated on the piano or organ.

The Wa'wa^{n} Ceremony

The Omaha name for this ceremony, Wa'wa^{n} ("to sing for some-one"), refers to one of the marked characteristics of the ceremony, the singing of songs accompanied by rhythmic movements of the two peculiar objects essential to the ceremony, the *nini'ba we'awan* (*nini'ba*, "pipe;" *we'awa^{n}*, "to sing with.")

According to the Sacred Legend, it was while a council was being held between the Omaha, including the Ponca, the Cheyenne, the Arikara, and other tribes, to bring about friendly relations, that this ceremony, with all its peaceful obligations, became known to the Omaha. The extent of country over which this rite once held sway has been referred to. (See p. 74.) It was a ceremony which made for the securing of peace between unrelated groups through the establishment of a ceremonial tie which should be regarded as of a nature as inviolable as that between father and son.

The two objects essential to this ceremony were similar to pipe-stems and ornamented symbolically but they were not attached to bowls and were never used for smoking. Still they partook of the significance of pipes in their sanctity, they were spoken of as pipes, and were held in the greatest reverence.[a] Songs formed an important feature of the ceremony and the singing was always accompanied by rhythmic movements of the pipe bearers and also of the pipes. This movement was spoken of as *nini'ba bazho^{n}*, "shaking or waving the pipes."

Each stem was of ash; a hole burned through the entire length permitted the passage of the breath. The length was seven stretches between the end of the thumb and the tip of the forefinger. The stem was feathered, like an arrow, from the wing of the golden eagle. Around the mouthpiece was a band of iridescent feathers from the neck of the duck; midway the length was a ruff of owl feathers; over the bowl end were stretched the head, neck, and breast of the mallard duck, tied in place by two bands of buckskin painted red, with long, flowing ends. Beyond the owl ruff were three streamers of horsehair dyed red, one at the tip of the stem, one at the owl feathers, and one midway between. These hair streamers were bound on by a cord made of the white hair from the breast of the rabbit. From each stem depended a fanlike arrangement of feathers from the tail of the golden eagle, held together and bound to the stem by two buckskin thongs; the end, which hung from the fan-shaped appendage, was tipped with a downy eagle feather. One of these fan-shaped feather arrangements was composed of ten feathers from the tail of a mature golden eagle. These were dark and mottled in appearance and were fastened to the blue stem; this pipe (fig. 87, *a*) represented the

[a] Throughout this section these articles will be referred to as pipes.

feminine element. The other stem, which was painted green, had its appendage of seven feathers from the tail of the young golden eagle. The lower part of these feathers is white; the tips only are dark. These were the feathers worn by men as a mark of war honors and this pipe (fig. 87, *b*) symbolized the masculine forces. It is to be noted that among the Omaha, as among the Pawnee, the feathers which were used by the warriors were put on the stem painted green to represent the earth, the feminine element, while those which were from the mature eagle and which stood for the feminine element, were fastened to the stem painted the color of the sky, which represented the masculine element; so that on each pipe the masculine and feminine forces were symbolically united. Near the mouthpiece

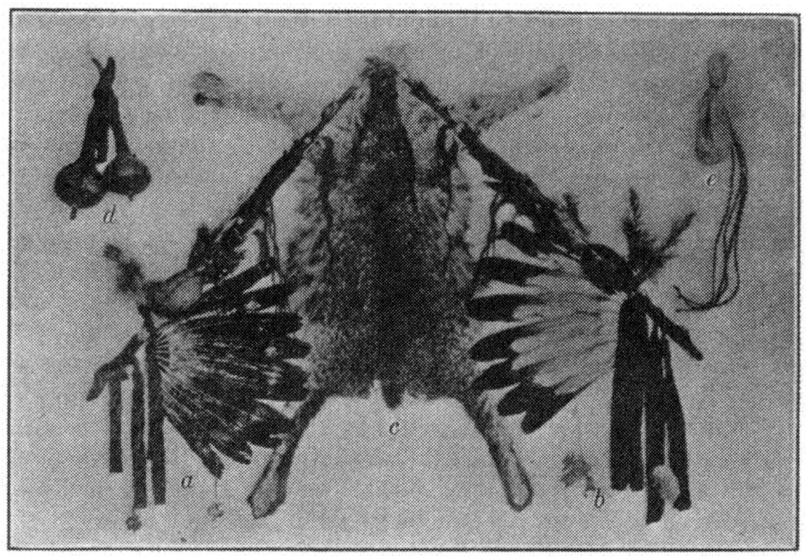

FIG. 87. Objects used in Wa' waⁿ ceremony.

was tied a woodpecker head, the upper mandible turned back over the red crest and painted blue. The pipes were grasped by the duck's neck, the mouthpiece pointing upward. When they were laid down, the stems rested in the crotch of a small stick painted red, which was thrust at the head of a wild-cat skin spread on the ground. This skin (fig. 87, *c*) served as a mat for the pipes when they were not in use and as a covering when they were being transported. The wild-cat skin was required to have intact the feet and claws, and also the skin of the head. Two gourd rattles (fig. 87, *d*), a bladder tobacco pouch (fig. 87, *e*) to which was tied a braid of sweet grass, a whistle from the wing bone of the eagle, and three downy eagle feathers completed the articles required for use in the ceremony.

Two parties, composed of persons having no blood relationship, were the principals in the ceremony. One was associated with the man who presented the pipes, the other with the man who received them. Among the Omaha the first was called *wa'wa^n aka,* "the one who sings;" the second was spoken of as *a'wa^n iaka,* "the one who is sung to." A man of one gens could carry the pipes to a man of another gens within his own tribe but not to a man belonging to his own gens; or he could take the pipes to a man of another tribe. The relation ceremonially established by taking and receiving the pipes was equivalent to that of father and son and the two parties were spoken of by these terms.

Only a man who had had the Wa'wa^n pipes presented to him four times was considered to be sufficiently instructed in the rites of this important ceremony to inaugurate a Wa'wa^n party. Before he could take definite action looking toward gathering the party together, he had to obtain the consent of the Seven Chiefs (see pp. 206, 376), particularly if he proposed to carry the pipes to another tribe.

A large amount of property was required to make up the gifts which must attend the presentation of the pipes; consequently the man who initiated the party was generally assisted by his relatives or close friends. The gifts that went with the pipes were eagle-feather bonnets, bows and arrows, red pipestone pipes, embroidered tobacco bags, otter skins, robes, and, in later years, brass kettles, guns, and blankets. The return gifts were horses (in earlier days burden-bearing dogs), bows and arrows, pottery, robes, and skin tent-covers. All these gifts, because they helped toward the peace and welfare of the tribe, could be counted as *wathi^n'ethe* either toward chieftainship or toward admission into the Ho^n'hewachi and thus the assistance given the "father" or the "son" of a Wa'wa^n party accrued to the giver's benefit by adding to his "count."

A Wa'wa^n party consisted of a dozen or more men. Sometimes the wives of a few of the leading men accompanied them and assisted in the work of the party. All the members contributed toward the gifts to be made and also toward accumulating provisions that would be needed on the journey, if a distant tribe was to be visited, and for the feasts to be given the receiving party during the four days and nights occupied by the ceremony. Ponies were sometimes taken as pack horses and occasionally the visiting men rode but generally the journey was made on foot. The pipes, incased in the catskin cover, were carried by their bearer, who with the leader of the party walked in advance, the other members following closely. If game was abundant, hunting was permitted to some extent; otherwise the party moved rapidly to its destination. No songs were sung on the journey but in those sung during the ceremony there were references to the traveling and the various events preparatory to the actual ceremony.

Owing to the loss of the Omaha ritual used when "tying the pipes"—a loss consequent on the death of the old men who knew it—a comprehensive comparison between the Pawnee version, already secured,[a] and the Omaha form of the same ceremony is impossible. While nearly all the articles used and their symbolism are identical, yet the absence of the ear of corn from the Omaha ceremony forms the most striking difference between the two. With the Pawnee the corn is spoken of as "Mother," and typifies Mother Earth, to whom the whereabouts and fortunes of man are known (op. cit., p. 44 et seq.). In the Omaha ceremony the corn has no place. With the latter tribe the eagle is the "Mother." She calls to her nestlings and upon her strong wings she bears the message of peace. With the Omaha, peace and its symbol, the clear, cloudless sky, are the theme of the principal songs and the desirability and value of peace are more directly expressed in the Omaha songs than in those of the Pawnee of this ceremony. It is the custom among the Omaha, when preparing the feathered stems, to draw a black line near the bowl end. The line does not show, for it is covered by the neck of the duck, but it is there, with its symbolism. It represents the neck or throat of the curlew. This bird in the early morning stretches its neck and wings as it sits on its roost, and utters a long note. This sound is considered an indication that the day will be cloudless. So, to all the other emblems on the stem this prophetic call of the curlew is represented as adding its song to the forces that make for the symbol of peace. In the I^{n}ke'çabe gens, which had the keeping of the tribal pipes, the name Ki'ko^{n}to^{n}ga, "curlew," is found. The name refers to this symbolic mark on the Wa'wa^{n} pipes. An old Omaha explained that "the eagle, whose feathers are on the pipes, and the wild cat, whose skin is their covering, are both fierce creatures and do not fail to secure their prey; but here, with the pipes, all their powers are turned from destruction to the making of peace among men."

Another emphasis of peace in the Omaha ceremony is found in the signification of the name given the child, who plays the same part in both the Pawnee and the Omaha version of the ceremony. Among the Omaha as with the Pawnee, the child represents the coming generations, the perpetuation of the race; but the Omaha emphasize the innocent character of the child, the absence of the warlike spirit. The name given the child is Hu^{n}'ga, the Ancient one, the one who goes before, the leader. In this name the continuance of the human family is implied but the name in this ceremony becomes the synonym for peace because "the child thinks no harm." The word Hu^{n}'ga forms a refrain in nearly all the Omaha songs of the ceremony. The meaning of the word and of the refrain were explained to the

---

[a] See The Hako, in the *Twenty-second Annual Report of the Bureau of American Ethnology*, pt. 2.

writers as given above. A like refrain does not occur in the Pawnee ceremony. The prominence given to peace in the Omaha version apparently confirms the account given in the Sacred Legend, that this ceremony was introduced to the people when a great council was being held in the interest of establishing peace among several tribes. This council seems to have taken place at a period in the history of the Omaha when the thoughtful members of the tribe were concerned for the very existence of the tribe itself, owing to the breaking away of groups, and "the old men" were devising means by which to hold the people more firmly together. This ceremony, which could take place only between unrelated persons, and which had a wide recognition among many tribes scattered over a vast territory, laid special stress on peaceful relations. So while among the Pawnee we find the teachings of peace embodied in the ceremony, they were not emphasized and dwelt upon with the same degree of insistence as among the Omaha. This difference becomes explicable when we consider the internal condition of the Omaha tribe and their relations to other tribes at the time the ceremony appears to have been adopted by them.

Among the Omaha the symbols on the stems were interpreted as follows: The green color represented the verdure of the earth; the blue color represented the sky; and the red color, the sun, typifying life. The straight groove, painted red, that ran the length of both stems stood for the straight path, representing the path of life and was interpreted to mean that if a man followed the straight path the sun of life and happiness would always shine upon him. The red streamers were the rays of the sun; the white cords that bound them the light of the moon, for night was believed to be the mother of day. The eagle was the bird of tireless strength. The owl, again, represented night and the woodpecker the day and sun; these birds stood also for death and life respectively. The downy feathers at the end of the thong that bound together the fan-like appendages were sometimes spoken of as symbolizing eggs and again, as the feathers of the young eagle, which fell from the bird when it matured and was able to take its flight. The gourd represented eggs and the reproduction of living forms. The band and the four lines painted on these were symbolic of the boundary line of the sky, the horizon, and the four paths of the four winds, at the four directions over which help comes to man. The tobacco pouch was similarly painted and to it were attached a braid of sweet grass, and a mat of buffalo hair such as falls from the animal when shedding its coat. The latter symbolized food and clothing and meant: "If you accept and follow the teachings of this ceremony, you shall go forth to search for food in safety and in peace." The sweet grass was used for its scent and was added to the tobacco when a pipe was smoked during the ceremony.

As has already been mentioned, in the Omaha form of the ceremony the eagle is the prominent figure; it supplants that of the corn in the Pawnee version. In the latter the pipes are taken up from their resting place on the wild-cat skin without song or ceremonial movement. In the Omaha ceremony the pipes are taken up wrth movements representing the eagle rising from her nest. These motions are accompanied by songs, some of which are of musical interest and beauty.

If the Wa′waⁿ party were taking the pipes to another tribe, when they were within a days journey four men were chosen to carry the tobacco pouch, which was painted symbolically with the circle and four dependent lines, and to which the braid of sweet grass and the mat of buffalo hair were attached. All four men wore the buffalo robe with hair outside, girded about the waist; the one who carried the tobacco pouch wore a downy eagle feather tied to his scalp lock. This person was called Ninia′thiⁿ (from *nini*, "tobacco," and *athiⁿ*, "to carry"—"tobacco carrier"). The four passed on rapidly to the lodge of the man whom the leader of the party had designated. Having arrived there, they entered the lodge and passed around the fire by the left. The tobacco pouch was placed in front of the man visited. The four then took their seats to the right of the entrance, filled a pipe (but not from the pouch brought), and offered it to their host. He then inquired who had sent him the tobacco bag. The bearer gave the name of the leader of the party and discoursed on the value of peace and peaceful relations between the two tribes. The host then sent for his relatives and followers to consult as to whether they could make the return gifts requisite and so accept the pipes. Only the inability to give the twelve to thirty ponies required as presents, or a recent death in the family, was considered a sufficient reason for honorably refusing the honor of receiving the pipes. If, however, the consultation with his relatives and friends resulted in a favorable decision, the host said to the young men: "Bid them hasten. Come, we are ready." The leader of the party was spoken of as *wa′waⁿ u′zhu* but he was addressed as "Father" and all of his followers as "Fathers." The man who received the pipes was addressed as "Son" and his party as "Sons."

The messengers hastened back and met the Wa′waⁿ party, who had slowly continued their journey. When very near the village the party halted, took the pipes from their covering, and placed them at rest on the crotched stick and the cat skin and sat down. They were met here by their host or one of his relatives, always a man of prominence, who bade them welcome. Then the party arose and two of the three principal singers took the pipes; the third stepped between them, holding the cat skin, in which was wrapped the crotched stick. The leader and other members took their places behind. Then the following song was sung:[a]

SONG OF APPROACH

Harmonized by John C. Fillmore to translate the music on the piano

♪ = 132 (Aria sung in octave unison)

f

The-thu ha - i - ba

f Trem.

Con Ped.

Huⁿ - ga

Huⁿ - ga

[a] The aria is sung in unison; the harmonization is added to translate the song to our ears and is so preferred by the Indians when played on a piano. The bass should be played lightly.

Thethu haiba
Thethu haiba thethu haiba the haiba a he
Thethu haiba the haiba
Thethu haiba Huⁿga
Thethu haiba a he
Thethu haiba the haiba
Thethu haiba Huⁿga

Literal translation: *Thethu*, here; *haiba*, they are coming: *Huⁿ'ga* refers to the child as a symbol of innocence, docility, and peace.

The song refers to the approach of the pipes. The people welcome the party, crying: "They are coming here!"

In singing this song the stems are waved to the rhythm of the music and the rattles are shaken with an accented beat but no drum is used. At the close of the song the party moves forward a little space, then a halt is made, and the song is repeated. There are four halts, at each of which the song is sung. The fourth halt is made at the entrance of the lodge, which has been prepared and stands ready for the ceremony. The actual entrance is in silence. When the west side of the lodge is reached, the pipe bearers stand facing the east and sing the following song:

Literal translation: *Ho!* exclamation; *ithathe*, I have found; *tha*, end of sentence. The words of the song are few but their meaning was explained to be: "Ho! I have found the man worthy to receive the pipes and all the blessings which they bring—peace, the promise of abundant life, food, and happiness." The words also imply a recognition of the qualities which make the man worthy of the selection, and which instigated the choice by the leader.

The following song was sung as the host and his relatives entered the lodge:

The huwine the huwine the huwine a he Huⁿ'ga
The huwine the huwine a he Huⁿ'ga

Literal translation: *The*, this; *huwine*, I seek; *a he*, vocables; *Huⁿ'ga* refers to the child, here the symbol of peace.

This song refers directly to the host and again implies that the one who was sought was one to whom peace was considered of great value; that the man's character was such as to hold the respect of his people and whose influence was for order and peace. The refrain *Huⁿ'ga* has a double reference—to the ceremony and to the character of the one to be made a "son."

After the singing of this song the pipes were laid at rest. The wild-cat skin was spread a little distance back of the fireplace, the crotched stick thrust into the ground at the head of the animal, and the stems were laid in the crotch; the pipe with the white feathers, representing the masculine force, lay uppermost. The rattles were placed under the winglike appendages; the ends with duck heads rested on the skin. After the skin had been spread and the stick put in place, the song used laying down the pipes was sung. In swaying the pipes the rhythmic movements simulated the eagle descending, then rising and again descending, until it rested on its nest.

There are no words to these songs; only vocables are used.

The pipe bearers now took their seats behind the pipes, which were never left alone throughout the entire ceremony (fig. 88). After the pipes were at rest the host left the lodge and the rest of the party busied themselves with unpacking and getting settled. The men usually occupied the lodge where the ceremony was to take place; if there were women in the party, a tent was prepared for them near by.

Soon after sunset the host reentered the lodge and took his place on the north side not far from the door. His relatives and friends were seated on both sides, the older men nearer the center, the young men toward the door. The Wa'waⁿ party sat between the pipe bearers and their host's party; the leader's seat was toward the north.

The servers of the party sat on both sides of the entrance. It was their duty to fill the pipes and attend to the fire and the cooking.

About the door were gathered the poor and the onlookers, who had no part in the ceremony. A feast had been prepared by the Wa'wa^{n} party but it was not served until near midnight. The pipes could not be taken up until some one of the host's party should rise and say: "Fathers, you have come to sing; we desire to hear you." This invitation required the gift of a horse. Then the leader of the Wa'wa^{n} party and the host both arose and advanced to the man who had spoken, as the act implied a gift. The host, standing before him, lifted both hands, palms outward, and then dropped them slowly. He then

FIG. 88. Pipe bearers and pipes in Wa'wa^{n} ceremony.

passed his right hand over the left arm of the giver from the shoulder to the wrist and repeated the movement with his left hand on the man's right arm, the sign of thanks. He then walked slowly in front of his kinsmen and friends, speaking to each man by a term of relationship, raising his right hand in further token of his thanks. The leader of the Wa'wa^{n} party then advanced to the giver and repeated the same movement indicative of his thanks. Raising his right hand, palm outward, he turned toward the left and then toward the right, to give thanks to all the host's relatives and friends gathered in the lodge. While this was going on within, an old man of the poorer class arose and passed out of the lodge, beginning as he went a song of thanks and finishing it outside the lodge. He introduced the name of the donor of the horse and to make sure that it was heard he called the name twice at the close of the song. This triple form of thanks was observed whenever a gift was made to the Wa'wa^n party.

At the conclusion of the thanks the pipe bearers arose and the pipes were taken up ceremonially. The movements simulated the eagle rising from its nest and making ready for flight. There are no words to the songs used to accompany these movements. These songs were repeated four times. The beauty of this part of the ceremony was greatly enhanced when the pipe bearers were graceful and could imitate well the flying, circling, rising, and falling of the bird. The feather appendages moved like wings as the pipes were swayed and both the eye and the ear were rhythmically addressed.

The following is one of the songs sung on raising the pipes. Only vocables are now used when singing these songs. Note the closing cadence when the eagle is up and away.

When the pipes were raised the three bearers, with the two pipes and the wild-cat skin, turned to the left and circled the lodge. The other members of the party followed, bearing the drum. A rhythmic side step was taken as the party faced their seated hosts, and the pipes were swayed so that the feathers moved like the wings of a bird slowly flying. The fire was always replenished just as the pipes started, so that the flames as they leaped filled the lodge with light and the shadows cast by the moving feathered stems seem to make real their simulation of the eagle's flight. If the song was familiar, as often happened, it was taken up by all present as the pipes approached and passed before the sitting people.

The following noble choral has been heard sung by three hundred or four hundred voices, male and female; no one is excluded because of sex or age, for, it is said, "The pipes are free to all." The volume of tone, the variety of voice quality, the singing in octaves, gave strong harmonic effects, and it was not surprising that the Omaha objected to such songs being given on an instrument as unsupported arias. The following harmonization was added to meet the demands of Omaha singers, who only gave their approval when the song was played as here presented. "Now it sounds natural" was their simple but unmistakable verdict.

The akede hiao tha
Ho tha kede hiao tha
The akede hia the he
Hiao tha kede hiao tha kede hia thehe

Literal translation: *The*, this; *awake*, what I meant (*wa* omitted in singing); *de*, sign of past tense; *hia*, here it is; *o*, vocable; *tha*, end of sentence. The second line has the same meaning as the first, the sounds being changed for ease in singing. The literal translation of the words of this song gives little idea of its meaning, but to the Omaha the song had a profound significance and its import as explained by the old men is borne out by the character of the music. The past tense refers to the teaching given in the past, to the fathers, whereby the blessing of peace could be secured, and this blessing is now brought here by the "tireless eagle" who bore it from the past, bears it in the present, and brings it to the "Son" with whom it will remain as a gift from Wako^{n}'da. Once, at the close of this song, a venerable man turned to the writers (all had been singing as the pipes passed around the lodge) and said: "Truly the pipes are from Wako^{n}'da."

The music of this choral presents points of interest, particularly as indicating what we term modulation, that is the passing from one key to another. On this point the late John Comfort Fillmore, a musical scholar of ability, wrote in 1892: "The song begins in the key of B flat. . . . the original key is kept until the fifth measure, in which the first clause ends with the relative minor chord. The next phrase of three measures is in the key of E flat (subdominant), the third measure effecting a transition to the key of F by means of the chord of G (over-third of E flat), followed naturally by the chord of C (dominant in F). The last clause begins in F, modulates to C, in the second measure and closes the period in that key. This key, the major over-second of B flat, the original keynote, would seem to be so remote as to make it impossible to preserve unity within the limits of a short 12-measure period. But the melodic flow is so smooth and the harmonic connections so natural that I, at least, do not get from it the impression of anything forced, harsh or unpleasant, nor do I feel the need of a return to the original tonic."[a] Much study was bestowed on this song by Professor Fillmore and many harmonization experiments were tried on Omaha Wa'wa^{n} singers during Professor Fillmore's visit to the Omaha reservation in Nebraska. The arrangement here given met with the expression of approval, "It sounds natural," when it was played to them on a reed organ, the only instrument there available.

---

[a] In A Study of Omaha Indian Music, in *Archæological and Ethnological Papers*, Peabody Museum, Harvard University, I, 295, Cambridge, 1893.

After the close of the preceding choral the pipe bearers again moved about the lodge, waving the feathered stems to the rhythm of the following song:

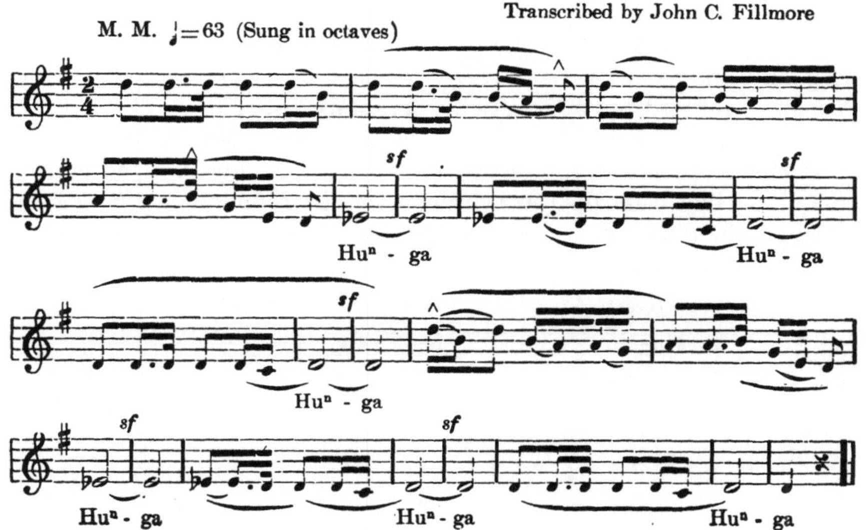
Transcribed by John C. Fillmore
M. M. ♩=63 (Sung in octaves)
Huⁿ - ga
Huⁿ - ga
Huⁿ - ga
Huⁿ - ga
Huⁿ - ga
Huⁿ - ga

The awake tha we the awake tha we
Tahesha we the awake tha we
Hu^{n}ga the awake tha we Hu^{n}ga
The awake tha we Hu^{n}ga
Tahesha we tha awake tho we
Hu^{n}ga the awake tha we Hu^{n}ga
The awake tha we Hu^{n}ga

Literal translation: *The*, this; *awake*, what I mean; *tha*, oratorical end of sentence; *we*, vowel prolongation; *tahesha*, an old word the meaning of which is lost. This word appears as a personal name in the I^{n}ke′çabe gens, which had charge of the Sacred Tribal Pipes. It probably had a symbolic meaning connected with the articles or with the teaching of this ceremony. *We*, vowel prolongation; *Hu^n′ga*, the name of the child who has a part in this ceremony.

This song followed and supplemented the preceding choral, which referred to a teaching that had been handed down. In this song the subject of this teaching was enunciated: "This is what I mean" (the present tense is used)—"*Hu^n′ga*," peace, which is to be accepted with the docility of the child. The song was a favorite one and was often expatiated on to the writers, particularly the teaching of the *Hu^n′ga*. This word is a modification of Ho^n′ga, a name (as already noted) which played an important part in the history of the Omaha and cognate tribes. It means "one who went before," an ancestor; also "one who goes before," one distinguished and important, a leader. The meaning of *Hu^n′ga* in this ceremony is made up of many aspects, all of which go to impress on the Omaha mind that from the beginning, down through the ages, and at the present time, that which preserves the race, even as does the child, is peace. Such was the explanation of the old men concerning this word so frequently used in these songs.

At the close of the song the pipes were laid to rest with ceremonial song and movements, as already described. Then the feast was served. Not far from midnight the company dispersed. The Wa'wa^n party remained in the lodge with the pipes and slept there.

At the first sign of the dawn the pipes were raised ceremonially and after they were up the bearers sang the following song as they stood in their places, facing the east, and swayed the pipes to the rhythm of the music:

(Sung in octaves)
Um - ba ya tho Ku - the go^n u - ho^n ga um -
ba ya tho Ku the go^n u-ho^n ga Um - ba ya tho
Ku the go^n u-ho^n ga um - ba ya tho Ku the go^n u-ho^n ga

Umba ya tho
Kuthe go^n uho^n'ga
Umba ya tho
Kuthe go^n uho^n'ga
Umba ya tho
Kuthe go^n uho^n'ga
Umba ya tho
Kuthe go^n uho^n'ga

Translation: *Umba*, day or dawn; *ya*, coming; *tho*, oratorical end of sentence; *kuthe go^n*, to move quickly, to make haste; *uho^n*, to cook, to prepare food; *ga*, sign of command. "Day is coming! Arise, hasten to prepare the food!" This song was repeated the second and third mornings of the ceremony.

No special ritual was observed on the second day. As gifts are generally made at this time, the songs used implied gratitude both for the gifts and for the promised success of the ceremony. The six songs that follow were sung on the second day.

Most of the *wa'wa^n* songs have but few words; they are supplied with vocables only. It was explained that these vocables are syllables representing words formerly used. As it was the custom among the Omaha to secure good singers to be the pipe bearers and leaders in the music, which was a special feature of the ceremony, the songs were not in the keeping of a priest; it was explained that syllables had been substituted for the original words to keep most of the words from the knowledge of the people. This statement may account for the paucity of words and the lack of particularity in the songs. Their meaning was general rather than related to some special and ritual action. The few words in this song and in all those sung on the second day were: *The*, this; *howane*, what I seek; *Huⁿ'ga*, peace.

The following three songs are interesting musically. No. 1 gives the theme in its simplest form; nos. 2 and 3 are variants. These three songs are regarded by the Omaha as distinct musically and are here given in order to show how little change is required to make songs sound differently to the native ear. They also throw a side light on the accuracy demanded in rendering songs and in their transmission, a marked peculiarity in Omaha music. It would be very easy for one of the white race to interchange these three songs as the difference between them is not striking.

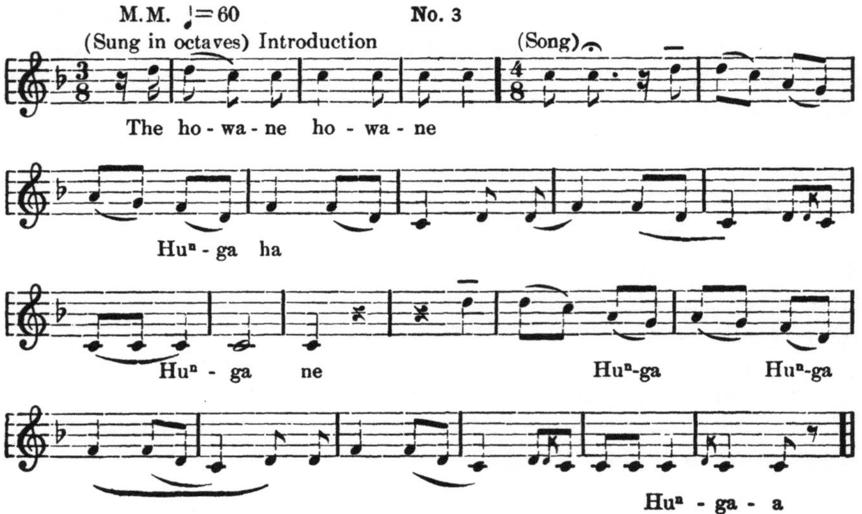

The rhythm in the following song is particularly strong and lends itself finely to the customary unison singing in octaves:

The following songs refer to peace under the symbol of the clear sky, *ketha*. This symbol embraces a reference to Wakoⁿ'da, who gives to man the sunshine, the clear sky from which all storms, all clouds, are removed. In this connection it should be remembered that the black storm clouds with their thunder and lightning are emblematic of war. The clear sky therefore represents the absence of all that could relate to war. Among the syllables sung to the music of these songs appear the words *ketha*, clear sky or peace, and *Huⁿ'ga*, childlikeness and peace. It is to be regretted that all the exact words of these songs are lost; they might have revealed something of the ritualistic progression of the ideas embodied in the ceremony. The fact that the only two words that remain stand for peace—one, *ketha*, peace as symbolized in nature, and the other, *Huⁿ'ga*, peace as symbolized by a little child—indicates that the peaceful teaching of the ceremony was that which appealed most strongly to the Omaha mind. Other phases, as can be observed in the Pawnee version, if they were ever a part of the Omaha version have been lost.

Flowingly, with feeling Double beat = 126
(Aria sung in octaves) Harmony by John C. Fillmore for translation on the piano
Ke - tha ya Huⁿ - ga Ke - tha Huⁿ - ga
Huⁿ - ga ke tha Huⁿ - ga
Huⁿ - ga Ke - tha Huⁿ - ga
Huⁿ - ga Ke-tha Huⁿ-ga Huⁿ - ga

Some of these *ketha* songs are gentle and pastoral in character, particularly this one; the words of the song were explained as meaning: "Fair as is the clear sky, the green grass, yet more fair is peace among men;" and the music bears out this interpretation.

(Aria sung in octaves) Harmonized by John C. Fillmore for interpretation on the piano

Double beat ♪ = 126 With dignity
Ke - tha ke - tha ke - tha ha
Ke- tha - a Huⁿ - ga - a - ha

Ke-tha - a Huⁿ - ga

The foregoing spirited choral is wonderfully stirring when sung by two hundred or three hundred voices, as the writers have heard it many times. It is spoken of as a "happy song."

When the weather was rainy, the following plea for a clear sky was sung:

(Sung in octaves)
Ke-tha we tha Huⁿ - ga
Huⁿ - ga
Huⁿ - ga
Huⁿ - ga
Huⁿ- ga
Huⁿ - ga
Huⁿ - ga

The only words are *ketha*, "clear sky," and *Huⁿ'ga*. It was greatly desired to have the sun shine during the ceremony, so when clouds gathered this prayer for clear weather was sung with much earnestness.

On the evening of the third day the gifts brought by the Wa'waⁿ party were presented to the host, who distributed them among his party.

On the morning of the fourth day the ceremony in reference to the child took place. There was no song nor any cooking of food. All must fast. The leader, or "Father," and the pipe bearer went to the lodge of the host, the "Son;" as they walked thither the following song was sung:

(Sung in octaves)

If this song ever had words, they are lost. Having arrived at the door of the lodge, they paused and sang as follows:

Atie tha weane
Atie tha weane
Atie tha weane
Zhi^{n}ga thi uwine the Hu^{n}ga
Atie tha weane
Atie tha weane
Zhi^{n}ga thi uwine the Hu^{n}ga

Literal translation: *Atie tha, atia tha,* I have come; *tha,* end of sentence; *weane,* a changed form of *uwine,* I seek you; *zhi^{n}ga,* little one, child; *thi,* you.

The party then entered the lodge where the little child, with its parents, was awaiting them. The leader carried clothing for the child and the skin pouches that contained the red and black paint. First the child was clothed; then a member of the Wa'wa^{n} party who could count honors won in defensive warfare was designated to paint the child. The pipes were waved to the following song as this ceremony took place:

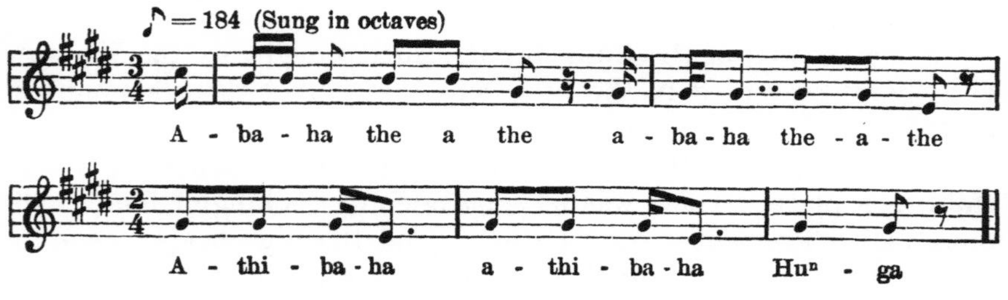

1

Abaha the athe, abaha the athe
Athi baha, athi baha Hu^{n}ga

2

Athaha the athe athaha the athe
Athethaha athethaha Hu^{n}ga

Literal translation: *Abaha*, to show; *the*, this; *athe*, I make; *athi baha*, to show you, *Huⁿ'ga*; *athaha*, to adhere; *the*, this; *athe*, I make; *athithaha*, to make adhere to you.

During the singing of the first stanza the man held the paint in its receptacle over the head of the child and showed it to all present. He first made a feint as if to touch the child with it. As the second stanza was sung he put red paint over the face of the child, then he drew a band of black across the forehead, a stripe down each cheek, one down the nose, and one at the back of the head. This design had the same meaning as that on the gourds. The band across the forehead represented the line of the sky; the stripes were the paths at the four directions whence the winds start; the red paint symbolized the light of the sun and the gift of life; the lines signified the winds—the breath of life, giving motion and power. In this connection the ceremony of Turning the Child should be remembered. (See p. 117.) This style of painting was called *Huⁿ'ga kioⁿ*, "Huⁿ'ga painting" (fig. 89). The dead of the Nini'batoⁿ subdivision of the Iⁿke'çabe gens were sometimes so painted for entrance into the life after death.

Fig. 89. Huⁿ'ga painting.

Then was sung the song which accompanied the act of tying the *hiⁿxpe'*, a downy eagle feather, on the child.

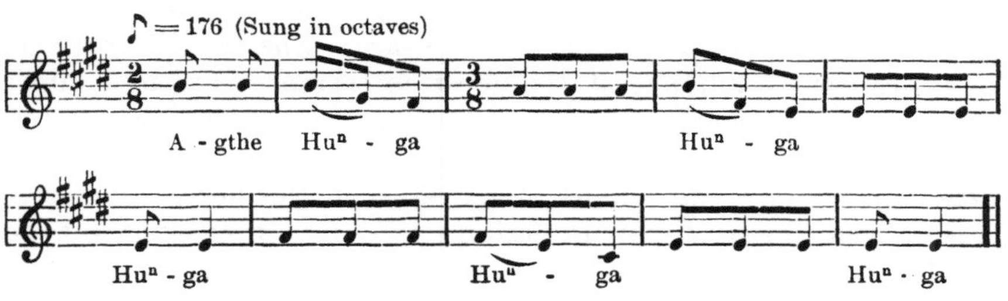

A'gthe Huⁿ'ga, etc.

Literal translation: *Agthe*, to put on something and make it stand.

Eagle down was sprinkled over the head of the child, making it look like a callow bird. The warriors counted their honors, and while they were telling of their deeds of valor performed in defensive warfare the following song was sung:

Harmonized by John C. Fillmore for interpretation on the piano

♪ = 176 (Sung in octaves)

Hu^n - ga ha - ne no tho Hu^n - ga ha - ne

Con. Ped.

D.C. ad lib.

no tho Hu^n - ga ha - ne no tho Hu^n - ga ha - ne

Hu^n'ga hani

Literal translation: *hani*, you have. Vocables fill out the measure of the music.

The meaning of this song and act was explained as follows: The reason why only honors won in defensive warfare could be counted at this time was that those men who had won such honors had done so because they had risked their lives for the defense of the women and children of the tribe; they had done deeds to promote safety and so to secure the perpetuation of the race. The act was symbolic and was considered one of the most important. It had a direct bearing on the teaching of the ceremony. If by any chance the Wa'wa^n party did not have a man who could recount deeds done in defensive warfare and honors so gained, then the host, "the Son," was obliged to seek a man to perform this part in the rite, for the child could not be lifted up and carried to the lodge where the ceremony was to be completed until a man had counted over it honors won in defensive warfare. This explains the meaning of the words

Huⁿ'ga hani—"you have the Huⁿ'ga," i. e., because of my acts the children live, "you have" them.

Note the change of key in the music and its implied harmonic modulation.

After the counting of honors the following words were sung:

Shoⁿ wiiⁿa tha

Literal translation: *Shoⁿ*, it is done; *wiiⁿa*, I carry you; *tha*, oratorical end of sentence.

The child was then taken on the back of a man, who followed the swayed pipes as this song was sung:

Zhiⁿga thi uwine Huⁿga, etc.

Literal translation: *Zhiⁿga*, little one, child; *thi*, you; *uwine*, I seek.

When the lodge was reached, the leader took his place outside at the right of the door and held the child between his knees. The singers took their seats at the left of the door. Two young men of the party were selected to perform the final dance. They were divested of clothing except the breechcloth. A red circle was painted on the breast and back, a *hiⁿxpe'* feather tied on the scalp lock. Each dancer carried one of the feathered stems.

Meanwhile all those who had made gifts of horses to the Wa'waⁿ party gathered their ponies and decked themselves in gala dress, and approached the lodge to witness the final dance. The singers started the music and the two young men, holding the feathered stems high above their heads, with a light, leaping step danced in two straight lines to and from the east, simulating the flight of the eagle. The line taken by the dancers signified that by following the teachings of the ceremony, the straight red line on the pipes, one could go forth and return in peace to his lodge and have no fear. As the young men leaped and danced—a dance that was full of wild grace and beauty—it might happen that a man would advance and stop before one of the dancers, who at once handed him the pipe. The man recounted his deeds and laid the pipe on the ground. The dance and music ceased, for the act was a challenge and the pipe could be raised only by one who could recount a deed equal in valor to that told by the man who had caused the pipe to be laid down. This stopping of the dance often led to spirited contests in the recital of brave deeds. While the dancing was going on, the ponies were led by the children of the donors to the leader and the little *Huⁿ'ga* stroked the arm of the messenger in token of thanks. When all the ponies had been received the final dance came to an end.

The man who had recounted his deeds and painted the *Huⁿ'ga* entered the lodge alone with the child and closed the door. He took the pipes, which had been folded together, and made four passes on child—down the front, back, and both sides. He then turned the child four times, and led it outside the lodge. This act of blessing the child was secret and no outsider but the host could be present. The pipes and all their belongings, wrapped in the wildcat skin, were then handed by the man who had blessed the child to the leader, who presented them to the host, saying: "My son, you have made me many gifts but they will disappear, while that which I leave with you will remain and bring you the blessing of peace." The "Son" then gave away the pipes, the wildcat skin, the tobacco pouch, and the rattles to those who had taken part with him in receiving the pipes. He retained none of the articles. Only by this act could he receive all the honor and advantage to be derived from the reception of a Wa'waⁿ party and enjoy all the promised benefits of the rite. The visitors then gathered their ponies, which were apportioned by the leader, and moved off. When a mile or two away they camped and partook of their first food after a fast of nearly twenty-four hours and then made their way home as rapidly as possible.

Many are the stories told by men and women of their experiences when they were *Huⁿ'ga*—of how tired they became, of the tidbits doled to them by the leader to keep them contented, of how when they rejoined their playmates the latter plucked at the down which clung to their hair and made sport of their queer looks. Nevertheless in after life it was regarded as an honor to have been a *Huⁿ'ga* and the inconvenience was remembered only to make merry with.

The Omaha Wa'waⁿ, while lacking some of the elaborateness of the Pawnee version of the same ceremony, was not without beauty and dignity. It was a ceremony that was dear to the people. It was held in a reverence free of fear and strongly tinctured with the spirit of kindliness and happiness. Its songs, being free to both sexes and to all ages, were widely known in the tribe and greatly enjoyed.

THE CEREMONY AMONG THE PONCA

According to a Ponca tradition, the Wa'waⁿ ceremony was instituted at the time the seven pipes were distributed at the formation of the tribe as it is at present. This tradition would seem to place the event about the time that the ceremony was accepted by the

Omaha when peace was made through it with the Arikara and other tribes. (See p. 74.) This ceremony was known and observed by the Ponca as among the Omaha and the same songs were used, for the Ponca had none of their own composition belonging to it. According to Hairy Bear the closing act, "blessing the child," which was secret among the Omaha, was open with the Ponca and differed in some of its details. After the pipes had been folded together and wrapped in the wildcat skin they were raised high over the head of the little *Huⁿ'ga*, then brought down slowly so as to touch the forehead of the child and passed down the front of the body to the feet until the mouthpiece rested on the toes, which it was made to press strongly on the ground; then the pipes were laid for a moment on the ground in a line toward the east, as the following words were spoken: "Firm shall be your tread upon the earth, no obstacle shall hinder your progress; long shall be your life and your issue many." The movements with the folded pipes were repeated on the right side of the child from its head to its feet and the pipes laid in a line toward the south, as the promise was repeated. The movements were next made on the back of the child and the pipes laid in a line toward the west, while the promise was given. Lastly the pipes were passed over the left side of the child and then laid in a line toward the north, as once more the promise was given to the child, who stood at the intersection of the four symbolic lines, "in the center of the life-giving forces." The child was then told to "walk four steps toward the sun." [a] When this was accomplished the little one was dismissed and the Wa'waⁿ ceremony came to an end.

[a] The taking of the four steps suggests the rite of Turning the Child (see p. 121).

X

WARFARE

Influence on Tribal Development

Two classes of warfare were recognized among the Omaha, defensive and aggressive. Each had its distinctive rites, its rank, and its duties in the tribal organization.

Defensive warfare was called *ti'adi,* meaning "among the dwellings," or *wau'atathisho*^{n} (*wau,* "women;" *ata'thisho*^{n}, "toward or pertaining to;" that is, "fighting for the protection of the homes, the women, and the children"). The Omaha word for "tribe," already explained (p. 35), was derived from fighting of this kind. In the use of this word one can get a hint of the growth and influence of defensive warfare. Self-protection naturally expanded toward the protection of one's family and to extend this protection to a group of families living near together was a logical progression and leading naturally to an appreciation of the necessity for permanency in the group to be protected. When therefore the thought expressed by the Omaha word for "tribe" had taken hold of the people so strongly as to become the name of a community held together at the risk of life against outside aggressors, that community had ceased to be a congeries of people and had become a more or less stable association of persons among whom political ideas could take root.

It has been shown that the Omaha tribal organization was based on certain fundamental religious ideas pertaining to the manner in which the visible universe came into being, and is to be maintained, and to man's relation to the Cosmos and to living forms. All these ideas were conceived anthropomorphically, for the Omaha projected his self-consciousness on nature. These conceptions were more or less clearly expressed in dramatic ceremonials, ceremonials that tended to bind the people together as expressions of a common faith.

The disintegrating tendencies of aggressive warfare, particularly the quarrels and schemes of ambitious men, were checked by the inculcation of the idea that war is allied to the cosmic forces and under their control. The storm, with its destructive lightning and deafening roar of thunder, was regarded as the manifestation of the war phase of the mysterious Wako^{n}'da. As has been shown, all Omaha males in their childhood were consecrated to Thunder as the god of war. The warrior was taught that it was this god, not man, who decreed the death on the field of battle; this mode of death was called *i^{n}'gthu^{n}gaxthi* (*i^{n}'gthu^{n}*, "thunder;" *ga*, "action by the hand;" *xthi*, "to bruise," as with a club), the term applied also to death caused by lightning. In this connection should be remembered the reference to the "Grandfather's club" in a song used in the Wate'giçtu (p. 437) and also the round stick bound to the ancient cedar pole (fig. 57). The application of this term to death on the battlefield probably had a double significance; it referred to the teaching that the life of a warrior was in the keeping of the Thunder god (see p. 126) and to the time when the club was the only weapon of the man. The word is said to be an old term, as evidenced by its transference to a warrior's death by an arrow or a gun. This teaching tended to change, in the Omaha mind, the character of warfare; it placed the warrior under a supernatural power over which he had no control, and, while it did not eliminate from him the spirit of revenge or hatred, it curtailed a man's estimate of his own ability to exploit vengeance on his fellows. This teaching was formulated in rites the performance of which was essential to the initiation of aggressive warlike expeditions, rites that became an effective means of establishing and maintaining tribal control over warfare.

The close connection between Thunder and the Sacred Tent of War was confirmed in popular belief by coincidences that were interpreted to indicate the watchfulness of the Thunder god over the war rites of the tribe. Within the last century the keeper of the Sacred Tent of War died and the man to whom the office descended was so afraid of the Tent and its duties that he refused to assume the office and kept away from the Tent. His brother was the next in the hereditary line, but he also feared the responsibility and left the Tent standing alone and uncared for. Shortly afterward both men were killed by lightning, and their deaths were regarded as a punishment sent by the Thunder god for the disrespect shown the office of keeper by their neglect of duty toward the sacred rites committed to their care. The punishment was believed to apply only to this life; it shortened the days of the offenders but did not affect their life after death.

Aggressive warfare was called *nuatathisho^{n}* (*nu*, "man;" *ata'thisho^{n}*, "in the direction of;" that is, "war with men"). The use of the word *nu*, "man" or "male," is noteworthy, particularly in connection with a ritual song used in according honors to the warrior, where again the word is employed, indicating that war was waged against men. While it is true that in attacks on villages women and children were sometimes killed they were not invariably put to death

WAI$^{N'}$WAXUBE

Aggressive warfare was under the control of rites which were connected with the *wai$^{n'}$waxube*, or Sacred Packs of War. (*Wai$^{n'}$* was the common name for a pack—a receptacle made of skin, frequently of parfleche, in which articles could be laid away and kept safely; *waxu'be*, "sacred"). There was another name applied to these packs: *wathi'xabe*, "things flayed," referring to the contents of the packs, which were the skins of certain birds. It was the presence of these bird skins, which represented the species and the life embodied in the species, that made the *wai$^{n'}$*, or pack, *waxu'be*, or sacred.

There is no tradition as to the origin of these packs. Probably none of those now existing in the Omaha tribe are much more than two centuries old. The pack itself was not sacred, only the contents. The association of birds with the powers of the air is very ancient. Particular birds were thought to be in close relation with the storm and the storm cloud, the abode of Thunder, the god of war. The flight of the birds brought them near the god and they were regarded as his special messengers; moreover, from their vantage point these denizens of the air could observe all that occurred on the earth beneath. When the warrior went forth to battle the birds watched his every act and through them the Thunder became cognizant of all his deeds. The swallows that fly before the coming tempest were regarded as heralds of the approaching god. The hawk and other birds of prey were connected with the destruction caused by the death-dealing storm. The crow and other carrion birds haunted the places where the dead lay and were allied to the devastating forces of the god of war. Upon this ancient belief relative to the connection between the birds of the air and the manifestations of the powers dwelling in the sky (the wind, the thunder, and the lightning) the war rites of the Omaha were built. It was only after the performance of certain ceremonies connected with these packs, wherein were kept the representatives of the birds which could act as officers, so to speak, of the Thunder, that the Omaha warrior could go forth to aggressive warfare with the sanction of the recognized war power of the tribe. How important this sanction was is revealed in the responsibility and punishment accorded the war leader who omitted to secure it for his venture. If a man among the Omaha who organized a war party secretly and stole away to carry out his designs of revenge or the acquiring of booty, in the battling chanced to lose a member of his party, he was accounted and punished as a murderer. In any event, no matter how bravely he might have acted, none of his deeds could receive the public honor which otherwise he would have secured.

Early in the last century such an unauthorized party stole away. They met with disaster and one of their number was killed. This misfortune placed the lives of the survivors in jeopardy. Realizing the trouble he had brought on himself and his companions, the leader secretly returned to the tribe and went to his father, one of the chiefs, for help. The chief, approaching his son, bade him and his companions to strip off all their clothing and put clay on their heads, and in this guise publicly to enter the village. They were met by the people with taunts and angry words; the only reply of the returning warriors was to lift their hands in an appeal for mercy. They were driven through the village by the incensed people but through the influence of the chief they escaped serious consequences as murderers. At last the chief declared that they had been sufficiently humbled and punished for their disobedience to tribal law. Gifts had to be made to the relatives of the deceased member of the party. In olden times members of an unauthorized war party which had lost any of its number, on their return were forced to strip themselves, put clay on their heads and faces, crawl on their hands and knees to the lodges of the principal chiefs, and there cry for mercy. During the last century a man well on toward high rank as a chief yielded to temptation and joined an unauthorized war party. He returned successful, but his progress toward chieftainship was arrested and during the lifetime of Big Elk (p. 83) the man was not allowed to meet with the chiefs or to take any part in tribal affairs. Other instances could be given of the debasement of men who joined unauthorized war parties, even if successful.

AUTHORIZATION OF A WAR PARTY

When a man wished to lead a party out on aggressive warfare, either to avenge an injury received or to obtain booty from an enemy, it was his duty to go to the keeper of a *wai^{n}'waxube*, or Sacred Pack of War, and invite him to a "feast." The term "feast" is used in a limited sense only; it does not imply a sumptuous meal but a repast, always very simple as to the food, partaken of in honor of an action or a person. This feast had to be repeated four times. After the fourth feast the keeper of the Sacred Pack opened it before the would-be leader, explained to him his duties, instructed him as to the rites he must perform morning and evening and how to organize and conduct his party as to scouting and attacking the enemy. Not infrequently some one of the sacred birds was given the leader to carry on the war path and on his return he was required to take it back to the keeper of the pack.

Besides the birds, there were certain charms concealed in small bags in these packs that were believed to help the leader and his men. What these little skin bags contained was a secret not imparted even to the man to whom they were loaned. Generally these charm bags were put into a pouch, which was carried by one of the party. When, however, the men were about to make the attack, each man fastened his own charm bag on his person.

There were four of these Sacred Packs among the Omaha. A difference of opinion existed among the old men as to the rank of these packs; but, taking all the evidence obtainable into consideration, it seems probable that the pack which belonged to the Sacred Tent of War, in charge of the We′zhi^{n}shte gens, had the widest authority and significance. Its rival was a pack that was the hereditary charge of Geu^{n}′habi, of the Wazhi^{n}′ga itazhi subgens of the Tha′tada gens. This pack was associated with a remarkable man named Wa′baçka, who lived in the eighteenth century and who led a memorable fight against the Pawnee. On that occasion, not only did Wa′baçka obtain authority for his war party from the keeper of this special pack but he carried the pack with him. It was because of the association of the pack with this historic event that it became specially honored by the Omaha tribe. As the story illustrates Omaha customs and is well known to the people, it is here given:

The Omaha and the Pawnee were at peace, when some Pawnee men raided the Omaha village and drove off a number of horses. At that time horses were not so plentiful as they became later; they were a comparatively new acquisition and were very valuable. Wa′baçka was not a chief but a man of position and had what might be called wealth, as he owned several horses. All these were driven away by the robbers. Thinking that the act was committed by some thoughtless, adventurous young men—for the two tribes were on friendly terms—Wa′baçka, accompanied by a few men who also had suffered loss, started for the Pawnee village to lay their grievance before the principal chief, who they felt would surely require the young men to restore the property taken from a friendly tribe. There are different stories told of what happened on this visit but all show that the chief did not take the matter so seriously as the Omaha thought he should. He said that his young men were in need of horses and had borrowed them, and bade the Omaha go back home and make arrows for the Pawnee (the Pawnee were not as good arrow and bow makers as the Omaha) and in the spring they might come again and the Pawnee would return the horses for the arrows. Another story runs that a Pawnee chief, to whom one of the party appealed, placed before the Omaha a large bowl of beans, and, laying beside it a war club, bade the Omaha eat all the food on pain of death. In any event, the Omaha felt themselves insulted—they had come peaceably and were willing to condone the Pawnee action if only the property were restored. When they were bidden to come again with arrows to exchange for their own horses, Wa′baçka said he would go back and make arrows and return with more than the Pawnee would care to see. As he left the Pawnee village the boys and young men laughed at him and his friends because of their fruitless errand.

On the way back Wa′baçka threw away his moccasins, leggings, and shirt, cut off the corners of his robe, and on entering the Omaha village went to the chief's house and stood there wailing, his hands lifted to heaven. He cried aloud of the insult that had been put on the Omaha by the Pawnee and called on the people to avenge the wrong done. The people listened but said nothing. At length a young man who was greatly moved composed a song telling of the occurrence, and went about the village singing it. He called on the people to rise and wipe out the insult put upon them.

This song has not come down to the present time. Finally the people were aroused; every man began to make arrows and the women to make moccasins. Wa′baçka hewed a club and said he would use this weapon only against the offending Pawnee. So great was the fervor created in the tribe, that the chiefs temporarily set aside their office and all the people were given into Wa′baçka's control without reserve. It is said that this is the only instance known in which the control of the people was given to one man. Meanwhile Wa′baçka had received authority from a sacred pack, and also had secured permission to take it with him. When the time came to start, the whole tribe went with Wa′baçka—men, women, and children. The women composed a song which was sung on the march across the country. This song has lived and as it has been used by the women since that time as a *we′ton waan*—a song to send strength to the absent warrior on the battlefield—it is probable that it originally belonged to that class of songs.

Uhe kithame
Wa′baçka ha xage wathastaⁿ zhiadaⁿ he
Kithame
He kithame

Literal translation: *Uhe kithame,* they yielded to his request; *ha,* vowel prolongation; *xage,* to cry; *wathasta*ⁿ *zhiada*ⁿ, he ceased not, for that reason.

Free translation

His call they obeyed!
Wa′baçka raised his voice, nor ceased to cry aloud.
Come with me!
They all obeyed.

As horses were scarce and the skin tents heavy, when about half a days journey from the Pawnee village the people halted and on the banks of Maple creek (a branch of the Elkhorn river, Nebraska) they buried their tents; this act gave rise to the name Ti′haxaike, which the stream still bears among the Omaha.

Before day the warriors, led by Wa′baçka, started for the Pawnee village, which was surrounded by a strong palisade. This they leaped and rushed in on the sleeping Pawnee. Tearing away the sods from their earth lodges, they set fire to the straw that covered the wooden structure beneath and as the smoke drove the people out they were slaughtered. Wa′baçka went direct to the lodge of the chief who had slighted the peaceful overtures made the year before and clubbed him to death. The battle was fierce; many were slain on both sides. The Omaha were avenged. They took all the booty they could carry; but the battle cost them the life of their leader, Wa′baçka, who fell, fighting to the last for the honor of his tribe. His death brought the battle to a close.

The club made and used by Wa′baçka is said to be preserved in the pack he carried at that time. An old man who, before the middle of the last century, had been instructed as a war leader from this pack, said that it contained one bird hawk, one blackbird, one swallow, one crow, and a bladder tobacco bag. This old man's party killed a Dakota and brought back the man's scalp; when the victory dance was being held some blackbirds came and alighted on the pole to which the scalp was attached and swallows swept over and about the camp. As the old man saw the birds, he called to the people: "They have come to greet us!" He had carried on the warpath a blackbird and a swallow from the pack Wa′baçka had used and he believed that the living representatives of the birds he took to watch over him had come to approve and to welcome the victorious party; all the people rejoiced at this favorable omen and believed it had been sent by the Thunder god.

ORGANIZATION OF A WAR PARTY

A war party varied in numbers from eight or ten up to a hundred warriors. A man seldom went on the warpath alone unless under the stress of great sorrow, as that caused by the death of a child or other near relative. He might then go forth to seek opportunity to kill some one who would be a spirit companion for the one who had recently died. If it was a child whose loss sent the father to seek an enemy, the little one's moccasins were taken along in the father's belt. If he found a man and killed him, he placed the moccasins beside the dead man and, addressing the spirit, bade it accompany the child and guide it safely to relatives in the spirit land.

All members of a war party were volunteers. As soon as a man determined to become one of a war party and gave notice of his determination, tribal custom obliged him to observe strict continence until his return to the tribe; disobedience of this requirement, it was believed, would bring disaster to him or to the people. The old men explained that this rule was based on the same reason as that which forbade marriage at such a time (p. 325); moreover if the man were married and should be killed, he might leave an unborn child to come into life without a father.

War parties were of two classes—those organized for the purpose of securing spoils and those which had for their object the avenging

WOLFSKIN WAR ROBE WORN BY ZHI^N^GA'GAHIGE

of injuries. The latter were held in higher esteem than the former, and the men who took part in them were regarded with more respect by the tribe.

The *nudo^n'ho^{n}ga,* or war leader, was the commanding officer. He directed the movements of the party and had to be ready to sacrifice his life for its safety if circumstances required. A war leader who in any way sought his own convenience and security or provided for himself first, incurred lifelong disgrace. The members of the war party were addressed by the war leader as *ni'kawaça,* a very old word indicating those who are not officers—similar to the term "privates." The leader assigned men to certain duties. There were four classes of service:

(1) The hunters, whose duty it was to provide game for the food of the party.

(2) The moccasin carriers. A large number of pairs of moccasins were necessary; otherwise the men would become footsore on the long journeys undertaken.

(3) The kettle carriers. These had charge of all the cooking utensils.

(4) Those who built the fires, brought the water, and carried the provisions of the party.

For services 2, 3, and 4 men of strength rather than agility were chosen.

DRESS OF WARRIORS

The warriors formerly wore a white covering for the head, of soft dressed skin; there was no shirt, the robe being belted about the waist and tied over the breast. For this latter purpose strings were fastened to the robe, the place where they were sewed being marked by a round piece of embroidery. When the war leader had once tied over his breast these strings that held the robe together, custom did not permit him to untie them until the scouts reported the enemy in sight. No feathers nor ornaments could be worn. In actual battle the warriors wore only moccasins and breechcloths unless they put on some skin connected with their vision. (See p. 131.) The accompanying illustration (pl. 54) shows a wolf skin worn by Zhi^{n}ga'gahige. A slit at the neck of the skin admitted the wearer's head, the wolf's head rested on the man's breast, and the decorated skin hung over his back.

When an enemy had been slain, the war leader painted his face black. Later, on the return to the village, all who had taken part in the fight put black paint on their faces.

Occasionally the wives of a few of the men accompanied a large war party. They assisted in the care of the moccasins and in the cooking. The women of a war party were allowed a share in the spoils taken because they had borne their part in the hardships of the journey.

The following *mi'kaçi* (wolf) song refers to this custom:

(Aria as sung) Harmonized by John C. Fillmore for interpretation on the piano
Hé-a e yaw ha - a hi-a e - yaw ha - a
Con Ped.
hi - a - e - yaw ha hi- a e - yaw ha a we tha he
he tho - i we - tuⁿ - gá de se - sa sa aⁿ - thuⁿ -
waⁿ- ge he ya hi - a e - yaw ha we - a - he tho

Hia e yaw haa
Hia e yaw haa
Hia e yaw haa
Hia e yaw ha a we tha he he thoi
Wituⁿga de sesasa aⁿthuⁿwaⁿgihe ya
Hia e yaw ha wea he tho

Literal translation: First four lines and last line, vocables. *Wituⁿ'ge*, younger sister; *se'sasa*, trotting; *aⁿthuⁿwaⁿgihe*, follows me.

Women were always spoken of as "sisters." The words picture the little sister trotting along with her share of the spoils, following the warriors. The lively music has a quaint charm.

SACRED WAR PACK AND CONTENTS

The Sacred War Pack, which was kept in the Tent of War, together with the other articles kept in this tent, was deposited in 1884 in the Peabody Museum of Harvard University, where they have been examined and photographed. This pack (fig. 90; Peabody Museum no. 37563) is of skin; it was so rolled as to present the

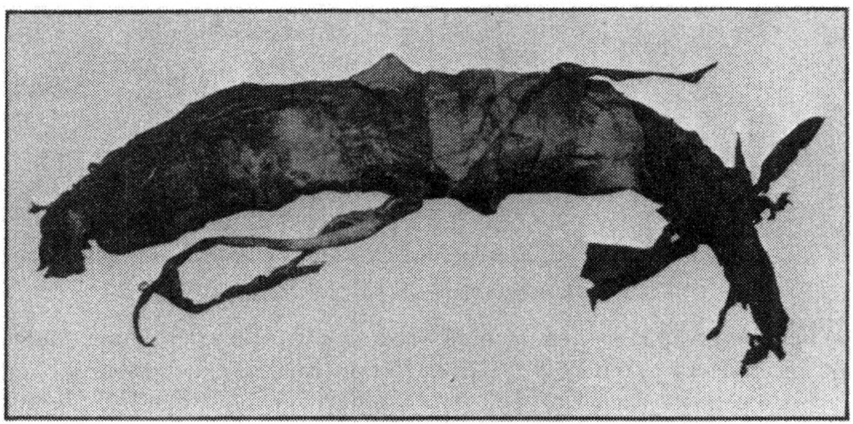

FIG. 90. Sacred War Pack (unopened).

appearance of a large, long-bodied bird, one end being fringed to represent the tail. It is 800 mm. long and 300 mm. in circumference; the length of the tail is 220 mm. The pack was held together by a band wound about it twice. A band about the middle had ends so looped that the pack could be hung up or carried, if necessary. There are a number of slits in one end of the skin covering through which a piece of hide was threaded in and out so as to gather the covering and form the neck of the bird; this end is the head. The other end is slashed to represent the tail feathers. The covering is wide enough to be wound twice about the contents and twisted at the neck end, but not at the tail end. It was folded over and tied by bits of hide knotted on the under side. When the pack was opened it was photographed with the contents in situ (fig. 91; Peabody Museum no. 47820).

The first article met with was a flag, carefully folded (fig. 92; Peabody Museum no. 47821); all efforts at identification of this flag have thus far failed. There is no knowledge of it in the tribe.

FIG. 91. Sacred War Pack (opened to show contents).

Whether it was captured, or presented to a war party by some trader in an effort to extend his business to the Omaha, is conjecture.

Six swallows, each wrapped in a bladder, four laid together (*c*) and two (*a, b*) below these, were beneath the folded flag (fig. 93; Peabody Museum no. 47817). Next was a falcon, the legs tied with a twisted cord of sinew, painted red. Below this was a swallow-tail kite (*Elanoides forficatus*) (fig. 94; Peabody Museum no. 47816). This bird is lined with cloth, native weaving of nettle-weed fiber. Several strands of native thread are fastened to the tail and a scalp lock is tied to the right leg. There were also a swallow-tail hawk (*Nauclerus furcatus*), a wolf skin, and seven skins of the fetus of the elk. The last-named are said to have been used by the chiefs in a ceremony now lost, which was not unlike some of the ceremonies of the Shell society, these elk skins taking the place of the otter skin.

FIG. 92. Flag found in Sacred War Pack. Inner rectangle represents flag. Dimensions: 6 ft. 9 in. by 4 ft. 9 in.; of corner rectangle, 2 ft. 6 in. by 2 ft. 9 in. Colors: darkest sections, red; lightest, yellow; remainder, blue.

The wolf skin is that of a young animal; in place of the feet, which had been cut off, was tied a tuft of elk hair, painted red. The head also has been cut off and a thong run through holes made in the neck,

FIG. 93. Objects from Sacred War Pack.

FIG. 94. Swallowtail kite from Sacred War Pack.

to which is fastened a feather, the quill of which is painted in red bands and bound to the thong with a strip of porcupine work and a tuft of elk hair, making a kind of tassel at the end of the thong.

Near the hind legs holes have been made in the skin through which passes a thong. (Fig. 95; Peabody Museum no. 48256.)

FIG. 95. Wolf skin and other objects from Sacred War Pack.

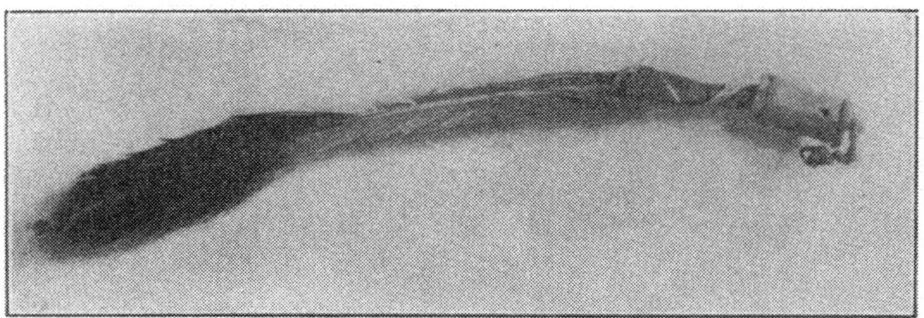

FIG. 96. Eagle feather in bone socket, from Sacred War Pack.

The wolf skin is said to have been used in augury by a war party. The banded quill of the feather forming part of the tassel was just above a bladder tobacco pouch, which was folded within the skin, as was also the eagle feather fastened in a bone socket for tying to the scalp lock. (Fig. 96; Peabody Museum no. 48264.) A war party sometimes resorted to augury to ascertain the conditions in the country to which they were going and to learn of their future success. The wolf skin was then used in the following manner: It was soaked in water and thus made pliable. Then it was put about the throat of one of the party, who was seated on the ground and supported at the back by another member. Two men, holding the ends of the skin wound about the throat of the seated man, drew it firm and taut but did not choke the man, who soon became unconscious. While in that condition he was supposed to be able to look into the future, viewing the country and the people whither the party were going, and discerning also what was to happen. The Winnebago were accustomed to use an otter skin for the same purpose and in the same manner.

While this pack could give authority to aggressive war parties, and, it is said, was sometimes taken along by the leader of a very large war

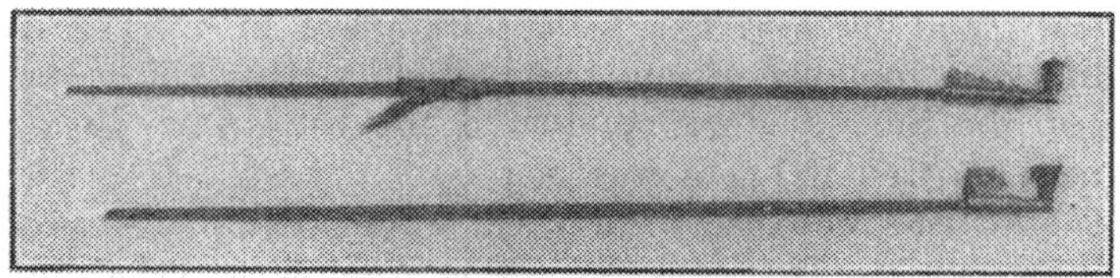

FIG. 97. Pipes from Sacred War Pack.

party, one of a hundred or more warriors (a *nuda*^{n}*' hi*^{n}*to*^{n}*ga*), it was the only pack entitled to authorize defensive warfare. When that was done the two pipes (fig. 97; Peabody Museum no. 37551) belonging to this pack were ceremonially smoked.

DEPARTURE CEREMONIES OF AN AGGRESSIVE WAR PARTY

When the leader of an aggressive war party had obtained authority from one of the four Sacred Packs, he was not held responsible for the death of any member of his party or for any disasters that might happen to it. Each one of the party, through the leader, had placed himself under the authority of the war power, the Thunder god, through his accredited representatives, the birds contained in the *wai*^{n}*'waxube*, the Sacred War Pack. We here find another illustration of the Omaha belief in the continuity of all life, so that a part could represent the whole and that all forms, animate and inanimate, were linked together by the pervading life-giving power of Wako^{n}'da. Because of this belief the Thunder and its representative birds, and the charms, or "medicines," which were generally some product of the earth, were able to influence men and their fortunes in all avocations. While this belief may seem strange and irrational, it was logical and vitally effectual to the Omaha and underlay his organization, ceremonies, and public and private acts. So when the leader and his followers had received instructions from the keeper of one of the Sacred Packs and had secured one or more of the sacred birds that would act as a medium between them and the Thunder god, they felt themselves ready to face any danger; and, in any event, the responsibility for their acts rested with the supernatural agencies they had invoked.

When a man applied for authority to lead an aggressive war party the keeper of the Sacred Pack invited the members of the Hoⁿ'hewachi to meet the party. The leader of the war party provided the feast. At this gathering songs and dances pertaining to the Hoⁿ'hewachi (night dance) were sung but not those related to the counting (p. 495) and tattooing ceremonies (p. 503). These songs were given to remove from the minds of the men about to go forth all fear of death by bringing before them the symbolism of night, which represented both death and birth. The feast took place in a large dwelling belonging to a member of the Hoⁿ'hewachi. On this occasion the keeper of the Sacred Pack conducted the ceremonies (which were sometimes omitted if haste was required). Just before they were ready to start, the men of the war party, led by their leader, performed the *mi'kaçi* dance (*mi'kaçi*, "wolf;" the wolf was regarded as connected with war). The dance was an appeal to the wolf that the men might partake of his predatory character, of his ability to roam and not be homesick. The dance was in rhythmic steps, more or less dramatic and imitative of the movements of the wolf—his rapid trot and sudden and alert stops. The music of the songs is lively, well accented, and inspiriting.

The first part of the following *mi'kaçi* song has no words, only vocables. The words in the second part are given below.

MI'KAÇI

Harmonized by John C. Fillmore

The upper line is the Aria as sung. The harmonization is preferred by the Indians when the song is played on the piano

MI′KAÇI—Continued

e - - gi - ma he a ha a ha e - ya e - ya
e - yau a ha e - yau he he ya A ha e ya
ha e ya a ha a ha e - ya e - ya e - ya ha e ya
A ha a ha e - ya e - ya e - ya a ha e - ya ha he ya

Mi′kaçi ama moⁿzhoⁿ nompa bazhi ba egima

Translation: *Mi'kaçi*, wolf; *ama*, they; *mo^n^zho^n^*, earth or land; *nompa*, fear; *bazhi*, not; *ba*, so; *e'gima*, I am like them, or I do likewise. "The wolves have no fear as they travel over the earth; so I, like them, will go forth fearlessly, and not feel strange in any land."

Homesickness was greatly dreaded by the warriors, as it unnerved them for action and presaged defeat. The above song and others similar in feeling were sung as a plea for help against this internal enemy of the warrior. The leader was constantly on the lookout for indications of nostalgia, and if he detected signs of this dreaded condition, if he found the men speaking of their sweethearts, he took means at once to cheer up the party. He would organize a dance, at which time songs of the following class would be sung, and in this way the men would be heartened and the party would go forward to success.

A ha i ya he, a ha i ya he
A ha i ya he, a ha i ya he
Ya ha i ya he
Ya ha i ya he
A he the he ya ho e tha he the he the thoe
E na! abthixe ko^n^btha thi^n^ nudo^n^ ithea he the
Ena! ithatabthe thi^n^ thethu thazhiahe
A he the he ya ho e tha he the tho

Literal translation: The first five lines and the last are vocables. *Ena!*, an exclamation used only by women; *abthixe*, I marry; *ko^{n}btha*, I wish or desire; *thi^n*, the one—the word indicates that the one spoken of is moving; *nudo^n*, war; *itheahe, ithehe*, has gone—the *a* is introduced to accommodate the word to the music; *the*, end of the sentence; *ena!*, feminine exclamation; *ithatabthe*, I hate; *thi^n*, the one moving; *thethu*, here; *thazhi*, has not gone; *a*, vocable; *he*, feminine termination of a sentence spoken by a woman.

Free translation

Ena! The one I wish to marry has gone to war.
Ena! The one I hate has not gone forth but remains here.

The *mi'kaçi* dance was the last public appearance of the war party. Their departure was kept secret. The leader designated a time and place where all were to meet and each man stole away to the appointed spot. This course was followed in order to prevent undesirable persons from joining the party and causing inconvenience.

Each leader of a war party was instructed in his duties by the keeper of the Sacred Pack to which he had applied for permission to go on the warpath. There were slight differences in the details of these instructions but the following, recounted by an old warrior from his own experience, may be taken as a fair picture of the general procedure:

At night, when on the march, after we had had supper and were about to go to bed, the leader selected four men, who were sent out from the camp to four designated places in the direction of the four cardinal points. The leader bade these men to go forth as directed and listen for the howling of the wolf. Toward midnight a man in the camp gave the cry of the wolf; he was answered by the four men from their posts, who then returned to the camp and all went to sleep. The guards did not watch all night. It was only during the first night that the party traveled; after that the men rested at night and went forward by day. On a morning when the party were near their destination, the Pack they had carried was opened ceremonially according to the instructions given the leader and eight men were selected and sent out as scouts; two were to turn back over the route that had been traveled and look for signs of people; two were to go out on one side, two on the other side, and two were to keep in advance of the party. The two in the rear were to follow at night and rejoin the party, which, thus protected in the rear, on the flanks and in front, traveled on all the day.

When one of the scouts discovered a village where there was a chance to obtain booty or other trophies of war, he at once ran to report to the leader, singing this song as he advanced toward the war party:

SCOUT SONG

The words are few and interspersed with vocables: *No^{n}zhi^{n}ga,* arise; *Nudo^{n}ho^{n}ga,* war leader; *uzhawe,* rejoice, be glad.

The attack was generally made in the very early dawn; such a fight was called *ti'gaxa,* "striking among the houses." This word appears as a name in the I^{n}shta'çu^{n}da gens. When a man was slain, his friends rallied around the body to protect it and to prevent honors being taken from it. Often the severest fighting took place over the body of a fallen companion. When possible the wounded were carried away, but those overpowered were generally killed. The dead were buried on the field of battle. Captives were not taken as there was no ceremony of adoption in the Omaha tribe.

THE WE'TO^{N} WAA^{N}

We'to^{n} waa^{n} is an old and untranslatable term used to designate a class of songs composed by women and sung exclusively by them; these songs were regarded as a medium by which strength could be transmitted to an absent warrior and thus assist him in becoming victorious over his enemies. When a war party was away it was the custom for women, particularly of the poorer class, to go to the tent of one of the absent warriors (sometimes that of the leader or one of the prominent men in the party), and, standing in front of the tent, there sing one or more of the *we'to^{n} waa^{n}.* It was believed that by some telepathic process courage and increased strength thus were imparted to the man who was battling. In return for the supposed benefits to the absent man, the wife of the warrior distributed gifts among the singers.

The following is a song of this class:

(Sung in octaves) Harmonized by John C. Fillmore for interpretation on the piano

Kage texi hai tho^{n}zha
Kage texi hai tho^{n}zha
He! Ishage waga^{n}ça bedo^n
Nu te texi hai tho^{n}zha
Kage tha ço^n ga tadu^n shu^{n}thathi^{n}she

Translation: *Kage*, little brother; *texi*, difficult; *hai, ai*, they say; *tho^{n}zha*, notwithstanding; *he!*, exclamation, as at a difficulty; *ishage*, old men; *waga^{n}ça bedo^n*, when they taught; *nu*, man; *te*, to be; *he*, vowel prolongation; *thaço^{n}ga*, you shall experience or realize; *sho^{n}thathi^{n}she*, therefore you are going. "Little Brother, the old men have taught that it is difficult to be a man; you are now going where you will realize this saying," implying that he will prove the truth of the teaching by his valor.

The custom of singing the *we'to^n waa^n* and belief in its efficiency obtains also among the Ponca and Osage tribes.

All the rites pertaining to defensive warfare were in charge of the We'zhi^{n}shte gens, whose place was on the south side of the opening into the *hu'thuga*. A tent was set apart as a repository for the ceremonial articles pertaining to war. This tent was pitched about 40 feet in front of the line of tents belonging to the We'zhi^{n}shte gens. The door of the tent was placed about the center of the invisible line that divided the two halves of the *hu'thuga*. This position of the Tent of War, shown in the diagram (fig. 20), was maintained only when the tribe camped in the ceremonial order of the *hu'thuga* on the annual tribal buffalo hunt. In the village the tent was pitched near the dwelling of the keeper. The office of keeper was hereditary in a certain family of the We'zhi^{n}shte gens. His duties were to provide the tent for housing the sacred articles and to protect them from the weather and injurious influences. When the tribe moved out on the hunt, he had to furnish proper transportation for the tent and its belongings. In his own lodge he was required to keep his doorway in order, to clean out his fireplace, and to sweep both every morning. His children had to be prevented from digging holes about the fireplace. Should he neglect these duties, calamity would befall him or his kindred.

All the sacred articles belonging to the Tent of War were kept in the rear of the tent, facing the door, with a skin covering to protect them from the weather. No one but the keeper was allowed to touch them. If during the bustle of travel any person or animal should run against the tent or any of its belongings, it was necessary, as soon as the Tent of War was set up, for the offender to go or the animal to be taken to the keeper to receive the ceremonial ablution. For this purpose warm water was sprinkled by the keeper over the offender with a spray of artemesia. If this should be neglected, the person or animal "would become covered with sores."

SENDING OUT SCOUTS

On the buffalo hunt when the tribe entered a region where signs of the trails of an unknown tribe were observed, this fact was at once reported to the leader of the hunt, who reported to the Seven Chiefs; these in turn notified the keeper of the Tent of War, who then sent for the leading men of the We'zhi^{n}shte gens to assemble in council, at which the Seven Chiefs were present. The chiefs reported to the council that signs had been seen which indicated that the people were on dangerous ground. The council without delay selected certain young men of the tribe, sons of leading warriors, to be called out to act as scouts. The herald of the gens was summoned. He responded, arrayed in the ceremonial manner—the robe worn with the hair outside and a downy eagle's feather fastened to his scalp lock. He took the pole on which the Pack Sacred to War, the *wai^n'waxube,* was hung (a crotched stick slightly taller than a man), and, going some 15 feet in front of the door of the tent, thrust the pointed end into the ground so that the pole stood firm; on it he hung the Pack Sacred to War. Then he took his place beside the pole with the pack and, leaning on a staff, called the names of the young men who had been selected for scouts, adding: *Mo^{n}zho^n i^n thega ço^{n}ga ta yathi^{n}ho!* (*mo^{n}zho^n,* "land;" *i^{n}thega ço^{n}gata,* "to examine for me;" *yathi^{n}ho,* "come hither"), "Come hither, that you may examine the land for me!". This command and explanation of the duty required were given after each name called. At the first sound of the herald's voice silence fell on the camp. Children were hushed or taken within the tents and every ear was strained to catch the words of the herald. When he had finished, he returned with the Sacred Pack to the tent and placed it in the center. Meanwhile the men who had been summoned did not stop to paint or ornament themselves but hastened from their dwellings to the Tent Sacred to War. If anyone who was called was thought too young for the task, his father responded instead. On their arrival those summoned entered the tent and sat in a circle.

The two pipes belonging to the Tent Sacred to War have bowls of red catlinite, with serrated ornamentations on the top; they are provided with stems of wood, 3 feet 4 inches in length, flat and painted (fig. 97). On one stem are fastened two narrow strips of skin ornamented with porcupine-quill work, from which depend a tuft of elk hair. The other stem is painted in red and black, the upper side red down the center, and a border of ten scallops on each side, of black; the under side of the stem is divided into nine sections. A black section is at the mouthpiece; the next is red, the next black, and so on until the red bowl is reached; the last block on the stem, where it joins the bowl, is black. The significance of these blocks of red and black is similar to those on the He'dewachi pole (fig. 62), symbolizing night and day, death and life.

The two Pipes Sacred to War were then filled from tobacco kept in an elk-skin bag, as the war ritual was recited. This ritual has been lost. The pipes were passed about the circle in the following order: One started at the left of the door and was passed by the left to the middle; the other started at the middle and was passed by the left to the door. The oldest men sat where they would be the first to receive the pipes. The smoking was in silence. Every man was obliged to smoke, as the act was equivalent to taking an oath to obey the custom and to do one's duty even at the risk of life. At the conclusion of the ceremony of smoking, one of the leading men of the We'zhi^{n}shte gens addressed the circle. He dilated on the responsibilities that rested on the scouts and reminded them of the necessity for truthfulness in making their reports, as their words would be heard by the unseen powers which never permitted a falsehood to go unpunished. He recounted the results that would follow any untruthful statement—the man would be struck by lightning, bitten by a snake, injured in the foot by some sharp object, or killed by the enemy. At the close of this charge the young men returned to their tents, where their friends had made haste to prepare food for them, packing pounded corn or meat in bladder bags. Extra pairs of moccasins were also provided. With these preparations the men were sent off in small groups to scour the country in every direction for a radius of 10 or 15 miles. Meanwhile the camp, thus protected, might move on, but the young men of the tribe were directed by the herald to wear their blankets in a given manner so as not to be taken for spies.

Generally speaking, an Indian was fond of going upon an elevation for the pleasure of looking over the landscape, but he did so only in localities free of enemies. When desirous of searching a region to ascertain whether or not it was safe, he might ascend to a vantage point, but while there he did not stand erect, making himself a conspicuous object to attract the attention of a hidden foe, but concealed himself that he might be able to see without being seen. It was accounted an honor to be called as a scout, the assignment ranking as high as participation in a war party. To have smoked the war pipe was an honor that could be "counted" when the reciting of brave deeds was permissible.

On the return of the scouts, the eldest, the one to whom the pipe had been offered first, went at once to the Tent of War, where the leaders of the We'zhi^{n}shte gens were gathered to hear the report. If an enemy had been discovered, a messenger was dispatched to summon all the leading warriors to a council of war. The report of the scouts was made known to the council and the necessary action determined. If the scouts reported that the enemy was in large force but was lingering about as if waiting for an opportunity to attack the camp, then it was debated whether it would be best to retreat or to send out warriors to attack them and meanwhile have the camp put in a state of defense. If the enemy was in small numbers, then the council might determine to send out a party to give them battle or drive them away. In either case the departing warriors would be led by a prominent warrior or perhaps a chief. It was only in defensive warfare that a chief of the Council of Seven could go to war. Such warfare was called *ni'ka thixe*, "to chase people."

If at any time enemies were suddenly discovered by a man who might be outside the camp looking after horses or otherwise employed, he hastened at once to a vantage point and waved his robe above his head. This sign was called *we'ça* ("to make a noise or give an alarm"). In such case the camp was prepared at once for defense. The women threw up breastworks with their planting hoes (*noⁿ'ça*, the word for "breastworks," later was applied to fences of all kinds). In the attack, if the warriors were hard pressed and there was danger of defeat, the men fell back to the breastworks. If the camping place was near timber, in case of disaster the women and children hastened to hide among the trees and the warriors sometimes followed. Instances have been related by old women of how, when the camp had been surprised, they thrust their children into holes and threw themselves on top as if dead. In one case a woman was stabbed with a knife while feigning death, but she made no movement and so saved her children; this woman recovered from the wound and lived to tell the story.

DEPARTURE OF A DEFENSIVE WAR PARTY

When the warriors went forth to battle in defense of their homes there were no public ceremonies or dances but here and there the voice of a woman would be heard singing a song to inspirit the men, and at its close she gave the cry of the bird-hawk to evoke the supernatural power of this bird, which was associated with the god of war.

The following is an example of these rally songs which are composed by women and sung solely by them to encourage their defenders on their departure to battle. Only vocables are used in the first part of the song, and these are employed to eke out the musical phrase of the second part.

RALLY SONG

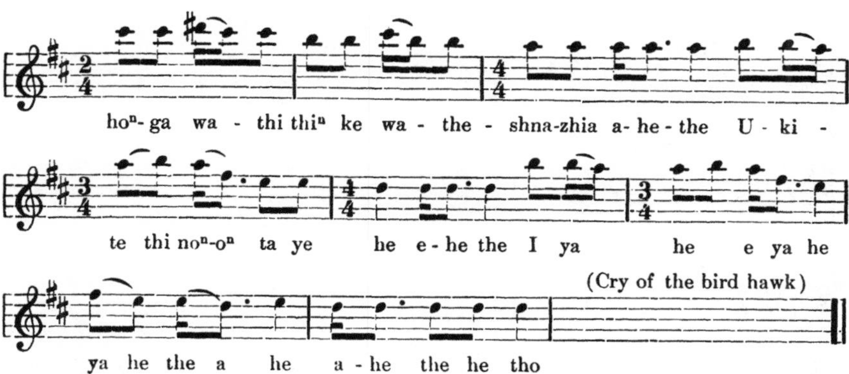
hoⁿ- ga wa - thi thiⁿ ke wa - the - shna-zhia a- he - the U - ki -
te thi noⁿ-oⁿ ta ye he e - he the I ya he e ya he
(Cry of the bird hawk)
ya he the a he a - he the he tho

NOTE.—The pitch is taken from the graphophone record made by the young woman. Her voice was a clear, strong, bell-like soprano, and her intonation remarkably true. The bird hawk is the war bird. The cry at the close of the song was a call to the bird to help the warrior going forth.

Nudoⁿhoⁿga wathi thiⁿke wathishna zhia ahe the
Ukite thinoⁿoⁿ da ye he ehe the (vocables)

Translation: *Nudoⁿhoⁿga,* leader; *wathi,* timid; *thiⁿke,* who is; *wathishna,* prominent, well known; *zhia,* not; *ahe,* I say; *the,* vocable; *ukete,* the tribe; *thinoⁿoⁿ,* hear you; *da,* let them; *ye he,* vowel prolongation; *ehe,* I say; *the,* end of sentence. "The timid leader never wins fame, achieves a prominent place. Let the tribes hear of you!"

In Omaha warfare there was no arrangement of the soldiers in lines, companies, or battalions. There was a recognized leader but each warrior marched and fought independently and although obedient to the leader's general orders he did not wait for any official command to take part in the fight. When a group of warriors moved out to defend the camp they did not go silently to the field of battle. Each man sang as he went. There was a class of songs which belonged exclusively to these occasions; these were called *na'gthe waaⁿ* (*na'gthe,* "captive;" *waaⁿ',* "song"). But the import of the term "captive" lies in the war customs of the people. If a man was taken captive, his fate was torture and death; therefore the captive song was synonymous with the death song. These songs were frequently composed by those who sang them, though occasionally one was handed down from father to son. Captive songs always expressed the warrior's feeling when contemplating the dangers of war and the facing of death. Other songs were sometimes sung by the men going forth, as an *hethu'shka,* or some favorite mystery song.

The *na'gthe waaⁿ* afford an opportunity to discern the ideals and beliefs which a man calls up before him when he seeks strength and courage to meet death. The three songs following are fair examples of the *na'gthe waaⁿ* class.

(Sung in octaves) Harmonized by John C. Fillmore for interpretation on the piano

Umba edaⁿ naⁿkuthe huⁿthiⁿbe ga
Umba edaⁿ naⁿkuthe huⁿthiⁿbe ga
He! Nudoⁿ hoⁿ ga a a zha a ma a te
Aye zhametho
Umba edaⁿ naⁿkuthe huⁿthiⁿbe ga

Translation: *He!*, an exclamation; *umba*, day; *edaⁿ*, approaching; *naⁿkuthe*, hasten; *huⁿthiⁿbe*, lead me; *ga*, sign of command; *nudoⁿ*-

ho^{n}ga, leader; *a a zha a ma a te*, vocables; *aye*, thus; *zhametho*, they may have said. "Have they not cried! Day approaches. He! Leader, lead me!" This song is the voice of the young and eager man who remembers the valiant warriors of the past as he sings.

(Aria as sung) Harmonized by John C. Fillmore for interpretation on the piano

Flowingly, with feeling ♩= 96

Ayezhame tho
Ayezhame tho
Ayezhame tho
Hi! wiço^{n}thu^n nu kede
Ayezhame tho
Ayezhame tho

Translation: *Ayezhame* (an elliptical phrase), they may have said, or, have they not said? The repetition of this phase is similar in effect to the chorus of our old ballads—it forms the setting of the picture set forth in the fourth line. *Hi!*, a woman's exclamation of surprise and delight; *wiço^{n}thu^{n}*, a term of endearment used by an elder sister to a young brother; *nu*, man; *kede*, lying. These words recall the birth of the man, the cry of joy of the elder sister as she enters the little secluded tent and sees that a man lies there. Now, as he enters the field of action, he is to prove himself a man worthy of the joy awakened at his birth. The music bears out the poetic feeling of the words. The climax of both poem and music is in the last phrase: "Have they not said, a Man!" This little song opens a rift into the inner life of the people and the social responsibility laid on the men of the tribe.

Harmonized by John C. Fillmore

The aria is as sung by the men. The harmonization translates the song, and is preferred by the Indians when it is played on the piano

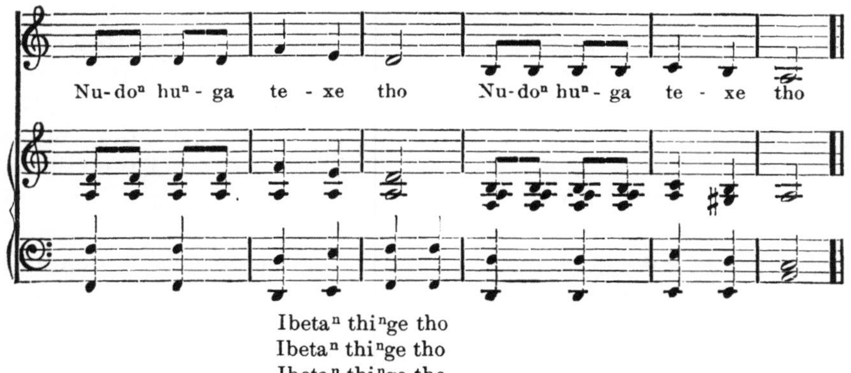

Ibeta^n thi^{n}ge tho
Ibeta^n thi^{n}ge tho
Ibeta^n thi^{n}ge tho
He! Ishaga ma waga^{n}çabeda^n
Ibeta^n she ahibite abazhete
Nudo^{n}hu^{n}ga texie tho
Nudo^{n}hu^{n}ga texie tho

Translation: *Ibeta^n*, to go around, as around an obstacle, or to circumvent or avoid a threatened disaster; *thi^{n}ge*, none; *tho*, vocable; *ishaga*, old man; *ma*, plural sign; *waga^{n}çabeda^n*, when they tell; *she*, yonder; *ahibite*, reached that (place) first; *abazhete*, have not said; *nudo^{n}ho^{n}ga*, leader; *texie*, the difficult, the hard to accomplish. "No one has found a way to avoid death, to pass around it; those old men who have met it, who have reached the place where death stands waiting, have not pointed out a way to circumvent it. Death is difficult to face!"

The words and the music are in feeling closely woven together around the thought of inexplicable birth and death. The seriousness and dignity of this song make it a notable composition.

Defensive warfare was graded higher than aggressive warfare and the man whose honors were won when defending the tribe was accorded a higher rank than the man whose honors were gained otherwise. No act entitling a man to a war honor, whether performed in defensive or aggressive warfare, could be claimed by him or its insignia worn until the honor had been publicly awarded in the ceremony called Wate′giçtu.

RETURN OF A WAR PARTY

An authorized aggressive war party was required to take a direct course toward its destination and after a battle to return by the same path. On the return journey of such war party, if successful, when a short distance from the village a fire was kindled, the rising smoke from which gave the signal of the victorious return of the warriors. If any of the party had been killed, a member stepped to one side and threw himself on the ground. This action indicated to the village the loss of one man. If more than one had fallen, the number lost was signified to the watchers by repeating this action. After this dramatic report, the leader designated a man to go forward and, when near enough to the village to be heard, to call out the names of those who had been slain. As the relatives of the dead heard the name of husband, father, or brother, they broke into wailing. When, later, the victorious party entered the village, the place resounded with shouts of welcome to the living and cries of sorrow for the dead.

The return of a defensive war party was less formal. Some one went in advance and reported to the camp the news of deaths or other disaster; the reception of the news, the shouts of victory, and lamentations for the dead were as already described. The victory celebration was the same in both cases.

If the returning party brought back the scalp of an enemy, the young men of the tribe at once made preparations for holding the *wewa'chi*, or victory dance. The scalp was tied to a pole and around it both men and women danced and sang together the songs belonging to this ceremony of exultation. The dance was a lively and exuberant motion. No dramatic episodes of war were acted out. The music was vivacious, and the words were frequently boasting or taunting in character. Sometimes they mentioned deeds that were heroic but they always referred to the acts of war. The following is a characteristic song of this dance:

VICTORY SONG

Harmonized by John C. Fillmore for interpretation on the piano

gaⁿ iⁿ - te - de tha xa - ge he ya the he tho - e U -
tha-de u - thi shoⁿ we - zhnoⁿ tiuⁿ waⁿ shu- she he ya tha ha
U-the - zha-zhe - gaⁿ iⁿ - te - de tha-xa - ge he ya tha ha tho

He a tha ha he ya he he a tha ha thoe
He a tha ha he ya he ya he the he ye tha ha
Uthazhazhegaⁿ iⁿtede thaxage, he ya tha ha tho e
Uthade uthishoⁿ wizhnoⁿti uⁿwaⁿshushe he ya tha ha
Uthazhazhegaⁿ iⁿtede thaxage he ya tha ha tho

Literal translation: *Uthazhazhegaⁿ*, you emulated; *iⁿtede,* and now, in consequence; *thaxage,* you weep; *uthade,* people, or tribes; *uthishoⁿ*, surrounding; *wizhnoⁿti,* I alone; *uⁿwaⁿshushe,* am brave. These words are interspersed with groups of vocables.

Free translation

You emulated me, and now you are crying, he ya tha ha tho e
Among surrounding tribes I only am the brave, he ya tha ha.
You tried to be like me—behold, you weep your dead, he ya tha ha tho.

83993°—27 ETH—11——28

Sometimes after an attack on the camp, an arm, leg, or head was brought from the neighboring battlefield and boys were made to strike or to step on the mutilated portion of the dead enemy, as though they were taking honors. This discipline was thought to stimulate a desire to perform valorous acts by familiarizing the youths with scenes of war.

The Wate'giçtu

The word *wate'giçtu* (composed of *wate*, "things accomplished," referring to the acts accomplished by the warriors; *gi*, sign of possession; and *çtu*, "to collect, or gather together") signifies "the gathering together of acts accomplished." All the acts of the warrior, having been duly authorized by the Wai^{n}'waxube (the Packs Sacred to War), belonged to and were possessed by the packs and until these deeds were ceremonially awarded to the warriors through the rites presided over by the packs they did not belong to the man to count or to claim as his own.

For his use in this ceremony each warrior prepared and painted red a stick about a span long, for each of the honors he was to claim. The four Packs Sacred to War were used in this ceremony placed side by side in the middle of the tent prepared for the occasion, semicircular in form and open so that the ceremony could be viewed by the people. The Pack from the Tent of War and that which had been carried by Wa'baçka were placed side by side in the middle, while on the sides were placed the packs from the Tapa' and I^{n}ke'çabe gentes. At the present time only two of the four packs are known to exist—the one now in the Peabody Museum of Harvard University and that which formerly belonged to Giu^{n}'habi, of the Tha'tada gens, which Wa'baçka carried in his battle with the Pawnee, already recounted. On this latter pack a piece of otter skin was tied, the string fastening it being so arranged as to fork. Into this fork the warriors aimed to drop their sticks at a given signal.

At this ceremony, which took place shortly after the return of the victorious warriors, the keepers of the Packs Sacred to War were the only officials. While chiefs could be present, they were there merely as onlookers and had no authority or part in the ceremony. The four keepers stood behind the packs, facing the east, while the warriors who were to claim honors stood before the packs. The claimants to the first-grade honors were in advance, those who claimed the second grade slightly behind these, the third grade behind the second, and so on. The keepers of the two middle packs then sang the following opening song:

Literal translation: *Shethu*, yonder; *agiba*, coming back here; *edado*ⁿ, things (their acts, or trophies); *athi*ⁿ*agibetha*, they are bringing.

The keepers admonished the men to speak the truth without fear or hesitation, for the omniscient birds present in the packs would hear and report their words to Thunder, the god of war. The penalties for exaggeration or false statement were then recounted.

Then the keepers sang the following song referring to Thunder, who is spoken of as Grandfather:

Thiti'go^n no^{n}pewathe! ga
Thiti'go^n no^{n}pewathe! ga
Thiti'go^n no^{n}pewathe! ga
Thiti'go^n weti^n ke gthi'ho^n ki no^{n}pewathe! ga
Thiti'go^n no^{n}pewathe! ga

Literal translation: *Thiti'go^n*, your Grandfather; *no^{n}pewathe*, fearful to behold; *weti^n*, club; *ke*, long; *gthi'ho^n*, lifts his; *ki*, when.

Free translation

Behold how fearful your Grandfather appears!
Your Grandfather is fearful, terrible to see!
Behold how fearful is he, your Grandfather!
He lifts his long club, fearful is he, your Grandfather gives fear to see!
Behold how fearful to see, fearful to see!

At the close of this song the man claiming the first honor stepped forward and began the recital of his deed, telling how he struck the body of the enemy. He held the red witness stick over the pack and all the people listened attentively to his words. At a signal from the keeper he let the witness stick drop. If no one had disputed his story and the stick rested on the pack, the people sent up a great shout of approval, for the omniscient birds in the pack had accepted his words as true. But if he was disputed and the stick fell to the ground, it was believed that the man had spoken falsely and that his words had been rejected by the birds. Then the people shouted in derision, his stick was tossed away and the man lost the honor he had sought to gain. If the stick remained on the pack, the keepers granted permission for the man to wear the insignia of the grade to which his deed belonged. These deeds were called *uo^n* ("acts accomplished"); the supernatural acceptance of his recital had been shown by the stick resting on the pack, therefore the man could claim his deed; it had been handed back to him, as it were, by the Sacred Pack.

GRADED WAR HONORS

Six grades of honors could be taken on the body of an enemy:

(1) The highest honor was to strike an unwounded enemy with the hand or bow. This feat required bravery and skill to escape unharmed. Only two warriors could take this honor from the same person.

(2) This honor required the warrior to strike a wounded enemy. Only two could take this honor from the same man.

(3) To strike with the hand or bow the body of a dead enemy. Only two could take this honor from the corpse.

(4) To kill an enemy.

(5) To take the scalp. This honor ranked with no. 3, since the dead man could not resist, although the friends of the slain might rally around the body and strive to prevent the act by carrying the man off. Two could scalp the same enemy.

(6) To sever the head from the body of an enemy.

WAR HONOR DECORATIONS

The decorations were called *u'kio*[n], (from *kio*[n], "to decorate one's self by painting or by wearing regalia or garments").

For the first grade the warrior was entitled to wear in his scalp lock, so arranged as to stand erect on the head, the white-tipped feather from the tail of the golden eagle.

FIG. 98. Deer-tail head-dress.

As the sign of having won the second grade, the warrior could wear the white-tipped feather from the tail of the golden eagle fastened to his scalp lock so as to project horizontally at the side of the head.

The third-grade honor entitled the man to wear the eagle feather so as to hang from the scalp lock.

The fourth-grade honor was shown by wearing an arrow through the scalp lock or by carrying a bow in the hand at certain ceremonial dances. Later, when guns were introduced among the Omaha, the man who killed the enemy with a gun wore a necklace of shavings; this represented the wadding formerly used in loading guns.

The fifth grade ranked with the third, and the eagle feather was worn hanging from the scalp lock.

The sixth grade was not marked by any regalia but the man who had performed the deed that constituted this grade was entitled to act as master of ceremonies at the feast held at the meetings of the Hethu′shka society of warriors.

Besides the wearing of the eagle feather, men who had won honors of the first, second, and third grades were entitled to wear on ceremonial occasions the deer-tail headdress (fig. 98). This was a sort of roach made of the deer's tail and the tuft of coarse hair from the neck of the turkey. The deer's tail was dyed red; the turkey hair was used in its natural color of black.

THE PONCA CEREMONY OF CONFERRING WAR HONORS

The ceremony of conferring war honors bore the same name among the Ponca as among the Omaha. The following account, given nearly twenty years ago by an old and leading man, whose honor count was next to the highest in the tribe, is presented to facilitate a comparison between the customs of the two tribes:

There were three ancient packs in the tribe. One was kept by Uno^{n}′baha, of the Mo^{n}ko^{n}′ gens; one by Ta′ikawahu, of the Thi′xida gens; and one by We′gaçapi, of the same gens. The keepers of the first two dreamed of Thunder. The last one descended to its keeper from his grandfather and it is said that all the old man's dreams were of the gray wolf. There are two modern packs, one kept by Shu′degaxe, of the Thi′xida gens, and the other by Sho^{n}′geçabe, of the Washa′be gens. These men had dreams of Thunder, so their packs were for the Thunder gods.

There was no fixed time for the ceremony. Sometimes several seasons would pass between one ceremony and the next. The keepers of the pack decided the time, which must be in the summer, when all animals, bugs, and snakes are out and above ground and the thunder has sounded.

When the ceremony was to take place the people were ordered to camp in the order of the gentes and to make the *hu′thuga* complete. When this was done all the men who had been on the warpath and had come back victorious and all the men who had been in defensive battle at home were placed in a line near the center of the tribal circle, facing the entrance. The keeper of the pack who was to confer the honors designated a man to carry the pack. Previously all the candidates for war honors had sent to the keeper of the pack that was to be used gifts of horses and goods, as fees for his services in the ceremony. The man with the pack took his place in front of the line of warriors, at a little distance from them, leaning on a forked staff which he planted on the ground, and maintained this position during the entire ceremony. The keeper of the pack then called one of the warriors and thus addressed him: "My servant, strengthen yourself and tell a straight story. If you do not tell a straight story, if you do not give the exact truth, the gods whom you hear crashing among the clouds will strike you dead. If you do not make your story in a straight path and tell all the truth, though you may feel your feet firm upon the back of this our grandmother [the earth], you shall stumble and fall [die]." The man then addressed the pack and told his story to it, not to any man. If no one present questioned, disputed, or corrected him, the keeper again addressed him as "My servant," and accorded to him the honor belonging to his action. The honors were as follows:

First honor: To strike an unwounded man. The sign of this honor was an eagle feather worn upright in the scalp lock; moccasin strings made of the skin of the gray wolf; the upper part of the body painted black; and authority given the man to nominate "soldiers." Soldiers were those whose duty it was to ride on the outside of the camp during any ceremony and to maintain tribal order.

Second honor: To be the first to strike a fallen enemy, one who had been wounded or who by some accident was prostrate. The sign of this honor was an eagle feather worn horizontal in the scalp lock, painting the body irregularly in black stripes, and to be called upon to serve as a "soldier."

Third honor: To be the second to strike a fallen enemy. There was no badge for this honor but the man was entitled to a seat in the gathering of soldiers and could eat with them. He had also the office of stopping the camp if the people continued to move and did not stop and camp where they had been ordered; also, when the camp was moving, if there were any stragglers, it was his duty to drive them up. (This duty referred to the time when the tribe was on the buffalo hunt.)

Fourth honor: To kill a man. If this was done with a gun, the slayer was to carry to the dances his gun with the end painted red, and to wear a necklace of shavings (the shavings represented wadding). He was entitled also to the cut of the buffalo meat called *i'nakuge,* which was taken from the back and included a part of the shoulders and of the hind quarter. It was roasted with the skin sewed about it and was considered a choice cut. If the killing was done with an arrow, the man was entitled to wear an arrow in the scalp lock, one-half of the shaft to be painted red. He was entitled also to the cut called *tezhu'*. He could wear this arrow badge of his honor when on the buffalo hunt, so that the people could see to what part of the animal he was entitled and set it aside for him.

Fifth honor: To take a scalp. The sign of this honor was to paint the face with a slight tinge of red and put black stripes across it and to be servant to the "soldiers." There was no fighting when a scalp was taken, for the man was dead; so there was little honor in taking a scalp. To wear scalps was not an honor from the pack. It was done on a man's own responsibility.

Sixth honor: Capturing horses from the enemy. The badge of this honor was to wear at the dances a coil of rope around the body and to paint on the body figures shaped like the impression of a horse's hoof. At any ceremonies that required the use of horses, the man could paint on his horse the prints of horses' hoofs.

The following incident was told many years ago by an old Ponca chief, now dead. The occurrence took place before the middle of the last century and throws light on the beliefs connected with this ceremony of bestowing honors.

I was present at the ceremony. The keeper of the Sacred Pack said to the honor candidates before him: "I appear before you as a representative of Thunder, whose loud voice you hear. Whatever words are to be spoken by you must be in strict accordance with the truth, so that the wrath of the Thunder may not fall on anyone. Any words spoken without regard for the truth will bring on the speaker death by the stroke of lightning, or he will be gored by a bull or be bitten by a snake, or in some way his life will suddenly cease." The candidates responded: "Thou god Thunder, who standest before us, hear the words I am about to give you before the people. I know the punishment I must expect if I should turn aside from the truth. I give to you my story as it is known to myself, with directness and without fear, knowing that I speak the truth." Two men then stepped forward, one with a gun and the other with a bow, and both claimed the same first-grade honor. The man with the gun said that he struck the enemy first with his gun and that the other claimant did not strike the enemy with his bow, but struck the gun instead. The man with the bow said he

"Crow" "Crow" and war bonnet.

WAR HONOR DECORATIONS

struck the enemy first and that the man struck the bow with his gun and did not strike the enemy. Other witnesses to the action gave their testimony and all agreed that the man with the bow struck the enemy first and not the man with the gun. Twice the keeper bade the two men repeat their stories, so that the one that was in the wrong might have a chance to withdraw his false statement and so escape punishment; but both men held to their original story. The stick was not dropped. The keeper then said: "I shall leave the question of the truth of this story to the Thunder god to decide. We shall know within the year which one of these men has spoken the truth." Summer came and during the tribal buffalo hunt a horse fell on the man who claimed to have struck the enemy with his gun, and he was killed.

The old narrator mentioned the names of the disputants and it was believed that the man on whom the horse fell had been supernaturally killed because he had spoken falsely.

"THE CROW"

A man who had attained more than once to honors of the first three grades became entitled to wear a peculiar and elaborate ornament called "the Crow." This was worn at the back, fastened by a belt around the waist; it was made with two long pendants of dressed skin painted red or green, which fell over the legs to the heels. On the skin were fastened rows of eagle feathers arranged to hang freely so as to flutter with the movements of the wearer. An entire eagle skin, with head, beak, and tail, formed the middle ornament; from this rose two arrow shafts tipped with hair dyed red. On the right hip was the tail of a wolf; on the left the entire skin of a crow. This composite decoration illustrated certain ideas that were fundamental to native beliefs, namely: That man is in vital connection with all forms of life; that he is always in touch with the supernatural, and that the life and the acts of the warrior are under the supervision of Thunder as the god of war. This relation was believed to be an individual one and any war honor accorded was the recognition of an individual achievement. Such a bestowal was the outcome of the native method of warfare, for there was no military organization, like an army, in the tribe and, strictly speaking, no commanding officer of a war party; when the battle was on, each man fought for and by himself. A valorous deed was therefore the man's own act and the honor which was accorded the kind of act performed was accredited by Thunder through the representative birds associated with Thunder, and contained in the Sacred Pack.

"The Crow" decoration (pl. 55) is said to symbolize a battlefield after the conflict is over. The fluttering feathers on the pendants represented the dropping of feathers from the birds fighting over the dead bodies. Sometimes the wearer of "the Crow" added to the realism by painting white spots on his back to represent the droppings of the birds as they hovered over the bodies of the slain. The two arrow shafts had a double significance: they represented the stark bodies and also the fatal arrows standing in a lifeless enemy. The eagle was associated with war and with the destructive powers of the Thunder and the attendant storms. The wolf and the crow were not only connected with carnage but they had a mythical relation to the office of "soldiers," the designation given to certain men on the annual tribal hunt, who acted as marshals and kept the people and the hunters in order during the surround of the herd. These men were chosen from those who had the right to wear "the Crow" and this regalia was generally worn at that time. It was worn also at certain ceremonial dances.

The following ritual, secured in 1896 from an old Ponca chief (pl. 56) who has since died, used by the Ponca when soldiers were appointed for the tribal hunt, throws light on the relation of the crow and the wolf to the hunter as the provider of food and to the warrior as the protector of the people.

1. He! u′thito^{n} thakishkaxa bado^{n}, eçka
2. U′shko^{n} thakishkaxe tabado^{n}, eçka
3. Ni′kagahi, eçka
4. He! Wano^{n}she thakishpahi bado^{n}, eçka
5. He! Sho^{n}′to^{n}ganuga thathi^{n}she tho^{n}, eçka
6. Wano^{n}she thanudo^{n}ho^{n}ga abado^{n}, eçka
7. Ka′xenuga thathi^{n}she tho^{n}, eçka
8. Wano^{n}she thanudo^{n}ho^{n}ga abado^{n}, eçka
9. He! gaçi′ge shna bado^{n}, eçka
10. Gaçi′ge ke tho^{n} a′gaxthe thisho^{n} mo^{n}zhni^{n} ado^{n}, eçka
11. Sho^{n}′to^{n}ganuga thathi^{n}she tho^{n}, eçka
12. I^{n}deço^{n} tho^{n} titi uthagaçi^{n} titi mo^{n}zhni^{n} ado^{n}, eçka
13. Çi^{n}′de ke thiaathiko^{n} ego^{n} mo^{n}zhni^{n} ado^{n}, eçka
14. He! Ka′xenuga thathi^{n}she tho^{n}, eçka
15. Nu′dehi^{n} gaçaça ego^{n} mo^{n}zhni^{n} ado^{n}, eçka
16. Ni′kashiga Ho! ethabiwathe ego^{n} mo^{n}zhni^{n} ado^{n}, eçka
17. Utha′gthaa tigthagtha mo^{n}zhni^{n} ado^{n}, eçka
18. Thaki′gthiço^{n}tha the thatha agaxthe thisho^{n} ke thithe xti mo^{n}zhni^{n} abado^{n}, eçka
19. Wani′ta tho^{n}tho^{n}, eçka
20. Thue xti titho^{n} gaxa bado^{n}, eçka
21. Thi shkaxe eshe abado^{n}, eçka
22. He! Wani′ta tho^{n}tho^{n}, eçka
23. Wiaxchi shtiwo^{n} gthe tha bazhi ba, eçka
24. Ço^{n}ço^{n}de xti, eçka
25. T'ewatha bado^{n}, eçka
26. He! Wai^{n} agtha bado^{n}, eçka
27. Ushko^{n}′ ke tho^{n}, eçka
28. A′gaxthe thisho^{n} ke, eçka
29. Mo^{n}zhni^{n}′ado^{n}, eçka
30. Thiu′de agthe uwato^{n}ga, eçka
31. Tet'e ke tho^{n}, eçka
32. A′shpae itho^{n}tho^{n} bado^{n}, eçka
33. Thi′to^{n}thi^{n} xti paho^{n}′ga thagthate ithiko^{n}tha bado^{n}, eçka
34. Ushte′o^{n}tha agthai ke tho^{n} shnata bado^{n}, eçka
35. Zhi^{n}ga thego^{n} xti awa′gipaxe ko^{n}btha tho^{n}, eçka
36. U′zhawa xti awagi paxe tho^{n}zha wiewamo^{n} athi^{n}he eshe abado^{n}, eçka
37. Wi′to^{n}thi^{n} i ithagite athi^{n}he tho^{n}zha, eçka
38. Zhi^{n}ga, eçka
39. No^{n}′de giudo^{n} xti awa′gipaxe athi^{n}he eshe abado^{n}, eçka

PONCA CHIEF

Literal translation

1. *He!*, exclamation; *u'thito*^{n}, arrangement in which to work; *thaki'shkaxa*, you make for yourselves; *bado*^{n}, implies the accomplished; *e'çka*, an exclamation, I desire, or I crave, I pray for.

2. *U'shko*^{n}, rules or regulations by which to control action; *thaki'shkaxe*, you make for yourselves; *tabado*^{n}, that you may—the act not completed.

3. *Ni'kagahi*, chiefs.

4. *He!* *Wano*^{n}*she*, soldiers; *thak'ishpahi*, you select among yourselves; *bado*^{n}, act completed.

5. *He! Sho*$^{n\prime}$*to*^{n}*ganuga*, wolf male; *thathi*^{n}*she*, you are moving; *tho*^{n}, implies that action was long ago—the wolf moved in the distant past.

6. *Wano*^{n}*she*, soldiers; *thanu'do*^{n}*ho*^{n}*ga*, you are war leader; *abado*^{n}, they say—a tradition handed down.

7. *Ka'xenuga*, crow male; *thathi*^{n}*she*, you are moving; *tho*^{n}, the action was long since.

8. *Wano*^{n}*she*, soldiers; *thanu'do*^{n}*ho*^{n}*ga*, you are war leader; *abado*^{n}, they say.

9. *He! gaçige*, the gathering; *shna*, you went; *bado*^{n}, act completed.

10. *Gaçi'ge*, to gather or congregate; *ke*, lies; *tho*^{n}, in the past; *a'gaxthe*, when the wind blows leeward; *thisho*^{n}, toward; *mo*^{n}*zhni*$^{n\prime}$, you walked; *ado*^{n}, they say, tradition.

11. *Sho*$^{n\prime}$*to*^{n}*ganuga*, wolf, male; *thathi*^{n}*she*, thou moving; *tho*^{n}, in time past.

12. *I*^{n}*de'ço*^{n}, face; *ço*^{n}, white or pale; *ti'ti*, come, come—coming repeatedly to view; *utha'gaçi*^{n}, peering over a hill or bush; *ti'ti*, appearing repeatedly; *mo*^{n}*zhni*^{n}, you walk; *ado*^{n}, it is said.

13. *Çi*$^{n\prime}$*de*, tail; *ke*, long; *thia'athiko*^{n}, standing to one side as if blown to one side by the wind; *ego*^{n}, like; *mo*^{n}*zhni*^{n}, you walk; *ado*^{n}, it is said.

14. *He! Ka'xenuga*, crow, male; *thathi*^{n}*she*, you move; *tho*^{n}, past time.

15. *Nu'dehi*^{n}, hair or feathers of the throat; *gaçaça*, standing on end, spread out; *ego*^{n}, like; *mo*^{n}*zhni*^{n}, you walk; *ado*^{n}, it is said.

16. *Ni'kashiga*, people; *Ho!*, exclamatory address of admiration; *etha'biwathe*, to be thought as inspiring admiration; *ego*^{n}, like; *mo*^{n}*zhni*^{n}, you walk; *ado*^{n}, it is said.

17. *Utha'gthaa*, you shouted; *tigthagtha*, repeatedly at a distance; *mo*^{n}*zhni*^{n}, you walk; *ado*^{n}, it is said.

18. *Thakigthiço*^{n} *tha*, turning yourself; *the*, going; *thatha*, repeatedly; *a'gaxthe*, leeward; *thisho*^{n}, toward; *ke*, the lay of the land; *thithe*, joyfully; *xti*, verily; *mo*^{n}*zhni*^{n}, you walk; *abado*^{n}, it is said.

19. *Wani'ta*, animals; *tho*^{n}*tho*^{n}, groups.

20. *Thue*, near by; *xti*, verily; *titho*^{n}, come to a place, near by; *gaxa*, they make; *bado*^{n}, act completed.

21. *Thi shkaxe*, you make; *eshe*, you said; *abado^n*, it is said.

22. *He! Wani'ta*, animals; *tho^{n}tho^n*, group.

23. *Wiaxchi*, one; *shtiwo^n*, not even; *gthe*, go home; *tha*, to cause; *bazhi*, not.

24. *Ço^{n}co^{n}de*, close together, as in a line; *xti*, verily.

25. *T'e*, dead; *wa*, plural; *tha*, to cause; *bado^n*, completed action.

26. *He! Wai^n*, to carry; *agtha*, go home; *bado^n*, completed action.

27. *Ushko$^{n\prime}$*, the place where an action has occurred; *ke*, lying down; *tho^n*, in past time.

28. *A'gaxthe*, leeward; *thisho^n*, toward; *ke*, lying down.

29. *Mo^{n}zhni$^{n\prime}$*, you walk; *ado^n*, therefore, for that purpose.

30. *Thiu'de*, a deserted place, once the scene of activity; *agthe*, to go home; *uwa'to^{n}ga*, immediately.

31. *Te*, buffalo; *t'e*, dead; *ke*, lying; *tho^n*, past action.

32. *A'shpae*, you gathered in multitudes; *itho^{n}tho^n*, in bunches or groups here and there; *bado^n*, completed act.

33. *Thi'to^{n}thi^n*, you first; *xti*, verily; *paho$^{n\prime}$ga*, before or first; *thagtha'te*, you eat what is yours; *ithiko^{n}tha*, gives you power to live, to be animated; *bado^n*, completed action.

34. *Ushte'*, what remains over; *o^{n}tha*, abandoned; *agtha'i*, they went home; *ke*, lying scattered; *tho^n*, past time; *shnata*, you eat; *bado^n*, completed action.

35. *Zhi^{n}ga'*, little ones, children; *thego^n*, like this; *xti*, verily; *awagipaxe*, I make for my own; *ko^{n}btha*, I want or desire; *tho^n*, past action.

36. *U'zhawa*, rejoicing, the possession of that which brings comfort or pleasure; *xti*, verily; *awa'gipaxe*, I make for my own; *tho^{n}zha*, yet; *wie'wamo^n*, I caused it, was responsible for it; *athi^{n}he*, the one moving; *eshe*, you have said; *abado^n*, it is said.

37. *Wi'to^{n}thi^n*, I first; *i*, mouth; *ithagite*, with I touch; *athi^{n}he*, the one moving; *tho^{n}zha*, nevertheless.

38. *Zhi^{n}ga'*, little ones, children.

39. *No$^{n\prime}$de*, heart; *giudo^n*, delighted; *xti*, verily; *awa'gipaxe*, I make for my own; *athi^{n}he*, the one moving; *eshe*, you have said; *abado^n*, it is said, traditionally.

Free translation

1. He! Government you made for yourselves, it was accomplished—*eçka!*
2. Rules you made that shall control action—*eçka!*
3. Even chiefs—*eçka!*
4. He! Soldiers you have selected among yourselves—*eçka!*
5. He! Great male wolf, in ages past you were "moving"—*eçka!*
6. Of soldiers you were a war leader, it has been said—*eçka!*
7. Male crow, in ages long ago you were "moving"—*eçka!*
8. Of soldiers you were a war leader, it has been said—*eçka!*
9. Where were congregated our desire (the herds of buffalo), you went—*eçka!*
10. They (the herds) were gathered leeward, where the wind blows you walked, it is said—*eçka!*

11. Great gray wolf, thou wert then "moving"—*eçka!*
12. Your pale face, it is said, peered over the hill again and again as you walked—*eçka!*
13. Your long tail blown by the wind to one side as you passed on, it is said—*eçka!*
14. He! Male crow, you long ago were "moving"—*eçka!*
15. The frayed feathers ruffled at your neck as you walked, it is said—*eçka!*
16. The people cry Ho! in admiration, as you walk, so it was said—*eçka!*
17. You shouted again and again back to them from the distance, it is said—*eçka!*
18. Turning yourself again and again as joyfully you walked to leeward on the broad land, it is said—*eçka!*
19. The herds of animals—*eçka!*
20. Verily you cause them to come near—*eçka!*
21. This have you done, so it is said—*eçka!*
22. He! Herds of animals—*eçka!*
23. Not even one may escape—*eçka!*
24. Verily, close together do they stand—*eçka!*
25. Slaughtered were they—*eçka!*
26. He! Many were carried home—*eçka!*
27. The field lay vast, it is said—*eçka!*
28. Ever toward leeward, O wolf—*eçka!*
29. For that purpose you walk—*eçka.*
30. A deserted place immediately becomes the scene of your activity—*eçka!*
31. The buffalo lying dead—*eçka!*
32. In great flocks here and there crows gather together—*eçka!*
33. Verily, what is yours you eat and the food gives you new life—*eçka!*
34. The remainder lay scattered, that which was left you ate—*eçka!*
35. Verily, like to this do I desire for my children—*eçka!*
36. Verily, I would make them to rejoice, that do I strive to bring to pass—*eçka!*
37. Although I have first touched food with my mouth—*eçka!*
38. Nevertheless, the little ones, the children—*eçka!*
39. Their hearts would I make glad, with my power (moving), so you said, it is said—*eçka!*

In this ritual, the wolf and the crow address the people as "little ones," "children," and by their help bring the herds near to furnish food and sustain life. The office of "soldier" on the tribal hunt made it possible for all the people, old and young, rich and poor, to be "made glad" by abundant food.

The refrain, *eçka*, is equivalent to "I desire," "I crave," "I ask or pray for." It is ritualistic and responsive to that which precedes. Each line is not complete in itself, yet it conveys the picture, or a part of the picture, of the help offered once and for all time by the wolf and the crow and tends to impress on the warrior his dependence on these supernatural helpers. In line 5, and again in line 7, the wolf and the crow are said to be "moving" in a time long past. This use of the word "moving" brings the crow and the wolf into mythical relation with Wako^{n}'da the power that "moves," that gives life to all things; the time when these creatures were "moving" was in the distant past and their action had in it something of the creative character.

The ritual also perpetuates the story of the time when the office of "soldier" (those who were to guard the people and regulate the hunting) was created, as well as the mythical promise of the crow and the wolf to help men in battle and in the hunt. To preserve the story of this association and promise, the war ornament, "the Crow," was devised. The Ponca and the Omaha claim to have been joint originators of this insignia, which has since been adopted by other tribes.

The following was told by a Ponca chief (pl. 57), more than ten years ago:

It is said that when the Crow came to offer his services to the people he had in his bill a *wahin'çon*—a ball of white down from the brant. This he laid before the leader of the people as a token of his ability to fulfill his promise of help.

When the leader of a war party wishes to practise augury to ascertain whether or not he will be successful, he relies on the wolf or the crow to reveal to him future events. The following story is told of Shu'degaxe and Mixa'çka, who years ago led a party against the Pawnee:

"One evening a wolf was heard howling and Shu'degaxe listened to it for a long time, when he said to his warriors: 'The wolf which you have heard howling has promised me success if I would vow to feast with him. I now give such vow and I will eat a part of the flesh of any enemy we may slay.' In two days the war party encountered the Pawnee and completely routed them. Many Pawnee were killed and many of their horses taken. True to his vow, Shu'degaxe took a bit of the flesh of an enemy he had himself slain and in the presence of his men undertook to keep his word. After much singing (which is often done before a great undertaking) the leader dropped the bit of human flesh down his throat, but threw it up after writhing in pain. He made two unsuccessful attempts. At last he wrapped the bit of flesh in a piece of buffalo fat, when he was able to keep it down.

Another story is told of a warrior to whom the crows offered their services as scouts. "These crows," said the leader to his men, "have promised to go in search of our enemy. They say that they want to feast on human flesh. They will return to us on the morning of the second day after this. Notice how yonder crow is marked; one feather is missing from his right wing. By this mark you will recognize him on his return day after to-morrow." The birds returned on the morning set for the report. They gave to the leader even the number of the people he would encounter and how many were to be slain. It all came true and the war party returned successful.

These two, the crow and the wolf, offered their company to the people and it was for mutual aid. The crow and the wolf were to direct the people in finding enemies and game and the people were to make sure of killing so that the wolf and the crow could feast on the flesh left on the field of battle or in the chase.

THE FEATHER WAR BONNET

There was one ornament which stood for the social relation, the interdependence of men, and which was not directly connected with the supernatural. This was the imposing eagle-feather war bonnet (pl. 55). The right to possess and wear this regalia could be obtained only by the consent of a man's fellow-warriors. To be sure, the person to whom the right was given must have already received, publicly, war honors; but he must also have gained the respect of the leading men of the community.

The materials required to make the bonnet were gathered by the man who wished to possess it but its manufacture depended on the

PONCA CHIEF

assistance of many persons. A sort of skull cap was made of dressed deer skin, with a flap hanging behind; a border of folded skin about the edge formed the foundation for the crown of golden eagle feathers, which were fastened so as to stand upright about the wearer's head. Each one of these feathers stood for a man; the tip of hair fastened to the feathers and painted red represented the man's scalp lock. Before a feather could be fastened on the bonnet a man must count his honors which entitled him to wear the feather and enabled him to prepare the feather for use in decorating the war bonnet.

As so many persons were required ceremonially to prepare the feathers to be used in making a war bonnet, the man who desired to have such bonnet prepared a feast and invited to his lodge his warrior friends; these partook of the feast and then counted their honors on the eagle plumes and so made them ready for use. Formerly only the man who had taken a scalp could put the tip of red hair on the eagle feathers, so that every feather thus ornamented stood for two honors—the feather itself for one of the first three war honors, the tip for the taking of a scalp. When a warrior counted his honors, he held up the feathers which were to represent these honors, saying: "In such a battle I did thus," etc. At the conclusion of the recital the feather was handed to the man who was manufacturing the bonnet, who put the feather in the proper place. As many of these bonnets contained fifty or more feathers, and as each feather must have an honor counted on it and no honor could be counted twice, the manufacturer of a war bonnet required a number of helpers and the task took considerable time—often several days. Strips of ermine, arranged to fall over the ears and cheeks, were fastened to the bonnet. The ermine represented alertness and skill in evading pursuit. A bird or some other symbolic object could be fastened on the crown of the skull cap. This object was generally some feature of the man's vision, through which he believed he received supernatural aid in time of need. Sometimes the flap was embroidered with porcupine work or painted with symbolic designs. Songs were sung during the making of the war bonnet. Before the advent of horses the flap of the bonnet did not extend below the waist, thus avoiding interference with walking or with the wearing of other ornaments, as "the Crow;" but after horses became plentiful the flap was extended to a man's feet when standing; when the man was mounted, it lay on the back of the horse.

A noted warrior might arrange to have a war bonnet made in order to present it to a valiant and well-known man who had a son. Such an act was regarded as a great honor to the family, and in acknowledgment valuable gifts would be bestowed on the donor. The presentation to the son was a challenge to him to achieve honors similar to those won by the warrior who made the gift. As such honors could be gained only by risking one's life, when the young man was brought into his father's lodge to receive the bonnet the women of the family gathered about the lodge and as he entered wailed for him as dead, cutting their hair and making all the demonstrations of grief in recognition of the dangers he must face to make good the challenge of the war bonnet.

The war bonnet was worn on ceremonial occasions and sometimes in defensive warfare when the village or camp was attacked. A story was told by an old man of an adventure in his youth. A party of warriors had gone out to defend the village and one of the leading men had worn his war bonnet. In the fight he found the bonnet in his way, so, calling a lad, he bade him take the bonnet back to the village. The boy did so and entered the camp wearing the war bonnet, amid the laughter and jokes of the people. Being a fun-loving lad, he paraded about and played the part of a victorious warrior to the amusement of all; as the event proved, he was really the herald of a notable victory by the Omaha.

In former times a man could not deck his leggings or shirt with a fringe of hair except by the consent of the warriors. Honors had to be counted on the strands of hair as on the feathers used in making a war bonnet, therefore each lock or tuft of the fringe stood for a war honor and no honor could be counted twice. It was this custom that made garments of this character so highly valued. The hair for the fringe was generally furnished by the man's female relatives. Each of the locks forming the fringe usually sewed in a heading of skin, frequently ornamented with quill work.

Weapons

The weapons of the Omaha were the bow and arrow, the shield the club, and the spear.

The club, called *zhoⁿpa'zhna* (fig. 99), was generally made from the root of the ash. It was well shaped, and not infrequently a weasel was carved on top above the rounded end.

The lance, or spear, was called *moⁿ'dehi* (*moⁿ'de*, "bow;" *hi*, "tooth"). This name bears out a tradition that in ancient times the Omaha used to attach a blade to one end of the bow, to be used like a bayonet, for thrusting.

It is said that different kinds of wood have been tried in making the bow. Hickory proved to be worthless, as changes in the weather caused it to warp or to lose its strength. Experience has shown that ash and ironwood make the best bows. These woods polish easily and the bows made from them remain true. When these were not available a kind of elm was used, "that having the drooping branches." The parts of the bow which were to be bent, were well oiled and bent into shape by pressure with the feet while held over live coals. A bow strung without being shaped in this manner would break the string, however strong. The head of the bow was bent or curved more than the foot. A good bow should be slightly curved at the middle of the back. Two notches (*ma'çki*) were made on the head of the bow and one on the foot. The stringing and unstringing of the bow were termed *unoⁿ'xpe*, "to loosen," a word applied only thereto. To preserve the elasticity and strength of the wood, the unstrung bow was bent backward before returning it to the sheath. The bow and the bowstring were kept always dry; moisture weakens a bow and causes the string to pull apart.

The bowstring was made from the sinew that lies on the muscle beside the backbone of the buffalo or the elk from the shoulders to the base of the spine. This sinew was prepared by soaking it over night in water slightly mixed with glue, after which the sinew was stripped into strands and all the water squeezed out. A strand composed of many threads was measured off twice the length of the bow. A pole having on it a small branch was driven into the ground and the strand looped over this branch. The maker of the bowstring took the ends one in each hand, twisted them between his fingers, and swung them twisting until the two strands tightened; then he twisted the cord firmly together into one string and knotted the ends. A loop remained where the cord was over the branch on the pole; this loop was for the head notches on the bow; the other end was left free for convenient adjustment. The bowstring was called *moⁿ'de koⁿ*, literally, "the bow tendon." Every man kept two strings for his bow—one fastened on the bow, the other carried in the quiver (fig. 100) for use in emergencies.

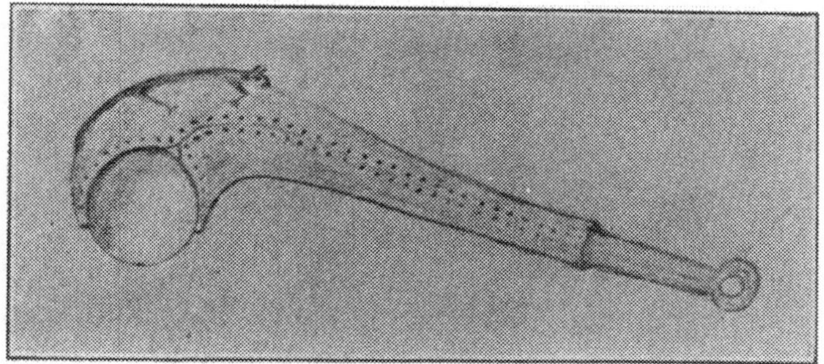

FIG. 99. War club (native drawing).

Dogwood and ash saplings were used in making arrow shafts. The first process in making arrows was to whittle the shafts down to a proper size; they were then hung over the fire for seasoning. Next, all the knots in the wood were cut out or scraped down level with the surface and the shafts rounded on a sandstone. In later times two pieces of perforated tin were used for this purpose. Fine sand was formerly employed to polish the shafts; later sandpaper

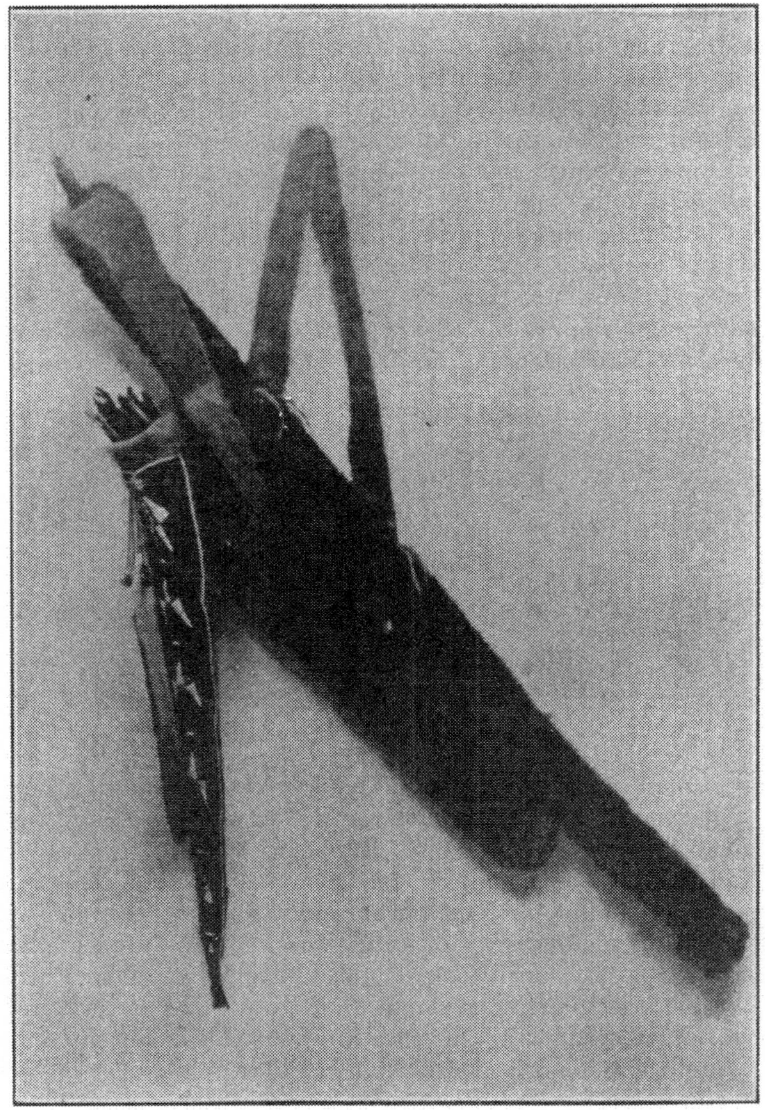

FIG. 100. Quiver.

became the substitute. The length of the shaft was the distance from the inside of the elbow of the left arm to the tip of the middle finger of the left hand and from the tip of this finger over the back of the hand to the wrist bone. This measurement was made on the wood itself; no string or other device was used. The shaft was then cut at this length and a notch was made, called *mo^{n}i'taxe zho^{n}ka* (*mo^n*, "arrow;" *itaxe*, "tip;" *zho^{n}ka*, "branched or forked"); after that a slit, *mo^n'hideugthe* (*mo^n*, "arrow;" *hide*, "shank;" *ugthe*, "to insert"), was made to receive the shank of the arrowhead. Into this slit the arrowhead was inserted, and fastened with sinew soaked in glue. The sinew was dried by the use of burnt mica, which was called *tako^n'iço^{n}the*, a descriptive term meaning "whitening for the sinew." The glue (*hi^{n}pa*) used with the sinew and to fasten on the feathers was made by boiling horn, turtle shell, or rawhide. The ends of the feathers used in arrowshafts were wound around smoothly and closely with sinew soaked in glue water, *hi^{n}pani* (*hi^{n}pa*, "glue;" *ni*, "water"). Burnt mica was used for whitening as well as for drying the sinew. The arrow maker took pride in finishing his work neatly and without soiling the sinew. After the arrowheads were attached, waving lines or grooves were made along the length of the shafts. This was done in order to prevent the wood from springing back to its natural bent and not, as has sometimes been stated, to allow the blood to flow along the arrowshaft, or for a symbol of the lightning. Arrowshafts were straightened by passing them through a hollow bone.

There were three kinds of arrows, all which were spoken of by the general term *mo^n*, "arrow". Two were known by descriptive names: (1) Arrows having heads of flint or stone were used for big game and for defensive warfare. These were always spoken of simply as *mo^n*. (2) *Hide'gapai* (*hide*, "foot;" *gapai*, "sharpened"). These arrows had no heads; the foot was sharpened. They were used for small game—as squirrels, rabbits, and prairie chickens, and also by both men and boys in practising to secure skill in aiming. Shooting at a mark for stakes (*mo^{n}ki'de ikiko^n*—*mo^n*, "arrow;" *kide*, "shoot;" *ikiko^n*, "gamble with each other") was a common mode of gambling. The stakes were usually arrows. In such games many men might engage in the sport. The first player set up the mark, provided there was no boy to serve the party. If there was a boy, he stuck an arrow into the ground at the distance agreed on, generally 200 to 400 yards; this mark was called *washa'begthe* (*washa'be* "a dark object;" *gthe*, "thrust in" the ground). The aim was to strike the arrow where it entered the ground. If an arrow fell beyond the mark, the marksman lost. A stick was used to measure the distances. When the stakes in a shooting match were goods (robes, saddles, etc.) or horses, then only two men could contest. An arrow set up in the ground was always the mark. (3) *Hide'tashe* (*hide*, "foot;" *tashe*, "knobbed"). These arrows were without heads; the shafts were knobbed at the foot. They were used by boys only, generally to kill birds.

For the purpose of identifying the slayer of an animal when hunting, arrows were always decorated in pairs. This custom gave rise to an expression—*mo^{n}wi^n'do^n* (literally, *mo^n*, "arrow;" *wi^{n}do^n*, "together, or united")—to indicate that things were similar. Among the Omaha the decoration of an arrow was always individual; there was no mark common to a gens. Among the Ponca, as has already been mentioned, certain gentes painted their arrows in a prescribed manner. Sometimes arrows were identified by the shape or color of the stone arrowhead, shaped as a "turtle's tongue," red, black, or white in color. An unfinished arrow shaft was called *mo^n'ça.*

Feathers for arrows bore the exclusive name *itha'thage,* an old term. The act of putting on the feather was spoken of as *a'tha,* also an old term. Before the advent of horses bows and arrows were made long, in order to insure accuracy. After the horse came into use the hunter could shoot at closer range and a shorter bow was employed; moreover, the long bow was inconvenient to handle on horseback.

The quiver (*mo^n'zhiha*), figure 100, was made of skin; a broad strap fastened at the open end and worn over the shoulder served to hold it. Quivers made from otter skins and ornamented with quills or beads were used on dress occasions.

The shield, which was circular, was made of rawhide cut from the shoulder of the buffalo bull. The piece intended for use was held over a fire, where it was allowed to shrink gradually, meanwhile being pulled until there was no spring left in the hide. It was then cut to the proper size. The cover was made of deer skin painted to represent a vision that had come to the owner when fasting.

Contents of the Tent of War

In June, 1884, the entire contents of the Tent of War were committed to the writers by the surviving hereditary keeper, to be placed in the Peabody Museum, Harvard University, where they now are. The ceremonies connected with these articles had become obsolete owing to the changed conditions brought about by the occupancy by white settlers of the country adjacent to the Omaha reservation; yet the objects were regarded with respect and a sort of superstitious awe. The older men remembered the days when these articles were potent in the tribal life; the younger generation knew of them vaguely, but had inherited a fear of their mysterious power. The keeper, Mo^n'hi^{n}thi^{n}ge (fig. 101), found the charge of these things a serious care and anxiety. He kept them in a tent near his little house, and as he was becoming old and feeble he feared they might inadvertently suffer harm and the tribe be supernaturally punished for the accident. Because of these fears and of the changes that had already taken place and were still going on—as, that chieftainship in the tribe had been abolished; the buffalo had been exterminated, so that hunting was no longer possible; wars were at an end; the tribal lands were being divided into individual holdings—he was brought to realize in no uncertain way that the past life of the people was irrevocably gone. Face to face with these evidences of change, the old man met the situation with thoughtful dignity. With his own hands, still as hereditary keeper, he laid away his sacred charge

FIG. 101. Mo^{n}'hi^{n}thi^{n}ge, last keeper of the Tent of War.

where the articles, no longer needed to promote tribal unity and tribal safety, would be made to serve the study and the preservation of the story of his people, saying, as he did so:

These sacred articles have been in the keeping of my family for many generations; no one knows how long. My sons have chosen a path different from that of their fathers. I had thought to have these articles buried with me; but if you will place them where they will be safe and where my children can look on them when they wish to think of the past and of the way their fathers walked, I give them into your keeping. Should there come a time when I might crave to see once more these things that have been with my fathers, I would like to be permitted to do so. I know that the members of my family are willing that I should do this thing and no others have a right to question my action. There are men in the tribe who will say hard things of me because of this act but I think it best to do as I am doing.

It was late in the afternoon when the writers went to get the articles. The old man was sitting alone outside his dwelling. He had carefully gathered the contents of the Tent of War and was taking his last look at them in the fading light. Then with his own hands and with quiet haste, he lifted them into our wagon. "They are all there," he said, and turned away as the round moon rose over the valley. This act of Mo^{n}'hi^{n}thi^{n}ge drew a sharp line that marked the close of a chapter in Omaha history. It is fitting that the name of one who was brave enough to draw that line should be remembered with honor and sympathy for his courageous act.

FIG. 102. Bag containing Sacred Shell.

THE SACRED SHELL

On the reorganization of the tribal government the rites of defensive warfare were placed in charge of the We'zhi^{n}shte gens. This gens had probably held an important place in the previous tribal order to have had given to it such prominence in the new order. It is likely that the earlier prominence was connected with the rites that were the special care of this people—rites which must have commanded a tribal recognition—and the ancient name of the gens, judging from tribal custom, probably referred to these rites. Both the name and the rites which gave the name have long been lost, but out of the dim past a ceremonial object has come down as a heritage of the gens—the Sacred Shell. No one knew what it stood for, but everyone held it in superstitious dread; in all the tribe there was not a person exempt from fear of this shell. The superstitions that clung about it indicated that its rites related to the cosmic forces and to fundamental beliefs relative to life and death. When it became known in the tribe that the keeper of the Tent of War had committed its contents to the writers, men drove 30 and 40 miles to give cautions concerning the handling of this shell, as dire consequences would follow any carelessness or undue freedom in touching it.

The shell was encased in a sort of leather bag made from a piece of dressed skin, folded together, the sides fringed and the fringe braided so as to form the receptacle. This bag (fig. 102; Peabody Museum no. 37557) was always hung in the tent, never being allowed to touch the ground. It was believed that should this happen a terrible heat would follow, so great as to dry up the water courses and kill the fish. Mankind would hardly survive the result of the impact of the shell and the earth. When the tribe moved out on the buffalo hunt the Tent of War with its contents was always taken along. The shell was carried on the back of a boy. Promising children in the gens were selected for this purpose, in the hope that the shell might influence the boy's dreams or visions and so bring good fortune not only to the lad but through him to the tribe. He was given a pointed stick with which to steady himself as he walked and when he sat down to rest he stuck the stick into the ground and hung on it the bag containing the shell. If by any chance, as sometimes happened, he tripped and fell as he ran, he must at once utter this prayer: *Hei! mo*^{n}*no*^{n}*'ƀthi*^{n}, "I have strayed" (as if one were lost in the woods). The words are applied to an action which may bring disaster, but which is accidental. This acknowledgment on the part of the boy was supposed to avert the consequences which would happen if the shell should touch the ground. Men who in their youth had carried the shell have told of having fallen, thus causing the bag containing the shell to strike stones, but because of this prayer no trouble followed.

FIG. 103. Bag opened to show Sacred Shell.

When the bag containing the shell was examined at the Peabody Museum, it was opened by being cut at the back, as the skin was too stiff and old for the ends to be unbraided and it was desirable to preserve the outward appearance of the bag. It was photographed before anything was disturbed. (Fig. 103.) The bag is about 6 inches wide and 9 inches deep. There are indications of a reddish stripe having been painted down the center from the top to the bottom. There appeared to be an inner bag, which was wrapped about four times with strips of tanned skin three-fourths of an inch wide having sprays of cedar tied in. This lining seems to have been painted

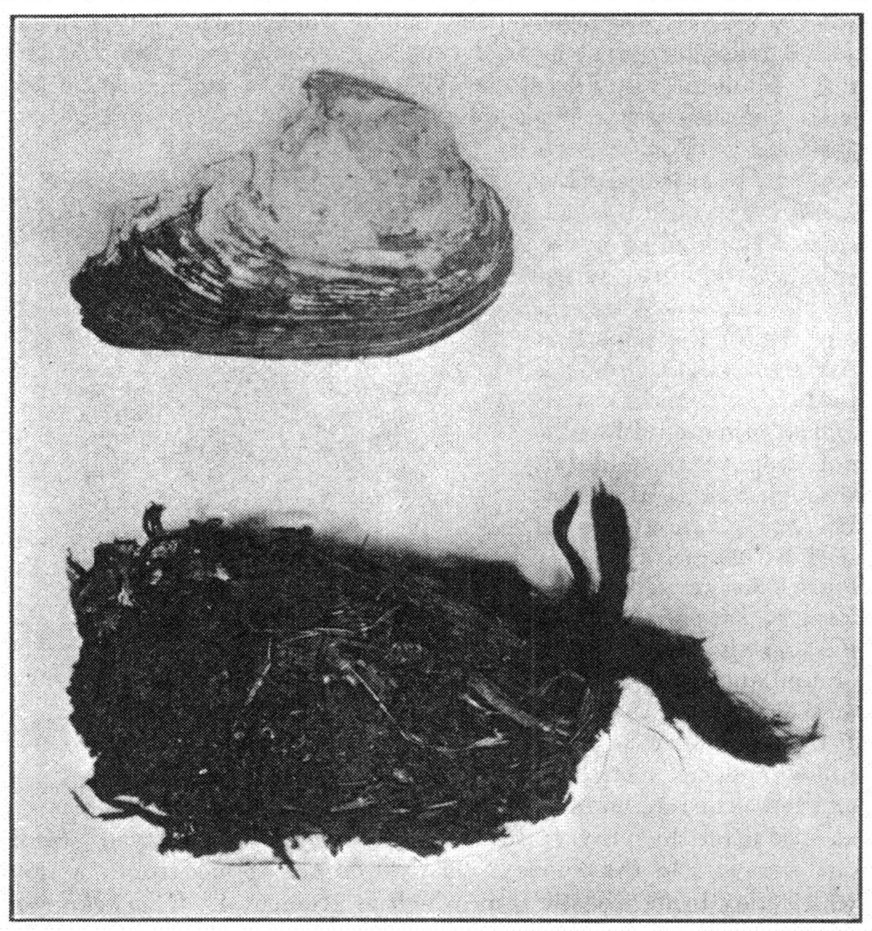

FIG. 104. Sacred Shell and contents.

red next the shell. On being removed, the shell and its undisturbed contents were photographed. (Fig. 104.)

The shell (pl. 58 and fig. 104; Peabody Museum no. 47822) was found to be a *Unio alatus*, a species that occurs in the Ohio, Missouri, and northern Mississippi valleys and in the Great Lakes; hence it is not probable that it came to the people from an outside source. The shell is not entire. "The winglike projection which extends

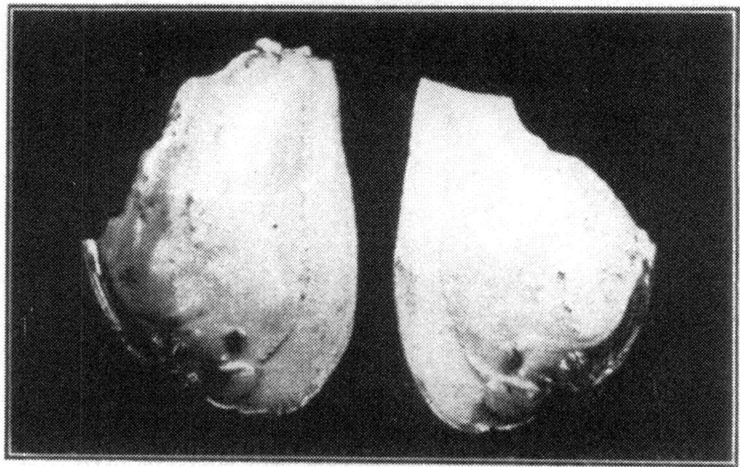

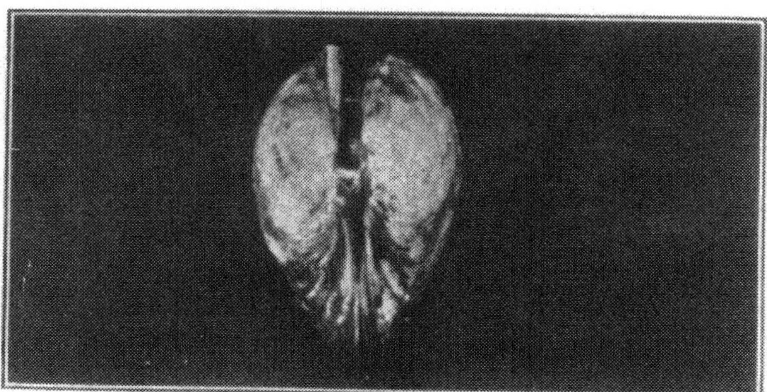

THE SACRED SHELL

from the beak of the shell had been broken or cut away; the surface had been rubbed down." It is possible that the condition of the shell may be due to human agency, although it may be accounted for otherwise—the break, by a fall on stones of the boy to whom the bag containing the shell was entrusted (an accident said to have occurred more than once during the last century), and the rubbed appearance, by the friction caused by long contact with the bag.

The contents (fig. 104) of the shell were wrapped in two pieces of matting, the warp of which is twisted vegetable fiber and the woof, rush. The outer matting is coarse and shows a selvage; the inner wrapping is of the same material, but of finer weave. Near the hinge of the shell was a scalp lock, tied with sinew and doubled over; beside it was a small skin receptacle, greatly compressed, containing a dark substance, probably earth, in which were a few seeds, fragments of what may have been grass, and some hairs. There is no tradition of this bag having been opened or of the shell having been exposed. The bag was said to contain a shell; nothing more concerning it was known.

Shells were formerly used to carry coals of fire. In the ancient ceremonies in which this shell had a part it may have served some such purpose either actually or symbolically. That it was connected with fire seems probable from the superstition that it could cause great heat. The fragments of cedar and the scalp would indicate some association with thunder and death. In the account of the Shell society (p. 509) it will be seen that the shell was connected with death and the continuation of life after death, as well as with water and the beginnings of life. Osage myths associate the shell with the introduction of life on the earth.

If additional light is ever thrown on this Sacred Shell of the Omaha tribe it will probably be the result of study of some of the cognate tribes, which may have preserved some tradition of a ceremony in which a shell of this kind was used.

THE CEDAR POLE

An ancient cedar pole (fig. 57) was also in the keeping of the We′zhi^{n}shte gens, and was lodged in the Tent of War. This venerable object was once the central figure in rites that have been lost. In Creation myths the cedar tree is associated with the advent of the human race; other myths connect this tree with the thunder. The thunder birds were said to live "in a forest of cedars." The phenomenon of lightning striking a tree was explained as, "the thunder bird has lit on the tree." What, if any, relation existed between the rites connected with the Cedar Pole and those of the Sacred Shell can not now be ascertained among the Omaha. The fact that both these relics of past ceremonials were in charge of one gens would seem to indicate some sort of connection.

This Cedar Pole was called Waxthe'xe, a name afterward transferred to the Sacred Pole in charge of the Ho^n'ga gens. The Sacred Pole symbolized the power of the chiefs and it is not improbable that the Cedar Pole stood for the power of Thunder, the god of war.

The Cedar Pole was 1 m. 25 cm. in length. To it was bound by a rope of sinew a similar piece of rounded cedar 61 cm. long called the *zhi'be*, or "leg." In the middle of the pole was bound another rounded piece of the wood, steadied by a third and smaller one, as three round sticks can be bound together more firmly than two. It is said that the pole typified a manlike being. As stated above, the lower piece was called "the leg," and it may be that the stick bound to the middle represented a club. The Thunder god, we are told, used a club for a weapon. One of the ritual songs used in the ceremony for awarding honors says:

> Behold how fearful is he, your Grandfather.
> He lifts his long club, fearful is he.

There is a tradition that in olden times, in the spring after the first thunder had sounded, in the ceremony which then took place this Cedar Pole was painted, with rites similar to those observed when the Sacred Pole was painted and anointed at the great tribal festival held while on the buffalo hunt. If this tradition is true, these ceremonies must have taken place long ago, as no indication of any such painting remains on the Cedar Pole. (See p. 229).

XI

SOCIETIES

There were two classes of societies among the Omaha—social and secret.

Membership in the social class was open to those able to perform the acts required for eligibility. To this class belong the warrior societies as well as those for social purposes only.

The secret societies dealt with mysteries and membership was generally attained by virtue of a dream or vision. Some of these secret societies had knowledge of medicines, roots, and plants used in healing; others were noted for their occult and shamanistic proceedings and furnish the only examples of such practices in the tribe.

There were no societies composed exclusively of women.

Social Societies

THE HETHU'SHKA

Among the societies of the social class one of the largest and most important was the Hethu'shka. Tradition and song indicate that this society was known when the Omaha, the Ponca, and their close cognates were living together as one tribe. Among the Omaha the ceremonies of the Hethu'shka formerly partook of tribal importance. The Ko^{n}'çe, or "Wind people," were the custodians of the two pipes sacred to the rites observed in the opening ceremonies when the members met together. There were occasions when the Hethu'shka members moved in a procession around the *hu'thuga* (tribal circle), following their two pipes, borne by their Ko^{n}'çe keepers. The office of keeping and filling the two pipes was hereditary in a family of the Ko^{n}'çe gens that to-day is represented by one surviving member. It is said that the object in establishing the Hethu'shka society was to stimulate an heroic spirit among the people and to keep alive the memory of historic and valorous acts. Thunder was the tutelar god of the Hethu'shka. The destructive power of the lightning, with its accompanying thunder and clouds so terrifying to man and beast, was recognized in the ceremonies and songs of this society. Among the Osage the Hethu'shka society is spoken of as the I^{n}gtho^{n}'ushko^{n}, "those who partake of the nature of the thunder." The society is known not only to the close cognates but to the Iowa and Oto tribes as well.

During the last century or more the Hethu'shka has spread among other branches of the Siouan family; tribes differing in language and customs have adopted it, so to speak. Among these are the Pawnee, who, according to tradition, were at one time close allies of the Omaha; they still call the Hethu'shka by its Omaha name. They and other tribes, who, to this day, delight in dancing to the rhythmic cadence of its songs, have songs of their own composition; but all these songs follow the model of the original Omaha songs. Any tribe familiar with the Hethu'shka "dance" at once recognizes one of its songs no matter in what tribe the song was composed. It is important to note that, although the Hethu'shka has so wide a popularity, it is only in the tribe in which it originated that the religious rites and songs of the opening ceremonies are observed; outsiders omit these observances and make use only of the dramatic dance, the songs, and the feast that closes the gathering of the members.

The membership of the Hethu'shka in the Omaha tribe was restricted to warriors; it included chiefs and "privates" but all were on an equal footing. The one requisite for eligibility was that the man should have received public war honors before the Packs Sacred to War. Entrance to the society was by unanimous consent. A desirable candidate was "picked" by a member and invited to a meeting, where, if no one offered objection to his joining the society, he was accepted as a member from that time.

The officers of the society were the hereditary keepers of the Hethu'shka pipes held as sacred, a leader, and a herald. The leader held his office during lifetime or until he chose to resign. When the office became vacant, the aspirant for the position had to be a man high in the respect of the tribe and a successful leader in war. The candidate made known his desire for the vacant office by inviting the members to a feast. At the feast his candidacy was discussed and if no objection to him were raised, he was accepted as leader. The herald had to be a reputable warrior and possessed of a strong, clear voice so that his messages might be distinctly heard. At each meeting the leader appointed two or more young men to act as servants in attending to the fire and assisting in the ceremonies. These servants were sometimes young men who had not yet attained to the distinction requisite for membership and it was considered an honor to be thus chosen and permitted to serve.

The meetings were held at irregular intervals, usually about once a month, always in the same place—in the commodious dwelling of some member who was respected in the tribe. He did not contribute anything besides shelter to the society, except when he chose to be the host, or feast-giver. Some member always volunteered to act in this capacity for each meeting; it was the duty of the host to furnish the requisite food for the "feast" and the tobacco for the pipes, though he could not fill these or prepare them for smoking, as that could be done only by the hereditary Ko^{n}'çe keeper. The host had also to prepare the black paint, made of charred box-elder wood mixed with water, and put it ready for use into a wooden bowl, the property of the society, kept for this purpose.

At the meetings of the society each member had his appointed place in the circle within the lodge. The leader, who must always belong to the highest grade of warriors, sat in the middle at the back part of the lodge, opposite the door. The men who were his equals in their grade of war honors sat next to him on his right and left; then came those of the next lower grade and so on, by grades, down to the door. The honors by which the places of the members were graded were those that had been publicly given the warriors at the Wate'giçtu (see p. 434). On each side of the entrance sat the servants appointed by the leader. Near the door on the right as one entered was the place set apart for the host or feast-giver of the meeting. Regardless of rank, the leader or anyone else had to leave his appointed seat and occupy this place on the evening when he acted as host.

The drum was placed at the left of the leader's seat. The men singers, two to four of whom used drumsticks, were grouped around it. Immediately behind the men sat a few women who possessed fine voices. This choir led in the singing of the songs, in which all the members, when not dancing, generally joined.

No clothing except the breechcloth was worn by the members and a long bunch of grass representing scalps the wearer had taken was fastened to the belt at the back. Later, but how long ago it is now impossible to ascertain, the members entitled to wear the scalps substituted therefor the bunch of long grass. In time this decoration became part of the Hethu'shka dress or regalia and as such was worn by all the members without regard to personal achievements. When the "dance" became known to the Dakota tribes and the Winnebago, the significance of the bunch of long grass having been forgotten, they gave the name "Grass dance," or the "Omaha dance," the latter name in recognition of the tribe from which the "dance" had been obtained. Each man painted himself in accordance with the directions given him at the Wate'giçtu and wore the decorations conferred on him at that public ceremony when he received his grade of war honors. The leader had to be of sufficient rank to be able to wear "the Crow" (see p. 441), a decoration of the highest order. Sometimes bells were tied about the legs and ankles, adding a sort of clicking, castanet accompaniment to the song and dance.

Not only were the members of the Hethu'shka chosen from among the brave men but the rules and influence of the society tended to enforce peace and harmony in the tribe. If a member became quarrelsome, a disturber of domestic or tribal affairs, the herald was sent to proclaim him to the people. He would give the man's name and say: "My friend, the door of the society is closed against you, that you may remain among the common people where such acts [naming his offense] are committed." This punishment was considered a great public disgrace.

When a meeting was to be held, all the belongings of the family were removed from the lodge for that evening and the place was left vacant for the society. The young men who had been appointed servants brought the necessary wood for the fire and the host sent the food to be cooked, for nothing was prepared beforehand. Just before the hour for assembling the host placed the bowl of paint and the two pipes, which had been filled and made ready for smoking, before the place belonging to the leader. Everything was then in readiness. When all the members were in their places the leader took up the bowl of black paint and the following song was sung by all present:

Mysteriously **Harmonized by John C. Fillmore for interpretation on the piano**

Double beat ♪ = 138 (Aria as sung in octaves)

Nu^n-xthe the-te hi-tha-ki-u^n te thu^n-ahi-de nu^n-xthe-the te

Con Ped.

hi-tha ki-u^n - te thu^n-ahi-de nu^n-xthe the - te

Nu^{n}xthe the te hithakiu^{n}te thu^{n}ahide
Nu^{n}xthe the te hithakiu^{n}te thu^{n}ahide
Nu^{n}xthe the te hithakiu^{n}te thu^{n}ahide
Nu^{n}xthe the te hithakiu^{n}te thu^{n}ahide
Nu^{n}xthe the te hithakiu^{n}te thu^{n}ahide

Literal translation: *Nu^{n}xthe,* charcoal; *the te,* this standing before me; *hithakiu^{n}te,* to paint or decorate himself with; *thu^{n}ahide,* I wearily wait, or wait until I am weary.

Free translation

Before me stands, awaiting my touch, coal-black paint,
Heavy black clouds filling all the sky o'er our head.
Upon our faces now we put the black, coal-black cloud.
Honoring war, wearying for the fight, warriors' fight,
Waiting to go where the Thunder leads warriors on.

The words were not intended to convey the idea that the members were literally tired of waiting for the wood to char in order that the ceremony of painting might take place, but rather that the desire for action was so strong within the warrior's breast that he was weary of the restraint, of the lack of opportunity that withheld him from heroic deeds of war. The music expresses more than the words alone convey. It expresses not only the warrior's eagerness but the portentous stir that filled the air with flying birds when the black storm clouds arose. The song strikingly suggests both the psychical and natural influence of the symbolic thunderstorm, the visible sign of the warrior god. During the singing of the song the leader dipped the fingers of his right hand into the paint and touched his forehead, cheeks, and chin, and both sides of his chest. Then the bowl was passed by the servants about the lodge and as the song was repeated each member put on himself the black paint, the insignia of the Thunder god.

When all had been painted, the leader took the pipes, dropped some tobacco on the earth, lifted the stems upward, paused a moment, and slowly turned and pointed them to the north, east, south, and west; he then lighted the pipes and handed them to the servants while this prayer was sung:

(Sung in octaves) Harmonized by John C. Fillmore for interpretation on the piano

Wakoⁿ'da thani ga the ke
Wakoⁿ'da thani ga the ke
Wakoⁿ'da thani ga the ke
Eha thani hiⁿga we tho he thoe
Wakoⁿ'da thani ga the ke
Wakoⁿ'da thani ga the ke
Wakoⁿ'da thani ga the ke
Eha thani hiⁿga we tho he thoe

Literal translation: *Wakoⁿ'da*, the power that moves and gives life; *thani*, modification of *nini*, tobacco; *ga*, here; *the*, this; *ke*, something long—indirect reference to the pipe; *eha*, now; *hiⁿga*, modification of *iⁿga*, to draw with the lips, as in smoking.

The indirect reference to the pipe indicates that the article is unimportant, a mere vehicle, the real offering being the tobacco smoke.

Free translation

Wakoⁿ'da, we offer this smoke,
Wakoⁿ'da, accept now our prayer,
Let the smoke rise upward to thee,
It bears our prayer, Wakoⁿ'da, to thee.

The words and music of this song are in marked contrast to the one that preceded. The descriptive character and the impatience expressed in the opening song here give place to stately measures in which the thoughts of the members are turned from the objective display of the Thunder gods toward the invisible Wakoⁿ'da, the directive life force which permeates nature and all forms of life. The beat of the drum is in 4/8 time while the music is in 6/8 time. The contrasting rhythm and syncopation express the restraining influence of the rite.

The pipes were passed in the following order: One pipe was started at the door and was smoked by all seated on the half of the circle between the left side of the entrance and the leader. The other was started with the leader and ended with the member at the right side of the door. As the pipes were passed among the members, the ascending smoke carried with it each warrior's appeal, voiced in the prayer to the invisible Wako^{n}'da. With this rite the opening ceremonies of the Hethu'shka came to a close.

Shortly after, the choir began a song in fast time and whoever was so inclined arose, dropped his robe in his seat, and stepped forth. Then, in a conventionalized pantomime he acted out one of his experiences in war from which he had gained a public war honor at the Wate'giçtu. A good dancer was light of foot and agile. A variety of steps was taken; the foot was brought down on the ground with a thud, making a synchronous accompaniment to the resonant drum beat and the voices of the singers; the limbs were lifted at sharp angles; the body was bent and raised with sudden and diversified movements, as in a charge, or as if dodging arrows or averting blows from weapons. In all this dramatic presentation of an actual scene there was not a motion of foot, leg, body, arm, or head that did not follow the song in strict time, yet keeping close to the story that was being acted out. The throb of the drum started the pulses of the spectator and held him to the rhythm of the scene as the eye followed the rapid, tense action of the dancer, while the ear caught the melody which revealed the intent of the strange drama, so full of color, movement, and wild cadences. The intense character of the dance made it impossible to sustain it for any considerable time; therefore the dance and song, although the latter was repeated, were always short. Rest songs, slower in time, followed a dance and during these songs the dancers sat muffled in their robes, often dripping with perspiration and panting to recover their breath.

When the food was ready, two men each of whom had broken the neck of an enemy, were designated by the leader to act as servers. Then the choir began the song that was the ceremonial call to the feast, to which the two men danced.

(Sung in octaves) Harmonized by John C. Fillmore for interpretation on the piano

Uhoⁿ thete nide tho
Uhoⁿ thete nide tho
Iⁿdakutha nide tho
Uhoⁿ thete nide tho he
Iⁿdakutha nide tho he tho

Literal translation: *Uhoⁿ*, the food now cooking, the feast; *thete*, this; *nide*, it is cooked or ready to eat; *iⁿdakutha*, an ancient term meaning friend or comrade; *tho, he, tho*, vocables.

Free translation

The feast awaits you—come, eat,
The feast is awaiting you,
Members, comrades, come and eat.
The feast awaiting stands before you, come,
Members, comrades, come and eat! He tho.

Two sticks were used in serving, and the choicest pieces were given the bravest man present. After all had been served except the host, or feast-giver (for he observed the tribal custom of not partaking of the food he had provided for his guests), the leader arose and made an address, in which he thanked the feast-giver and discoursed on the need of food for the preservation of life. He told of the trials, dangers, and hardships encountered in securing food, so that the quest represented both a man's valor and his industry; and, since no one could live without it, food was a gift of the greatest value. Therefore no one should partake of it without thanking the giver and he should not forget to include the giver's wife and children who relinquished to outsiders their share in this great necessity of the family. At the close of this speech each member partook of the food provided. When the repast was over, the member who had received the choicest part of the meat held up the picked bone and acted out in a dramatic dance the story of his exploit. Sometimes this exhibition was of a remarkable histrionic character.

When the time to disperse came, usually shortly after this dance, the choir began the song of dismissal. During the singing of the first part the members rose in their places and at the beginning of the second part the member who sat with the door to his right passed around the lodge and fire place and was the first to leave, each one following in his turn, all singing as they walked and passed out under the stars. When all had gone, the choir rose from about the drum and left the lodge in silence. This dismissal song is choral in character and yet has the rhythm of a march.

Harmonized by John C. Fillmore for interpretation on the piano

1

Kotha no^{n}zhi^{n} the
Kotha no^{n}zhi^{n} the
Kotha no^{n}zhi^{n} the
Eha no^{n}zhi^{n} hi thame tho he thoe

2

Kotha mo^{n}thi^{n} the
Kotha mo^{n}thi^{n} the
Kotha mo^{n}thi^{n} the
Eha mo^{n}thi^{n} hi thame tho he thoe

Literal translation: *Kotha*, an archaic term for friend; *no^{n}zhi^{n}*, arise or stand; *the*, vocable; *eha*, now; *hithame*, they say; *eha he*, vocables; *thoe*, close of stanza; *kotha*, friend; *mo^{n}thi^{n}*, walk. The words indicate that the members address one another: "Friend, we stand; Friend, we will walk."

Free translation

1

We say, Friend, arise!
Arise, Friend, we say.
Arise, Friend, and stand.
We say, Now arise and stand.

2

We say, Friend, now walk,
Now walk, Friend, we say.
We say, Friend, now walk.
We say, Friend, now walk we away.

The songs of the Hethu'shka are of much interest musically and they have also an historic value. It was a rule of the society that when a member performed a brave deed the society was the authority to decide whether the name of the doer and the record of his deed should be preserved in song. No one would dare to have a song composed in his honor without this consent. When consent was given, the song was composed, learned by the members, and then became a part of the record of the Hethu'shka society. In rendering such a song, when that part was reached where the warrior's name was mentioned the drum was not struck, that the name might be the more distinctly heard.

The words of the songs of the Hethu'shka were never intended to be complete in themselves, being for the sole purpose of recalling the incident or story which the song commemorated. Frequently a single word referred to a known tribal ceremony or recalled a teaching or precept, so that to the Omaha the word was replete with meaning and significance. For this reason a literal translation of the songs can not be made intelligible to an English reader; moreover, an attempt to make them thus intelligible would take from, rather than unfold, the meaning of the original and would rob the words of their native sense and dignity.

The songs of the Hethu'shka society number a hundred or more, each one commemorating some historical incident or bringing to mind the duties that devolved on the warrior members. Some of the songs reveal the ideals held up to inspire the conduct of the warriors. Although the songs belonged to the society, they were not restricted to the membership, non-members also being permitted to use them. By this custom the teachings set forth in the songs spread beyond the membership and so tended to enforce the Hethu'shka standards of conduct throughout the tribe.

The following eight songs are selected to show how the young men were stimulated to loyalty to the Hethu'shka society, to the tribe, to the family, and to perform acts which accorded with the Omaha ideal of a brave man:

First Song—Brotherhood and Loyalty

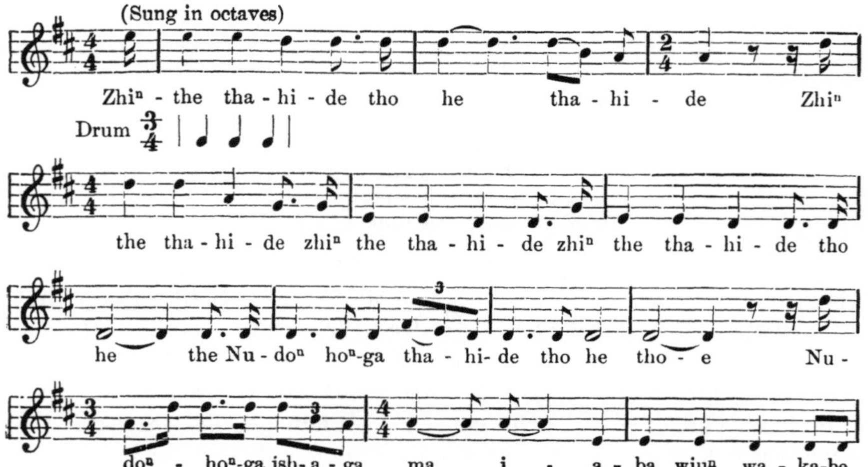

1

Zhiⁿthe thahide tho he thahide
Zhiⁿthe thahide zhiⁿthe thahide
Zhiⁿthe thahide tho he the
Nudoⁿhoⁿga thahide tho he thoe

2

Nudoⁿhoⁿga ishagama iaba
Wiuⁿwaka be tho
Zhiⁿthe thahide tho he the
Nudoⁿhoⁿga thahide tho he tho

Translation: *Zhiⁿthe,* older brother; *thahide,* I longingly wait; *tho he,* oratorical close of sentence; *nudoⁿhoⁿga,* leader, captain; *ishagama,* old men (*ma,* a plural sign); *iaba,* they spoke; *wiuⁿwaka,* they refer to me; *he tho,* oratorical ending of sentence. "Elder brothers! I longing wait [to share in the duties of the society]. Captains! the old men have spoken [of these duties]; their words now refer to me. Elder brothers! Captains! I longingly wait to take part in them [the duties]."

This song enforced the bond of brotherhood which bound together the members of the Hethu'shka. There were two ways in which the relation of brother could be expressed in the Omaha language: "Elder brother" and "younger brother." In the song the newly admitted member speaks, addressing the members of the society as "elder brothers." As war honors were requisite to membership, those whom he addressed were all men of more or less distinction. In his form of address he not only recognizes this but also his own inclusion in the brotherhood and proclaims his eagerness to do his part in maintaining the honor of the society and to share in its duties. By calling his "elder brothers" *nudoⁿhoⁿga,* "captains," he not only acknowledges their attainments but expresses his willingness to follow their leadership. In the second stanza he lays claim to share in the traditions of the society, that he may in his own career carry out the exhortations of the aged men whose words have been an inspiration to his "elder brothers" and "captains."

SECOND SONG—THE HETHU′SHKA, REPRESENTING THE TRIBE, DEFY THE ENEMY

(Aria as sung in octave unison) Harmonized by John C. Fillmore for interpretation on the piano

Song ♩. = 60

She - thu i ba u^{n} - wo^{n} ne - a ma she - thu i ba u^{n}

Drum beat ♪ = 120

Con Ped.

wo^{n} ne - a-ma tho he......... Ha - i - ba She- thu i ba u^{n} -

wo^{n} nea - ma tho he......... tho - e U - mo^{n} - ho^{n} thi^{n} a -

wa - thiⁿ iⁿ thiⁿ ge she - a i ba doⁿ The-thua - noⁿ - zhia
tha Du - da i ge tho he - - - tho

Shethu i ba uⁿwoⁿ neama
Shethu i ba uⁿwoⁿ neama tho he
Haiba shethu i ba uⁿwoⁿ neama tho he thoe

U'moⁿhoⁿ thiⁿ awathiⁿ iⁿthiⁿge
Shea i ba doⁿ thethu anoⁿzhia tha
Duda i ge tho he tho

Literal translation: *Shethu,* there, yonder; *i ba,* coming; *uⁿwoⁿ neama,* are seeking for me; *tho he,* oratorical end of sentence; *haiba,* they are coming; *U'moⁿhoⁿ thiⁿ,* the Omaha; *awathiⁿ,* where is he?; *iⁿthiⁿge,* they are saying of me; *shea i ba doⁿ,* yonder they come; *thethu,* here; *anoⁿzhia,* I stand; *tha,* end of sentence; *duda,* hither; *i ge,* come; *tho he tho,* end of sentence.

In this song the Hethu'shka personifies the tribe. The enemy is pictured as advancing from all sides, angrily calling: "Where are the Omaha?" The Hethu'shka, the men in whom "the fear of death has been dispelled," shout back as one voice: "Here I stand; come hither!" While the song is defiant, there is also in it the note of tribal unity as against enemies.

THIRD SONG—THE HETHU′SHKA THE PROTECTORS OF THE WOMEN AND CHILDREN

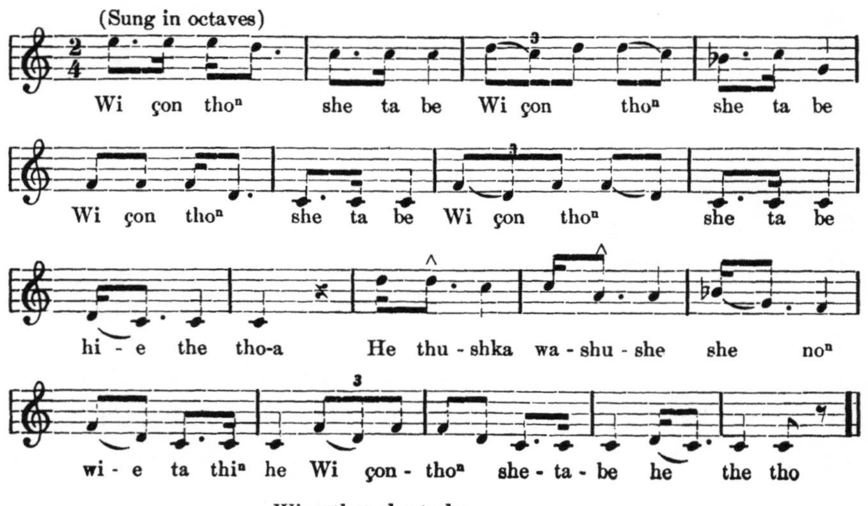
(Sung in octaves)
Wi çon tho^n she ta be Wi çon tho^n she ta be
Wi çon tho^n she ta be Wi çon tho^n she ta be
hi - e the tho-a He thu - shka wa - shu - she she no^n
wi - e ta thi^n he Wi çon - tho^n she - ta - be he the tho

Wiço^{n}tho^n she ta be
Wiço^{n}tho^n she ta be
Wiço^{n}tho^n she ta be
Wiço^{n}tho^n she ta be tho he tho
Hethu′shka washushe sheno^n
Wie ta thi^{n}he
Wiço^{n}tho^n she ta be tho he tho

Literal translation: *Wiço^{n}tho^n—wi*, my; *ço^n*, abbreviation of *itho^{n}ga*, younger brother; *tho^n*, a term of endearment; *she*, abbreviation of *eshe, shetabe*, you shall cry; *Hethu'shka*, the society; *washushe*, brave; *sheno^n*, of; *wie ta thi^{n}he*, so shall I be (the younger brother, who has become an *Hethu'shka*, speaks).

This song sets forth the obligation that rested on the Hethu′shka as the protectors of the women of the tribe, who were spoken of collectively under the term "sisters;" this term is implied in the song. It is the women, the "sisters," who "cry" to the "younger brothers." In the song the women are bidden to call on the younger brothers when danger threatens, the young and active men, "the younger brothers," those who were free from domestic responsibilities and at any moment could spring to the cry of sisters in trouble. The song tells who the younger brothers were to whom the sisters could always appeal when a foe came near—they were of the brave Hethu′shka, who were in duty bound to be ready at all times to guard the women and children of the tribe.

FOURTH SONG—MAN'S LIFE IS TRANSITORY

(Sung in octaves)
Mo^n - zho^n sho^n-ge - te tho mo^n- zho^n sho^n - ge - te tho he tho Ho^n -
thi^n - ge de sho^n ge te tho Mo^n - zho^n sho^n - ge - te
tho mo^n - zho^n sho^n ge - te tho he tho Sho^n-
ge - te tho he tho Ho^n thi^n - ge de sho^n ge te tho Mo^n -
zho^n sho^n- ge te tho mo^n - zho^n sho^n - ge te tho he e tho

Mo^{n}zho^n sho^{n}gete tho
Mo^{n}zho^n sho^{n}gete tho he tho
Ho^{n}thi^{n}ge de sho^{n}gete tho
Mo^{n}zho^n sho^{n}gete tho
Mo^{n}zho^n sho^{n}gete tho he tho
Sho^{n}gete tho he

Literal translation: *Mo^{n}zho^n*, the land, the scene one beholds; *sho^{n}gete,* shall long endure; *tho he tho,* oratorical end of sentence; *ho^{n}thi^{n}ge de,* when I am gone.

This admonitory song was explained as follows: "The natural fear of death that is in every individual sometimes so overpowers a man that in a time of danger he may lose self-control and abandon to their fate those whom he is in duty bound to protect. To drive away the fear of death and to vitalize the courage so necessary to a man who by nature and by tribal law is obligated to protect his family and the families of the tribe, the example of men who had hazarded their lives in the performance of duty was held up by the society; the members were persistently taught that man's life is transitory, and being so it is useless to harbor the fear of death, for death must come sooner or later to everybody; man and all living creatures come into existence, pass on, and are gone, while the mountains and rivers remain ever the same—these alone of all visible things abide unchanged. The song represents the Hethu'shka as saying: 'I shall vanish and be no more but the land over which I now roam shall remain and change not.'"

FIFTH SONG—AN ADMONITION

Harmonized by John C. Fillmore for interpretation on the piano

Kaga wigiçitha thiⁿhe no
Wigiçitha thiⁿhe no
Wazhiⁿga shti thithiⁿge doⁿ, wigiçitha thiⁿhe no
Wakoⁿda da i doⁿ hegoⁿ ta thiⁿhe no
Kaga thethu hoⁿbaçkitha thiⁿhe no
Wigiçitha thiⁿhe no
Wazhiⁿga shti thethiⁿge doⁿ wigiçitha thiⁿhe no
Wakoⁿda da i doⁿ hegoⁿ ta thiⁿhe no
Kaga thethu hoⁿbaçkitha thiⁿhe no
Wigiçitha thiⁿhe no

Literal translation: *Kaga*, friend; *wigiçitha*, I remember you who are mine; *thiⁿhe*, as life passes; *no*, vocable; *Wazhiⁿga*, a personal name; *shti*, you also; *thithiⁿge*, you are no more; *Wakoⁿda da*, the thunder gods; *i*, they; *doⁿ*, when; *hegoⁿ*, so shall my acts conform (to their decrees); *thethu*, here; *hoⁿbaçkitha*, I am angry.

The burden of this song is the remembrance by the Hethu′shka of comrades slain in battle and the strong desire for revenge stirred by such memories; but the men are reminded of the teaching that to the Thunder gods belongs the power to decree death and that man must conform his acts to the will of the gods even though his spirit chafes under the restraint. It is thought that the song is a very old one and that several names were used, one superseding another as the memory of the fallen hero faded. Wazhiⁿ′ga, who is mentioned in the song, was killed before the middle of the last century.

Sixth Song—Necessity for Alertness

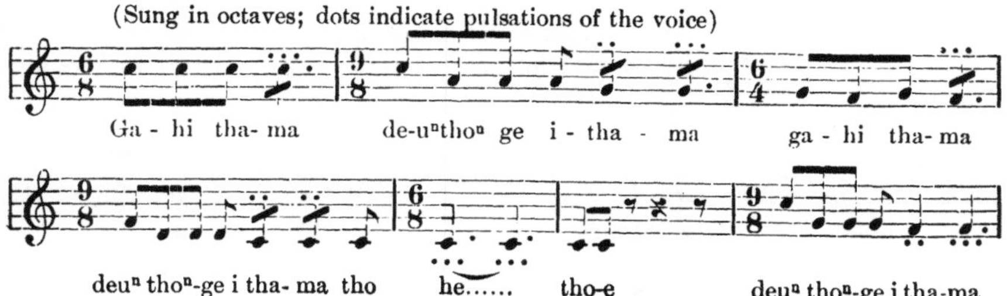
(Sung in octaves; dots indicate pulsations of the voice)
Ga - hi tha- ma de-uⁿthoⁿ ge i - tha - ma ga - hi tha- ma
deuⁿ thoⁿ-ge i tha- ma tho he...... tho-e deuⁿ thoⁿ-ge i tha-ma

a-zho^{n} mi-ke di pa nu hu wi^{n} a me tho he........... um ba
i da u gtha i - tha- me tho he........ tho.

Gahithama deu^{n}tho^{n}ge ithama
Gahithama deu^{n}tho^{n}ge ithama tho he thoi
Deu^{n}tho^{n}ge ithamaazho^{n} mikide panuhu wi^{n}a me tho he the
Umba ida ugtha ithame tho he tho

Literal translation: *Ga'hithama,* yonder far away (the voices I hear); *deu^{n}tho^{n}ge,* they are saying something to me; *ithama,* they send (their words); *azho^{n}*, I lay; *mikide,* where; *panuhu,* owl; *wi^{n}a me,* one speaks; *tho he the,* vocables; *umba,* morning; *ida,* comes; *ugtha,* shout; *ithame,* directed toward one.

The song may refer to the time when the Omaha were a forest people; it preserves the memory of a timely discovery by which a disaster was averted and a victory won. The story runs as follows:

The Omaha were camped in a forest. One dark night a warrior was awakened by the hooting of an owl. He was an observant man, familiar with the cries of birds and the sounds made by animals. As he listened, he heard answering hoots in the distance. He thought the sounds not genuine, but imitations probably made by men. He arose silently, slung his quiver over his shoulder, took his bow, and crept among the trees. At a distance from the camp he detected signs of men—enemies. He stealthily made his way back and awakened the sleeping warriors of the tribe, who at once made themselves ready for defense. At daybreak the enemy rushed from all sides on the Omaha camp but the men were prepared and met the onslaught so successfully that few of their foes escaped.

The song commemorates the alertness of the man whose ear was trained to know the calls and cries of birds and holds him up as an example.

Seventh Song—Fidelity to Parents

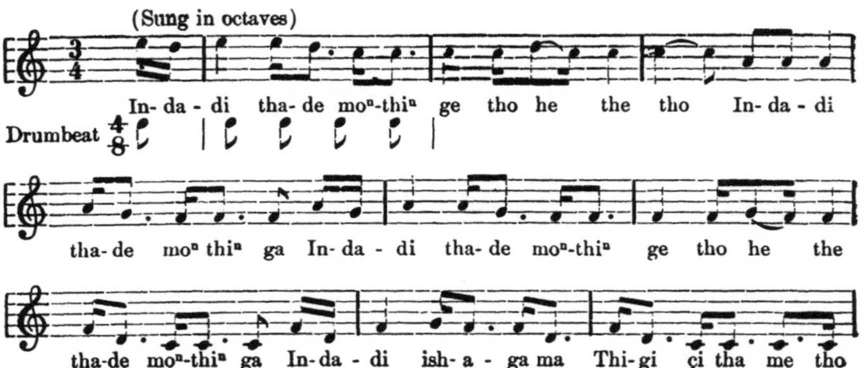
(Sung in octaves)
In- da - di tha- de mo^{n}-thi^{n} ge tho he the tho In- da - di
Drumbeat
tha- de mo^{n} thi^{n} ga In- da - di tha- de mo^{n}-thi^{n} ge tho he the
tha-de mo^{n}-thi^{n} ga In-da - di ish- a - ga ma Thi-gi çi tha me tho

he the tho-e Tha- de mo^n-thi^n ge tho he - the tho
Wa- zhi- da - thi^n i - zhi^n - ge i thi^n - ga be tho In - da
di tha de mo^n-thi^n ge tho the he tha - de mo^n-thi^n - ga In- da -
di ish - a - ga ma thi - gi çi - tha me tho he the tho

Indadi thade mo^nthi^nge tho he e the tho
Indadi thade mo^nthi^nga
Indadi thade mo^nthi^nge tho he e the
Thade mo^nthi^nga
Indadi ishaga ma
Thigi çithame tho he thoi
Thade mo^nthi^n ge tho he the tho
Wazhidathi^n izhi^nge ithi^nga be tho
Indadi thade mo^nthi^nge tho he the
Thade mo^nthi^nga
Indadi ishaga ma
Thigi çithame tho he the tho

Literal translation: *Indadi,* my father; *thade,* call forth, proclaim; *mo^nthi^nge, go; ga,* sign of command; *tho he e the tho,* vocables; *ishaga ma,* the aged men; *thigi çithame,* they will remember you; *Wazhidathi^n,* personal name; *izhi^nge,* his son; *ithi^nga,* say of me.

The words of the song are few and impossible to render literally. They are mnemonics merely but they serve to carry the memory of the act which the song commemorates. The song is said to be very old and has been handed down through many generations, an indication of the estimation placed on the teaching it sets forth—the unselfish regard for the fame of his father shown by the hero of the story and song. The account runs as follows:

A young man, whose name, according to his expressed wish, is unknown, said to his comrades as he lay dying on the field of battle, where he had fought valiantly: "When you proclaim my death," referring to the custom of calling out the names of the slain when the war party returned to the village, "speak not my name, but that of my father. Say, 'The son of Wazhi′dathi^n is slain.' " Having made this request, the young man spoke again but as if he were addressing his father. He said: "Father, in my death shall the aged men remember you!" The aged men were the historians, so to speak; they were the ones who treasured the memory of tribal incidents and passed them on to younger generations. By this act of the son he caused his father's name to be held in remembrance, but at the same time his own act was such that he was held up to future generations as an example of filial regard.

EIGHTH SONG—AGAHAMO^{N}THI^N

The song is eulogistic of a warrior hero.

Shethi^n the thi^n do^{n}ba ge tho he
Shethi^n the thi^n do^{n}ba ga
Ha! do^{n}ba ga Ha! do^{n}ba ge tho he the
Agahamo^{n}thi^n do^{n}bage tho he thoe

Literal translation: *Shethi^n*, yonder; *the*, one; *thi^n*, going; *do^{n}ba*, behold; *ge*, *ga*, sign of command; *tho he the the*, vocables; *ha*, exclamation; *do^{n}bage*, behold him; *Agahamo^{n}thi^n*, personal name; *do^{n}bage*, behold him.

The words are few, an exclamation bidding the people to behold, to look on A′gahamo^{n}thi^n!, and would be quite unintelligible but for the story which gave rise to the song. A′gahamo^{n}thi^n died in the early part of the last century. He was a man of great valor. He had won and received all the public war honors but he was not satisfied. At each meeting of the Hethu′shka society all through one fall and winter he would rise and declare: "During the next battle in which I take part I will drag an enemy from his horse or die in the attempt!" The following summer, when the Omaha were on the buffalo hunt, the tribe was attacked by the Yankton and a fierce encounter took place. True to his word, A′gahamo^{n}thi^n charged the line, dragged a Yankton from his horse, and slew him. Almost immediately A′gahamo^{n}thi^n was killed. In emulation of his courage the Omaha made a desperate charge on the Yankton and defeated them. This song was composed to commemorate the warrior who made good his promise and in so doing saved his people. Of A′gahamo^{n}thi^n it was said, "He spoke a word and chased it to his death."

THE PU′GTHO^{N}

Chiefs only could become members of this society. It was, therefore, what might be called exclusive, as compared with the more democratic Hethu′shka, which was open to every man who had won public war honors. The songs of the Pu′gthoⁿ society were restricted to the members, outsiders not being permitted to sing them. The society ceased to exist some fifty years ago; the few members who were living twenty years ago clung to their exclusiveness and were chary of speaking about or singing the songs. For this reason only a few songs were obtainable, and also for another reason, which, it is said, had much to do with the final breaking up of the society. There was an officer in the organization known as the keeper of the songs. This office was held for life and it was the duty of the keeper to train his successor in the knowledge of the songs and their stories. Through a series of coincidences a superstition grew up that whenever the keeper sang one of the old songs death would visit his family. Members became loath, therefore, to take the responsibility of asking for the songs and whenever the request was made it was accompanied by large gifts; these gifts were offered the keeper to atone for any ill fortune that might come to him because he had sung the songs. As all the songs referred to the acts of chiefs, such songs were historical and were of tribal import. Moreover, these songs were necessary for the ceremonial dances that could be performed only at meetings of this society. On these occasions the chiefs wore their full regalia and headdresses made from the head of the buffalo, which partook of the nature of a mask. This was the only society among the Omaha in which headgear that approximated the character of a mask was used. It is said that the last time the keeper was prevailed on to sing an old song, while he was in the act of singing a Sioux warrior crept stealthily into the camp, made his way to the singer's tent, and there shot dead the daughter of the keeper. This event put an end to the meetings of the society. No one knows for whom or by whom the Pu′gthoⁿ songs were composed or the events they celebrated. Not a half dozen of the songs survive and of these the incidents which gave rise to them all but one are lost. The Pu′gthoⁿ songs are unlike the Hethu′shka songs in that they do not present contrasting rhythms, which so frequently occur in the latter. The rhythm is simple and forceful and the music wilder than in any other class of Omaha songs.

The songs that survive are warlike in character and their marked rhythm is attractive, but they are rather bombastic in both words and music, as became the expressions of a society composed exclusively of chiefs—men who had won distinction and achieved public recognition and who enjoyed their power and position. These songs afford an interesting contrast to those belonging to the Hethu'shka society. While many of the latter's songs referred to war, as befitted a society of warriors, they did not emphasize personal distinction but generally appealed to the people through some heroic experience or by the expression of some valorous feeling, frequently of a noble and self-forgetful character. Their songs therefore cover a wider range of musical expression than do the Pu'gthon songs, which bear the stamp of self-consciousness and self-satisfaction.

First Song

PU'GTHON

Harmonized by John C. Fillmore for interpretation on the piano

Ya e hi tha e hi the Ya e hi tha e hi the..............

Yae hi tha e hi the
Yae hi tha e hi the
Yae hi tha e hi the
Yae hi tha e hi the
I^{n}dakutha wahato^{n}ga eame
Yae hi tha e hi the
Yae hi tha e hi the
Yae hi tha e hi the

Literal translation: *I^{n}dakutha* is an old word meaning "friend;" *wahato^{n}ga,* shield; *eame,* they say; *yae hi,* etc., are vocables.

It is probable that Wahato^{n}ga was a personal name and the song plays on the meaning of the word. The meaning of the song was said to be that Wahato^{n}ga was a friend and a shield to the people.

Second Song

(Sung in octaves) Harmonized by John C. Fillmore for interpretation on the piano

♩. = 84 *Dignified*

Shu - pi da hu - a - ta na-zhi^{n} the Shu - pi - da hu -
ff Con Ped.
a - ta na- zhi^{n} the a - e the tha e the he the
p

E - he hu - a - ta na-zhi^n the e the tha e the hi the
f

Shupida huata nazhi^n the
Shupida huata nazhi^n the
Aethe tha ethehi the
Ehe huata nazhi^n the
Ethetha ethe hi the

Literal translation: *Shupida*, when I come; *huata*, I shout; *nazhi^n*, stand, meaning to stand in a given place; *ehe*, I say or command.

Free translation

When I come to the battle I shout,
I shout as I stand in my place,
I shout my command as I stand.

THIRD SONG

(Sung in octaves) Harmonized by John C. Fillmore for interpretation on the piano

♩= 100 Dignified
Shu - pe - da wea - wa - ta tha - wa - the Shu - pe -
ff
Con Ped.
da wea wa - ta tha - wa - the Pa - tha - ga - ta
ff

tha - wa - the a he the hi the a - hi - the

Shupida weawata thawathe
Shupida weawata thawathe
Pathagata theawathe
Ahe the hi the ahi the

Literal translation: *Shupida*, when I come; *weawata*, where; *thawathe*, do I send them; *pathaga*, to the hills or mounds (i. e., graves); *ta*, yonder; *thawathe*, all the rest are vocables.

Free translation

When I come, where do I send them?
When I come, where do I send them?
To their graves do I send them!

This song is very old, dating back perhaps to the time when the Omaha and Ponca were one tribe. The Ponca claimed the chief and told the following story: The people had been attacked and some women had been killed. The chief this song commemorates came late on the scene and by his valor turned the tide of the battle. He was armed with a long lance of ash wood, the end of which was pointed and hardened by grease and scorched in the fire. With this lance he rushed on the enemy, thrusting it between the legs of a man and tossing him in the air to be killed by the fall. His great strength and courage caused the death of many. The song was composed to commemorate his coming and by his spirited action sending the foe "to their graves."

THE KI′KUNETHE

The name Ki′kunethe (*ki′ku*, "to gather together;" *nethe*, "to build a fire") indicates the social purpose of the society—to gather about a fire. This society was composed of the leading men of the tribe. There was no formal membership. There was an officer, a sort of "chairman" or leader, who was chosen to preside. The gathering was for social pleasure and to talk over and discuss subjects of interest. There was a custom which may refer to some ancient forms once observed. The place in the middle at the back part of the lodge was always kept vacant. This was the seat that would be assigned to an honored guest. Before this empty seat was placed a bowl or platter with a horn spoon. It was explained that this place was kept in recognition of Wako^{n}'da, the provider and ruler of mankind, who was thus present with the men as they met together and talked. This society was given up about 1870, when the changes incident to contact with the white settlers and the Government had begun seriously to affect the tribe.

THE T'E GA'XE

T'e ga'xe (*t'e*, death; *gaxe*, to make, to simulate—to simulate death) was the name of an ancient social society that disappeared before the middle of the last century. This society had songs which were sung at its gatherings but they are lost, together with the customs once observed.

THE MO^{N}WA'DATHI^{N} AND THE TOKA'LO

The Mo^{n}wa'dathi^{n} (Omaha term for Mandan) and the Toka'lo (meaning unknown) were social societies that were borrowed or introduced from the Dakota. Both of these societies ceased to exist about the middle of the last century. The meetings of both were public; they had a formal membership open to any man of good repute. The members sometimes paraded on horseback around the camp, moving to the rhythm of the songs of the society. Their dances were said to be dignified rather than dramatic—a statement borne out by the surviving songs. Whether the music was composed by the Omaha or came from the Dakota is not known. There are no words to the songs, a fact which makes it probable that the music was adopted from another tribe, the foreign words being dropped.

SECRET SOCIETIES

All of the secret societies had to do with mysteries and were spoken of by the general term Xu'be wachi, (*xube*, "sacred," "mysterious," "occult;" *wachi*, "dance"—that is, rhythmic movements of the body keeping time with the melody sung and also expressive of the emotion aroused by the music).

THE MO^{N}CHU' ITHAETHE

Entrance into the Mo^{n}chu' ithaethe (*mo^{n}chu*, "bear;" *i'thaethe*, "to show compassion"—"those to whom the bear has shown compassion," by appearing in a dream or vision and giving power) society was by virtue of a dream of the bear. To this society belonged the knowledge of the practice of sleight of hand, as the thrusting of wands down the throat and similar performances. This knowledge was said to have been gained originally from the animals. This society should not be confused with the Waca'be itazhi (Bear subgens) of the Tha′tada gens, which took part in the ceremonies held in the Sacred Tent in charge of the We′zhi^{n}shte gens when the thunder first sounded in the spring. The two were distinct and unrelated. The Mo^{n}chu′ ithaethe society has been extinct for half a century. The following song belonged to this society:

BEAR SONG

(Sung in octaves)
The thu a-ti a no^{n}-zhi^{n} i tha e he tha...... thethu tia no^{n} zhi^{n} i tha e he tha Xu - ga b'thi-a the-
thu a-ti a no^{n} zhi^{n} i-the e tho^{n}-be pi-a-do^{n} the-thu a- ti no^{n}-zhi^{n}

Literal translation: *Thethu*, here, at this place; *ati*, I came; *ano^{n}-zhi^{n}*, I stood; *xuga*, badger (this word was sometimes used to designate animals with claws; in this instance the grizzly bear was really meant); *bthia*, I was; *etho^{n}be piado^{n}*, as I appeared.

The words refer to the time when the man went out to fast. When he came to a particular place (*thethu*), the grizzly bear appeared as he stood there and the man felt that he was mysteriously related to the bear. The song set forth the man's credential or title to membership in the Bear society.

THE TE′ ITHAETHE

To the Te′ ithaethe (*te*, "buffalo;" ithaethe, "to show compassion"—"those to whom the buffalo has shown compassion," by coming to them in a vision and giving power) society was committed the knowledge of medicines for the curing of wounds. Membership was accorded to persons of both sexes to whom the buffalo appeared in dreams. The roots of the wild anise, the hop (*Humulus lupulus*), and *Physalis viscora* were used for healing. Bits of these roots were ground between the teeth, then water was taken into the mouth, and the medicated liquid was blown with force into the wound.

The following account by one of the writers details a scene witnessed in his boyhood when one of his playmates was accidentally shot by a young man who, with some companions, was firing a pistol at a mark:

After the shooting the excitement was intense, and above all the noise could be heard the heartrending wails of the unfortunate man who had wounded the boy in the head. The relatives of the lad were preparing to avenge his death, and those of the man to defend him. I made my way through the crowd, and, peering over the shoulders of another boy, I saw on the ground a little form that I recognized. Blood was oozing from a wound in the back of the boy's head and from one under the right eye near the nose. A man ordered the women to stop wailing and bade the people to stand back. Soon through an opening in the crowd I saw a tall man wrapped in a buffalo robe come up the hill and pass through the space to where the boy lay. He stooped over the child, felt of his wrist, and then of his heart. "He is alive," the man said; "set up a tent and take him in." The little body was lifted on a robe and carried by two men into a large tent that had been hastily erected. Meanwhile a young man had been sent in all haste to call the buffalo doctors. Soon they were seen galloping over the hill on their horses, one or two at a time, their long hair flowing over their naked backs. They dismounted and one by one entered the tent, where they joined the buffalo doctor who lived near by and had already been called. A short consultation was held. The sides of the tent were drawn up to let in the fresh air and to permit the people to witness the operation.

All the buffalo medicine men sat around the boy, their eyes gleaming over their wrinkled faces. Then one of the men began in a low voice to tell how in a vision he had seen the buffalo which had revealed to him the secret of the medicine and taught him the song he must sing when using it. At the end of every sentence the boy's father thanked him in terms of relationship. Then he compounded the roots he had taken from his skin pouch and started his song at the top of his voice. The other doctors, some twenty or more, joined in, and sang it in unison with a volume that could be heard a mile away. The song was accompanied by a bone whistle imitating the cry of the eagle. After the doctor had started the song he put the bits of roots into his mouth, ground them with his teeth, and taking a mouthful of water he approached the boy bellowing and pawing the earth like an angry buffalo at bay. When near the boy he drew in a long breath, and with a whizzing noise forced the water from his mouth into the wound. The boy spread out his hands and winced as though he had been struck. The man uttered a series of short exclamations: "Hi! hi! hi!" Then the father and the man who had wounded the boy lifted their outspread hands toward the doctor to signify their thanks. During the administration of the medicine all the men and two women doctors sang with energy the following song which had been started by the operator:

(Sung in octave unison)
Ni - uⁿ shka-xe ni - uⁿ shka - xe the- xe ni - uⁿ shka-xe
he the he........ E - gon the-thu toⁿ the - a...... the e-gon the
thu kom btha tha the he kom btha he he the - a...... the

Literal translation: *ni uⁿshka xe* (*nia*, part of me, hurt; *uⁿ*, me, you; *shkaxe*, make—you hurt me); *egoⁿ*, then; *thethu*, here; *toⁿ*, from; *theathe*, I send; *kombtha*, I want or desire—from here I desire to send it.

A second doctor now repeated the treatment and started his song, all the others joining in the singing as before, while he administered the remedy.

At the completion of the song a third doctor made ready to give his application, starting his song and all the other doctors joining as before in the singing.

At the end of the song the fourth doctor began to compound the roots, and when he was ready he began the following song, which was taken up by all the others and sung with forceful energy:

(Sung in octave unison)
Ni thuⁿ tha-de a-ma Ni thuⁿ tha-de a - ma......... u - he-ke the i the
e a ma e tho he Ni thuⁿ tha - de e - a - ma tho he

Literal translation: *ni*, water; *thu*ⁿ, round; *thade*, to designate; *ama*, they; *uhekethe*, to yield to him; *itheama*, they say.

This song conveys to the Omaha mind a picture of the prairie, the round wallow standing like a pool with water, and the wounded buffalo being healed near it by its companions. There is a belief among the Omaha that the buffalo cure their wounds with their saliva; therefore the doctors prepare the herbs in the mouth and blow the water into the wound.

The doctors remained all night, applying their medicine and dressing the wound. Four days the boy was treated in this manner. On the evening of the third day the doctors said the lad was out of danger, and that in the morning he would be made to stand and meet the rising sun, and so greet the return of life.

I went to bed early, so as to be up in time to see the ceremony. I was awakened by the sound of the singing, and hurried to the tent. Already a crowd had gathered. There was a mist in the air, as the doctors had foretold there would be, but as the dawn drew nearer the fog slowly disappeared, as if to unveil the great red sun that was just visible on the horizon. Slowly it grew larger and larger. The boy was gently lifted by two strong men, and when on his feet was told to take four steps toward the east [note the resemblance to the ceremony of Turning the Child, p. 121], while the doctors sang the mystery song which belonged to this stage of the cure. The two men began to count as the boy feebly attempted to walk—one, two, three. The steps grew slower, and it did not seem as if he could make the fourth, but he dragged his foot and made the fourth. "Four!" cried the men; "It is done." Then the doctors sang the song of triumph.

The fees were then distributed. These were horses, robes, bear-claw necklaces, eagle feathers, embroidered leggings, and other articles of value. Toward these the relatives of the man who shot the boy contributed largely. One or two doctors remained with the boy for a time. In a month or so he was back among us, ready to play or to watch another pistol practice by the young men.

THE WANOᴺ'XE ITHAETHE

Men and women to whom ghosts appeared in dreams or visions were eligible to membership in the Wanoⁿ'xe ithaethe (*wanoⁿ'xe*, "a form that is transparent," "a ghost;" *i'thaethe*, "shown compassion by"—"those to whom ghosts have shown compassion") society. Members were believed to have the power to *wathigthoⁿ*, divine or foretell events, particularly approaching death. If death was foretold, the relatives of the doomed person might ask the member foretelling the death to seek to avert it. To bring about this result he heated water as he sang his songs and then cast the water on the ground to the right or the left of the entrance of the lodge of the threatened person—never in a straight line from the door. By this act the spirit is thwarted in its onward progress toward the spirit world and is forced to return, so that person continues to live. The members of this society could also stop rain. This power was exercised only by request. When a member was asked to stop the rain, he filled a small, unornamented pipe (in token of his modesty in addressing the cosmic forces), elevated the stem, and smoked, singing his song as the smoke was wafted upward; the act was believed to secure the desired result.

The following is one of the songs of this society:

GHOST SONG

Translation: The first eight measures are vocables. *Ho^n*, night; *thi^n*, moving; *thethi^n*, yonder moving; *i*, come; *ne*, modification of *thi^n*, moving; *thethu*, here. "Night is moving toward us here." Night refers to death, by which one enters the realm of ghosts.

THE I^{N}GTHU^N′ ITHAETHE

Membership in the I^{n}gthu^n′ ithaethe (*I^{n}gthu^n*, "Thunder;" *ithaethe*, "shown compassion by"—"those to whom the thunder has shown compassion") society was open only to the man or woman who had heard the Thunder beings in dreams or visions. It was believed that through this medium occult powers were imparted and that by means of the songs given the elements could be controlled—rain could be brought or the storm driven away. Future events could also be foretold, for in most of these secret societies magic powers were supposed to be exercised. Sometimes the members pitted their powers against one another. The following song commemorates one of these contests, which occurred many years ago when a number of the Omaha went on a visit to the Ponca. Among the visiting party was a member of the Thunder society noted for his occult powers. In the Ponca Thunder society was a man who had a similar reputation. These two men met and while they feasted each other they secretly sought each other's death by means of their magic. The Ponca drew on the ground a picture of the Omaha and struck it with his club (the club being the weapon of the Thunder beings), at the same time calling on the Thunder beings similarly to strike the original of the picture. The Omaha suspected some magic attempts, so he sang his songs, relying solely on them for his protection. The visit of the Omaha party came to an end and the people returned home; a few days afterward the Ponca who had drawn the picture of the Omaha and invoked the Thunder was himself struck by lightning. The incident became speedily known to the Omaha magician and this song was composed to commemorate the event. The name of the Ponca, Gati′demoⁿthiⁿ, is mentioned in the song, where he is represented as weeping because his request to the Thunder beings to strike the Omaha had been turned upon himself.

THUNDER SONG

He! Kage tede xage ame tho he
He! Kage tede xage ame tho he, the ha
Xage ame tho he the e ha tha
Thethu hiⁿwiⁿtha ma he tho
Gati′demoⁿthiⁿ hoⁿthixu hiⁿtha moⁿzhia tha
Xage ame tho he he a tha
Thethu hiⁿwiⁿtha ma he, tho

Literal translation: *He! kage, He!* friend; *tede,* a contraction of *intede,* and now, or for that cause; *xage,* weep or cry; *ame,* they say; *tho,* musical syllable; *he,* end of sentence; in the second line *the ha,* vocables; *thethu,* here; *hi^{n}wi^{n}tha,* tell me; *ma,* they; *he,* end of sentence; *Gati'-demo^{n}thi^n,* a Ponca personal name, that of the man who was the subject of the song and drew the picture; *ho^{n}thixu,* a picture or sketch; *hi^{n}tha,* pleased; *mo^{n}zhia,* I not; *tha,* end of sentence.

The song represents the Omaha narrating the experience. "My friend, they say Gati'demo^{n}thi^n made a picture of me. I was not pleased; here they tell me that he it was who cried."

A member of this society dreamed that the Thunder gods wanted to take him but, not wanting to go to the gods, he persuaded them to take a substitute. Shortly afterward a friend of his was killed by lightning, an incident which he regarded as the result of his appeal. This incident is preserved in the following song:

Words

Wi shutheakithe a
Wi shutheakithe
Wi shutheakithe a
Paho^{n}gamo^{n}thi^n shutheakithe a
Wi shubtha mo^{n}zhie tho he thoe
Wi shutheakithe a
Wi shitheakithe a

Literal translation: *Wi,* I; *sh^{u}theakithe,* send to you; *Paho^{n}ga-mo^{n}thi^n,* name of the man struck by lightning; *wi,* I; *shubthamo^{n}zhie,* do not come; *tho he thoe,* vocables.

The above songs can not be classed with those which were regarded as potent and as directly connected with the Thunder beings, although they refer to incidents which might be regarded as showing the power of man's appeal.

The following song refers directly to the dream experience of the singer and is of the class that was believed to bring a direct response from the Thunder beings:

THUNDER SONG

E tho he
Wako^{n}da hi^{n}wi^{n}tha me tho he
Wako^{n}da hi^{n}wi^{n}tha me tho he
Hi^n kage ha! xage thi^n hi^{n}wi^{n}tha me e e tho he thoi
Wako^{n}da hi^{n}wi^{n}tha me tho he
Wako^{n}da thi^n xage thi^n hi^{n}wi^{n}tha me e e tho he tho

Literal translation: *E tho he!* exclamatory syllables but subjective in character; *Wako^{n}da*, here does not refer to the permeating life and power throughout nature but to the manifestation of power in the thunder; *hi^{n}wi^{n}tha*, told me; *me*, they; *tho*, musical vocable; *he*, end of sentence; *hi^n kage ha*, my friend; *xage*, to weep or cry; *thi^n*, sign of one moving; *hi^{n}wi^{n}tha*, tell me; *me*, they; *e tho he the*, vowel prolongation; *thoi*, vocable marking the close of the musical clause; *tho* in the last line marks the close of the song.

This song speaks of the time when the man went out to fast and pray; as he went the Thunder beings spoke to him and called him "friend." The music presents points of interest, as to both rhythm and melody, as expressive of the meaning of the song.

THE HO$^{N'}$HEWACHI

This was the name of a society or order of honorary chieftainship, composed of men who had accomplished one hundred or more *wathi$^{n'}$ethe* (certain prescribed acts and gifts; see p. 202). To achieve membership in this order was accounted one of the highest honors a man could secure, although it carried with it no political prominence.

The literal translation of the name is: *Ho$^{n'}$he*, "in the night;" *wa'chi*, "dance;" but this does not convey the true meaning of the word. *Wa'chi* does not mean "dance" in our sense of the word but dramatic rhythmic movements for the expression of personal emotion or experience, or for the presentation of mythical teachings. *Ho$^{n'}$he* refers to creative acts, for through the mysterious power of Wako^{n}'da night brought forth day. Night was therefore the mother of day, and the latter was the emblem of all visible activities and manifestations of life. The feminine cosmic force was typified not only by night but by the heavenly bodies seen by night, as the masculine cosmic force was symbolized by day and the sun. The credential of a man's attainment to membership in the Ho^{n}'hewachi was the right to tattoo on a maid certain cosmic symbols of night and day. The woman thus tattooed was called a *Ni'kagahi wau*, woman chief (*ni'kagahi*, "chief;" *wau*, "woman"). The origin of the Ho^{n}'hewachi is lost in antiquity; it is said to have been "given by Wako^{n}'da to help the people." This society exists in some of the cognate tribes and is as highly regarded among them as among the Omaha.

So great were the requirements demanded of a man for admission to the Ho^{n}'hewachi that the successful candidate was said to have been "pitied" (compassionately helped) "by Night," as otherwise he could not have accomplished the tasks required. The symbols tattooed on the girl were designated *xthexe*, an untranslatable name meaning a mark of honor or of distinction. It will be remembered that the Sacred Pole (see p. 219) was called *Waxthe'xe*, signifying "that which has the power to bestow honor or distinction." The Sacred Pole, as its name implies, was representative of the authority which was the fount of honor in the tribe. Permission to place this mark of honor on a girl had to be given by the Seven Chiefs, as well as by the members of the Ho^{n}'hewachi. The Ho^{n}'hewachi is claimed to be very old and in connection with this claim it should be remembered that the ancient name of the Cedar Pole (see p. 219) was *Waxthe'xe*, and that the name of this ancient and sacred object, whose ceremonies had become lost, was transferred to the new Sacred Pole when the latter emblem was set up in the interests of tribal unity and stability of government. The ancient pole of cedar, according to tradition and myth, was allied to ceremonies connected with Thunder and with the creation of the human race. It was kept, as was the Sacred Shell, in the Sacred Tent in charge of the We'zhi^{n}shte gens. According to traditions and beliefs, the rites pertaining to the Shell were connected with the cosmic forces which brought the universe into being and maintained its life. While it is impossible clearly to trace connection between the Ho^{n}'hewachi and the ceremonies that once clustered about the ancient Cedar Pole and the Sacred Shell, yet the name given to the mark of honor, (*xthexe*), the symbols used, and the sex of the person on whom they must be tattooed, as well as the name of the society to which they belonged, all afford a strong probability that the ancient cosmic rites, long since lost, were related to the Ho^{n}'hewachi, if they do not in part survive in the ceremonies of this society, ceremonies which in songs and symbols refer to the creative cosmic forces typified by night and day, the earth and the sky, forces which were also represented in the fundamental ideas on which the tribal organization rested.

The One Hundred Wathi^{n}′ethe

As has been said, the requisite for entrance into the Ho^{n}′hewachi was that the candidate should be able to count at least one hundred *wathi^{n}′ethe* (see p. 202); but in making this "count" he could not include those *wathi^{n}′ethe* (gifts) which he had made to the Seven Chiefs in order to insure admission into the order of Ni′kagahi xu′de, as he had made these gifts for another purpose, one that pertained solely to his ambition to become a chief. The *wathi^{n}′ethe* which could be "counted" in order to secure entrance into the Ho^{n}′hewachi were similar in character to those already described as requisite to entrance into the Ni′kagahi xu′de but they were not directly connected with the Seven Chiefs. Among the classes of acts and gifts that "counted" and ranked high were those benefiting the tribe and those made to a very poor man or woman.

The following story was told of Waha′xi, a noted chief who died before the middle of the nineteenth century: One day an old woman came to his tent, entered, and sat down near the door. No one noticed her for quite a while, but presently the chief bade his wife clothe the old woman. So the packs were opened and Waha′xi's wife took out various garments, dressed the woman in fine leggings, a tunic of red cloth, and wrapped about her a red blanket. Then the chief arose and placed corn in her hand and sent her home. The appearance of the gayly clad old woman bearing corn attracted the attention of the people, and the chief, already of high rank, was permitted to "count" this act of clothing the beggar as a *wathi^{n}′ethe*.

Making contributions for bringing about peace both within and without the tribe was an act of public merit and could be "counted;" so also could gifts which were made to put an end to a period of mourning, as the following will illustrate: On the death of a member of the tribe who was greatly respected all societies suspended their meetings and all dances ceased. Sometimes a year might pass, the village keeping silence to honor the memory of the dead. At length a chief would call the people together and whoever chose to contribute toward the gifts to be made to the mourners could "count" his gift. The collected gifts were borne by two men to the lodge of the mourners. For the honor of bearing the gifts each of these men gave a horse. When the bearers of the gifts arrived at the lodge, the relatives of the deceased were thus addressed: "You have grieved many days. Your hair has grown long. We have brought these gifts that you may cut your hair and return to the people." Then the chief mourner cut his hair, put on gala dress, and distributed the gifts among his near kindred, while the herald proclaimed throughout the village: "You, the people, are told to be joyous again!" Songs and dances were resumed and the people made merry after their long silence. This ceremony has not been performed since the middle of the last century.

Another form of giving was to place a robe on the arm of a child and bid it take the gift to the lodge of a leading man, who, on receiving the gift, would emerge from his tent and call aloud the name of the giver.

All contributions to a Wa′wa^n party, or gifts made through this ceremony, could be "counted," as these were in the interest of peace within and without the tribe. For similar reasons the gifts made during the festival of the He′dewachi were "counted"

Gifts of horses were accounted among the most valuable. Sometimes the "count" of a horse was connected with peculiar circumstances, as in the following case: Waha′xi had a son whom he hoped would one day be a chief, but who died prematurely. At his funeral a fine white horse was about to be killed, when the father of Kaxe′no^{n}ba brought forward a mule and asked that it be killed and the fine horse spared. Knowing that the mule also could not well be spared by the man, Waha′xi decided not to kill either the horse or the mule but bade the man to "count" both horse and mule as *wathi^n′ethe*. Such gifts were classed as "gone to see the dead."

The We′ku feast offered another occasion for men to make gifts which could be "counted." This feast occurred when there had been a difference between two tribes and the chiefs wished to make peace. The Seven Chiefs called the various chiefs and young warriors together and told them of the proposed We′ku feast, to which the tribe with whom there had been trouble had been invited. The men then volunteered to make gifts toward receiving the tribe. He who intended to offer a large gift would say, "I will give some small article." Those who could make only a small donation said nothing. When all the gifts were gathered, three or four of the donors who were men of rank and respected by the people were sent to invite the other tribe to the feast. As the guests were seen approaching, all the men who had contributed gifts mounted their horses and rode out to meet the coming tribe, charging upon them as if upon an enemy. The leader bore a pipe prepared for smoking and offered it to the leader of the guests who, after it was lighted, accepted it. The gifts were then distributed, the feast eaten, and peace concluded between the tribes. After the feast the guests were entertained as individuals among Omaha families. All gifts made on such an occasion could be counted as *wathi^n′ethe*. The We′ku feast took place for the last time shortly before the middle of the nineteenth century.

Another act that could be counted as *wathiⁿ'ethe* and that ranked among the highest was saving the life of a comrade in battle or preventing his capture, as such an act could be done only by risking one's life.

A thrifty man could seldom "count" his hundred before he was near middle life, even though he wasted no opportunity. During all the years of his preparation he must work silently and not reveal his purpose to anyone for fear he might fail. Nor did he tell which maid he had chosen to receive the mark of honor. There was a general belief that if a man made his choice known before he was ready to have the tattooing done, either the girl would die or some misfortune would befall him.

Passing the long test required for entrance into this society was regarded as proof not only that the members were favored by Wakoⁿ'da but that they possessed will power capable of producing results; consequently a form of punishment, *wazhiⁿ'agthe* (*wazhiⁿ*, "directive energy" or "will power;" "*agthe*," "to place upon"), was exercised by them. A disturber of the peace within the tribe or one whose acts were offensive to the chiefs was sometimes punished by the concerted action of the Hoⁿ'hewachi through *wazhiⁿ'agthe*, the members fixing their minds on the offender, placing on him the consequences of his actions so that he was thrust from all helpful relations with men and animals. Misfortune and death were believed to follow as the result of this treatment. *Wazhiⁿ'agthe* belongs to the same class of acts as *wazhiⁿ'thethe* (p. 583); the former was believed to send disaster and the latter to help by the exercise of will power.

The Watha'wa (Feast of the Count)

When a man had all his arrangements made, could "count" the required number of *wathiⁿ'ethe*, had accumulated the required fees, and had secured the food necessary to entertain the chiefs and other guests for the initiatory ceremonies, which lasted four days, he notified the man whom he had selected to be his sponsor. The sponsor called together the members of the Hoⁿ'hewachi, the candidate furnishing the food for the required feast, and the candidate's name was then proposed. If no objection was made, he was told that he could prepare for the ceremony of initiation.

The tribal herald summoned the Council of Seven and the members of the Hoⁿ'hewachi to the lodge of the candidate, which had been prepared for the ceremony. On this occasion every article except those intended as gifts to the chiefs and members of the order must be removed, as the candidate could retain nothing that was in the lodge at the time the Seven Chiefs entered, wearing their robes in the ceremonial manner and bearing the pipe to be used in the ceremony. A buffalo skin was placed back of the fireplace, on which were two bunches of grass that were to serve as rests for the pipe. Near the fire at the edge of the robe was a board on which the tobacco to be used in filling the pipe was placed. The two Ni′kagahi u′zhu took their seats in the center at the back of the lodge and the other members of the Council of Seven occupied their official places. Next to them, on both sides of the lodge, sat the members of the Hoⁿ′hewachi. The candidate took his seat by the door to the left as one entered. On the opposite side of the door sat the herald.

During all the years that the candidate had been preparing for this occasion he had kept a number of willow sticks about a foot long, each one of which represented a *wathiⁿ′ethe*. These hundred or more sticks, tied in a bundle, were handed by the candidate to the herald, who laid them before the Ni′kagahi u′zhu. The *u′zhu* chief to the left, representing the Hon′gashenu side of the *hu′thuga* (tribal circle), took up the bundle and passed it to the other *u′zhu*, representing the Iⁿshta′çuⁿda side, who in turn handed it to the chief next to him. In this way the bundle representing the candidate's "count" was passed by the left around the circle. When it again reached the *u′zhu* chief who first took it up, he called the herald, who came and received the bundle of sticks from the Ni′kagahi u′zhu and carried it back to the candidate sitting at the door.

Meanwhile the concourse outside the lodge had steadily increased in numbers and among them were those who secretly aspired to the honor of becoming members of the Hoⁿ′hewachi. The immediate relatives of the candidate moved anxiously about, desirous of helping his memory during the ordeal of "counting," for his statements could be controverted by the outsiders and there were always those who were envious of his attainments and sought to confuse and disconcert him. The excitement outside the lodge contrasted sharply with the decorum within, where the candidate stood before the assembled chiefs, muffled in their robes, and the members of the Hoⁿ′hewachi, who sat closely watching the man as he took up reed after reed and told what kind of gift it represented, when, where, and to whom it was made. All the *wathiⁿ′ethe* had to be classified as to kind in this public recital. First the candidate "counted" the gifts of horses. When the statements regarding a gift were controverted, a witness was called to testify to the truth of the statements. Robes, bows and arrows and quivers, pipes, and shell disks were "counted" in groups or classes. The "count" began in the early morning and lasted all day. It was a severe tax on a man's memory, for these gifts often extended over a period of ten or twenty years. At the close of his "count" the chiefs bade the man enumerate the articles he had gathered for fees. The chief then sent the herald to proclaim the completed "count" to the people. He would state that So-and-so (naming the candidate) had given away so many horses, so many robes, and so on through the list of classified gifts. Thus the man's record was made public and thereafter no one could challenge his "count" as it was then given forth.

The ceremony of smoking the pipe followed the completion of the count. This was in the nature of a formal presentation to Wakoⁿ'da of the *wathiⁿ'ethe* which had just been publicly "counted;" it also represented the taking of an oath of membership. The smoking was a solemn and elaborate ceremony. A firebrand could not be used to light the pipe, for which purpose a live coal was taken from the fire with a split stick. When ready to be lighted the pipe lay with the stem toward the south. The herald took it up and held it for the Ni'kagahi u'zhu who sat toward the south while the latter lighted it. The herald then passed the pipe in turn to the Ni'kagahi u'zhu who sat toward the north, and to the chief at the latter's left. While being smoked the pipe was always held by the herald. It was said: "The pipe must pass in an unbroken circle from south to north, and when laid down after this circuit the stem must point to the north." A pause followed the smoking; then the herald took the pipe from its grass rest and walked with it around the fireplace. He held it up to the zenith before laying it to rest with the stem to the north. The chief who had lighted the pipe now grasped its stem in his left hand and the bowl in his right, and swung the pipe slowly in a circle from right to left until it was in an upright position at the left side of his body. Then he proceeded to clean the pipe and lay it back on its grass rest on the robe, with the stem to the south. The herald then took up the pipe and again walked with it about the fire. At the completion of the circuit he laid it beside the fireplace. The chief who had cleaned it then rose and put it back on the buffalo robe. This last act completed the ceremony of smoking. The varied and complicated movements connected with passing the pipe and placing it at rest had reference, it is said, to the movements of the heavenly bodies. The herald then arose and put together the grass rest of the pipe and the bundle of sticks used in the counting and laid them in the back part of the lodge.

Members of the candidate's family outside the lodge now filled two large wooden bowls with a kind of porridge made of pounded maize and passed them through the door into the lodge. The herald took one of the bowls and placed it in front of the chief who had lighted the pipe. The latter took four spoonfuls of the food and passed the bowl to the next chief without lifting it from the floor. The other bowl was passed from the door up to the chief who had partaken first from the first bowl. Each person took four spoonfuls of the porridge. Care was taken by all not to spill any of this sacred food and not to make a noise with the lips in eating. When the second bowl reached the chief who sat toward the south, he poured a few drops of the food into a depression in the ground near the fireplace made by the knuckle of the forefinger of the right hand.[a] The other bowl was now brought from the door and the two bowls were placed side by side in front of the two Ni′kagahi u′zhu. Considerable food remained in both of the bowls. The chief toward the south then designated a chief on the north side of the lodge, to whom one of the bowls was taken; next he selected a chief on the south side to whom the other bowl was taken. Then the herald was called and bidden to take the bowls to the lodges of these chiefs. Outside of the tent the herald was relieved of his burden by the wives and daughters of the chiefs designated, who carried the food to their homes. After the bowls were emptied they were brought back and placed near the door of the lodge, to be returned to their owners.

At this point, if any chief of the Council of Seven was not a member of the Hoⁿ′hewachi he was excused. He at once arose, thanked the assembly, and left the lodge, which now contained only the candidate and the members of the Hoⁿ′hewachi.

The Feast of the Hoⁿ′hewachi

The candidate now selected two of the bravest men to act as his heralds and to summon all the chiefs who were entitled to be present at the Feast of the Hoⁿ′hewachi. The heralds put on the buffalo robes with the hair outside, girding them about the waist, painted their faces black, and placed eagle down on their heads. Then they proceeded to the lodges of the chiefs entitled to attend the feast, addressing them by name, and giving the official call of invitation: *Waçkathiⁿ ho!* The meaning of this word is lost. When the heralds had passed around the camp circle they returned to the lodge of the candidate, where the feast was to be held. Even if all who had been thus invited were already present in the lodge, the two heralds went to the door of the tent and again gave the official call of invitation, mentioning the names of those who had the right to attend the feast. The leader of the Hoⁿ′hewachi then ordered the drum, rattles, and bells to be sent for and food to be prepared for those present, as they had been sitting since early morning and had only eaten ceremonially of the "Feast of the Count." If the count lasted more than one day this feast could not take place until the count was completed. The right to "beat the drum" belonged to the man who could count the highest war honors. It has become diffi-

[a] Note the resemblance between this taking of food and pouring of drops into a depression made by the knuckle and the Ponca ceremony at the Feast of Soldiers (p. 309).

cult in recent years to complete this ceremony after the ancient manner, on account of the dying out of the men who could count war honors, for these honors had to have been accorded a man in the public ceremony of Wate′giçtu, already described (see p. 434). The story is told of an Oto who, in order to complete the ceremony of initiation, had to send to a cognate tribe to secure the services of a man who was properly entitled to "beat the drum."

After the meal had been eaten the chiefs and members resumed their seats, the drum was placed, and the following song was sung:

U - thi - tha sha - ya ma U - thi - tha sha - ya ma
E-goⁿ-shoⁿ doⁿ u-thi-tha sha-ya ma U-thi-tha sha-ya ma
U - thi- tha sha - ya ma U - thi- tha sha - ya ma

1

Uthitha shaya ma
Uthitha shaya ma
Egoⁿ shoⁿ doⁿ uthitha shaya ma
Uthitha shaya ma
Uthitha shaya ma
Uthitha shaya ma

Literal translation: *Uthitha,* to tell you; *shaya,* coming; *ma,* he, they; *egoⁿ,* now, for that reason; *shoⁿ,* done, completed; *doⁿ,* therefore.

The words of this song are meager and difficult to translate. Their meaning was explained to have reference to the sponsor coming to the members of the Hoⁿ′hewachi and reporting that the candidate for whom he stood had now completed the required number of *wathiⁿ′ethe,* or prescribed gifts, and awaited their acceptance of him.

2

Athigi shaya ma
Athigi shaya ma
Egoⁿ shoⁿ doⁿ uthudoⁿbe taya ma
Athigi shaya ma
Athigi shaya ma
Athigi shaya ma

Literal translation: *Athigi,* to fetch, bring, cause to come; *shaya,* coming; *ma,* they; *egoⁿ,* now, for that reason; *shoⁿ,* done; *doⁿ,* therefore; *uthudo*ⁿ*be*, to consider, to look into; *taya ma*, coming for that purpose, they.

This stanza was explained as referring to the response to the official call of the herald which caused the chiefs and members to gather together for the purpose of considering the count of the man who aspired to become a member of the Hoⁿ'hewachi, and who was publicly to present the record of his acts.

3

Thidoⁿ be shaya ma
Thidoⁿ be shaya ma
Egoⁿ shoⁿ doⁿ uthudoⁿ be taya ma
Thidoⁿbe shaya ma
Thidoⁿbe shaya ma
Thidoⁿbe shaya ma

Literal translation: *Thido*ⁿ*be*, see you, as the result or outcome of a decision; *shaya*, coming; *ma*, they; *uthudo*ⁿ*be*, to look into, to consider, to judge; *taya ma*, coming for that purpose, they.

This stanza refers to the final judgment of the men who had come together to consider the claim of the candidate to membership. In this stanza the three preliminary steps already taken are summed up. It was during this summing up that the young girl on whom the mark of honor was to be placed entered and danced before the assembled Hoⁿ'hewachi. The act dramatized the awakening of the feminine element—an awakening everywhere necessary for a fulfillment in tangible form of the life-giving power. This dance of the girl constituted the fourth and last step in the movements recounted in the three stanzas of the song—the step that led directly to the consummation of the candidate's long years of effort. Generally the girl chosen was the daughter of the candidate; but if he had no child of a suitable age he could select the daughter of a relative or of a close friend. She must be a virgin who had recently reached puberty. She was clad in gala garments made for the occasion, formerly a skin tunic embroidered with porcupine quills. She was frequently accompanied on her entrance and dance by two or three young women who had received the "mark of honor."

With the meaning of the acts connected with the singing of this song should be considered the important fact that the song gives the rhythmic model after which all songs that pertain to the Hoⁿ'hewachi were fashioned. It therefore represented the fundamental rhythm that expressed the musical feeling concerning those ideas or beliefs for which the Hoⁿ'hewachi stood in the native mind. It may here be stated that a similar rule was observed in the songs connected with any given society or rite—they all conformed to the rhythmic standard peculiar to the society or the ceremonial. As a result, an Indian could classify at once a song by its rhythm, as belonging to the Hethu'shka the Wa'wa^{n}, the Ho^{n}'hewachi, or any other society or rite with which he was familiar. This custom has restricted freedom in musical composition and thus has retarded its development among a remarkably musical race. It has tended to make the songs of the tribe monotonous and this tendency has been enhanced by certain beliefs concerning the function and power of music entertained by the native peoples. Every member of the Ho^{n}'hewachi was required to compose a song which had to conform to the rhythmic standard of the Ho^{n}'hewachi initial song. The song had to be an expression of the man's personal experience, and frequently, though not invariably, it referred to a dream or vision that came in answer to his supplication.

The chiefs and members remained all night at the lodge of the candidate. They continued to be his guests until the completion of the ceremony of tattooing. Meanwhile the family of the candidate occupied a tent near by, and two women, on whom the "mark of honor" had been placed, were designated to cook the food required for the assembled guests.

THE TATTOOING

Early in the morning two scaffolds were set up outside the candidate's lodge, one on each side of the door. On these were suspended the articles to be given as fees. Among them had to be 100 knives and 100 awls. These were male and female implements. The knives were thrust into the ground around one side of the fireplace and the awls were similarly placed on the other side. Back of the fireplace a bed was made of the costliest robes and a pillow was placed toward the east. After the morning meal had been eaten by the guests and the girl had eaten with the family, she was brought in and laid upon the bed, facing the west, for, being emblematic of life, she had to lie as if moving with the sun. The two heralds stood at the door of the lodge and called the names of those who were to sing during the tattooing. These must be men who had received public war honors. The official cry already noted was given with each name called, whether the men were already in the lodge or not.

The charcoal to be used in making the coloring preparation was placed in a wooden bowl and taken to the man who was to do the tattooing. Usually one of the chiefs performed this duty. The figure was first outlined by means of a flattened stick dipped into the solution made from the charcoal; then it was pricked in with needles. Steel needles are now employed; formerly flint points were used. The needles were tied in a bunch, to which small bells were fastened; formerly the rattles of the rattlesnake were used. After the pricking the charcoal was put over the surface, which was then pricked a second time. This completed the tattooing. The round spot was first put on the forehead; this represented the sun. While this was being done the following song was sung:

Mithoⁿ shui the tha
Mithoⁿ shui the tha
Mithoⁿ shui the tha
Mithoⁿ gathu ti thoⁿde shui thetha
Mithoⁿ shui the tha
Mithoⁿ shui the tha

Literal translation: *Mithoⁿ*, the sun, the round sun; *shui*, comes, speaks, or says; *gathu*, yonder point; *ti thoⁿde*, when it comes; *shui the*, comes, speaks, or says.

This ancient song, as was explained, refers to the sun rising to the zenith, to the highest point; when it reaches that point it speaks, as its symbol descends upon the maid with the promise of life-giving power.

After the symbol of the sun was placed on the girl's forehead the outline of a four-pointed star (fig. 105) was marked on her chest as the following song was sung:

Hoⁿthiⁿ the tha
Hoⁿthiⁿ the tha
Hoⁿthiⁿ the tha
Umba ia tho
Umba ia tho
Umba ia tho

Literal translation: *Ho*ⁿ, night; *thi*ⁿ, moving; *the*, going; *tha*, end of sentence; *umba*, day; *ia*, is coming; *tho*, oratorical end of sentence.

The meaning of the song is: Night moves, it passes, and the day is coming.

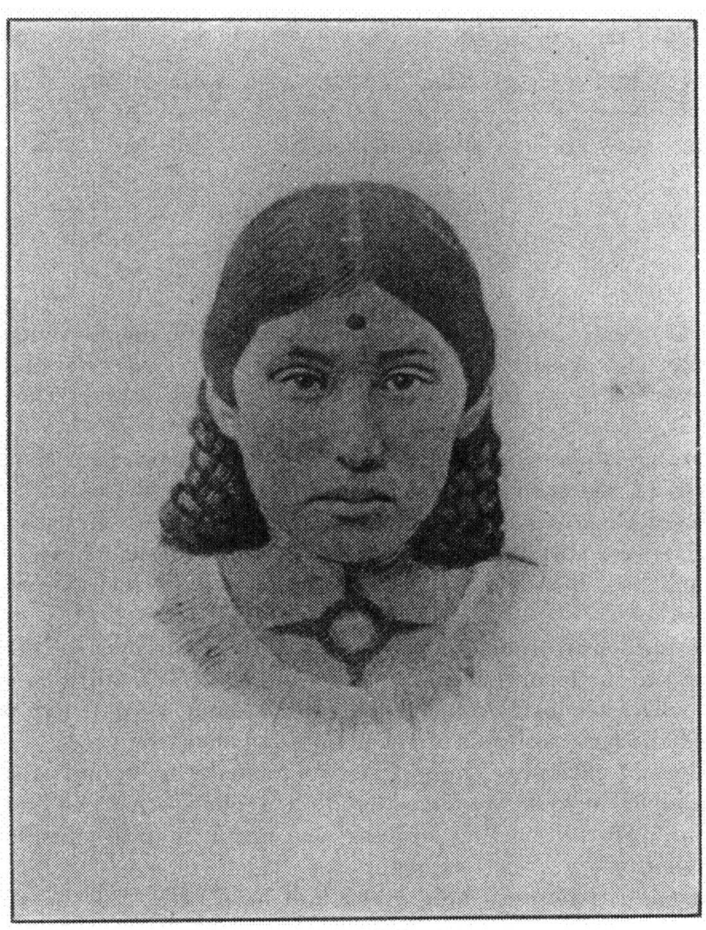

FIG. 105. Tattooed design—"mark of honor."

The star is emblematic of the night, the great mother force, its four points representing also the life-giving winds into the midst of which the child was sent through the ceremony of Turning the Child, already described (see p. 117).

During the completion of the tattooing of the symbols of day and night the following song was sung:

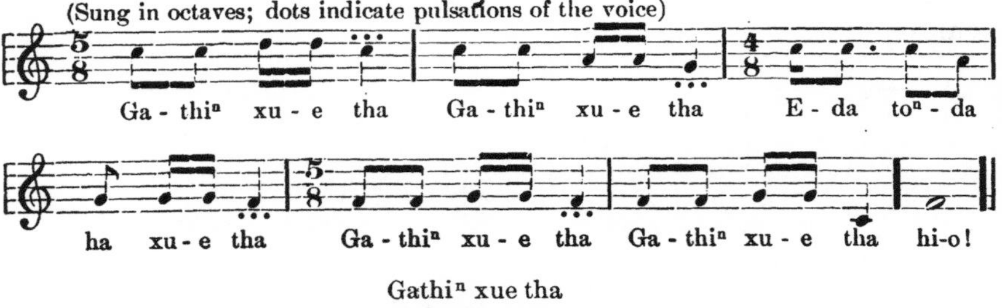
(Sung in octaves; dots indicate pulsations of the voice)
Ga - thiⁿ xu - e tha Ga - thiⁿ xu - e tha E - da toⁿ - da
ha xu - e tha Ga - thiⁿ xu - e tha Ga - thiⁿ xu - e tha hi-o!

Gathiⁿ xue tha
Gathiⁿ xue tha
Eda toⁿda ha xue tha
Gathiⁿ xue tha
Gathiⁿ xue tha hio

Literal translation: *Gathiⁿ*, yonder unseen is one moving; *xue*, noise; *tha*, end of sentence; *eda*, a modified form of *edoⁿ*, for that reason; *toⁿda ha*, over the earth; *xue*. noise; *hio*, the cry of the living creatures.

This song, it was explained, referred to the serpent, here the representative of the teeming life that "moves" over the earth. (Note the tabu of the lost subgens of the Iⁿshta'çuⁿda gens and its meaning.) Because this life is "moving" it makes a noise. Even the sun as it "moves," it is said, "makes a noise," as does the living wind in the trees.

Sometimes a crescent moon was tattooed on the back of the girl's neck and a turtle on the back of her hands. The turtle was connected with rites pertaining to water and wind, as noted in the account of the Ke'iⁿ subgens of the Tha'tada gens (see p. 161). During the ordeal of tattooing the girl strove to make no sound or outcry. If she should do so it was considered as evidence that she had been unchaste. If the healing process was rapid, it was considered a good omen.

After the ritual songs here given had been sung, the members of the Hoⁿ'hewachi sang their individual songs. In the Ponca tribe the men who had dreamed of buffalo sat on one side of the lodge; those who had had other dreams sat on the opposite side; and the songs were sung first by a man on one side and then by one on the other. This order was not regularly followed among the Omaha. After the noon hour food was cooked and served to the chiefs, while the herald called the families of these men to receive their share. Much food was consumed and distributed on this occasion.

When the tattooing was finished the girl left the tent. Then the herald brought in all the articles that were hanging on the scaffolds outside the tent and piled them in the middle of the lodge. All the uncooked food was placed near the door. The leader distributed the gifts. A knife and an awl were given to each person. In apportioning the fees the person who did the tattooing received the largest share, and all the food, both cooked and uncooked, that remained became his property.

The accompanying design (fig. 106) tattooed on the hand of a Ponca girl strikingly sets forth the meaning of the Hoⁿ'hewachi: Here are the emblems of day and night and between them stand the forms of children. By the union of Day, the above, and Night, the below, came the human race and by them the race is maintained. The tattooing of this figure was said to be "an appeal for the perpetuation of all life and of human life in particular."

FIG. 106. Design tattooed on hand of Ponca girl (native drawing).

At the meetings of the Hoⁿ'hewachi, even when there was no initiation of a member or tattooing of a maid, only those men who had received war honors could "beat the drum" for the singers. Before a man could sing his song he had to relate his war honors, telling what they were and what were the acts for which they had been publicly awarded. While he sang the women who had received the "mark of honor" danced. Only women danced at the meetings of the Hoⁿ'hewachi. This was because the order was one in recognition of Night, of the feminine force or principle. The man recounted his deeds, for they were "performed in order to insure to the woman that safety which was requisite for the performance of her duties as wife and mother." The rites and symbols of the Hoⁿ'hewachi epitomized the fundamental ideas on which the tribal organization was based. The requirements for admittance to membership afforded undisputed proof of a man's valor and industry—the two factors necessary for the preservation and the prosperity of the tribe. The word for tribe, it will be remembered, indicates that it was composed of those who were banded together to fight against attacks from the outside. Valor, therefore, was necessary to hold the tribe together and industry to maintain it. These manly requirements were emphasized in the honors accorded through the Hoⁿ'hewachi, which also dramatically set forth the essential place occupied by woman in promoting the general welfare. Many of the manufactured articles which went to swell the man's "count" were the product of woman's industry.

The following song is an example of the class of songs which were composed by members of the Hoⁿ'hewachi. This song commemorated the experience of the composer—an experience which left its mark on his subsequent life. A sister whom he greatly loved died. He missed her companionship sorely. Without her the world seemed to him a blank. He used to go alone to the hills and there weep and pray for his sister's presence. At last one day, as he lay on the hillside weeping, he became conscious of some one near him. Lifting his eyes, he beheld his sister's face, and heard her voice saying: "I have been seeking for you over the breadth of the land." Then the man knew that his sister's spirit yet loved and guarded him. He arose comforted, dried his tears, ceased from that day to mourn, and cheerfully resumed his appointed duties. This incident was the theme of the song which he composed as his song of membership in the Hoⁿ'hewachi. He used to sing it when he met with the members. The man himself related this story to the writers and sang them his song. He died a number of years ago.

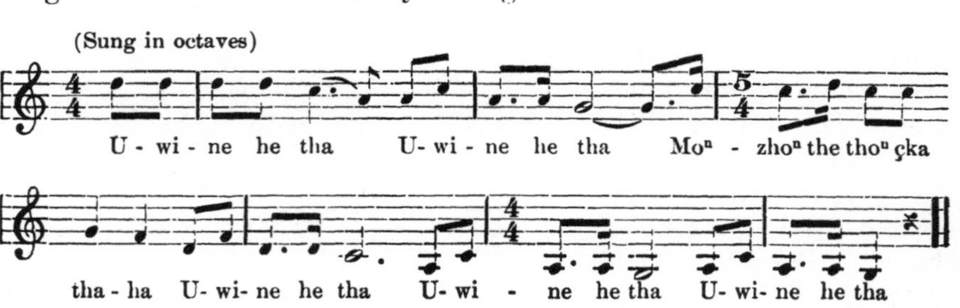

Uwine he tha
Uwine he tha
Moⁿzhoⁿ thethoⁿçka thaha
Uwine hetha
Uwine hetha
Uwine hetha

Literal translation: *Uwine he*, I seek for you; *tha*, end of sentence; *moⁿzhoⁿ*, earth; *thethoⁿçka*, expanse, great size; *thaha*, over.

Sometimes a song descended to a new member, particularly if the new member took the place of a deceased father or elder brother.

It was accounted good fortune and an honor to marry a woman bearing the "mark of honor." She not only belonged to a family that had achieved tribal reputation but it was believed that she would become the mother of many children who would live to grow up. If a buffalo bearing white spots or a white buffalo was killed, only women bearing the "mark of honor" dressed the skin of the animal, which was presented to the Sacred Tent to renew the Sacred White Buffalo Hide then in use.

THE WASHIS'KA ATHI^{N} (SHELL SOCIETY)

All the secret societies among the Omaha, as has been stated, dealt more or less with magic as well as healing by means of herbs and roots. Even if natural remedies were used, the songs sung when they were gathered and when they were administered were supposed to increase their efficacy. In some instances this efficacy was attributed to magic; in others the song was an appeal somewhat of the nature of a prayer.

The account here given of the Shell society, Washis'ka athi^{n} (*washis'ka*, "shell;" *athi^{n}*, "they have"—"those who have the shell") as it existed in the Omaha tribe is very nearly complete; sufficiently so, it is hoped, to permit of a comparative study of somewhat similar societies which exist among cognate tribes, the Winnebago and the Oto. The "Grand Medicine" of the Chippewa seems to have aspects in common with this society.

Origin

The following is the Omaha story of the origin of the Shell society:

Once (an indefinite and long time in the past) a stranger came to the village. He was entertained by the chief and all the prominent men. There was living in the tribe a man who, while a good hunter, was a quiet man who never pushed himself into notice. His modest behavior was a source of anxiety to his wife, who was ambitious and did not share her husband's aversion to notice. She learned of the stranger's presence, and noted how much was made of him, and she determined to have her husband also entertain this man. She said to her husband: "You will never become an important man in the tribe if you do not push yourself forward. You must ask this stranger to our lodge. I will prepare a feast, and you can entertain him as all the great men are doing." She called her eldest son, and said: "You are to go to the chief's house and tell him that his guest is invited to your father's house. Mention your father's name." She then set about to make the tent clean and put everything in order. She cooked food, spread a robe on the seat of honor, and was ready for the guest. The boy did as his mother told him. When he delivered his message the chief, who knew the retiring nature of the lad's father, asked him: "Did your father send you?" The boy answered "Yes." In due time the stranger came. He wore his hair roached, his leggings were yellow and embroidered, his moccasins were black; he had no shirt, but wore his robe with the hair outside. He had a fine bow, and at his back a quiver of otter skin filled with arrows. The man, his wife, and the four children were all clad in their best, and waiting to receive the stranger. Of the children, the eldest two were boys, the third was a girl, and the youngest a boy—all of them healthy and well formed. The wife set before their guest deer meat and beans cooked with raccoon fat. He ate, and talked with the family, then he returned thanks to them and left. Soon he departed from the village and was heard of no more all that summer or the following winter. When spring came the stranger again appeared, and was treated with honor by the chiefs and leading men. And again the woman took the initiative in inviting the stranger to her lodge, and again the chief questioned the son who brought the invitation: "Did your father send you?" The boy again answered "Yes." The stranger responded as before. He returned his thanks, but he gave no explanation of himself, and departed. Another year passed and the spring came, and so did the stranger. Once more the son carried the invitation and the chief asked the same question and received the same answer. The stranger came, partook of the hospitality offered, and departed, leaving the man and his wife in ignorance as to who and what he was. Nor did anyone know aught of the stranger. The fourth spring came, and so did the stranger, and the same invitation was extended, to be questioned by the chief and answered by the lad as before. The stranger was received as he had been for three years; but now as he made his thanks he said: "I am a being of mysteries. I have been seeking for the proper persons whom I may instruct in the knowledge of these mysteries. You have shown an interest as to what I have to bring, for this knowledge can only be given to those who seek for it. You have four times entertained me at the proper season. I have observed you, and am satisfied that you are the ones to receive knowledge of the mysteries. Everything now is in readiness for me to fulfill my purpose. It is now the time when the people go away to hunt. I wish you to stay where you are. After the people have gone, then we will travel for a season. During that time I shall teach you of these mysteries. I shall expect a return from you. What it must be I will make known at the proper time."

The tribe moved off to hunt, and the man and his wife and the stranger remained behind. At night, as they all lay down to sleep, the father kept wondering about the stranger, and lay awake watching him. The stranger pretended to sleep, but he, too, watched. When the morning came the stranger arose, went for water, returned with it and gave it to the children to drink, and also to the father and mother. Then he combed the children's hair and washed them. These actions perplexed the parents, but the stranger remained silent as to his motives. The next day after the tribe had gone the stranger bade the father and mother make ready to move, and they all did so, going whither the stranger directed. As they traveled, the stranger pointed out the different trees, told of their fruits, and also of the herbs and roots that were good for food and those that were good for medicinal purposes, and bade the couple observe and remember them. The stranger said to the man: "You are to go to a certain place on the other side of that stream where there are scattered elm trees, thickets, and vines of wild beans, and look about and see if there are any animals." The man started off, as he was directed, and when he reached the place he saw a deer. Taking aim, he shot it. It was a young buck about 4 years old. He looked about and saw other deer. He killed 12, making 13 in all. He drew the carcasses to a place where he could camp, and started back for his family. On the way he met his wife and three of the children and the stranger, who was carrying the youngest on his back.

When they reached camp, the stranger told the man to roast four shoulders. When this was done, he gave a shoulder to each child and another cut to the father and mother, and bade that the rest of the meat be dried before the fire and then cached. In the morning the stranger went for water, as before, gave them all to drink; then he combed the hair of the children and washed them, to the great perplexity of the father and mother.

The stranger told the man to go to a place where there were sand hills and scattered cottonwood trees and see if there were animals there. The man went, and as he drew near he saw an elk feeding. He shot it. It had forked horns and was 4 years old. As he looked about, he saw deer and he killed several. He dragged the carcasses to a camping place and started back to his family. He met them as before, the stranger carrying the youngest child. The stranger told the man to take the heart and tongue of the elk and lay them aside, for that night they would have a ceremony, and sing. The father did so, and put the heart and tongue where the children could not meddle with them. After sundown the stranger bade the woman go and get water and cook the heart and tongue of the elk. The stranger cleared the fireplace and took a seat at the south side of it. Next on his left sat the father, on his left the mother, the children on her left, beginning with the eldest, down to the youngest. The stranger sang twenty-two songs and taught them to the father and mother. During the pauses between the songs the cries of the different animals with which the stranger was associated could be heard, showing their satisfaction at the progress the stranger was making. They sang all night. The two little children went to sleep but the two older ones kept awake. When they were through singing they sang a song by which to go out, and the stranger bade them to remember this song.

After about four days, when the meat was dried, the stranger told the man to go on to a creek that ran through ravines where there were great elms and knolls with stumps, and see if there were any animals there. The man went as directed and peering round from behind a stump he saw a buffalo cow. Drawing his bow, he shot it through the heart. It was about 4 years old. The man was greatly astonished at the sight of the animal, as he had never known buffalo in that vicinity. He saw several deer and killed them. He dragged the carcasses to a camping place and started back to his family. On the way he met them. The stranger was carrying the youngest child. "What have you killed?" he asked. The man told of the buffalo. The stranger bade the man take the heart and tongue and put them aside. When they reached camp and the sun was down, the stranger told the woman to go for water and to cook the heart and tongue of the buffalo.

When the heart and tongue were cooked the stranger took his seat at the south side of the fireplace; the father sat at his left, the mother at the father's left, at her left the children, from the eldest down to the youngest. They ate of the heart and tongue. That night they sang other songs. All night they sang. The little children fell asleep; the two older boys joined in the singing. Between the songs the cries of the animals were again heard. At the end they sang the song to accompany their going out. The stranger told the father and mother never to forget to sing that song before going out.

The next day, as usual, the stranger rose early, procured water, gave them all to drink and then combed the children's hair and washed them. By this time the stranger had won the confidence and the affection of the children but the father was getting anxious. He was puzzled by the stranger's behavior and he and his wife talked together and wondered about the man. They came to the conclusion that he must be thinking of his own children and that was why he was so attentive to their little ones. He had already brought them great good fortune in hunting, and they not only wanted to show gratitude and appreciation for what he had done, but they wanted to test him, to see if he was really human. They had not much to offer him, as they were not well provided for when the stranger became their guest, but they determined to offer him what they had. So they said to him: "We have not much, but we have these things," showing him their store, "and we have our children. Take your choice, for we offer you all." They felt sure he would never choose their children, but to their surprise he handed them back all their goods and said: "Since you have offered them, I will take the children." Then the stranger went on to say to the couple: "I am an animal, and have been sent by all the animals that live near the great lake to secure your children and to make you great in your tribe. All the animals living near this great lake have had a council and I am their messenger." Then he went on to tell the man that there were seven leaders in this council—the black bear, the buffalo, the elk, the deer, the cougar, the gray wolf, and the skunk. These were specially connected with the man. There were seven other animals that would be connected with the woman; these were the otter, the raccoon, the mink, the swan, the silver fox, the squirrel, and the owl. Of these animals, the black bear, the buffalo, the elk, and the deer are for food; the cougar has strength and courage, it rises with the sun and goes forth to get food for its young; the gray wolf does the same; the skunk is a hunter; it dwells in a snug house and is clean. The otter hunts in the water; the raccoon hunts along the streams and takes of the fruit growing there; the mink does the same. The swan provides clothing that gives comfort and also beauty. The silver fox is a hunter; squirrels live on food from trees; and the owl hunts at night.

At this council, the first seven counseled with the second seven and all agreed to help man. Then the sun was appealed to, and the sun consented that the animals should help man, give him of their own powers, so that by their powers he should have power to become like them and to partake of their qualities. The sun said: "I shall stay above and look down on my children." The moon was appealed to, and the moon gave consent, and said: "I shall stay above and look down on my children." The lightning agreed to make paths, the small paths for the elk, the deer, the buffalo, and the bear, and a wide path for all the other animals. Then all said: "Go, search for the proper person to whom to give this power." This was the explanation the stranger gave to the father and mother when he accepted the gift of their children.

After the meat secured by the father had been dried and cached, the family moved on, and came near the borders of a great lake. Willows were growing on its banks and it was beautiful to look upon. In the lake was a high rock and there was also an island with trees growing on it. There was a smooth beach, on which the water was lapping the shore and the fish were jumping in the sunlight. The stranger bade the father search for animals. He went off, and finally he spied a black bear. He took aim, shot, and killed it. Just then he saw something descending; it was an eagle that dropped and lit on a cottonwood tree. Then the eagle spoke to the man and asked that he be allowed to share in the food and he would come and be one of them. The family of the man had stopped on the second bench above the lake. The man cut up the bear and carried it all up to his family; he left nothing, not even the blood. The stranger bade him set aside the heart and tongue of the bear. Then the father went forth and killed deer. At sunset the wife brought water and cooked the heart and tongue and again the stranger sat at the south of the fireplace, the father on his left and the mother at the father's left, the children at her left from the eldest to the youngest, and all partook of the meat. The stranger sang songs, and taught them to the father and mother. They sang all night and the youngest children fell asleep. The two older boys joined in the singing. At the close they all sang the song they had been bidden to do.

On the evening of the third day the stranger told the father and mother that he had long been seeking for such a family as theirs to whom to give his magic gifts by which they should find plenty of game, accumulate wealth, and become chiefs in the tribe. He said: "I am going away, and shall take your children that you have given me. But I shall come again; you will find me on the lake shore; I shall be in what you find there." The morning of the fourth day the stranger rose early. There was no wind and the water of the lake was perfectly still. He got water, gave them all some to drink, then he combed the hair of the children and washed them. He told the mother to put on the children's best clothing, to make the tent tidy and in order, and to spread a skin at the back of the fire with its head to the west. He told the mother to sit on the south side of the fireplace near the door, on her left her husband and at his left the stranger took his seat. He told the children to all go out and play, but to stay within sound so they could hear when they were called. Then he talked to the father and mother. He bade them remember all he had taught them and to tell no one. After a while the man could choose seven men, and the woman could choose seven women, and initiate them; then they must wait four years, when another seven could be chosen. They would have power, when they initiated the others, to impart the power he had given them. When he had finished his instructions he sang a song and all the animals living by the high rock beat on the drum and sang the same song. Four songs were thus sung by the stranger, and to each the animals on the rock sounded the drum and sang. They were joined by all those that dwelt on the island. When the songs were finished the stranger ordered the mother to call to the tent her eldest child. She circled the lodge, went outside, and called her son. Then she came in and took her seat. Soon his springing steps were heard approaching the tent. He lifted the door flap to enter. The stranger cried "Hah!" and the lad fell forward, striking the pole that stood by the fireplace, and lay dead. The stranger bade the father and mother lift the boy and lay him on the south side of the skin, his head to the west. Then the stranger arose and painted the boy. He made a red line across the mouth from the right ear to the left, then drew a red line from the left ear down the left arm to the thumb; then a similar line from the right ear down the right arm to the thumb; then a red line over the chin down to the heart, where a red circle was made; then a red band across the forehead to the ear. Then he painted the body blue from the waist up to the neck and the elbow up to the neck. When the painting was completed he took his seat and then bade the mother call her second child. Again she circled the lodge and passed outside and called her second son to come to the tent and returned to her seat. Soon he was heard coming rapidly along. As he stooped to enter the stranger cried "Hah!" and the boy fell as his brother had done. The stranger bade the father and mother carry the boy and lay him on the skin to the left of his brother. Then the stranger arose and painted the second child, making the same red lines; but when he came to paint the body he put the blue paint on in spots. When he had finished the stranger resumed his seat. Then he bade the mother call her third child, and she arose as before, circled the tent, went without, and called her daughter to come to the lodge, reentered, and took her seat. Soon she heard the little girl skipping toward the tent, singing as she came. As she put her head in, the stranger cried "Hah!" and the little girl fell dead as had her two brothers. Again the father and mother at the bidding of the stranger lifted the child and laid her on the skin at the left side of her brothers. The stranger then arose and painted the red lines across the face and on the arms, and from the chin down to the heart, as on her brothers, but put blue in spots on her body and cheeks and tied a sash across her heart, and returned to his seat. Then he bade the mother call her youngest child. She rose as commanded, circled the tent, went outside and called the little boy and returned to her seat. She had hardly reached her place when they heard the little boy running to answer the call. He poked his head into the tent, the stranger cried "Hah!" and the child fell prone and dead. Again at the stranger's bidding the parents carried the little boy and laid him on the skin at the left of his sister. Then the stranger rose and painted the child as he had all the others, except that the body and arms above the elbow were made the color of the earth. The stranger told them that the red lines were the rays of the sun that give life; the blue on the body of the eldest boy was the clear sky; the blue spots on the body of the second son, the night sky; the blue spots on the girl, the moon and the night; the brown spots on the youngest child, the earth. The stranger further explained that the painting on the body of the eldest son, which represented the day, the clear blue sky, was related to the painting on the body of the girl above the sash and on her cheeks, which stood for the moon, the power at night. The painting on the body of the second son, which represented the night sky, spotted with stars, was related to the painting on the body of the youngest child, which was the color of the earth, for the earth and the stars were brothers; he bade them observe the circle of stars (near the handle of the Great Dipper); this circle of stars were all brothers. Moreover, he told them that the shells were like the stars. He said there was a holy bird which was the leader of all the animals about the lake. This holy bird was the white swan and the birds flocked in sevens and fives. He said that the down near the left wing should be worn on the head. The left wing of the bird would be a symbol of its power. He bade them notice that the water of the lake was still; so the mind of man, he said, must be quiet, like to the lake, where dwell the mysterious animals, that they could give to man of their powers and by means of this magic bestowal he was to be able to perform strange and mysterious acts. He told the father and mother they were to remain where they were four days. When the stranger had finished his instructions he sang two songs and all the animals about the lake joined in the singing and those on the rock struck the drum. When the singing was over the stranger bade the father and mother take up the eldest boy, carry him out of the lodge, and lay him on the beach, face downward, his head toward the water. When they had done so, he bade them bring the second son and lay him down so that his head would be at the feet of his elder brother. When they had done so, he bade them bring the girl and lay her, like the others, face downward, her head to the feet of the second son. When they had done so, he told them to bring out the youngest child and place him face downward, with his head at the feet of his sister. Then the stranger entered the tent and left there his robe and came forth and walked on the water to the place where the sky and water meet and disappeared beyond. Soon a great wave arose and rolled over the quiet waters until it reached the shore where the children lay. It covered the body of the eldest boy and drew it in. The parents stood silently watching and as they looked, in the far distance they saw the stranger loom up and disappear. Then a second wave rolled up in the east and swept over the lake, which had become tranquil again. On it rolled until it came to the beach, when it lapped over the body of the second child and drew it in. As the wave receded and the lake became still, the stranger rose and looked at the parents and disappeared. Then came another wave that rolled on and on until it reached the body of the girl, covered it, and drew it in; and once more the lake became quiet as at first, while in the distance rose the form of the stranger. As he disappeared a mighty wave uprose and rolled over the lake, reached the beach, and swept the body of the youngest child from the beach where it lay, and again the lake became still. The father and the mother had watched these proceedings in a wondering state of mind. They made no sound nor did they speak. The silence of the lake and of all sounds, the absence of the stranger, the empty place where the children had lain, brought an overpowering sense of desolation to the parents and they gave way to violent demonstrations of grief. They cut their hair, threw away their clothing, and wailed as they walked beside the placid silent lake. Night came on; still the man and woman wailed, until from exhaustion they slept. Before the sun was up the woman arose and began to wail afresh. Her husband joined her, wailing as he came. The lake lay quiet, but covered with a mist. As the woman walked she remembered the words of the stranger and began to search, hoping she might find something as he had said she would. Her eye caught sight of a gleam in the water. She stooped and took from the water a white shell, exclaiming as she did so: "I have found it! I have found it!" Her husband heard her cry of joy, and he began to search. By and by he saw a dark object in the water; he stooped and took from the water a dark shell. Then he exclaimed: "I have found it!" Just then as they stood holding their shells, the mist parted, making an opening down the lake like a path and in the path stood the four children, well and happy. As the parents stood gazing in wonder, the children spoke, and said: "Do not grieve for us. We are content. Death is not to be dreaded. It is not as you think it to be. In course of time you will be coming and then you will know for yourselves." And as their voices died away the mist closed the path and they were seen no more but in the mist, as through a veil, they saw the outline of a strange animal (fig. 107). It seemed as big as the great lake. Its skin was covered with hair and was brown like that of the deer. The ridge of its back was serrated with tufts of hair. It had branching horns and hoofs like the deer, and a slender tail with a tuft at the end, which swept toward the sky to the farthest end of the lake. At last this mysterious shadowy figure melted away and the lake lay quiet before the astonished couple. Then the man said to the woman: "We have found the mystery, let us go home." His wife consented; she was now content. She had seen the children and what they had said dwelt in her mind. So they returned to their tent to abide there as the stranger had said. The man went out to hunt. He knew where to find game and they had a large store of meat and many pelts. While they were still camped beside the lake there came to their tent a messenger from their tribe. He said that he had been sent by their people to seek for them. They had remained behind the others with a stranger and their kindred

FIG. 107. Mythic animal in legend of Shell society (native drawing).

feared that they might have been lured into danger and some ill befallen them. "Where are your children?" the messenger asked. "They are dead." "Where is the stranger?" "He has gone away, but he has given us all that you see, and he has promised to give us more when this supply is gone. Go back and tell the people what the stranger has done for us."

When the messenger saw the great store of meat and the many caches filled with dried meat, the pelts, and all the wealth given to the man and his wife, he was astonished and returned to the tribe to tell what he had seen and heard. Then the man and his wife left their camp, and, taking all they could with them and caching the rest until such time as they could return for it, they started back to rejoin their tribe. When they were once more with their people they determined to organize a society, as the stranger had told them to do, that they might give to the members of the magic power which they had received. The first lodge was composed of seven, the man and his wife and the four children, under the leadership of the mysterious stranger with the magic power. The man and woman each initiated seven others. Then they waited four years, as they had been told to do. They made packs in which to keep the articles they must wear when the society met and also the medicinal roots which the stranger had pointed out to them. Some of these roots were to heal diseases; others were poisons which were to be used to punish offenders by causing them to die. A knowledge of all these roots and herbs was given as secrets by the stranger to the man and his wife, never to be imparted except to those who should be initiated into the society. Not only could the man and his wife thus impart this knowledge, but they could also give to those who were initiated a share in the magic power bestowed on them by the mysterious stranger, who was the messenger of the council of animals that dwelt in and about the great lake.

Such is the story of the origin of the Shell society.

Organization

The society seems to have been organized in order to preserve the story upon which it was founded and its dramatic presentation forms the basis of the ceremonies observed at a regular meeting.

The membership was composed of five "*ti*," or lodges, each presided over by a *nudo*^{n}'*ho*^{n}*ga*, "leader" or "master." Each lodge had its place in the dwelling set apart for the meetings of the society. This was originally a large tent, afterward an earth lodge, and in recent years a circular wooden building arranged like the latter.

The leaders of four of the lodges personated the four children (pl. 59) of the story and the lodges were spoken of as the lodge "of the eldest son," "of the second son," "of the daughter," and "of the youngest son." The fifth lodge was presided over by the *u'zhu*, or principal leader, who was at the head of the entire society. It is said that "in early times the office of *u'zhu* was filled by a woman, because it was the woman, the wife of the man in the story, who took the initiative and sent her son to invite the stranger to her house, prepared the feast, and entertained him; and also because it was to the woman, the mother, that the children addressed themselves when they appeared in the path on the lake after they had been "shot" by the mysterious stranger. But as time went on the women became too timid to fill the place so it was taken by men.

The place of the *u'zhu* was facing the east in the middle at the back of the dwelling. On his right toward the south sat "the eldest son" and his lodge. On his left toward the north were "the second son" and his lodge. To the latter's left on the north side sat "the daughter" and her lodge, and on the opposite side on the south to the right of "the eldest son" sat "the youngest son" and his lodge. (Fig. 108.)

The position of these four lodges had a cosmic significance. The manner in which the mysterious stranger of the story painted the four children bore out this same significance. He painted the body of the eldest son blue to represent the clear sky with no clouds to obstruct the passage of the sun's rays—so the sun was thus indi-

"THE FOUR CHILDREN," SHELL SOCIETY

rectly represented, it is said. The youngest son was painted the color of the earth. Both these children and their lodges are on the south side of the dwelling, the side "where the sun travels and causes the earth to bring forth." This side is spoken of also as "the masculine side." The second son was painted to represent the night sky and the daughter had the moon painted on her. These two children had their places on the north side of the lodge, the side which typified "the night and the feminine forces." The position assigned these "children" occurs in ceremonies observed in other tribes, which represent cosmic relations in that the related groups are placed diagonally and not directly opposite each other. Here the "eldest son," typifying the sun, the masculine power of the day, is diagonal to the "daughter," who stood for the moon, the feminine power of the night; and the "second son," representing the stars, is diagonally opposed to the "youngest son," who represented the earth. The mysterious stranger declared that "the earth and the stars are brothers."

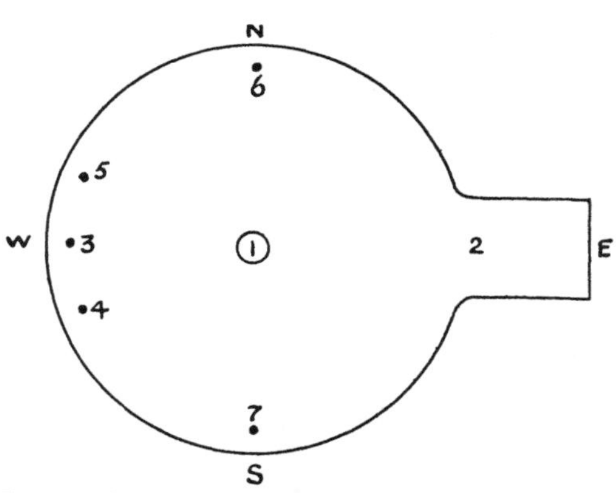

Fig. 108. Diagram illustrating meeting of Shell society. 1, Fireplace; 2, entrance toward the east; 3, *u'zhu;* 4, "eldest son" (the sun); 5, "second son" (the stars); 6, "daughter" (the moon); 7, "youngest son" (the earth).

All the offices of the society were obtained by purchase and were not elective. When a person holding an office felt that age or ill health made it difficult to fulfill the duties required, the office was sold, generally to a relative. Many of the present officers are descendants of those who formerly held these places. The present holder of the office of "eldest son" is the fifth in direct descent to hold the place. He is now a man over 50 and his father and grandfather lived to be old men. The other offices have been in the families of the present occupants for three or four generations. The five principal officers had to be present personally at all meetings. No substitutes were allowed, so the absence or sickness of one of these persons prevented a meeting being held. Besides these offices there were minor positions, the holders of which had certain duties connected with the dramatic rites. Sometimes a person bought and held several of these positions: The right to place the four "children" before the fireplace; to beat the drum; to have charge of the wooden bowl belonging to the society, which is said to be very old; to fill this bowl with water; to examine the water; to pass the bowl; to select the servers of the feast; to designate to whom the choice pieces of meat were to be given; to invite guests to be present at the public part of the ceremony. The right to wear certain regalia had also to be purchased. Some of these articles have descended with the office, and the man who bought the office generally purchased the right to wear the regalia that had been worn by his predecessor.

No dream was requisite for membership. A member "must be able to keep a secret and not be of a quarrelsome disposition." The unanimous consent of all the members was necessary to admission to membership. In former times four years had to elapse between the presentation of a name and the acceptance of a person as a member, but of late years the time has been shortened. Other changes seem to have crept in. It is said that there should be seven lodges. The mysterious stranger told the man and his wife they were each to initiate seven members, seven men and seven women; then they were to wait four years, when seven more of each sex could be taken in. The seven initiation sticks still used are said to refer to this direction of the stranger. How the change to five lodges came about could not be learned and it is a question if it is now known. Of the animals that held a council with the stranger and agreed to give magic power to man, the four which were to give themselves as food seem to be associated with the lodges of the four "children." That of the "eldest son" is sometimes spoken of as the black-bear lodge, that of the "second son" as the elk lodge, the "daughter's" as the buffalo lodge (it is said that the "moon led the Omaha to the buffalo"), and the "youngest son's" as the deer lodge. The eagle belonged to the *u'zhu*, the head of the society, because "the eagle descended and spoke to the man after he had killed the black bear and said he would come and be one of them and give supernatural power."

It was formerly the custom that when a man was initiated he was required to bring the skin of an otter, a mink, or a beaver to represent the water, the skin of a squirrel or a badger to represent the earth, and that of a crow or an owl to represent the air. So, too, whenever a member shot a bear, an elk, a deer, or a buffalo, he saved a portion of the meat for use at a meeting of the society, in memory of the fact that these animals were closely connected with the rites.

Each lodge possessed a pack, or parfleche case, in which articles belonging to that lodge were kept. The regalia the right to wear which had been purchased by members, medicine for curing diseases, and poisons for punishing offenders were kept in these packs. Of the five packs belonging to the five lodges three are gone. One was captured a long time ago in a battle. One was burned accidentally near the beginning of the last century, and one that was formerly in charge of Big Elk is now in the Peabody Museum (no. 37560) of Harvard University. The contents of the other two packs have

MEMBERS OF THE SHELL SOCIETY

MEMBERS OF THE SHELL SOCIETY

MEMBERS OF THE SHELL SOCIETY

MEMBERS OF THE SHELL SOCIETY

MEMBERS OF THE SHELL SOCIETY

been divided, so that now each lodge has a substitute for its lost pack.

The dress of the members varied with their ability to possess fine garments. The men were expected to wear only the breechcloth and moccasins. While a few observed this rule, most of the men wore shirts or leggings. In that case the line of paint which ran down each arm to the thumb was drawn on the sleeve of the shirt. The skin tunic of the women of early days was usually replaced in later times by a calico or other cloth sack and skirt, embroidered with ribbons which reproduced in color and design the old porcupine-quill embroidery, or by a gown of the style commonly worn by white women. Still later, rather bizarre designs much used by the Oto and some other tribes, which showed considerable white influence, became "fashionable" as "foreign importations." (Pls. 60–64.)

The painting on the face, the line from the mouth to the ears, representing a ray of the sun, and the lines down the arms typifying the lightning were in accordance with the manner in which the mysterious stranger painted the children; and the putting of down (which should be from under the left wing of the swan) upon the head constituted the peculiar decoration of the members.

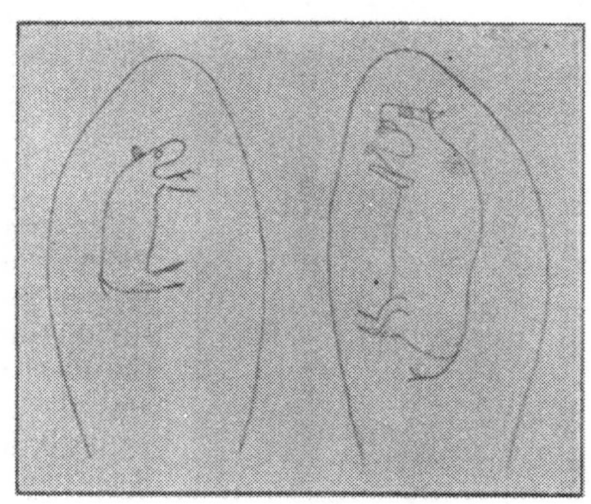

FIG. 109. Moccasin design belonging to "eldest son's" regalia, Shell society (native drawing).

Among the regalia the right to wear which was purchased by men were an otter-skin cap, a beaded cap with a feather in front that slants to the left, a black-squirrel-skin bag, a red-squirrel-skin bag, a pair of black skin moccasins with a bear embroidered on the left foot in black beads on a background of white beads, the head being toward the toe, and a buffalo similarly embroidered on the right foot (fig. 109). The right to wear these descended to "the eldest son;" they may be seen in plate 59. The right to carry a silver-fox-skin bag was purchased by a woman. Each member had his own otter-skin mystery bag (fig. 110; Peabody Museum no. 53054) and a left wing which represented the wing of the "holy bird," the swan. (This use of the wing is regarded by some persons as an innovation, as it is said "the wing belongs to the Pebble society.") The mystery bags were not buried with the dead, but were generally handed down and passed on with the place taken by a new member. Two shells were used, *Olivia nobilis* Reeve, which is white and was regarded as female, and *Olivia elegans* Lam., which is dark and was considered the male. How these "male" and "female" shells were divided among the members was not explained.

Besides the wooden bowl already mentioned there was a board (*nini'amashude*) about a foot square with the edges embroidered; this was used for the preparation of the tobacco for smoking. The drum was formerly of the native type described on p. 371; later a keg was substituted but the employment of water and heat in tuning was still practised. Two gourd rattles, and two pillows on which to strike the rattles, were kept with the drum. All these articles were the property of the society and each had its special keeper.

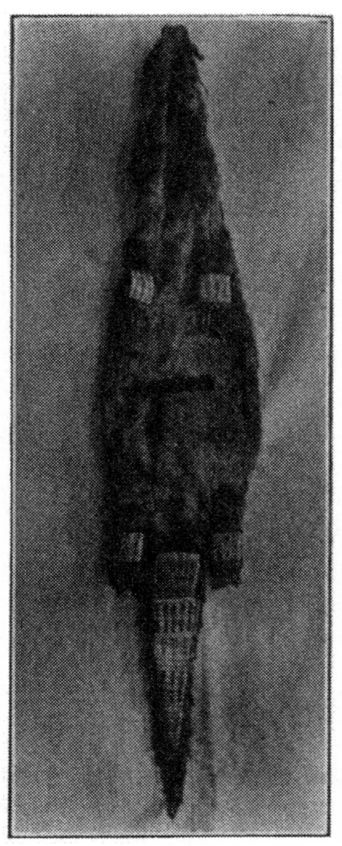

FIG. 110. Otter-skin bag, Shell society.

Each lodge had a pack, as stated above, and to each pack belonged two pipes and four sticks (*nini'uthubaçki*), the latter being used in filling and cleaning the pipes.

Regular Meetings

The regular meetings of the society were held in the months of May, June, August, and September, these being the mating seasons respectively of the black bear, the buffalo, the elk, and the deer. At other times, particularly in the fall and winter, meetings had to be held at night and were informal in character.

When a member decided to invite the society to hold a regular meeting he acted as host and prepared the required feast. Every regular meeting had its host. The host not only provided the food for the feast, but gifts to be distributed among the members. In olden times these gifts were the skins of animals connected with the society as shown in the story of its origin. In recent times calico, blankets, and broadcloth were substituted. After the man had accumulated the required materials he sent for the four servants of the society and bade them tell the members that on such a day a regular meeting of the society would be held. When the day arrived he sent a servant of the society to procure the tobacco board and four sticks used for the pipes belonging to the pack of his *ti*, or lodge and bade him place these articles in his (the host's) appointed seat in the lodge. The food was placed outside the dwelling where the society met and there was made ready for cooking. The gifts were spread within; the bowl, drum, and rattles obtained by the servants from their keepers were deposited in their proper places. Then the servants were dispatched to tell the members "all is ready."

Then the members entered the dwelling, passed around the fire by the left and took their places with their respective lodges; the last to enter was the host, who took his accustomed seat. (Fig. 111.)

THE OPENING CEREMONY

The pipes belonging to the pack of the lodge of which the host was a member were brought to him. He took one, filled it with tobacco which he had prepared on the board, and handed it to a servant, who took it to the *u'zhu*. The latter lighted the pipe, smoked it, and passed it to the person on his left, who smoked and passed it to the left. Meanwhile the host filled the second pipe and sent it by a servant to one of the masters of one of the other lodges, whichever one he pleased. No special order was observed. The master lighted, smoked, and passed the pipe to his left. Soon the first pipe was returned to the host, who refilled and sent it to another master, who lighted, smoked, and passed the pipe on. In this way the pipes were filled, smoked, and passed four times around the assembly.

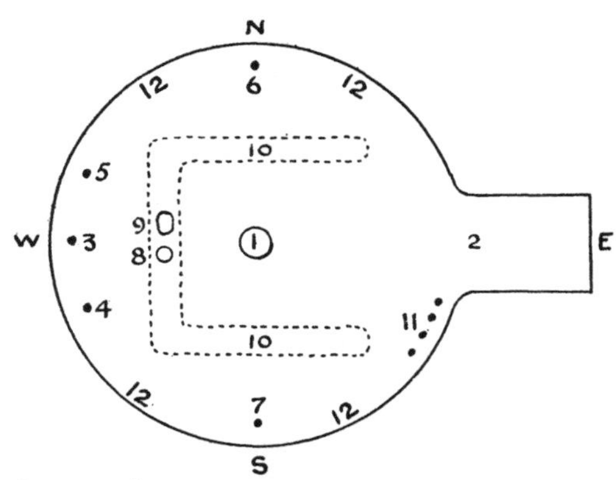

FIG. 111. Diagram showing positions of officers and of ceremonial articles at meeting of Shell society. 1, Fireplace; 2, entrance; 3, *u'zhu;* 4, "eldest son;" 5, "second son;" 6, "daughter;" 7, "youngest son;" 8, drum; 9, rattles; 10, gifts; 11, servants; 12, members.

Next, the host called a servant and handed him the seven invitation sticks. These sticks were made by each host and were never used twice. They were squared at both ends and the length was "the measure of a clenched fist." The servant took the sticks in his left hand, circled the fire, and went to the master who personated the "eldest son" and held the sticks before him. He received them in his left hand, removed one stick, laid it down before him, and handed the six back to the servant, who, holding the six sticks in his left hand, circled the fire and went to the master of the lodge of the "second son," and held the sticks before him. The "second son" received them in his left hand, took out one, and handed the five back to the servant, who circled the fire, went to the "daughter," and held the sticks before her. She received them as the others had done, took one, laid it down, and handed the four back to the servant, who for the fourth time circled the fire, went to the "youngest son," and held the sticks before him. He took them in the same manner, removed one, laid it down, and handed the three sticks back to the servant, who carried them back to the host.

The packs belonging to the several lodges were then taken up by their keepers, held by the ends, and turned four times from left to right "so that all the animals and roots within the packs might move from north to south." Then the keeper took a pinch of tobacco with his left hand and made a line from the bottom to the top of the pack, sprinkling a little of the tobacco as his hand moved. Four of these lines were made on the side of the pack and then he let fall the remainder of the tobacco on the pack. Next he struck the pack with his open palm four times and lifted the pack slightly. After these movements the packs were untied. The "eldest son" and the "daughter" manipulated the strings and bindings of their packs in the same way. The "second son" and the "youngest son" untied their packs differently from the first two, but both observed the same method in opening their packs. When all these motions were completed the regalia was distributed by the officers who had the right to perform this duty. At this time any "medicines" required by the members (such "medicines" as were kept in the packs) were given to those who desired them. This done, the packs were put behind the seats occupied by the masters of the lodges.

The host then gave the red and green paint he had provided to a servant, who put them on a cloth laid on the top of the drum. This was set directly in front of the *u'zhu*. The *u'zhu* summoned a servant, gave him some of the red clay used for paint, and bade him take it to the woman who sat at the extreme end on the south side; and she at once began to comb her hair. This represented the act of the mysterious stranger who thus cared for the children in the story. All the members then made ready to put on their regalia, while the woman to whom the paint was sent arose and, taking her otter-skin mystery bag, went by the left around the circle of members and, with her left hand outspread toward each person in turn, mentioned the term of relationship by which she was entitled to address him. Meanwhile the *u'zhu* had mixed some of the green or blue clay with water in a small wooden bowl and sent it to the master of the woman's lodge, who represented the "youngest son." After the woman had returned she was painted by the master, who then painted all the members of his lodge. While the painting of the members was in progress the *u'zhu* directed a servant to gather up the mystery bags of the members by fours, and lay them before him; he then painted with the blue paint the head of the animal whose entire skin formed the bag. When this was done the servant advanced to the drum, made four feints, and then struck the drum four times. This represented that part of the story in which the animals in the lake and on the island struck their drums when the children were painted. The ceremony of gathering and painting the bags and striking the drum was the same for all the lodges.

Then the master representing the "eldest son" rose (he had painted his invitation stick red), having completed his duty of painting the members of his lodge, and, holding up his invitation stick, he passed by the left around the fire followed by all the members of his lodge. When they reached the entrance at the east they paused, faced the west and the fireplace and sang the following song, led by their master who held the painted stick aloft. The drum was not used to accompany any of the songs belonging to the opening and second part of the ceremony.

M. M. ♩=120 (Sung in octaves)
Transcribed by Edwin S. Tracy
Moⁿ wi - ta - we he she - wa - the - ke - he Ha - thi thi - u -
de the - ka noⁿ ge Ga - moⁿ - de she - wa - the
ke Ha thi thi - u - de the - ka noⁿ ge Ga - moⁿ
de she - wa - the - ke Ha - thi thi - u - de the - ka noⁿ
ge Ga - moⁿ - de she - wa - the - ke Ha - thi thi - u
de the - ka - noⁿ - ge Ga - moⁿ - de she - wa - the

ke Moⁿ - wi - ta - we he she - wa - the - ke he
Ha - thi thi - u de the - ka noⁿ - ge

Moⁿ witawe he! Shewatheke he
Hathithiude thekanoⁿge
Ga'moⁿde shewatheke
Hathithiude thekanoⁿge
Ga'moⁿde shewatheke
Hathithiude thekanoⁿge
Ga'moⁿde shewatheke
Hathithiude thekanoⁿge
Ga'moⁿde shewatheke
Moⁿ witawe he! Shewatheke he
Hathithiude thekanoⁿge

Translation: *Moⁿ*, arrow; *witawe,* mine; *he,* vocable; *shewatheke,* as you have bidden; *hathithiude,* deserted or abandoned; *theka noⁿge,* you who have been; *ga'moⁿde,* this I shall do. "You who have been deserted [or abandoned] have given me an arrow which you have bidden me to use, and this I shall do as you have bidden me."

This refers to the instructions given by the father and mother to the members of the society when they first organized it. The song speaks of them as the "abandoned ones," as they were left all alone when the stranger and the four children disappeared among the waters. The "arrow" refers to the shell, which was shot as an arrow.

At the close of the song the lodge marched around the fire and the master returned the invitation stick to the host, after which they moved to their places.

Then the master who represented the "second son" arose, holding his painted invitation stick. All his lodge rose and followed him around the fire to the entrance, where they turned, faced the fire, and sang the song belonging to their master and lodge. This song the writers were not able to obtain. After the singing of this song the "second son" circled the fire and returned his painted invitation stick to the host, when he and his lodge went back to their appointed seats.

The "daughter" then arose, as did her lodge. They circled the fire to the entrance, where they turned, faced the west and the fire, and sang their song. This song the writers were not successful in obtaining. At the close they circled the fire and the "daughter" returned her painted stick to the host; then she and her lodge passed on to their seats.

The "youngest son" arose, and with his lodge circled the fire, paused at the entrance, turned, faced the fire and the west, and, holding up his red painted invitation stick, sang the following song:

Transcribed by Edwin S. Tracy
M.M. ♩ = 120 (Sung in octaves)
Mi - the - ga ha ha ha ha doⁿ mi - the - ga ha...... ha
ha e ya ha......... ha ha ha - doⁿ mi - the - ga ha ha
ha e ya ha...... ha ha the - ge u ha mi - the he he
he mi - the he mi - the he - he he ha doⁿ the - he - he
he a ha ha ha ha doⁿ mi - the ga ha ha ha - doⁿ

Mithega ha ha ha hado^n! Mithega ha ha ha e ya ha ha ha hado^n
Mithega ha ha ha e ya ha ha ha thege uha
Mithega he he he mithega ha mithega ha ha ha hado^n
Mithega he he he mithega ha mithega ha ha ha hado^n
Mithega hado^n

Literal translation: *Mithega*, I go; *ha*, vocable; *hado^n*, behold, see; *thege* yonder; *uha*, to walk as in a path.

When the song had been sung they circled the fire by the left, returned the stick to the host, and then took their accustomed seats.

A servant was next dispatched with the wooden bowl to fill it with water. This bowl is said to represent the earth, which held the lake spoken of in the story, and the water had to be taken from a spring, a lake, or other quiet body. When the servants returned with the bowl the water was examined by the officer whose duty it was to attend to having the water correctly furnished. Meanwhile the officer who had the right to place the four "children" before the fire went to the man representing the "eldest son," who arose and followed the officer. They two circled the fire and went to the place where the "second son" sat. He arose and followed them, and the three circled the fire and went to the "daughter." She arose, fell into line, and the four passed about the fire and then went to the "youngest son." He arose, fell in behind the "daughter," and the five passed around the fire. When they reached the west they paused and stood facing the east.

The officer who led the "children" then took the bowl of water and handed it to the "eldest son," who took four sips and passed it to the "second son." He took four sips and handed it to the "daughter;" she did likewise and passed the bowl to the "youngest son." After taking his four sips he handed the bowl to the officer, who carried it to the member sitting at the left of the row of members, the one who first combed her hair. She took four sips and passed the bowl to the person at her left, who also after four sips passed it on to the left, and so the bowl went entirely around, each member taking four sips. Finally the bowl was given to its keeper.

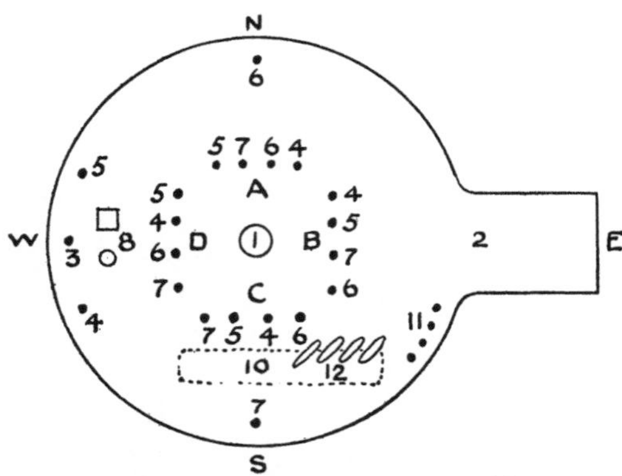

FIG. 112. Diagram showing arrangement and four ceremonial movements of officers at meeting of Shell society. 1, Fireplace; 2, entrance, facing the east; 3, *u'zhu;* 4, lodge of "eldest son;" 5, lodge of "second son;" 6, lodge of "daughter;" 7, lodge of 'youngest son;" 8, drum and rattles, moved back;" 10, gifts; 11, servants; 12, "children" ejecting shells on gifts after encircling lodge four times. *D, A, B, C,* successive positions of "children" before the fire; *D*, last position, like the first.

The drum was then moved back and the goods were spread toward the south. Then began a series of circlings of the fire by the four "children," during which a song was sung to each of the four directions; the "children" shifted their places and finally returned to the position occupied at the beginning. The accompanying diagram (fig. 112) may help to make clear this movement, which is not without dignity as the people perform it.

All standing at the west, the "eldest son" turned, faced the north, and sang the following song:

ELDEST SON'S SONG

M. M. ♩= 72 (Sung in octaves) Transcribed by Edwin S. Tracy

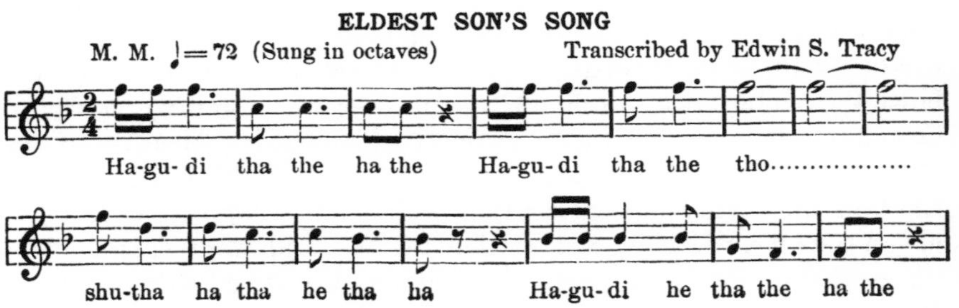

Ha - gu - di tha the tha.................... Shu tha ha the
he tha ha Ha- gu- di he tha the tha..............................
slow
Cry of Mystic Ancients
Ha!
ha ha ha

Hagudi thathe ha the
Hagudi thathe tho
Shuthahatha he tha ha
Hagudihe thathe ha tha
Hagudi thathe tha
Shuthahathe he tha ha
Hagudi he thathe tha

Translation: *Hagudi*, where? *thathe, theathe*, I send, I make to go; *hathe*, this (refers to the shell, with the secret power); *shuthe athe, shuthahathe*, in your direction; *he*, vowel prolongation; *tha*, end of sentence. "Where do I send this (the shell)? I send it in your direction."

The "eldest son" then led the way, the others following in single file, to the north side of the fire. When all were standing in line facing south he left his place, circled the fire alone, and on his return took his place beside the "youngest son."

The "second son" then turned, faced the east, and sang the following song:

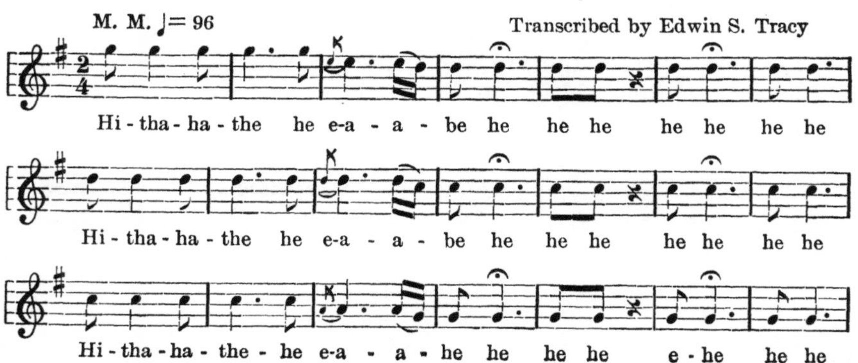
M. M. ♩= 96
Transcribed by Edwin S. Tracy
Hi - tha - ha - the he e-a - a - be he he he he he he he
Hi - tha - ha - the he e-a - a - be he he he he he he he
Hi - tha - ha - the - he e-a - a - he he he he e - he he he

Hi-tha-ha-the he e-a - a - be he he he e-he he he

Hi-tha-ha-the he e-a - a - be he he he e-he he he

Hi-tha-ha-the he e-a - a - be he Hi-tha-ha-the he

e-a - a - be he he he e-he he he Hi-tha-ha-the he

e-a - a - be he he he e-he he he oh (Cries of the

Magic Ancients)

ha he ho ho ho ho ho ho

Hithahathe he eabe he he he ehe he he

Literal translation: *Hithathe,* I have found it; *eabe,* said. Vocables are introduced to stretch the words to the music.

The song refers to the mother finding the shell and exclaiming, "I have found it!", as recounted in the story.

At the close of the song the "second son" led toward the east, the others following in single file. When they were all standing in line he left his place, circled the fire alone, and on his return took his place to the right of the "eldest son."

The "daughter" then turned, faced the south, and sang the following song:

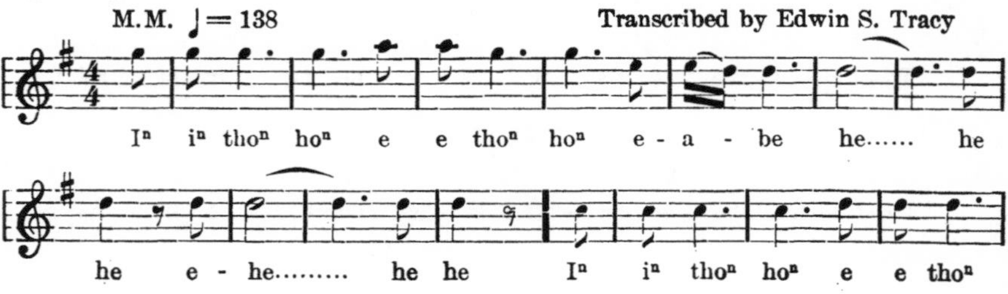
M.M. ♩= 138
Transcribed by Edwin S. Tracy
Iⁿ iⁿ thoⁿ hoⁿ e e thoⁿ hoⁿ e-a-be he...... he
he e-he......... he he Iⁿ iⁿ thoⁿ hoⁿ e e thoⁿ

hon^n e - a - be he......... he he e - he......... he he

I^n i^n tho^n ho^n e e tho^n ho^n e - a - be...... hio

o.................... In i^n tho^n ho^n e e tho^n ho^n e - a - be

he......... he he e - he......... he he I^n i^n tho^n

ho^n e e tho^n ho^n e - a - be...... hio - o..........................

I^n i^n tho^n ho^n e e tho^n ho^n eabe he he he
Ehe he he
I^n i^n tho^n ho^n e e tho^n ho^n eabe he he he
Ehe he he
I^n i^n tho^n ho^n e e tho^n ho^n eabe hio
I^n i^n tho^n ho^n e e tho^n ho^n eabe he he he
Ehe he he
I^n i^n tho^n ho^n e e tho^n ho^n eabe hio

Literal translation: *I^n*, stone; *tho^n*, round; *eabe*, it is, they say.

This song refers to the mother finding the shell. It is to be noted that the shell is here spoken of as a round stone. This song, as well as other points in the story it dramatizes, raises the question as to the relation between the Shell and Pebble societies. If they are related the Pebble society bears marks of being the older. Its rituals deal with more fundamental conceptions than does the story on which the Shell society is said to be founded.

After the song the "daughter" led toward the south, and the others followed her in single file. When all were in line she left her place, circled the fire alone, and on her return took her place on the right of the "second son."

The "youngest son" then turned and faced the west, and sang the following song:

Transcribed by Edwin S. Tracy

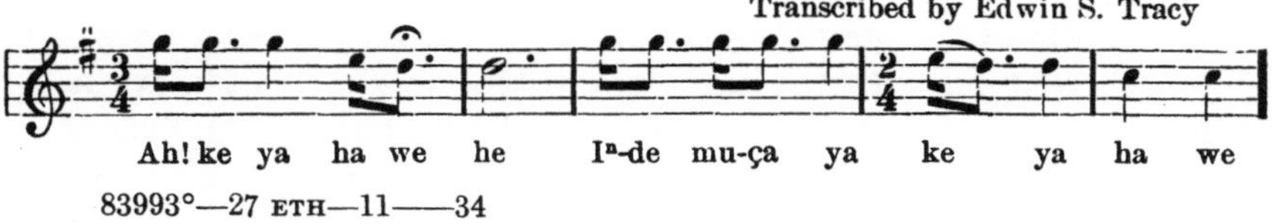

hi - a I^{n} de mu-ça ya Ke ya ha we hia
slow
quicker
hia
hia
Cry of Magic Ancients
ha
e ho..............

Ah! ke ya ha we he
I^{n}de muça ya ke ya ha we hia
I^{n}de muça ya ke ya ha we hia

Literal translation: *Ah ke,* now then; *ya ha we he,* come, let us gather together; *i^{n}de,* face; *muça,* to shoot: *hia,* magical cry. Some of the words are archaic.

This song refers to the completion of the purposes of the stranger and the organization of the society. In it the members are bidden to "come now and shoot each other in the face." The otter-skin from which the shell was supposed to be "shot" was always aimed at the mouth, whence comes the breath, the sign of life in man. The Pebble people shot at any part of the person; the Shell people only at the face.

At the close of the song the "youngest son" led toward the west, the others following. When all were in line he circled the fire alone, and on his return took his place to the right of the "daughter." All four were then in their first position.

Standing before the fire and facing the east, the four laid their mystery bags down in front of them. Then, beginning with the "eldest son" (no. 4), they coughed in order as they stood. The cough was repeated four times in the same order and at the fourth cough the shell was ejected. The four coughs were said to be for the purpose of gaining strength to reach the four hills of life leading to old age. The palms of the hands were then moistened, the bag was picked up with the right hand, the shell held in the left. Then all four started around the circular dwelling at a trot, with one breath uttering the magic cry *Chochochooo* until they reached the middle of the north side. There they took breath, then, with the same cry, trotted to the middle of the east, took breath, and with the same cry and movement went to the middle of the south side, where they again paused to breathe and then went on with the same cry to the west. This movement about the dwelling with the four stops and prolonged magic cries was repeated four times. After a brief rest the four started again. With the same magic cry they circled the fire without pausing until they reached the south side, where the gifts of goods were spread. They there put their shells into their mouths and each one fell prone on the goods. This act represented the death of the children in the story.

The drum was then put before the *u'zhu*, and one of the minor officers started a song of the slow-time class called a "rest song." During its singing the four "children" stood motionless before the fire.

INTRODUCTORY TO DRAMATIC MOVEMENT

Dagohotha ha wiu^{n}thahakude he ga ha
He he ha ha u^{n}thahakude he ga
Mithega ha u^{n}thakude he ga ha
He he ha ha u^{n}thahakude he ga ha
He he ha ha u^{n}thakude he ga
Mithega ha u^{n}thahakude he ga ha
He he ha ha u^{n}thahakude he ga

Translation: *Dagotha*, an archaic term meaning "what is it?"; the vocable *ho* is introduced to stretch the word to the music; *wiu^n*, me; *thakude*, you shoot; *ha he ga ha* are vowel prolongations or vocables; *mithega*, I go forth. The meaning of this song is: "What is it with which you shoot me as I go forth?"

After this song, one in fast time was sung. All the lodge of the "eldest son" joined in the singing during which the following movements took place: The four "children" passed around the fire four times, and then went to the lodge of the "youngest son" at the southeast and "shot" four members at the end of the line; the latter fell rigid but in a few moments arose, took their places behind the four "children" and in single file the eight circled the fire. The last four then "shot" four of the lodge of the "eldest son," who fell, arose, and followed the others, and the twelve circled the fire. Then the last four "shot" four members of the lodge of the "second son," who fell, arose, and took their places behind the others, and the sixteen circled the fire. Then the last four "shot" four from the lodge of the "daughter," who fell, arose, and followed the others and the twenty went around the fire.

Kutha e wako^{n}da ha
Shei^{n}gehe tha ha
Hino^{n}ge ta ha i^{n}ge tha ha
Kutha e wako^{n}da ha tha ha
Ashei^{n}gehe tha ha
Hino^{n}ge ta ha i^{n}getha ha
Kutha e wako^{n}da ha tha ha
Ashei^{n}ge tha ha
Kutha e wako^{n}da ha
Shei^{n}ge tha ha
Hino^{n}ge ta ha i^{n}ge tha ha ha

Literal translation: *Kutha*, a term of endearment for a wife, used only in great grief (the word for wife in ordinary address is *thanon'ha;* when spoken of, *wigaxthon*); *e*, he; *Wakon'da*, here used in the sense of "mysterious;" *sheingehe tha ha*, an archaic form difficult to translate, refers to all things yonder—the animals, the earth, and its teeming life; *hinonge*, let us run; the word used refers to the running of animals, not men. The lines are all composed of changes on these words.

The song refers to the incident in the story when, after the shell had been found, the husband in his grief called to his wife and said, "We will now run home." The movement was to put them in accord with that of the animals of the earth and of the magic and mysterious animals of the story; also, they were to be endowed with their swiftness and magic power. Beneath the story of the song lies another meaning, which relates to the imparting to the man and woman of added life, reproductive power, by means of the magic granted to them.

This dramatic movement completed the opening ceremony, which was closed to the public.

THE PUBLIC CEREMONY

At the close of this cumulative procession about the fire those members who chose to do so returned to their respective places. The drum was then taken to one of the lodges and the members of that lodge formed a choir while the drum was with them. Each lodge had its own songs, and there was an initial song for each lodge which had to be sung first when the drum was brought; subsequently the singers chose the songs they wished to sing, there being no fixed order after the first. The drum was beaten as an accompaniment to all the songs, which were divided into the slow, or rest, songs, during which the members sat and talked or rested; and fast songs, during which they passed about the fire, "shooting" whom they pleased. Whoever was "shot" fell rigid, lay a few moments in a tense attitude, then arose and took a place in the moving line about the fire, and "shot" whomsoever he wished. After the drum had remained a while with one lodge it was carried to another. The initial song of that lodge was sung, then other songs belonging to the lodge, according to the fancy of the choir, and the procession formed again. The drum had to pass to all the lodges during a regular meeting.

The following are the initial songs of the four lodges:

Initial Song of the Lodge of the "Eldest Son"

M.M. ♩= 72 (Sung in octaves)
Transcribed by Edwin S. Tracy
E - u - tha ki - da wi-hi the he......... he he wa
shi......... ge he...... he he E - u - tha ki - da wi - the
he...... he he wa - koⁿ - da wi - the he he he e - iⁿ
ga - we he........ he he E - u - tha ki - da wi - the
he........ he he iⁿ - ga - - we he........ he he E -
u - tha ki - da wi - the he...... he he wa - koⁿ - da wi - the
he he he e - iⁿ - ga we he...... he he E - u - tha ki - da
wi - the he...... he he iⁿ - ga - we...... he...........

Eutha kida wihithe he he he
Washige he hehe
Eutha kida withe he he he
Wako^{n}da withe he he he e
I^{n}gawehe hehe
Eutha kida wihithe he hehe
I^{n}gawehe hehe
Eutha kida wihithe he he he
I^{n}gawehe

Literal translation: *Eutha,* tell; *kida,* when home; *withe,* I cause you; *he he he,* vocables; *washige,* possessions or wealth; *wako^{n}da,* mysterious—refers to the mysterious stranger who gave the magic; *withe,* caused, appointed; *i^{n}gawehe,* speaking to me thus.

The song refers to the command of the stranger bidding the man and his wife to say when they went home that the mysterious stranger had offered them riches, possessions, through the magic power given them. The song implies that like powers will be passed on to the initiated.

Initial Song of the Lodge of the "Second Son"

Thege he hehe
Howane he he he
Athege he hehe
Howane he hehe
Athege he hehe
Howane hia
Nikathege he hehe
Howane he hehe
Thege he hehe
Howane hia
Ahehe hehe hehe hehe
Ahehe he ha

Literal translation: *Thege*, these; *howane*, I have sought; *athege*, behold these; *nika*, part of *nikathega*, people; *hia*, cry of magic animals; vocables and magic cries.

The song means: Behold the possessions I have sought and gained by the magic given by the mysterious stranger; behold the people I have gathered about me by his help. Reference is made to the magic help given to the initiated in the society.

INITIAL SONG OF THE LODGE OF THE "DAUGHTER"

Transcribed by Edwin S. Tracy

Awatedi thati e do^n o^n
Ho^{n}tho^{n}thathe ha
Awatedi thati e do^n o^n
Ho^{n}tho^{n}thathe ha
Awatedi thati e do^n o^n
Ho^{n}tho^{n}thathe ha
Awatedi thati e do^n o^n
Ho^{n}tho^{n}thathe ha
Wieha shetidi thati e do^n
Hiwithe ha
Awatedi thati e do^n
Ho^{n}tho^{n}thathe ha
Awatedi thati e do^n
Ho^{n}tho^{n}thathe a

Literal translation: *Awatedi,* at what place; *thati e do*^{n}, came you; *ho*^{n}*tho*^{n}*thathe,* and you found me; *wieha,* it was I; *shetidi,* at yonder place; *thati e do*^{n}, you came when; *hiwithe ha,* I found you.

This song refers to the initial incident in the story, the mother sending her son to invite the mysterious stranger. He asks: Where did you find me? I it was who found you at yonder place, the house of the chief from which the stranger came to partake of the feast prepared for him by the woman. In this song the "daughter" recalls the act of the mother which led to the formation of the society and the gift of magic.

INITIAL SONG OF THE LODGE OF THE "YOUNGEST SON"

Transcribed by Edwin S. Tracy
E wa-ko^n-da a gi-bo^n-thi-tho^n ha E wa-ko^n-da a gi-bo^n-thi-tho^n
E wa-ko^n-da a gi-bo^n-thi-tho^n ha E wa-ko^n-da a gi-bo^n-thi-tho^n
E wa-ko^n-da a gi-bo^n-thi-tho^n ha E wa-ko^n-da a gi-bo^n-thi-tho^n

E wako^{n}da a gibo^{n}thitho^n ha
E wako^{n}da a gibo^{n}thitho^n
E wako^{n}da a gibo^{n}thitho^n ha
E wako^{n}da a gibo^{n}thitho^n
E wako^{n}da a gibo^{n}thitho^n ha
E wako^{n}da a gibo^{n}thitho^n

Literal translation: *E,* he; *wako*^{n}*da,* mysterious; *a,* vowel prolongation; *gibo*^{n}*thitho*^{n}, called him.

This song refers to the calling of the youngest son into the tent, where he was "shot" as he entered, by the mysterious stranger, as told in the story. By that "shot" magic was given and can be transmitted by the representative of the youngest son, according to the claim of the society traditions.

These initial songs are among those said to have been taught by the mysterious stranger when the family were eating of the game that had been killed through the magic influence given the hunter to call the animals.

When the drum had passed around all the lodges the members took off their regalia, and while the disrobing was in progess the servants brought in the food for the feast. The *u'zhu* then took a wooden spoon, dipped up some of the broth, and dropped it into the fireplace. Then he circled the fire, and when facing the east, took another spoonful of the broth and carried it out of the lodge. At the entrance facing the east he held the food up to the sun, then poured out the offering at the entrance to the dwelling. Then he returned and, placing his finger on the spoon, touched with his moist finger the head of each of the mystery bags of the four masters and both moccasins of the "eldest son" and the "second son." After this ceremony all the articles which belonged to the packs were laid away where they belonged. The choice pieces of meat were then removed and given by the servants as directed by the officer who has that duty. Then all the members were served. Before anyone partook of his food each member arose and gave thanks to the host, beginning at the southeast end of the line. When the last person had spoken he took a bit and ate it; then each in turn followed, and all partook of the food without further ceremony. At the conclusion of the meal the gifts were taken to the "eldest son," who either distributed them or sent them to another master for distribution. The servants were always remembered in this division.

After the gifts had found their way to those who were to receive them, the songs of dismissal followed. These were the songs which the mysterious stranger bade the father and mother never to forget when rising from a feast. They were sung in the order of the "children," beginning with the "eldest son." Each song has two stanzas and there are four repetitions.

DISMISSAL SONG OF THE "ELDEST SON"

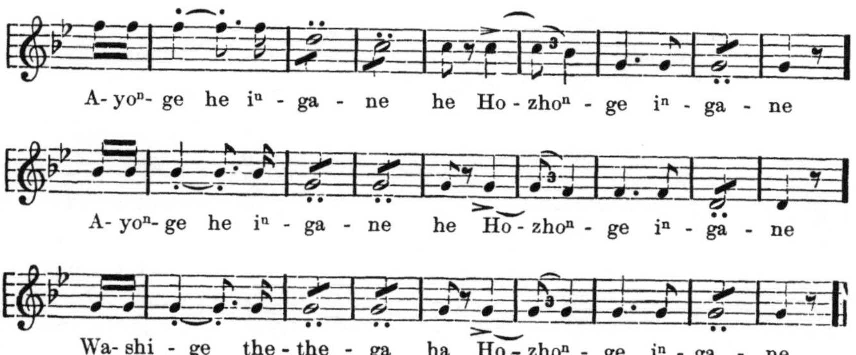

1

Ayoⁿge he iⁿgane he
Hozhoⁿge iⁿgane
Ayoⁿge he iⁿgane he
Hozhoⁿge iⁿgane
Ayoⁿge he iⁿgane he
Hozhoⁿge iⁿgane
Wakoⁿda thethega ha
Hozhoⁿge iⁿgane

2

Washige thethega ha
Hozhoⁿge iⁿgane
Ayoⁿge he iⁿgane he
Hozhoⁿge iⁿgane
Ayoⁿge he iⁿgane he
Hozhoⁿge iⁿgane
Washige thethega ha
Hozhoⁿge iⁿgane

Literal translation: *Ayoⁿge,* as it has been said; *he,* vowel prolongation; *iⁿgane,* spoken to me; *he,* vowel prolongation; *hozhoⁿge,* path; *he,* vowel prolongation; *wakoⁿda,* mysterious (refers to the stranger); *thethega,* go hither.

This song was explained to mean: "I rise to take the path pointed out to me by the mysterious messenger or stranger." The path refers to the path of life, with its avocations.

The second stanza is identical with the first except in lines 1 and 7. *Washige* in these lines means "possessions," the products of hunting gained through the magic imparted by the mysterious stranger to bring the animals.

Dismissal Song of the "Second Son"

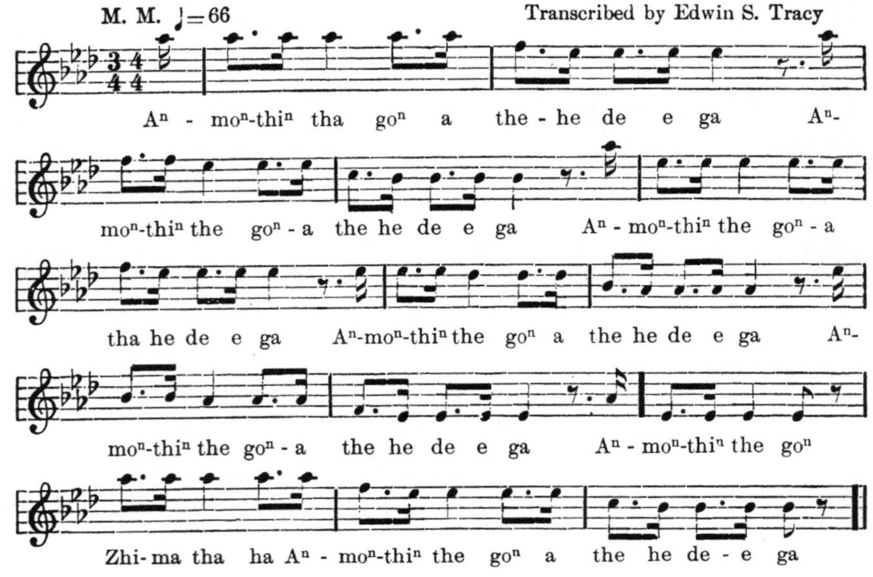

1

A^{n}mo^{n}thi^{n} thego^{n} athahede e ga
A^{n}mo^{n}thi^{n} thego^{n} athahede e ga
A^{n}mo^{n}thi^{n} thego^{n} athahede e ga
A^{n}mo^{n}thi^{n} thego^{n} athahede e ga

2

A^{n}mo^{n}thi^{n} thego^{n} athahede e ga
A^{n}mo^{n}thi^{n} thego^{n}
Zhimatha ha
A^{n}mo^{n}thi^{n} thego^{n} athahede e ga

Literal translation: *A^{n}mo^{n}thi^{n},* the other one; *thego^{n},* is gone; *athahede,* a longing desire; *zhimatha,* an archaic word; the remaining syllables are vowel prolongations and vocables.

The meaning of this song is said to be: "The other one, my brother, has gone, and I have a longing to follow him along the paths opened before us."

Dismissal Song of the "Daughter"

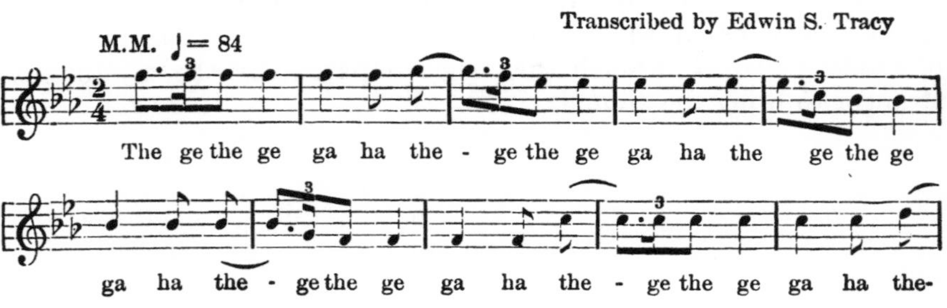

- - ge the ge ga ha the - ge the ge ga ha the - ge the ge
ga ha the - ge the ge ga ha the - ge the ge ga ha the-
- - ge the ge ga ha the - ge the ge ga ha mo^{n} - thi^{n} du-a
ge he we - shi-ge ha - a we - shi- ge ha a the - ge the ge he ga

1

Thegethe ge ga ha
Thegethe ge ga ha
Thegethe ge ga ha
Thegethe ge ga ha
Thegethe ge ga ha
Thegethe ge ga ha
Thegethe ge ga ha
Thegethe ge ga ha

2

Thegethe ge ga ha
Thegethe ge ga ha
Thegethe ge ga ha
Thegethe ge ga ha
Mo^{n}thi^{n} dua ge he
Weshige ha a
Weshige ha a
Thegethe ge he ga

The words of this song can not be translated. They are said to be old—at least, they are unintelligible to the Omaha of to-day. The meaning of the song is said to be: "We will again take this path." The word *weshige*, or one like it in sound, occurs. This word means "possessions" or "wealth," referring to the fruits of the successful hunter whose magic helped him to reach the animals in the story. "The path" therefore may refer to the possessions given through the magic imparted by this society.

Dismissal Song of "Youngest Son"

Transcribed by Edwin S. Tracy
M. M. ♩=88 (Sung in octaves)
She u - ha wi tha ha.......... ha ha She - u -
ha wi tha ha......... ha ha Ku - u - tha ha wi tha ha... ha
ha She - u ha wi - tha ha.......... ha ha Ku - u - tha
ha........ ha ha She - u - ha wi - tha ha........ ha
ha She - u ha wi tha ha...... ... ha ha mo^{n} zho^{n}
ha wi - tha ha........ ha ha She - u ha wi - tha ha...... ha ha
Ku - u - tha ha wi - tha ha ha ha She - u ha wi - tha
ha........ ha ha Ku - u - tha ha........ ha ha She - u -
ha wi - tha ha........ ha ha She - u - ha wi - tha ha ha

1

Sheuha withaha ha ha
Sheuha withaha ha ha
Kuutha ha withaha ha ha
Sheuha withaha ha ha kuutha ha ha ha
Sheuha withaha ha ha
Sheuha withaha ha ha

2

Mo^{n}zho^{n} ha witha ha ha ha
Sheuha withaha ha ha
Kuutha ha witha ha we ha
Sheuha withaha ha ha kuutha ha ha ha
Sheuha withaha ha ha
Sheuha withaha

Literal translation: *She*, those; *uha*, paths; *wethaha*, we go; *kutha*, wife; *mo^{n}zho^n*, land, earth.

The words of the song are few but the song is said to refer to the father and mother of the children speaking together after the death of their children, recalling the fact that before this strange experience they had traveled together but now they were to follow other ("those") paths over the earth, which had been pointed out to them by the mysterious stranger. That there was grief in facing the change is shown in the use of the term *kutha*, "wife," which, as already explained, was never used except in great sorrow, as at death.

At the conclusion of this song the lodge of the "youngest son" arose and went out first; then followed the lodge of the "daughter," next the lodge of the "second son," then that of the "eldest son," and finally the *u'zhu*.

In olden times a sweat bath was obligatory in washing off the paint but now it is removed with warm water.

The following eight songs belong to the lodge of the "eldest son" and afford a fair sample of the songs of the society. Three are of the slow class, "rest songs;" that is, there is no movement when they are sung. A song of this class always preceded one of the fast songs, during which the dramatic movement about the lodge took place, the members "shooting" one another. There is one special song in this group (no. 8) which is sung only when the thunder is first heard after the winter season. As the regular meetings of the society are not held during the spring, this song can not be classed with those usually sung at a meeting of the society, when any of the remaining seven songs of the following group could be sung while the drum was with this lodge. Of the songs here given some are evidently old, others are modern—at least, not quite a hundred years old. It will be noted in the explanation of these songs that throughout the story and practices of the society there runs a double thread, the dramatization of the story itself and a suggestion of the dual forces whose conjunction brings about living forms. The circle of life is also presented; its beginning, birth, is in mystery and it returns to the mystery of death. The magic side of the beliefs of the society is well brought out in songs nos. 3, 6, and 7.

Owing to the great difficulty and expense of obtaining material of this character, no attempt has been made to secure the songs of the other three lodges. The ritual songs of the secret ceremonies of the opening of a regular meeting are practically complete, as well as the customs and usages of the society. It is probable that the songs of the other lodges are similar to those here given. It is possible that some phase of the story or the beliefs may be emphasized in one lodge more than in another but the general scope is practically as here presented.

First Song—Slow Song, Introductory to Dramatic Movement in "Shooting" Members

1

(Sung twice)

Dagothaha waakude iⁿ ga we he he he
E he he he waakude iⁿ ga we he he he
E he he he woⁿage he ga ha
Waakude iⁿ ga we he he he
E he he he waakude iⁿ ga we he he he
E he he he
Dagothaha waakude iⁿ ga we he he he
E he he he waakude iⁿ ga we he he he
E he he he waakude iⁿ ga we he

2

(Sung twice)

Dagothaha waakude i^n ga we he he he
E he he he waakude i^n ga we he he he
E he he he I^{n}no^{n}ge he ga ha
Waakude i^n ga we he he he
E he he he waakude i^n ga we he he he
E he he he
Dagotha ha waakude i^n ga we he he he
E he he he waakude i^n ga we he he he
E he he he waakude i^n ga we he

Literal translation: *Dagotha*, what is it?; *wakude*, to shoot; *wo^{n}age*, an archaic word; *I^{n}no^{n}ge*, also archaic. The remaining syllables are vocables and vowel prolongations.

The song is said to be old. It refers to the shooting of the children by the mysterious stranger, as told in the story.

SECOND SONG—SLOW SONG, INTRODUCTORY TO A DRAMATIC MOVEMENT

M.M. ♩. = 104 (Sung in octaves) Transcribed by Edwin S. Tracy

No^n - ge shu the - tha - bi - ga ha ha ha he
he ha ha no^n - ge shu - the - tha bi - ga ha ha
ha he he ha ha U^n - da mo^n -
thi^n - du - wa - ge he No^n - ge shu the tha bi ga
ha ha ha he he ha ha No^n - ge shu the - tha
bi - ga ha ha ha he he ha ha No^n - ge - shu
the - tha - bi - ga ha ha he he ha No^n - ge shu -

the - tha - bi - ga ha ha ha he he ha ha Noⁿ -
ge - shu the - tha bi - ga ha ha ha

1

Noⁿge shuthethabiga ha ha ha he he ha ha
Noⁿge shuthethabiga ha ha ha he he ha ha
Uⁿda moⁿthiⁿ duwage he
Noⁿge shuthethabiga ha ha ha he he ha ha
Noⁿge shuthethabiga ha ha ha he he ha ha
Noⁿge shuthethabiga ha ha ha he he ha ha
Noⁿge shuthethabiga ha ha ha he he ha ha
Noⁿge shuthethabiga ha ha ha he he ha ha

2

Noⁿge shuithabiga ha ha ha he he ha ha
Noⁿge shuithabiga ha ha ha he he ha ha
Uⁿda moⁿthiⁿ duwage he
Noⁿge shuithabiga ha ha ha he he ha ha
Noⁿge shuithabiga ha ha ha he he ha ha
Noⁿge shuithabiga ha ha ha he he ha ha
Noⁿge shuithabiga ha ha ha he ha

Literal translation: (1) *Noⁿge*, running; *shuthethabiga*, going forth in your direction; *uⁿda moⁿthiⁿ duwage*, along the different paths they are running. (2) *Noⁿge*, running; *shuithabiga*, coming, returning.

The song refers to the rapid movements of the "four children" when they ran around the lodge and stopped at each of the four directions. The two stanzas are said to have another significance: The "running" indicates vigorous and abundant life, the birth of living things "going forth;" the second stanza refers to their "returning" to Mother Earth, moving along the different paths to final death.

The music is unusually attractive and melodious—in contrast to many of the songs of this society.

Third Song—Slow Song, Introductory to a Dramatic Movement

Transcribed by Edwin S. Tracy

M. M. ♩= 100
Shi-ge thi-noⁿ-ge-tha ha...... ha ha Shi the - thu
ha...... ha ha Shi the - thu ha ha ha
ha e he he he Shi-ge thi-noⁿ-ge-tha ha! ha

ha Shi the - thu ha! ha ha Shi the - thu
ha! ha ha e he he he
Shi-ge thi - noⁿ-ge - tha ha ha Shi the - thu
ha ha ha Shi the - thu ha ha ha e
he...... he he Shi noⁿ-ge-tha ha!..... ha ha Shi
(Spoken) Cry of Magic Ancients
the..... thu ha ha ho ho ho ho ho ho ho

(Repeated four times)

Shige thino^{n}gethaha! ha ha
Shi thethuha! ha ha
Shi thethuha! ha ha e he he he
Shige thino^{n}gethaha! ha ha
Shi thethuha! ha ha
Shi thethuha! ha ha e he he he
Shige thino^{n}gethaha! ha ha
Shi thethuha! ha ha
Shi thethuha! ha ha e he he he
Shi no^{n}gethaha! ha ha
Shi thethu ha!

Literal translation: *Shige*, again; *thino^{n}gethaha*, in an appointed direction you are running; *shi*, again; *thethuha*, here is the place; *no^{n}ge*, running. The remaining syllables are vocables and vowel prolongations.

This song refers to a meeting of the society at which the members by their magic turned themselves into birds and animals and flew and wandered over the earth. One member strayed off and was lost but was finally discovered, and this song refers to the calling of the members to the one that was lost, telling him that he was going in the opposite direction, and bidding him come "again" "here," that is, to the place where the other members were gathered.

FOURTH SONG—FAST SONG FOR DRAMATIC MOVEMENT

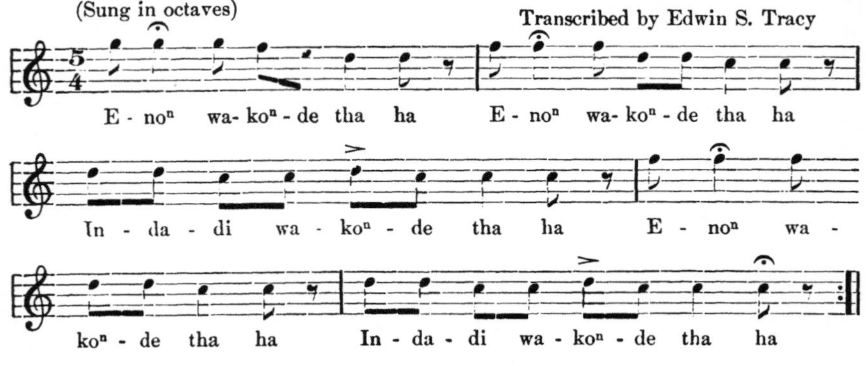

(Sung four times)

Enon wakonde tha ha
Enon wakonde tha ha
Indadi wakonde tha ha
Enon wakonde tha ha
Indadi wakonde tha ha

Literal translation: *Enon*, he alone; *wakonde*, mysterious; *tha*, is; *ha*, end of sentence; *indadi*, father (referring to the stranger).

In this song the stranger of the story is called "father" and he is declared to be mysterious and the giver of magic. The members of the society are as his children and receive from him the mysterious power. "My father is mysterious—he alone is mysterious!"

The fast songs are used for the movements about the lodge when the members "shoot" one another with the magic shells.

FIFTH SONG—FAST SONG FOR DRAMATIC MOVEMENT IN "SHOOTING"

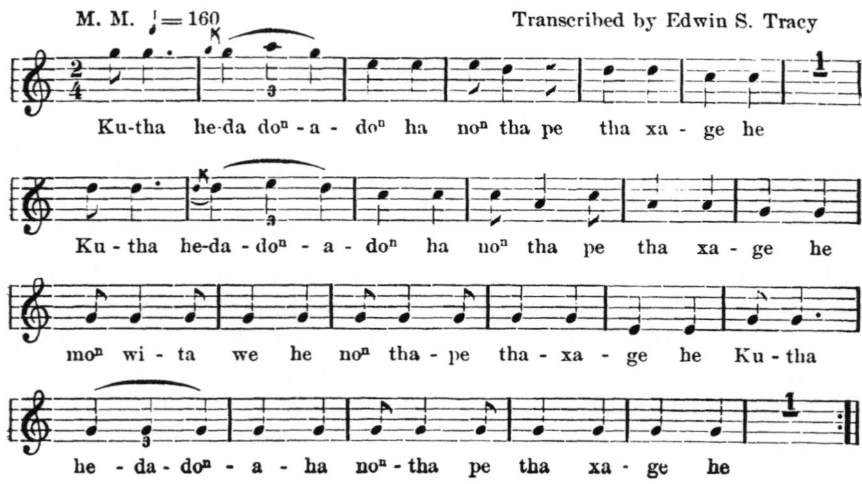

(Sung twice or more)

Kutha hedado^{n}ado^n ha
No^{n}thape thaxage he
Kutha hedado^{n}ado^n ha
No^{n}thape thaxage he
Mo^n wita we he no^{n}thape thaxage he
Kuça hedado^{n}a ha
No^{n}thape thahage he

Literal translation: *Kutha*, a term of affection applied only to a wife; *hedado^{n}ado^n ha*, what is it? *no^{n}thape*, afraid of; *thaxage he*, you cry; *mo^n* arrow; *wita*, my; vocables. The only changes for the second stanza are in the lines beginning with *kutha* and *mo^n wita*, and these are as follows: *Kutha shia dado^n ado^{n}ha*, "Wife, what else are you afraid of?" *Mo^{n}ko^n witawe no^{n}thape thaxagehe*—*mo^{n}ko^n*, medicine (not magic, but physic); *witawe*, mine; *no^{n}thape*, afraid of; *thaxagehe*, you cry. The magic power is here spoken of as an arrow.

This song is said to have a double meaning and to be phallic in character. This phase of the society was disapproved by a class of the older men of the tribe, as tending to licentiousness among the young people.

SIXTH SONG—FAST SONG FOR DRAMATIC MOVEMENT IN "SHOOTING" ONE ANOTHER

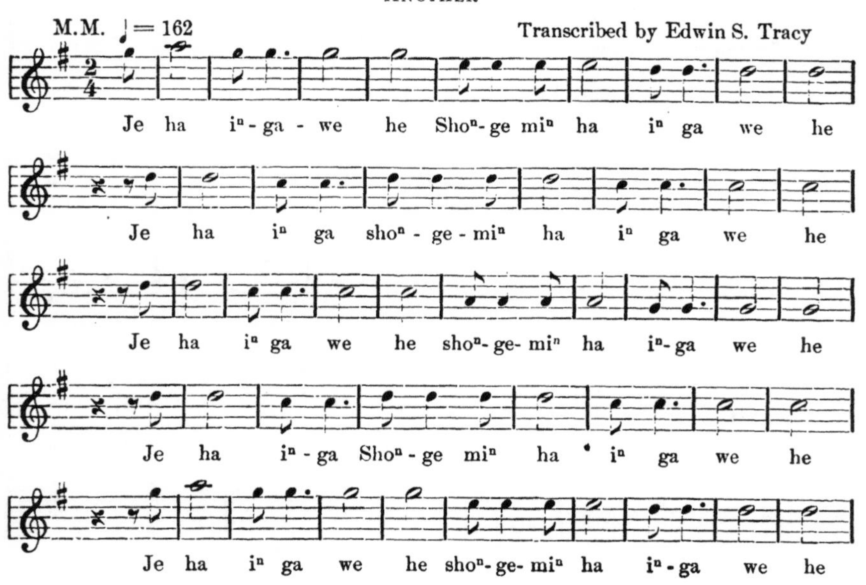
M.M. ♩ = 162
Transcribed by Edwin S. Tracy
Je ha iⁿ - ga - we he Shoⁿ- ge miⁿ ha iⁿ ga we he
Je ha iⁿ ga shoⁿ - ge - miⁿ ha iⁿ ga we he
Je ha iⁿ ga we he shoⁿ- ge- miⁿ ha iⁿ- ga we he
Je ha iⁿ - ga Shoⁿ - ge miⁿ ha iⁿ ga we he
Je ha iⁿ ga we he shoⁿ- ge- miⁿ ha iⁿ - ga we he

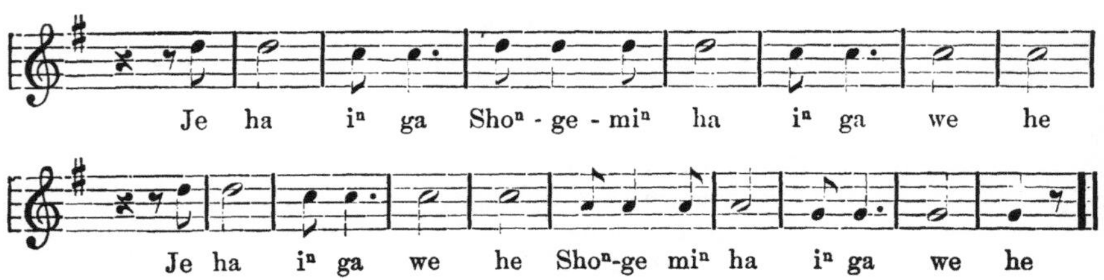

TEÇO^{N}'S SONG OF REVENGE

Je ha i^{n} ga we he sho^{n}ge mi^{n}ha i^{n} ga we he
Je ha i^{n} ga sho^{n}ge mi^{n}ha in ga we he
Je ha i^{n} ga we he sho^{n}ge mi^{n} ha i^{n} ga we he
Je ha i^{n} ga sho^{n}ge mi^{n}ha i^{n} ga we he
Je ha i^{n} ga we he sho^{n}ge mi^{n} ha i^{n} ga we he
Je ha i^{n} ga sho^{n}ge mi^{n} ha i^{n} ga we he
Je ha i^{n} ga we he sho^{n}ge mi^{n} ha i^{n} ga we he

This song refers to the killing of a horse by magic because the owner had offended one of the members of the society. The incident is said to have occurred early in the last century. The only recognizable word is *sho^{n}ge,* horse; the others are obscured by syllables.

SEVENTH SONG—FAST SONG FOR DRAMATIC MOVEMENT IN "SHOOTING" MEMBERS

M.M. ♩= 160 (Sung in octaves) Transcribed by Edwin S. Tracy

A- gu - di wa tha xta ha A- gu- di wa - tha

Dots indicate pulsations of the voice

xta ha Zhu - ga - di wa tha xta Zhu - ga - di

wa tha xta da ha A - gu - di wa tha xta ha

A - gu - di wa tha xta A - gu - di wa - tha

xta ha A - gu - di wa tha xta ha

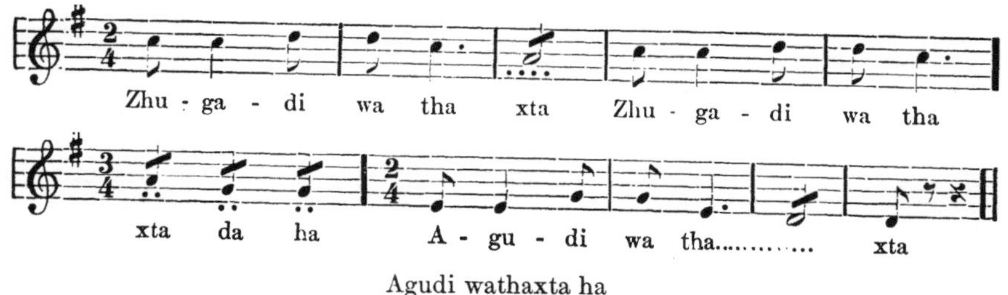
Zhu - ga - di wa tha xta Zhu - ga - di wa tha
xta da ha A - gu - di wa tha............ xta

Agudi wathaxta ha
Agudi wathaxta ha
Zhugadi wathaxta tha
Zhugadi wathaxta tha ha
Agudi wathaxta tha ha
Agudi wathaxta

Literal translation: *Agudi,* in what part of the body; *wathaxta,* shall I bite him; *zhugadi,* in the body.

The song relates to the story of two members of the Shell society who were determined to kill each other by the power of their magic. One of these men was fond of the wild potato and used to go at the proper season to a certain spot to gather them. His opponent knew of this habit and exercised his magic to have a rattlesnake hid in the grass near this place. When the man went to dig potatoes he was bitten by the snake and died—not of the bite, it was claimed, but from the effect of the magic that put the snake there. This song dates from the early part of the last century.

Eighth Song—Slow Song, Sung when Thunder is First Heard in Spring

♩ = 144 Transcribed by Edwin S. Tracy

I-e tha ha ha ha I-e she-moⁿ tha ha...... ha
ha I-e tha ha...... ha ha I-e she-moⁿ tha ha.........................
I-e tha ha...... ha ha I-e she-moⁿ tha ha...... ha ha
I-e tha ha...... ha ha I-e she-moⁿ tha ha......
ha ha...... I-e she-moⁿ tha ha...... ha ha...... I-e she-

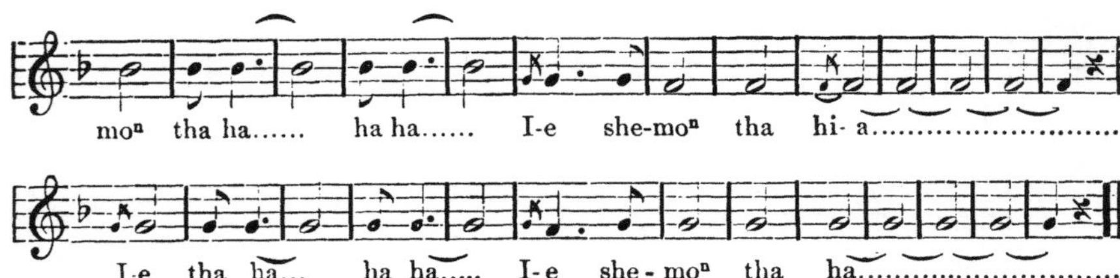
mo^n tha ha...... ha ha...... I-e she-mo^n tha hi- a........................
I-e tha ha... ha ha..... I-e she - mo^n tha ha........................

Ie tha ha ha ha
Ie shemo^n tha ha ha ha
Ie tha ha ha ha
Ie shemo^n tha hia
Ie tha ha ha ha
Ie shemo^n tha ha ha ha
Ie tha ha ha ha
Ie shemo^n tha ha ha ha
Ie shemo^n tha ha ha ha
Ie shemo^n tha ha ha ha
Ie shemo^n tha hia
Ie tha ha ha ha
Ie shemo^n tha ha

Literal translation: *Ie*, speech, or command; *shemo^n*, yonder moving; *tha*, plural sign; all the rest are vocables.

This song was sung by the members of the lodge of the "eldest son" when the thunder was first heard in the spring. This was the signal of the awakening to new activity of all the life on the earth. The words mean, it was explained, "the command of those yonder [the Thunder] I have obeyed."

The following account by one of the writers gives an eye-witness's picture of the dramatic movement at a meeting of the society:

When I was a lad at the mission school I used to steal away and go to the village to see the performance of the ceremony of the Shell Society. The meetings of this ancient organization were usually occasions of great interest to the tribe, for a general invitation would be given to the people to witness that part of the rite which was open to the public.

At these gatherings particular care was observed by young and old to appear in the best constumes that could be obtained, so that while waiting for admission to the spacious earth lodge the great concourse of spectators, clad in colors most pleasing to the savage eye, would present a brilliant appearance.

At the first sound of the resonant drum, and as the member of the society who was honored with the invitation to preside at that important instrument sang a bar or two of his song by way of leading and opening the ceremony, every man, woman, and child rushed for the long entranceway in order to secure the best positions in the lodge from which to observe the "dance" advantageously. Being small and active, I used to push my way between the legs of the grownup people, and thus manage to get in advance and find a good place where I could see the whole ceremony to my heart's content.

The first song and the accompanying initial procession of the members around the central fireplace of the great circular room—the men, tall and majestic, moving with stately tread to the measured rhythm of the music, and the women following modestly, but with no less dignity—never failed to impress my mind with the earnestness of the fraternity. Immediately following the termination of this opening procession, a song in faster time would be struck up and the solemn movements of the members would suddenly change to motions full of dramatic action. Each person would menacingly thrust forward an otter skin with grinning head, which he carried in his hands. The members seemed as though determined to destroy each other with the magic power contained in the otter, and everyone uttered a peculiar cry which gave efficacy to the sacred skin. Suddenly a man would fall rigid to the hard floor, trembling in every limb, as though shot with a gun or arrow; then another and another would fall, while those who did the "shooting" moved on with triumphant cries. After a moment of writhing in seeming agony those who had been "shot" would rise and take their turn at "shooting" others. All this "shooting" and falling and the uttering of mystic cries would overwhelm me with awe, for it was all so strange and so far beyond my understanding.

I often witnessed this peculiar ceremony when a boy, and, like other careless observers, I as often went away impressed only by the songs, the solemn procession, the rhythmic movements of the "dance," and the fine regalia of the society, with never a thought that beneath all this outward show there might be some meaning so profound in its nature as to support a member in the maintenance of his dignity while going through acts which on ordinary occasions would make him appear frivolous.

In later years, when I began the serious study of the customs and cults of my people, I learned that in this as well as in other rites there were, back of the ceremonies given publicly, teachings made known only to the initiated, teachings worthy of careful thought and reflection. Knowing this to be true, I sought in various ways to obtain a knowledge of the ritual and teachings of the Shell Society without having to become a member, but failed in each attempt. It chanced, however, in 1898, that a novitiate who had lost his shell, learning that I was to visit the reservation, wrote to me to bring him a shell. From the meager description he gave me I was not sure of the kind he wanted, so I purchased a few of several varieties and took them out with me. When I exhibited my collection the new member looked them carefully over, but was not sure which was the right kind. To his great relief, the member of the society by whom he was initiated appeared on the scene, and we placed before him the pile of shells. He separated the right kind from the others, and then waited for me to speak.

"I have brought these shells," I said, "for your friend and for you, but for my services I desire to know something of the inner teachings of your society."

"A request of that kind," he replied, "usually comes with proper fees and ceremonies observed by us all, and with the recommendation of members in good standing, but since you seem to be in earnest to know something about the teachings of our society, and as we are in need of the shells, I will waive all this and give you the beginning only of the story, which is long and beautiful. There are two kinds of shell used in our society," he continued, selecting two from the pile and holding them up; "one is male and the other is female. The distinction so made comes from the story I am about to tell you."

Then he proceeded to give me a paraphrase of the story of the origin of the society, which was later obtained in full, together with the ritual, songs, and account given in the foregoing pages.

Ceremonies on the Death of a Member

On the death of a member a meeting of the society was called, and the regular opening ceremonies already described (see p. 521) took place. It was said that "on such an occasion death is not simulated, but real for one of the members has passed from this life." The body of the deceased, arrayed in his best clothes, with his face painted, in accordance with the rules of the society, was carried to the dwelling in which the society held its meetings, where it was seated in the member's accustomed place. During the ceremony in the presence of the dead no one spoke except when the rites required, and all the members when not actively engaged sat with bowed heads. The dead man was the only one with head erect. On such occasions outsiders were afraid to go in when the doors were opened, for it was said that in times past onlookers had been killed by magic. All the regalia which the dead member had purchased the right to wear was removed from him at the proper time and returned to his lodge. Nothing of that character was buried with the dead. After the lodges had been dismissed in the manner already described, the dead body was removed and given the ordinary form of burial.

Magic Ceremony for Punishing Offenders

When the contents of the Sacred Tent of War were deposited in the Peabody Museum of Harvard University, a pack was found among

Fig. 113. Pack belonging to a lodge of the Shell society.

the articles which had no connection with the duties or ceremonies pertaining to the We'zhi^{n}shte gens as keepers of the rites of war. It has since been learned that this pack had belonged to one of the lodges of the Shell society. Big Elk was the keeper of this pack and as he was a chief and leading man not only in his own gens, the We'zhi^{n}shte, but in the Council of Seven, he felt at liberty to store this pack in the Tent of War. At his death and during the general disturbance of tribal customs which soon followed, the pack remained with the articles that properly belonged in the Tent of War and so passed into the possession of the writers in 1884 when these were given to them to be deposited at Cambridge, Mass. A photograph was taken of this pack (fig. 113; Peabody Museum no. 37560) as it came into the hands of the writers, just as it was left by Big Elk.

This pack had long been regarded with great fear, as it was believed to contain virulent poison. So great was this dread that a promise was exacted of the writers that if the pack was opened extreme caution should be used, as it was feared that whoever handled the contents would surely die in consequence of the sacrilege. The sprays of cedar thrust through the strings that tied the pack had nothing to do with it, so far as is known; these may have been added in recognition of

FIG. 114. Largest bag in pack (fig. 113).

the Tent of War in which the pack was kept. When the pack was opened at the Peabody Museum it was found to contain some queer little boxes made like trunks, evidently toys, dating from the early part of the last century, in which were little bundles containing red paint, a few shells, and dusty fragments impossible of identification.

Six bags were found in the pack; these were woven with two kinds of coarse yarn or twine, one of wool, the other of vegetable fiber. This material was of white manufacture and was probably obtained from traders; the weaving was native. The general hue of the bags is reddish brown.

The largest bag (fig. 114; Peabody Museum no. 48265) found in the pack measures 11 by 9½ inches; it contained a similar bag (fig. 115; Peabody Museum no. 48288) slightly smaller, its dimensions being 10 by 7½ inches. In this bag were various little boxes and bundles containing down painted red, such as is seen on the heads of the members of the Shell society.

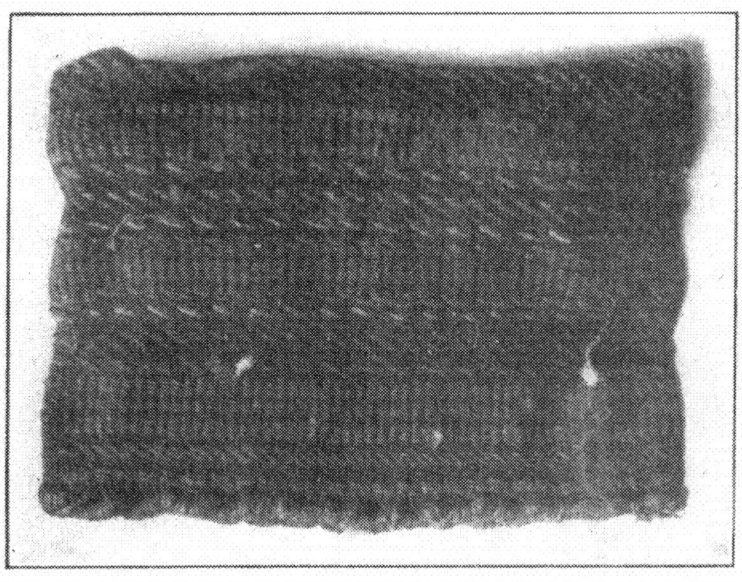

Fig. 115. Bag found in pack (fig. 113).

Fig. 116. Bag found in pack (fig. 113).

The next smaller bag (fig. 116; Peabody Museum no. 48318) is 7¾ by 6½ inches. Its contents were: A bladder package (fig. 117, *a;* Peabody Museum no. 48301) containing paint, probably carbonate of copper; a bladder package (fig. 117, *b;* Peabody Museum no. 48305) containing gum; a similar package (fig. 117, *c;* Peabody Museum no. 48300); a similar package (fig. 117, *d;* Peabody Museum no. 48306) containing two little brushes of stiff animal hair; a package of cloth (fig. 117, *e;* Peabody Museum no. 48292) containing gum and swan's-down.

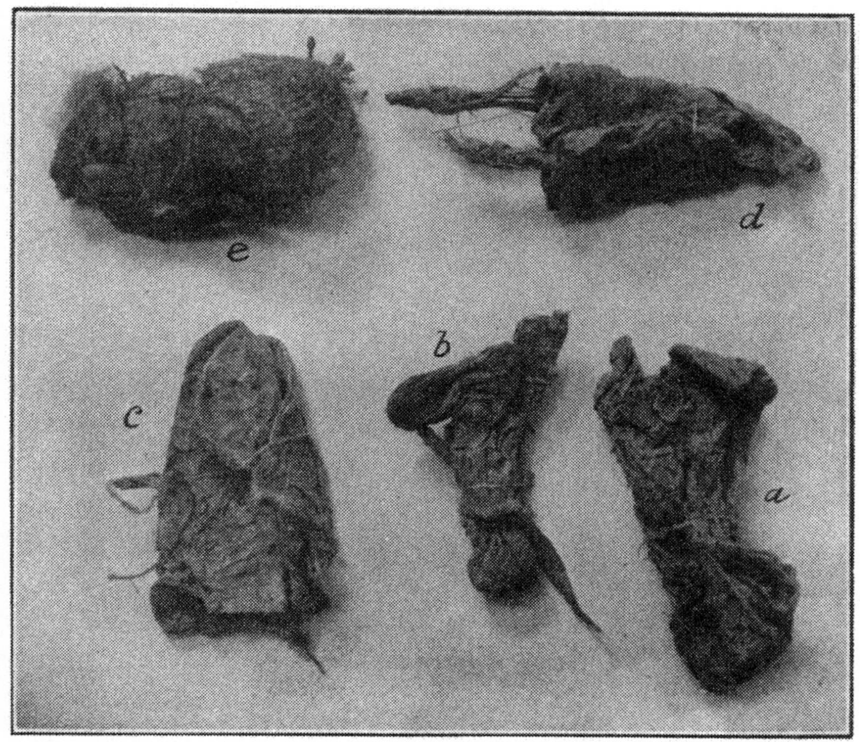

Fig. 117. Objects found in bag (fig. 116).

The fourth size bag (fig. 118; Peabody Museum no. 48289), 6 by 4 inches, is of a finer weave than the other bags and contained packages wrapped in corn husks. One of these (fig. 119, *a;* Peabody Museum no. 48281) inclosed a dried caterpillar. The contents of the other husk packages (fig. 119, *b*, *c*) had turned to dust; nothing else remained when the pack was opened.

The fifth bag (fig. 120; Peabody Museum no. 48319), 4½ by 4 inches, contained a package incased in a skin covering (fig. 119, *e;* Peabody Museum no. 48285) of red paint, a bit of cloth of native weaving, vegetal fiber inclosing a small piece of mica and tied up with shed buffalo hair and swan's-down (fig. 119, *d;* Peabody Museum no. 48286), and a red stone concretion attached to a long thong (fig. 119, *f;* Peabody Museum no. 48287).

The sixth bag (fig. 121; Peabody Museum no. 48295) measures only 4 by 2¾ inches; it contained small skin bundles in which were galena, green paint, and carbonate of copper. These bundles, which were tied together, may be seen in the illustration, projecting from the bag.

Besides the foregoing articles there is a tobacco bag (fig. 122, *a;* Peabody Museum no. 47818) embroidered with porcupine quills. The groundwork is yellow, the figure of the eagle is in red, the tip of the tail, the wings, and the beak white. The border is of alternating

FIG. 118. Bag found in pack (fig. 113).

blocks of white and reddish yellow, and the fringe is of buckskin. Near the bag lay a figure cut from dressed skin, about 17¾ inches long (fig. 122, *b;* Peabody Museum no. 47819). The headdress is slightly more than 2½ inches in height. The arms measure about 4½ inches in length. The figure is cut into two parts and sewed up on the sides of the arms, legs and body, and head, making it a bag with separate compartments. A slit in the back afforded the opening through which articles could be inserted or withdrawn. This figure remained a puzzle to the writers for a long time. Finally its photograph was recognized by a member of the Shell society and its purpose was explained by Pe′degahi, an old chief, no longer living, a member of the Shell society, who had seen this figure used by Big Elk (the latter died in

1848 or 1849). It is said that this figure-shaped bag had come down to Big Elk through eight generations. Pe′degahi remembered the names of six of the former owners of this interesting relic. He said that there used to be a ritual connected with the figure but that it had been lost.

It was explained that the figure represented the society. It was called *Gahi′ge to^{n}ga*, "great chief." The head stood for the *u′zhu*, leader or master of the entire society, whose symbol was the eagle. The left arm was the "eldest son," representing the sun and the black bear. In the bag made by this arm were kept the poisons used for

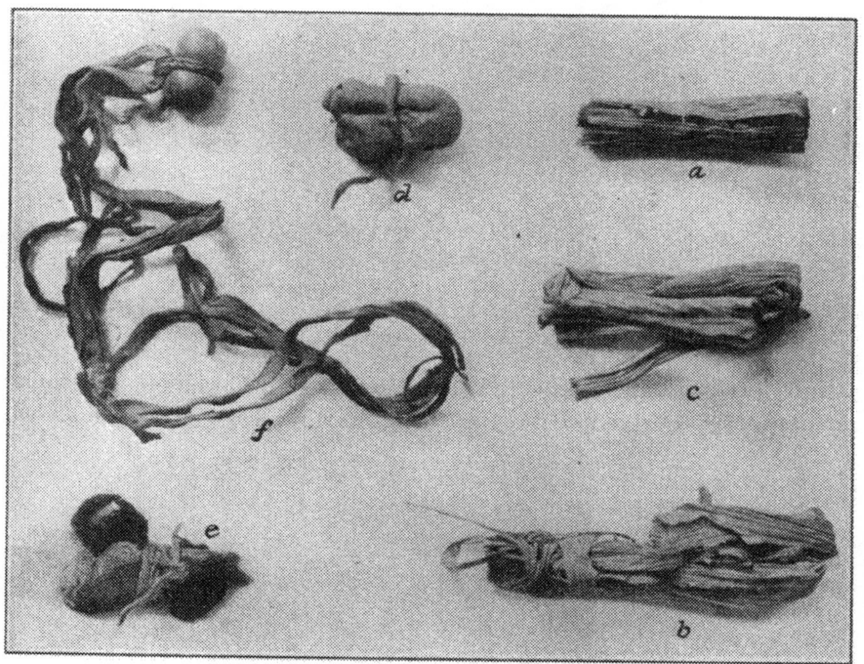

FIG. 119. Contents of bags (figs. 118, 120).

punishment. The right arm was the "second son," representing the stars and the elk. In this bag were kept the roots used as medicine for rheumatism. The left leg was the "daughter," representing the moon and the buffalo. In the bag formed by this leg were kept two shells, male and female. The right leg was the "youngest son," representing the earth and the deer. In this bag were kept medicines for curing diarrhea. It was explained that the left arm and the left leg "went together." It will be noted, as stated above, that these represented the "eldest son" and the "daughter"—the two that were placed diagonally to each other in the arrangement of places in the lodge. The arm contained poisons for punishment; the leg, the magic shells which made it possible to administer them, so that the functions of this left arm and leg, which "went together," were

FIG. 120. Bag found in pack (fig. 113).

also related and made effectual because male and female. The right arm and leg represented brothers, the earth and the stars, and both

FIG. 121. Bag found in pack (fig. 113).

contained medicines for healing. It was said in explanation that "the punishment (effected through this figure) was directed by Wako^{n}'da to keep the people in order and to check crime, as molesting wives or daughters and destroying property, and so causing mischief to arise in the tribe."

The statement concerning the poison was rather vague and it has not been possible to procure the plants for identification. The poison was made from the root of a vine of which there are four varieties. These were described as follows: "One grows on the ground, one runs on trees and has red leaves, the third has but few leaves, and the

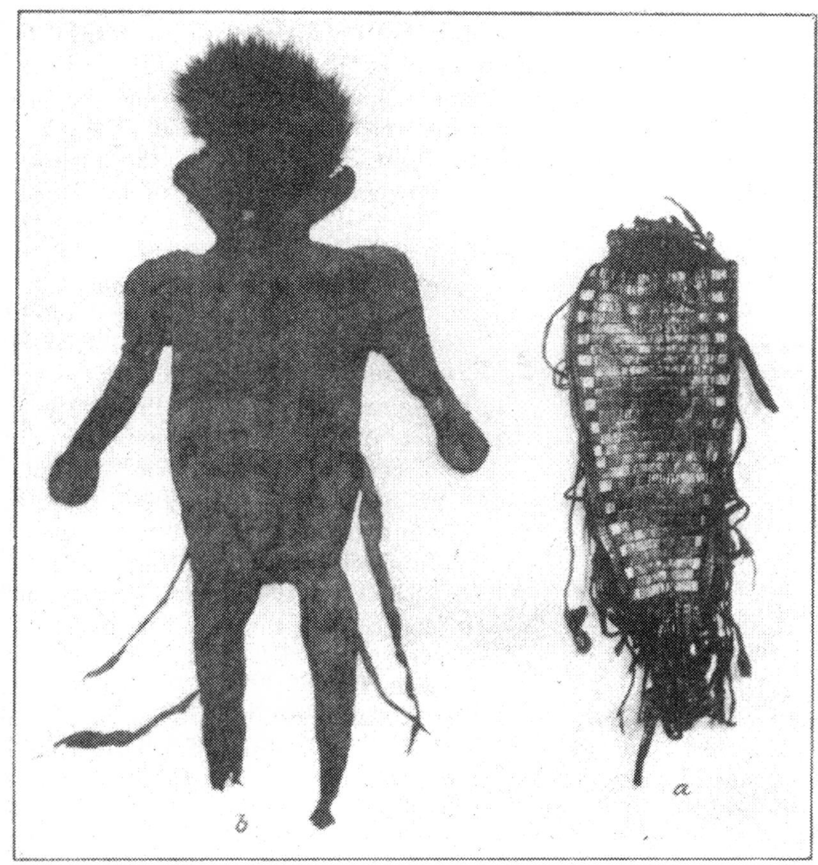

FIG. 122. Tobacco bag (*a*) and figure (*b*) found in pack (fig. 113).

fourth has many rootlets clinging to the bark of the tree. It is the root of the latter variety from which the poison was made." To this root was added the decaying flesh of the lizard and "a bug that swims on the surface of the water." These were said to be the ingredients of the poison kept in the left arm of the figure. It was explained: "The left is always first; we begin to paint ourselves on the left and follow the sun."

The figure has a roach of hair made of a bit of "bear skin," the hair so arranged as to stand up. The zigzag lines from the eyes were said to be tears. The moons on the shoulders were all the gibbous, or "dying," moon, and signified death. The circle represented the sun. In this figure of the sun was kept the bear's claw used when drawing the outline of the condemned man. The red lines down the arms represent the lightning. This figure was said to represent a man whom the Monster flayed, using his skin as a receptacle; and the Monster told the man and his wife to make this figure in imitation of the human-skin bag and to use it in this ceremony. It is said that Big Elk had a pair of moccasins made from the paws of the bear. Whether or not these moccasins were worn at the ceremony when this figure was used no one now living can tell nor do the moccasins now exist so far as can be learned. The lost ritual is said to have explained all the parts of the figure, even the use of the strings.

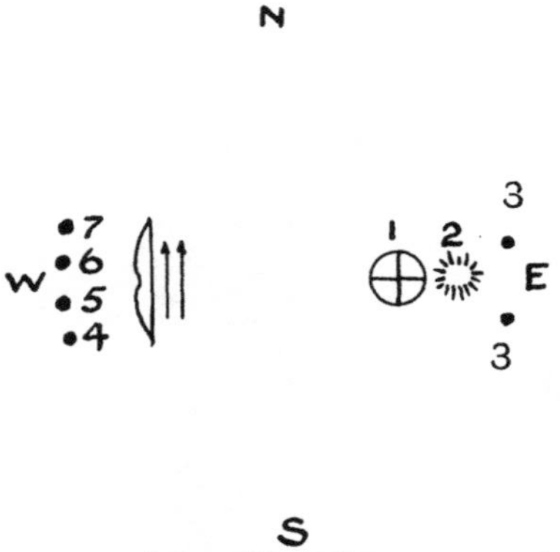

N W E S 1 2 3 3 4 5 6 7

FIG. 123. Diagram illustrating arrangement of Shell society at secret meeting for punishment of an offender. 1, Fireplace and four sticks; 2, pile of earth; 3, 3, servants; 4, 5, 6, 7, masters of the four lodges.

When a man committed an offense that seemed to demand punishment the society met at night to consider the matter, at which time both the act and the man's character were discussed. If the society determined to punish the man, then this figure was brought out. It seemed to stand as a symbol of the united purpose of the society, for on such an occasion the members had to act as a unit. The meeting when they were to take action occurred in the early morning. The servants had already been dispatched to a secret place where they had excavated a circular space for a fireplace and piled toward the east the earth taken out. Four sticks pointing to the four directions were laid in the fireplace. Before sunrise the members went forth singly from their homes and gathered quietly at the place appointed for the meeting. They sat in a circle. The four masters, representing the four "children," took their places at the west, facing the east. A small bow, about 2 feet long, and two arrows with flint points, provided with shafts about 2 feet long, were placed in front of the four masters. (Fig. 123.)

When all were seated, the man who had suffered the wrong laid his pipe down in front of the masters, west of the bow. He then ordered the servant to take the pipe and a live coal to a certain man and offer it to him. If the man accepted the pipe and lighted it, he signified that he was willing to draw the figure of the offender on the ground. The pipe had to be lighted with a live coal which was carried in a split stick. If the man refused to accept the pipe, the servant carried it back to the accuser, who designated another man. The servant then carried the pipe to the second man. If he refused, the accuser could select a third, fourth, and fifth person. These selections could be repeated four times. There is a tradition that twice the pipe was offered the full number of times and every time refused, so that the punishment of the offender had to be abandoned. Sometimes the pipe was accepted by the first man, but more often it was passed to two or three persons before one was found to accept it, for all must agree and promise to keep this session of the society and its action a secret. When the pipe was accepted it was lighted by the one accepting it and was smoked by all the members of the society, an act which signified that all consented. The accuser then refilled the pipe and ordered it taken to the leader of another lodge, all the members of which smoked it. It was then refilled and sent to the leader of still another lodge, all the members of which smoked it. Once more the pipe was refilled and sent to the fourth lodge, in which it was smoked by all the members. During this ceremony the pipe had started from each of the four lodges and had passed four times around the members, thus binding all, both as lodges and as individuals, to secrecy and to the fulfillment of the act contemplated. The pipe was then returned to the accuser. The latter then bade the servant take the bear's claw from the breast of the figure to the man who had accepted the pipe. Then the masters consulted together in order to determine how many days the offender should be allowed to live. After their decision was made, the man who had received the claw rose and recounted his faithfulness to the teachings of the society and that of his fathers before him. Then he turned to the left and laid his left hand on the head of each member, saying as he did so: "To trust you with my action." Then he stood at the north, where he intended the feet of the figure to be, and faced the north. Then he turned and placed the bear's claw at a point which would be the middle of the top of the figure's head; and without lifting his hand from the earth he made a continuous outline

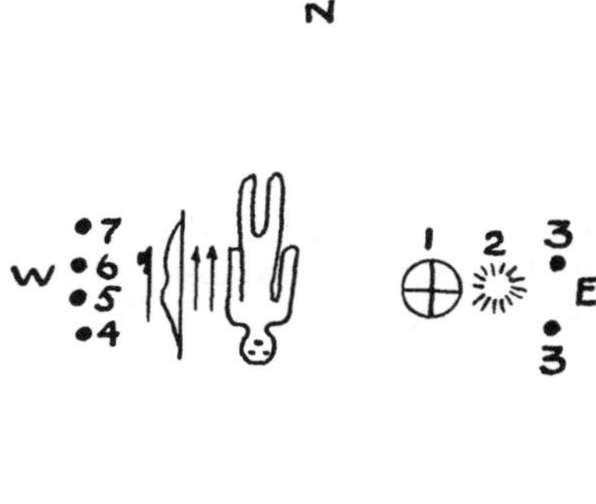

FIG. 124. Diagram illustrating final ceremony of secret meeting of Shell society. 1, Fireplace and four sticks; 2, pile of earth; 3, 3, servants; 4, 5, 6, 7, masters of the four lodges.

of a man, beginning at the left on the top of the head and passing to the right around the figure, ending at the point where he began. Next he made the left eye, then the nose, then the right eye, then the mouth, and from the lower lip he drew a line down to the heart, which was indicated by a circle, and above this the two lungs. (Fig. 124.) When the drawing was done, he laid the bear's claw on the left shoulder and then ordered the servant to pick it up and take it to the accuser.

The accuser now ordered the servant to take the bow and arrows from before the masters and hand them to the one who had drawn the figure. This man might refuse to receive them. If he refused, the servant was told to take them to another man. On his way to do this he had first to circle the fire. Sometimes the office of the bow and arrows was refused several times. At last a man was found who accepted them. He then arose and passing to the left laid his left hand on each member's head, saying as he did so: "To trust you with my action." When he reached his place, poison was brought him from the master and he poisoned the arrows. Then he stepped to the left of the figure, stooped, and fitted the arrows to the bow, pulled the string slightly, but did not shoot. He then passed around in front of the row of members and stopped again at the left of the figure and made another feint. This was done four times and at the last he shot the arrow into the heart of the figure and left it standing there, and returned by the left to his place.

The masters now rose and said: *Kiwashko^{n}iga ha!*—"Let each man take care of himself!"

The members then threw off their robes and each left singly, going his own way. The servants gathered up the robes and the other belongings of the officers and members and took them to their owners and keepers.

Two servants now watched the offender, "who was soon taken sick." When this occurred, it was reported to the four masters, who gathered at night in a tent, without fire, where they sang low and continued to sing until the man died.

A story is told that once when these rites were in progress, the offender—who chanced to be a member of the society—came upon the secret session. While he did not know certainly that he was to be the victim, he suspected it. He joined in the proceedings but moved about the wrong way in order to break the spell and so prevented the completion of the rites. The place where the meeting was held was on a high bluff overlooking the Missouri river. Suddenly some of the members rushed on the man, drove him to the edge, and threw him over, but by his magic he turned himself into a bird as he fell, and by this artifice gained in safety the other side of the river, whence he piped to the disappointed avengers. This story is repeated by members of both the Shell and Pebble societies as representing their own experience.

There are many stories of turning the otter-skin mystery bags (fig. 110) into live otters.

Some old men assert that the reason why the shell is sacred and is honored by this society is because the Omaha first lived beside the great water where the shells are found.

THE I^{N}'KUGTHI ATHI^{N} (PEBBLE SOCIETY)

The literal translation of the name of the I^{n}'kugthi athi^{n} (*i^{n}*, "pebble;" *kugthi*, "translucent;" *athi^{n}*, "to have or possess") society is "They who have the translucent pebble."

Membership was gained by virtue of a dream, or vision, of water or its representative, the pebble, or the water monster, received when fasting. The water monster was said to be a huge creature in animal form that lashed the water with its mighty tail. It was generally spoken of as living in a lake.

The members of the Pebble society wore very little clothing, sometimes only the breechcloth, but the body was painted with devices indicating the animals or monsters seen in the dreams. In this respect the Pebble society differed from the Shell society. The members of the latter made it a point to wear gaily ornamented apparel.

The meetings of the Pebble society were not held at stated intervals and only through the summer. The opening part of every session was secret; only members could be present.

Opportunity was once given to one of the writers to be present; while no portion of the proceedings was explained the following movements were observed:

Back of the fire calico was spread on the ground—a gift from the man who gave the feast and so made the meeting of the society possible. All the members sat around the sides of the lodge. When the members had gathered, some one announced that all were present. Then four men from different parts of the line of members went, one at a time, to a place on the south side of the lodge where there was powdered charcoal on a board. As each man came to this place he stooped and laid his hands on the earth and then passed them over his arms and over his body to the feet. The movement seemed to be similar to that made on a man who had just safely passed through some difficult and dangerous experience, in order to come in touch with one who had been the recipient of some great power. After this action he placed the fingers of his right hand in the charcoal and made a black line from his mouth down the length of one arm, and a similar line from his mouth down the other arm. After that he made black lines on his body with his blackened finger tips. Then he took some of the black powder in the palm of his hand and went back to his lodge. He then painted the symbolic black lines from the mouth down the length of the arm on all the members of his lodge. While he was doing this, another leader went to the south side, and standing before the black paint made the same movement with his hands on the earth and on his body; he then painted himself and returned to paint the other members of his lodge. When all four leaders had touched the earth and had painted themselves and the members of their lodges, they went to the rear of the lodge and stood facing the east, with the offering of calico at their feet. Then all four bent over and made movements as though retching. Finally they spat out their pebbles. They next circled the fire and passed to the end of the row of members on the south side and "shot" four with their pebbles. These four members fell rigid to the earth. The four leaders then circled the fire, as did also the four who had been "shot;" then these four "shot" another four, who after circling the fire "shot" still another four, and so on by fours until all had been "shot" and all the members were moving about the fire. No songs accompanied these complex movements. When all the members had been "shot," they took their respective places and sat down. The drum was then taken to the lodge sitting at the south and the members of the choir took their places about the drum and began a slow song. This was the signal that the secret session was closed.

After the secret ceremonies guests were admitted. The members rose in their places as the outsiders entered. The public part of the ceremony consisted in moving around the fire in single file and "shooting" one another with the pebble or some other small object. The hand which simulated "shooting" was shielded by the wing of an eagle held in the other hand. Any part of the body might be struck. The person "shot" immediately pressed his hand on the spot supposed to be touched, assumed a tragic attitude, then fell to the ground and lay rigid. Much more action was observed in the Pebble society by the person "shooting" and the person "shot" than in the Shell society, which made the exercises of the former the more dramatic. The magic cries also were different; those of the Pebble society were lower in tone and were considered to be more impressive. The songs of dismissal were differently rendered in the two societies. In the Shell society, it will be recalled, the master of each lodge led in the singing and each lodge had its song, which was sung in the order of the ages of the four "children." In the Pebble society each member had his own song of dismissal and when the time came for the meeting to close all sang simultaneously. The effect on an outsider was anything but agreeable—it was "like bedlam," and only when one looked into the faces of the members and noted their intense earnestness was it possible to conceive how each man could hold to his own song against that of his equally vociferous neighbor.

The exact organization of the society could not be definitely learned, except that it was divided into four groups or lodges.

The members of this society treated sickness by mechanical means—bleeding, sucking out the disturbing object, and practising

FIG. 125. Waki'dezhi^{n}ga.

a kind of massage which consisted in kneading and pulling on the region below the ribs, a rather severe and painful operation, called by the Omaha *ni'xathito^{n}*.

The rituals of this society could not be fully obtained. Each group seems to have had its ritual and these may have been parts of the entire ceremony. It is doubtful if the complete set of rituals is now known to any living Omaha. The following, a part of the opening ritual, was obtained some years ago from the former leader, Waki'-dezhi^{n}ga (fig. 125), who is now dead. It deals with Creation and the cosmic forces.

Opening Ritual

1. Mi i tho^{n} tathisho^{n}, ni′kashiga
2. A′wage ego^{n}, ni′kashiga
3. Wani′ta dado^{n}, to^{n}ga ke shti wo^{n}
4. Bthu′ga xti uthe′wi^{n} i ego^{n}, ni′kashiga
5. Wagthi′shka dado^{n} ke shti wo^{n}
6. Bthu′ga xti uthe′wi^{n} i ego^{n}
7. A′wa te ego^{n} i iei^{n} te
8. Eno^{n} xti o^{n} xti thi^{n}ke ego^{n}
9. Ethe′go^{n} wathe′ go^{n}
10. I^{n} ço^{n}′ to^{n}ga te tho^{n}
11. Mo^{n}′xe itha′ugthexti p’u′tho^{n}
12. Mo^{n}′xe itha′ugthexti
13. Zhi^{n}′ga the ui′the u^{n}gi′kaxe ta i te tho^{n}zha
14. Ato^{n}′ tha i te sheto^{n} ui′the u^{n}gi′kaxe ta i te
15. Eshe a bado^{n}

16. Edi uwa′to^{n} thi^{n}ke
17. Peto^{n}nuga tha to^{n} she, pa ke çnede′ a xti no^{n}zhi^{n} ego^{n}
18. Pa′hi ke e′to^{n} thi^{n}ge′ xti no^{n}zhi^{n} ego^{n}
19. A′wate ego^{n} to^{n}de ke uti^{n}′ ihe′the go^{n}

* * * * * * *

20. I′uçishto^{n} athi^{n}′ ga′ha i de
21. Ni′kashiga, ni′kazhide ma shetho^{n}
22. Zhi^{n}ga ui′the u^{n}gi′kaxe ta i te tho^{n}zha

23. Edi uwa′to^{n} sho^{n}′to^{n}ga nuga ede hu tithe′the ki
24. I′thapithi^{n} xti to^{n}′de ke, thap’o^{n}′de xti
25. Thapo^{n}′de uthi′shi xti, thapo’^{n}′de go^{n}
26. Ui′e ga′xa bi e go^{n}

27. Edi uwa′to^{n} he′ga ede, pa′hi ke zhi′de xti
28. I′thapithi^{n} xti, a′hi^{n} ke na′di^{n}di^{n} the no^{n}zhi^{n} ego^{n}
29. I′thapithi^{n} xti gaha′ itho^{n}tho^{n} ego^{n}
30. I′thapithi^{n} xti giu^{n}′ the go^{n}
31. I^{n}sha′ge we′utha ga′xa bi e go^{n}

Literal translation

1. *Mi*, sun; *i*, come; *tathisho^{n}*, in that direction east; *nikashiga*, people.

2. *Awage ego^{n}*, of whatever kind; *nikashiga*, people.

3. *Wani′ta*, animals; *dado^{n}*, every kind; *to^{n}ga*, great; *ke* indicates that they spread over the ground in vast numbers; *shti wo^{n}*, they also.

4. *Bthu′ga*, all; *xti*, truly; *uthewi^{n}*, gathered; *i ego^{n}*, it came to pass.

5. *Wagthishka*, insects; *dado^{n}*, of every kind; *ke*, spread (scattered over an extent of ground); *shti wo^{n}*, they also.

6. *Bthu′ga*, all; *xti*, truly; *uthe′wi^{n}*, gathered; *i ego^{n}*, it came to pass.

7. *A′wa*, how; *te ego^{n}*, what manner; *i*, come; *iei^{n}te*, did they come?

8. *Eno^n xti*, it alone; *o^n xti*, the greatest; *thi^{n}ke*, sitting; *ego^n*, like.

9. *Ethe'go^n*, to think; *wathe'go^n*, to cause.

10. *I^n*, stone; *ço^n*, white or pale; *to^{n}ga*, great, big; *te tho^n*, that stood.

11. *Mo^n'xe*, sky, heavens; *ithaugthe*, all the way up; *xti*, verily; *p'u'tho^n*, in a mist, as steaming.

12. *Mo^{n}xe*, sky, heavens; *ithaugthe*, all the way up; *xti*, verily.

13. *Zhi^n'ga*, little ones; *the*, this; *ui'the*, to speak of, as a theme; *u^{n}gikaxe*, they shall make of me; *ta i te*, shall; *tho^{n}zha*, however.

14. *Ato^n'*, whatever distance; *tha i te*, they travel; *sheto^n*, so long; *ui'the*, to speak of, as a theme; *u^{n}gi'kaxe*, they shall make of me (as an object of veneration); *ta i te*, shall.

15. *Eshe*, you have said; *a bado^n*, they have said.

16. *Edi*, there; *uwa'to^n*, next in order or rank; *thi^{n}ke*, sitting.

17. *Peto^{n}nuga*, male of the crane; *tha to^n she*, thou who standest; *pa*, beak; *ke* indicates length; *çnede'*, long; *a xti*, very; *no^{n}zhi^n*, stands; *ego^n*, like.

18. *Pa'hi*, neck; *ke*, the length; *e'to^n*, the same in length; *thi^{n}ge'*, none; *xti*, verily, in truth; *no^{n}zhi^n*, standing; *ego^n*, like, and so.

19. *A'wate ego^n*, in a manner; *to^{n}de*, ground, earth; *ke*, the (length); *uti^n'*, to pick at or strike; *ihethe*, quickly; *go^n*, like.

20. *Iuçishto^n*, words that are not true; *athi^n'*, to have; *ga'xa*, make; *i*, plural; *de*, shall.

21. *Ni'kashiga*, people; *ni'kazhide*, red people; *ma*, plural, they; *shetho^n*, you who are.

22. *Zhi^{n}ga*, little ones; *uithe*, a theme; *u^{n}gi'kaxe*, they shall make of me; *ta i te*, shall; *tho^{n}zha*, however.

23. *Edi*, there; *uwa'to^n*, next in order or rank standing; *sho^n'to^{n}ga-nuga*, male gray wolf; *ede*, a; *hu*, voice; *tithethe*, to send or utter; *ki*, and.

24. *I'thapithi^n*, without effort; *xti*, verily; *to^n'de*, the earth; *ke*, lying, or that lay; *thap'o^n'de*, to make to vibrate with the voice; *xti*, verily.

25. *Thap'o^n'de*, to make to vibrate; *uthi'shi*, impossible; *xti*, verily; *thap'o^{n}de*, to make vibrate; *go^n*, like.

26. *Ui'e*, something to speak of; *gaxa*, made; *bi e go^n*, they have.

27. *Edi*, there; *uwa'to^n*, next in order or rank; *he'ga*, buzzard; *ede*, a; *pa'hi*, neck; *ke*, long; *zhi'de*, red; *xti*, truly.

28. *I'thapithi^n*, without effort, slowly; *xti*, verily; *a'hi^n*, wings; *ke*, the; *na'di^{n}di^n*, dry; *the*, make; *no^{n}zhi^n*, stand; *ego^n*, like.

29. *I'thapithi^n*, without effort; *xti*, truly; *ga'ha itho^{n}tho^n*, rising up and down; *ego^n*, like.

30. *I'thapithi^n*, without effort; *xti*, truly; *giu^n'*, flying; *thego^n*, he went.

31. *I^{n}sha'ge,* old men; *we'utha,* example; *ga'xa bi,* they made; *ego^{n},* like.

Free translation

1. Toward the coming of the sun
2. There the people of every kind gathered,
3. And great animals of every kind.
4. Verily all gathered together, as well as people.
5. Insects also of every description,
6. Verily all gathered there together,
7. By what means or manner we know not.

8. Verily, one alone of all these was the greatest,
9. Inspiring to all minds,
10. The great white rock,
11. Standing and reaching as high as the heavens, enwrapped in mist,
12. Verily as high as the heavens.
13. Thus my little ones shall speak of me,
14. As long as they shall travel in life's path, thus they shall speak of me.
15. Such were the words, it has been said.

16. Then next in rank
17. Thou, male of the crane, stoodst with thy long beak
18. And thy neck, none like to it in length,
19. There with thy beak didst thou strike the earth.

* * * * * * *

20. This shall be the legend
21. Of the people of yore, the red people,
22. Thus my little ones shall speak of me.

23. Then next in rank stood the male gray wolf, whose cry,
24. Though uttered without effort, verily made the earth to tremble,
25. Even the stable earth to tremble.
26. Such shall be the legend of the people.

27. Then next in rank stood Hega, the buzzard, with his red neck.
28. Calmly he stood, his great wings spread, letting the heat of the sun straighten his feathers.
29. Slowly he flapped his wings,
30. Then floated away, as though without effort,
31. Thus displaying a power (a gift of Wako^{n}'da) often to be spoken of by the old men in their teachings.

The above, which bears the marks of antiquity, is unfortunately incomplete.

The old leader gave the following explanation of the teachings of the Pebble society, which may be a paraphrase of a ritual:

At the beginning all things were in the mind of Wako^{n}'da. All creatures, including man, were spirits. They moved about in space between the earth and the stars (the heavens). They were seeking a place where they could come into a bodily existence. They ascended to the sun, but the sun was not fitted for their abode. They moved on to the moon and found that it also was not good for their home. Then they descended to the earth. They saw it was covered with water. They floated through the air to the north, the east, the south, and the west, and found no dry land. They were sorely grieved. Suddenly from the midst of the water uprose a great rock. It burst into flames and the waters floated into the air in clouds.

Dry land appeared; the grasses and the trees grew. The hosts of spirits descended and became flesh and blood. They fed on the seeds of the grasses and the fruits of the trees, and the land vibrated with their expressions of joy and gratitude to Wako^n′da, the maker of all things.

Among the Osage there is a similar myth, in which the elk figures as a helper of mankind to find a place to dwell.

The sweat lodge was used as a preparatory rite and always when a member was about to minister to the sick. The following ritual was that used by Waki′dezhinga as he entered the sweat lodge to make ready for his duties toward the sick:

Ritual for Sweat Lodge, No. 1.

1. He! I^{n}shage′ eçka
2. I^n′e shni^{n}ke she eçka
3. I^{n}shage′ eçka
4. He! zhi^{n}ga′ wi ewe′po^{n}çe tho^{n}de
5. Ego^n bi eçka
6. I^{n}shage′ eçka
7. He
8. He! gthi^n a′bito^n thethe xti
9. Thagthi^n′ ado^n eçka
10. Tade′ ui′the the′no^n ha te tho^n eçka
11. Tade′ baço^n ego^n thagthi^n′ ado^n eçka
12. I^{n}shage′ eçka
13. He! xa′de zhi^{n}ga tho^n tho^n eçka
14. Uti′ e′thathe ego^n thagthi^n′ ado^n eçka
15. He! wazhi^n′ga a′zhazha xti thagthi^n′ ado^n eçka
16. Hi^{n}xpe′ a′gthagtha xti thagthi^n′ ado^n eçka
17. I^{n}shage′ eçka

18. Edi uwa′to^n eçka
19. Edi uwa′to^n eçka
20. He! ni nike she eçka
21. Ni nike ato^n adi′to^n
22. Gaçu′çe shni^n e i^{n}te eçka
23. He! du′ba thi′thiça i te
24. Utha thithi^n′ge te tho^{n}zha eçka
25. Zhi^{n}ga′ i′thite go^n′tha i te tho^{n}zha eçka

26. He! Ti thato^n she eçka
27. Ti thato^n she eçka
28. Wani′ta to^{n}ga eçka
29. He! itha′ kigthaxade eçka
30. Zhi^{n}ga′ ui′the u^{n}gi′kaxe ta i te eshe ama tho^n eçka

31. He! tishi thato^n she eçka
32. No^n′xahi thiba′gizhe xti
33. A′baku thiba′zhu tho^n
34. No^{n}t′u′ça xti
35. Zhi^{n}ga the uithe u^{n}gikaxe ta i te tho^{n}zha eçka
36. He! pehi^n′ bixa′xado^n eçka
37. No^{n}zhi′ha tho^n the′tho^n
38. Xa′de tho^n hi^n a′zhi ado^n eçka
39. Hi^n′tho^n çka do^n eçka
40. Hi^n a′zhi te tho^n e′waka i do^n eçka

41. He! mo^{n}thi^{n} ta i ke eçka
42. Wi^{n}′u^{n}wata uki′mo^{n}gtho^{n} i ke eçka
43. A′baku tho^{n} no^{n}t'u′ça xti
44. Uzho^{n}′ge no^{n}çta xti i ke
45. Pe a′ço^{n} githe ihe′thatha xti
46. Mo^{n}shni^{n}′ ado^{n} I^{n}shage′ eçka

47. He! zhi^{n}ga′ giko^{n}′tha bado^{n} eçka
48. Ithigiko^{n}′tha tabado^{n} eçka
49. Thie i′wigipathi^{n} ta mike tho^{n}zha eçka
50. I^{n}sha′ge eçka

He! is an exclamation involving the idea of supplication and distress; *eçka*, a refrain, meaning "I desire," "I crave," and, sometimes, "I implore."

Free translation

1. He! Aged One, eçka
2. Thou Rock, eçka
3. Aged One, eçka
4. He! I have taught these little ones
5. They obey, eçka
6. Aged One, eçka
7. He!
8. He! Unmoved from time without end, verily
9. Thou sittest, eçka
10. In the midst of the various paths of the coming winds
11. In the midst of the winds thou sittest, eçka
12. Aged One, eçka
13. He! The small grasses grow about thee, eçka
14. Thou sittest as though making of them thy dwelling place, eçka
15. He! Verily thou sittest covered with the droppings of birds, eçka
16. Thy head decked with the downy feathers of the birds, eçka
17. Aged One, eçka

18. Thou who standest next in power, eçka
19. Thou who standest next in power, eçka
20. He! Thou water, eçka
21. Water that hast been flowing
22. From time unknown, eçka
23. He! Of you the little ones have taken
24. Though thy mysteries remain unrevealed
25. These little ones crave thy touch, eçka

26. He! Thou that standest as one dwelling place, eçka
27. Even as one dwelling place, eçka
28. Ye great animals, eçka
29. He! Who make for us the covering, eçka
30. These little ones, thou hast said, let their thoughts reverently dwell on me, eçka

31. He! Thou tent frame, eçka
32. Thou standest with bent back o'er us
33. With stooping shoulders, bending over us
34. Verily, thou standest
35. Thus my little ones shall speak of me, thou hast said
36. Brushing back the hair from thy forehead, eçka

37. The hair of thy head
38. The grass that grows about thee
39. Thy hairs are whitened, eçka
40. The hairs that grow upon thy head, eçka
41. O, the paths that the little ones shall take, eçka
42. Whichever way they may flee from danger, eçka
43. They shall escape. Their shoulders shall be bent with age as they walk
44. As they walk on the well-beaten path
45. Shading their brows now and again with their hands
46. As they walk in their old age, eçka

47. He! This is the desire of thy little ones, eçka
48. That of thy strength they shall partake, eçka
49. Therefore thy little ones desire to walk closely by thy side, eçka
50. Venerable One, eçka.

In the ritual the primal rock, referred to in the opening ritual, that which rose from the waters, is addressed by the term "venerable man," whose assistance is called to the "little ones," the patients about to be ministered to. Line 7, with its exclamation of supplication and reverence, *He!*, opens the description of the rock, which sits from all time in the midst of the winds, those messengers of life-giving force. Note the use of the phrase "midst of the winds" in the ritual of Turning the Child (p. 120). The small grass refers to the means of heating the stones placed in the sweat lodge as a "dwelling place." Again, the abiding quality of the rock is referred to in lines 15 and 16: Immovable the rocks have remained while the droppings of the birds and their molting feathers have fallen season after season. In lines 20–25, "Thou water," "water that hast been flowing from time unknown," it is said, that "these little ones [the people] crave thy touch." The primal rock of these rituals is the theme of some of the songs of the Pebble society.

The standing house, the sweat lodge, is next spoken of; the animals who have given it a covering are remembered gratefully, the bent-over boughs are mentioned and compared to the bent shoulders of the old men whose long life is like "the well-beaten path." The prayer for the gift of life for the "little ones," whose health is desired, is curiously and poetically blended with this description of the standing house, wherein the power is sought by which they, the "little ones," "shall desire to walk closely" by the side of the long-lived rock, and, because of these supplications to rock and ever-flowing water, shall secure health and length of days. These rituals, naïvely poetic, reveal how completely man is identified with nature in the mind of the native.

The following was intoned as the sweat lodge was prepared for curative purposes:

RITUAL FOR SWEAT LODGE, NO. 2

1. He! I^{n}sha′ge, ′çka
2. Zhi^{n}ga′ wako^n′ditha ba ′do^n, eçka
3. Gthi ′tho^n′thigitha ba ′do^n, e′çka
4. Edi uwe′he ta mike xu′ka, edi uwe′he ta mike
5. Eshe′ ama tho^n d′eçka
6. Zhi^{n}ga wako^n′ditha ba′do^n eçka
7. I′thiginitha ta ba′do^n, eçka
8. Gthi ′tho^n′thigitha ba′do^n, eçka
9. I^{n}sha′ge, ′çka
10. He! Zhi^{n}ga ithigino^{n}zhi^n go^n′tha ba′do^n, eçka
11. Gthi ′tho^n′thigitha i tho^{n}zha, eçka
12. I^{n}sha′ge ′çka
13. Eda′do^n shti wo^n ′de ′shna ′zhi te
14. Uki′hi ′azhi tho^{n}ka eshne′go^n te
15. I^{n}sha′ge ′çka

Literal translation

1. *He!*, address to call attention; *i^{n}sha′ge*, old man, a term of respect addressed to the stones that are heated for the bath; *′çka*, *eçka*, I desire, implore.

2. *Zhi^{n}ga*, children; *wako^n′ditha*, being in distress; *ba*, they; *′do^n*, *ado^n*, therefore; *eçka*, I implore.

3. *Gthi*, at home, the arrival at home (refers to sweat lodge); *′tho^n′thigitha*, *itho^n′thigitha*, *itho^{n}tha*, something round placed on the ground (refers to the stones used in the sweat lodge, but the appeal is in the singular as the generic stone is addressed); *thi*, you (refers to the stone); *gi*, the possessive sign; *ba*, they; *′do^n*, *ado^n*, therefore, because of; *eçka*, I desire.

4. *Edi*, with them, there; *uwehe*, I shall join, or take part, or cooperate; *ta*, shall, it is my will; *mike*, I am or I be; *ta mike*, I shall be; *xu′ka*, to teach, instruct, initiate.

5. *Eshe′*, you have said; *ama*, they say; *tho^n d′*, *tho^n di*, an idiom meaning it can not be denied; *eçka*, I desire.

6. The same as the second line.

7. *I′thiginitha—I*, of, by, in; *thi*, you; *gi*, possessive; *initha*, to seek protection (*gi* implies a relation between the one speaking and the one addressed, something in common; if the appeal was to a stranger the *gi* would be omitted); *ta ba ′do^n* (*ta*, may; *ba*, they; *′do^n*, that), that they may—"That in you they may seek protection."

8. The same as the third line.

9. The same as the first, omitting *he*.

10. *He*, address to call attention; *zhi^{n}ga*, children; *ithigino^{n}zhi^n*, by means of you to stand (*no^{n}zhi^n*, to stand); *go^{n}tha*, to desire, applied to whatever supports life, health; *ba*, they; *′do^n*, *ado^n*, that.

11. *Gthi'tho^{n}thigitha* (see third line); *i*, plural, refers to "they," the children; *tho^{n}'zha*, although, nevertheless; *eçka*, I desire.

12. The same as the first line.

13. *Eda'do^{n} shti wo^{n}* (*eda'do^{n}*, things; *shti wo^{n}*, whatever), idiom—and whatever things; *'de, ede*, words; *shna*, to think; *'zhi, u^{n}kazhi*, not; *te*, do.

14. *Uki'hi*, learned; *'zhi, u^{n}kazhi*, not; *tho^{n}ka*, they are; *eshnego^{n}*, you judge; *te*, do.

15. The same as the first line.

Free translation

1. Oh! Aged One! I implore,
2. Your children being in sore distress, eçka,
3. Have brought you home, eçka.
4. "I shall be with them as an instructor, I shall be with them."
5. You have said, they say, it can not be denied, eçka,
6. Your children being in sore distress, eçka,
7. That in you they may take refuge, eçka,
8. Have brought you home, eçka,
9. Aged One! I implore.
10. Oh! Your children desire to arise by your strength, eçka,
11. Though they may have erred in their bringing you home, eçka,
12. Aged One! I implore.
13. And whatever you may think, do not reproach them,
14. But rather, judge them by their ignorance,
15. Aged One! I implore.

The following ritual was used when entering the sweat lodge before the initiation of a member of the Pebble society was to take place. According to ancient custom, one of the articles to be served at the feast given as part of the ceremony was a white dog; this was cooked as the stones were heated for the sweat lodge. During the preparation and cooking of the dog all the leaders of the society had to be present. The dog was painted before it was strangled; a band of red was put across the nose and the feet and tip of the tail were painted with the same color. Songs preceded the death of the dog, the dressing of it, and also the feast. Any mistake made in singing these songs or in reciting the ritual resulted in the early death of the offender. The songs which accompanied the feast have all been forgotten owing to the lapsing of the ceremony. The ritual here given was obtained from an old man who has now been dead many years.

Ritual for Sweat Lodge, No. 3

1. He I^{n}shage eçka
2. He I^{n} shnike tho^{n} eçka
3. I^{n}shage eçka
4. Wibthaho^{n} ta mike tho^{n}zha eçka
5. I^{n}shage eçka
6. He I^{n}shage eçka
7. Nito^{n}ga niuathite uthishi xti ke tho^{n} eçka
8. I^{n}shage eçka

9. Niuitha atithagthi^{n}ado^n eçka
10. I^{n}shage eçka
11. Agudi to^n tiedo^n ethego^n wathe shniki eçka
12. I^{n}shage eçka
13. Niuitha atithagthi^n ado^n eçka
14. I^n! I^n! eshe thagthi^n abado^n eçka
15. Zhi^{n}ga the awagi i^n tamike tho^{n}zha eçka
16. Ie waagino^{n}o^n agthi^n tamike tho^{n}zha eçka
17. Eshe abado^n eçka
18. Wi^n ie thashno^n ki zhi no^{n}gtho^{n}tha uthishi ago^n thethi^{n}ke zho^n tho^{n}zha eçka
19. To^{n}de ke kapiethe xti no^{n}gtho^{n}tha ta thi^n eshe abado^n eçka
20. I^{n}shage eçka
21. I^{n}dado^n piazhi ke tho^n eçka
22. Mo^{n}te shtiwo^n tha′zhi ado^n eçka
23. Ibe xi^n ego^n uxthitu ego^n thagthi^n ado^n eçka
24. I^{n}shage eçka
25. He I^{n}shage eçka
26. Wi^n u^{n}gthaho^n o^{n}gthapi ego^n de eçka
27. I^{n}shage eçka
28. Ithagishti^n tamike tho^{n}zha eçka
29. Gudiha ego^n the do^n eçka
30. I^{n}shage eçka
31. Baxu weduba ke tho^n eçka
32. Wethabthi^n, weduba ke tho^n eçka
33. Shetheathi^n tho^n etho^{n}be hi ta ma eshe aba do^n eçka
34. I^{n}shage eçka
35. He I^{n}shage eçka
36. Dado^n uto^{n}bathe ego^n thagthi^n ado^n eçka
37. Taki^{n}de çi^{n}tha ego^n thagthi^n ado^n eçka
38. Peçi^{n}tha ego^n thagthi^n ado^n eçka
39. Azhuhi igawa ego^n thagthi^n ado^n eçka
40. Zhi^{n}ga tho^{n}ka wi mike ego^n ta tho^{n}ka wi^n o^{n}gthaho^n o^{n}gthapi ego^{n}ki, I^{n}shage eçka
41. He I^{n}shage eçka
42. Tishi thato^n she tho^n eçka
43. Niko^{n}ha ke tho^n eçka
44. Apamo^{n}gthe xti aithagthi^n ado^n eçka
45. Itaxetho^n tho^n eçka
46. Niuthubido^n tigthagtha thagthi^n ado^n eçka
47. Tishi thato^n she eçka
48. Zhi^{n}ga wi^{n}achi thetho^{n}ka tho^n eçka
49. Wi^n aagigthi^n ta mike tho^{n}zha eçka
50. Edado^n piazhi ke eçka
51. Bthuga xti muçihi awagithe tamike tho^{n}zha eçka
52. O^{n}ba ukiho^{n}ge wi^n ibako^n thi^{n}ge xti ethumbe hi tama eshe abado^n eçka
53. I^{n}shage eçka
54. "He, dadi′ ha" eshe taya eshe abado^n eçka
55. Nisni ke tho^n eçka
56. He ni iti^n xti itho^{n}the niuthibthi itho^{n}the, ta t'i^{n}xe dado^n piazhi upethe ke tho^n bthuga xti agaha gthihe ado^n eçka
57. Mo^{n}te shtiwo^n tha zhi ado^n eçka
58. I^{n}shage eçka
59. Ebe i^{n}de wi^{n}achi wi^n i u^n thu^{n}gita i shte shte wo^n eçka
60. Edado^n piazhi ke tho^n eçka

61. Bthuga xti muçihi awagethe tamike eshe abado^{n} eçka
62. Xthuga duba ha te tho^{n} eçka
63. Bthuga xti thiexthua piazhi ke tho^{n} uçihi awagithe tamike tho^{n}zha eçka
64. Zhi^{n}ga eçka
65. Akiki ho^{n}ge etho^{n}be hi tama tho^{n}zha eçka
66. Kimo^{n}ho^{n} xti tade baço^{n} xti aino^{n}zhi^{n} tama eçka
67. Eshe abado^{n} eçka
68. I^{n}shage eçka

Free translation

1. Oh! Aged One, eçka
2. Oh! thou recumbent Rock, eçka
3. Aged One, eçka
4. To thee I shall pray, eçka
5. Aged One, eçka
6. Oh! Aged One, eçka
7. The great water that lies impossible to traverse, eçka
8. Aged One, eçka
9. In the midst of the waters thou came and sat, eçka
10. Aged One, eçka
11. Thou, of whom one may think, whence camest thou? eçka
12. Aged One, eçka
13. From midst the waters camest thou, and sat, eçka
14. It is said that thou sittest crying: I^{n}! I^{n}! eçka
15. Though I shall carry these my little ones, eçka
16. Though I shall sit and listen to their words, eçka
17. Because, they say, you have said, eçka
18. If one shall go astray in his speech, although here lies one on whom one's footsteps may seem impossible to stumble, eçka
19. Upon this, the earth, very suddenly he shall stumble, they say you have said, eçka
20. Aged One, eçka
21. The impurities, eçka
22. Shall not enter within, eçka
23. Shall drift, like filth, as thou sittest, eçka
24. Aged One, eçka
25. Oh! Aged One, eçka
26. If one of mine prays to me properly, eçka
27. Aged One, eçka
28. I shall be with him, eçka
29. Further along he shall go, eçka
30. Aged One, eçka
31. The fourth hill, eçka
32. The third, the fourth, eçka
33. Even in going they shall appear thereon, they say, you have said, eçka
34. Aged One, eçka
35. Oh! Aged One, eçka
36. Thou sittest as though longing for something, eçka
37. Thou sittest like one with wrinkled loins, eçka
38. Thou sittest like one with furrowed brow, eçka
39. Thou sittest like one with flabby arms, eçka
40. The little ones shall be as I am, whoever shall pray to me properly, eçka
41. Oh! Aged One, eçka
42. Oh! Thou Pole of the Tent, eçka

43. Along the banks of the streams, eçka
44. With head drooping over, there thou sittest, eçka
45. Thy topmost branches, eçka
46. Dipping again and again, verily, into the water, eçka
47. Thou Pole of the Tent, eçka
48. One of these little ones, eçka
49. I shall sit upon one, eçka
50. The impurities, eçka
51. All I shall wash away from them, eçka
52. To the end, without one obstacle, they shall appear thereon, they say, you have said, eçka
53. Aged One, eçka
54. It is said that you have commanded us to say to you, Our Father, eçka
55. Thou Water, eçka
56. Oh! Along the bends of the stream where the waters strike, and where the waters eddy, among the water-mosses, let all the impurities that gall be drifted, eçka
57. Not entering within, eçka
58. Aged One, eçka
59. Whosoever touches me with face or lips, eçka
60. All the impurities, eçka
61. I shall cause to be cleansed, it is said, you have said, eçka
62. The four apertures of the body, eçka
63. And all within the body I shall purify, it is said, you have said, eçka
64. Little ones, eçka
65. Through and through shall appear, eçka
66. Against the wind, in the midst of air, they shall appear and stand, eçka
67. It is said, you have said, eçka
68. Aged One, eçka

In this ritual the Primal Rock is addressed as "Aged One," sitting in the midst of water "impossible to traverse." The stones in the sweat lodge represented this Aged One, while the steam from the water symbolized the mighty water whence issued life and which had power to wash away all impurities. The almost tender mention of the willows that dip their branches "again and again" into the stream and that now constitute the framework of the lodge is noteworthy. So, too, the mention of the placing of the little ones "against the wind, in the midst of air," bears testimony to how deeply seated in the native mind is the religious idea of the life-giving power of the winds—the winds that stand at "the four directions" into whose "midst" is sent the child, that he may reach the four hills of life.

The ritual is very difficult to translate. It is highly poetic in the original, full of picture and movement. The refrain, *eçka*, "I desire," "I am drawn toward," "I seek," carries the idea of a movement urged on by earnestness on the part of the person speaking. The word *eçka* has no exact equivalent in English.

The following songs, recorded from various members of the society, give the peculiar rhythm characteristic of the songs that belong to the Pebble society. The first has been selected as giving the general theme or motive in its simplest form. The other songs show how this motive has been treated without sacrificing the peculiar rhythm. These songs were sung as the members moved about the lodge waving their eagle-feather fans and "shooting" the pebble, the magic power of which caused the one "shot" to fall rigid as the pebble was supposed to strike the body.

Hu wi-bthe tho ho the-ke atha... Hu wi-bthe tho ho the-ke atha... the-ke a-tha ho

Literal translation: *Hu wibthe,* I have told you; *tho,* end of sentence; *ho,* vowel prolongation; *theke atha,* here it lies; *ho,* vowel prolongation.

Mo^{n}-thi^{n} tha - the he shu-tha-the the he mo^{n}-thi^{n} tha - the he
shu-tha-the the he e a shu-tha the he shu-tha-the the he
mo^{n} thi^{n} tha - the he shu-tha-the the he tha ...... ha

Literal translation: *Mo^{n},* arrow; *thi^{n},* moving; *thathe,* I send; *he,* vowel prolongation; *shuthathe,* I send to you; *the,* end of sentence; *he* vowel prolongation. In this song the pebble is compared to the swift-moving arrow.

The-thu a-ti no^{n}-zhi^{n} ho^{n}-tho^{n} tha-the tha ha the - thu a-ti no^{n}-zhi^{n}
ho^{n}-tho^{n} tha- the tha ha ho^{n}-tho^{n} tha- the tha - ha ho^{n} - tho^{n} tha- the
tha ha ho^{n} - tho^{n} tha- the tha ha ho^{n} - tho^{n} tha- the tha - ha

Literal translation: *Thethu,* here; *ati,* come; *no^n^zhi^n^,* stand; *ho^n^tho^n^ thathe,* you have found me; *tha,* end of sentence; *ha,* vowel prolongation. This song represents the singer proclaiming: "Here where I stand the pebble has come and found me, struck me with its power."

Wa-koⁿ-da thoⁿ mi-ke aⁿ-thoⁿ-tha-the A-zhoⁿ mi-ke
thoⁿ tha-the he A-zhoⁿ mi-ke thoⁿ the-the he
A-zhoⁿ mi-ke thoⁿ-the-the ho tha ha A-zhoⁿ mi-ke an-thoⁿ-tha-the
Hu-hu mi-ke thoⁿ-tha-the he Hu-hu mi-ke an-thoⁿ-tha-tha he!
Cry of the Magic Ancients E hu-u-u hu

Literal translation: *Wako^n^'da*—this does not refer to the great Wako^n^'da but to the mysterious creatures, the givers of magic; *tho^n^,* as; *mike,* I am; *a^n^tho^n^thathe,* thou hast found me; *he,* vowel prolongation; *azho^n^,* I lay; *mike,* I am; *tho^n^thathe,* hast found me; *huhu,* fish; *mike,* I am; *a^n^tho^n^thathe,* thou hast found me; *e-hu-u-u-hu,* vibrations, cry of magic power.

This song refers to an experience of one of the members of the society who was one day bathing, when he caught sight of a hawk, and fearing it was an enemy he turned himself into a fish. The bird descended to get the fish, when the man eluded his fellow-magician by turning himself into a rock, and so escaped by his magic power, while his fellow-magician, the bird, hurt his bill on the hard rock. There are many songs which refer to these magical transformations.

The following song is said to preserve an incident in the early history of the society:

When magic was first given to the members the power was not strong. By and by the members felt that it had gained in strength and they determined to attempt to do something more than merely to exercise it on animals. So they agreed to try their magic power on men and two persons were chosen to experiment on. When these men were "shot" by the pebble the magic proved to be so powerful that one of them was killed. Then the society knew that they had really become possessed of the gift of magic.

Literal translation: *Awakide*, I shot at them; *tha*, end of sentence; *win*, one; *autha*, I wounded at once, or at the first shot; *tha*, end of sentence; *ha*, vocable; *wonshige*, man—an old word now in use among the Winnebago; *nonba*, two; *wakide*, shot; *betha*, they were; *on'mon*, the other; *kide*, shot or killed.

The song presents a point which may be of historic interest, in the word used for "man"—the one who was shot and killed—*wonshige*. This is said to be an old word. It has disappeared from the Omaha language but is used by the Winnebago, whose speech has been regarded as preserving an older form of the parent tongue than the present Omaha language. The keeping of this one word, which relates to the effect of the magic in killing a man, while the other words have changed, raises the question whether this song (said to be very old) has come down from a time when the Omaha and Winnebago were still together as parts of the parent body.

The rituals and the customs of the Pebble society are more primitive than are those of the Shell society and there are indications that the latter society has borrowed from the former. In one of the Shell Society songs, included in the preceding account of that society, the shell is spoken of as a pebble or stone.

As these two societies are the only ones in the tribe which observe shamanistic practices and as they both strongly emphasize magic. it is not impossible that at one time they may have been connected, If such was the case, it is probable that the Pebble is the older society of the two.

XII

DISEASE AND ITS TREATMENT

Among the Omaha hygienic and physiologic laws were practically unknown. Even the contagious character of some diseases was not recognized. It was this fact that made the scourge of smallpox so severe, and later measles laid hold of old and young, with a virulence unknown to our own comparatively immune race. Disease was regarded as more or less of a mystery; sometimes but not always magic was held to be responsible for sickness, but it alone was not depended on to insure a cure. Herbs and roots were used for medicinal purposes, but in gathering and administering these, certain formulas had to be used. These formulas were in the nature of a prayer to Wako^{n}'da and an invocation to the power dwelling in the healing herb, calling on it to become curatively active. The knowledge of such plants and roots and of their ritual songs and how to apply them had to be purchased, as a high value was placed on such knowledge. After payment the purchaser was shown the proper plant and directed to its locality, he was taught the songs used when gathering it and also the songs to be sung when it was administered. No one individual knew all the medicinal plants. Treatment of disease was specialized, so to speak, one person curing hemorrhages, another fever, and so on.

Bleeding was commonly employed in treating ailments; for this purpose gashes between the eyebrows were made with a flint knife or cupping on the back was effected by the use of the tip of a horn. A species of massage was also employed. The influence caused by the presence of women about a wounded person was deemed to be unfavorable; this influence (*wa'thite*) was regarded as related to the vital functions of woman. A similar influence was thought to arise by binding a wound, even in an emergency, with anything that had been near the genital organs of a man.

Herbs were used not only in the treatment of disease but for the purpose of healing wounds. That success often attended the cure of wounds and other injuries is well known. How the Buffalo society treated wounds has been described (p. 487). As all medical aid was given with more or less ceremony and with songs accompanied by the beating of a small drum, these noises evidently exercised a psychical influence on the patient and did not injuriously affect the nervous system, as they would have done in the case of one to whom the sound was without meaning. The patient knew that the songs were sung to invoke supernatural aid and that on the efficacy of the appeal he must largely rely for relief.

Although witches and witchcraft did not exist among the Omaha, disease was sometimes supposed to have its origin in the magical introduction into the human body of a worm or other object, which could be removed only by means of magical formulas, by sucking, or by manipulation. Certain individuals and certain practices were supposed to be able to bring disease and death to a person by means of magic. In such cases magic had to be used to dispel the imposed magic. Among the Omaha these magical practices were almost wholly confined to the members of the Shell and Pebble societies. Some of their practices were claimed to trench on the marvelous. They declared they could transform themselves into birds, animals, stones, or leaves and joined in tests of the strength of their respective magic powers. One form of test consisted in trying to jump or fly over one another; the one who succeeded in so doing was regarded not only as possessing greater magic but as controlling the one defeated. No authentic accounts could be obtained from anyone who had actually witnessed these feats, but many persons were ready to assert that they had certainly been performed.

There was another method by which death and disaster could be brought to a man. This power was vested in the Ho^n'hewachi (p. 497). In this case the invoking of disease and death was in the nature of inflicting punishment on a social offender by turning on him the consequences of his own actions. The method employed was connected with the belief that help could be sent from one person to another by the power of willing known as *wazhi^n'thethe* (*wazhi^n'*, "will—the power by which man thinks, feels, and acts;" *the'the*, "to send"). *Wazhi^n'thethe* therefore means to send one's will power toward another to supplement his strength and thereby affect his action. To this helpful exercise of will power belongs the class of songs called *we'to^n waa^n* (p. 421).

The exercise of will power for punishment, as practised by the Ho^n'hewachi, was called *wazhi^n'agthe* (*wazhi^n'*, "will;" *agthe*, "to place on"). The two words, *wazhi^n'thethe* and *wazhi^n'agthe*, might seem at first glance to have the same meaning. The former means, however, the will power of one person sent to help another, and the latter the will power placed on. In the latter case the Ho^n'hewachi wills that the consequences of a certain line of conduct shall fall on a person who of his own accord has determined on such a line of conduct; that is, the man is to be abandoned to the results of his own unwise behavior; he is to be thrust out from all helpful relations with men or animals. *Wazhi^n'agthe* would seem to have been expressive of a kind of excommunication pronounced by the men who had achieved position in the tribe, through valor and industry, against a man who had offended social order and endangered the peace of the tribe. This form of punishment, which blended social ostracism with a kind of magical power, was greatly feared and frequently resulted in the death of the victim.

The practice of midwifery belonged almost exclusively to women. In some exceptionally complicated or dangerous cases of parturition male doctors were called. In general women made rapid recovery from childbirth and within a week were able to resume their usual domestic duties.

Some Curative Plants

Among the roots used for medicinal purposes were the following:

Sweet flag (*Acorus calamus* S.), called by the Omaha *mo^{n}ko^n'ninida*. The root was chewed for disorders of the stomach. It was also put into the feed of horses when ailing. When on the tribal hunt the people came to a marshy place where the sweet flag grew, the young men gathered the leaves, made wreaths, and wore them about the neck or head because of the pleasant odor.

The outer covering of the root of the Kentucky coffee tree (*Gymnocladus canadensis*) was used in hemorrhage, particularly from the nose or during childbirth. This root was used also when the kidneys failed to act. The native name of the tree was *no^n'titahi*. The root, powdered and mixed with water, was administered to women during protracted labor.

The root of the large bladder ground cherry (*Physalis viscora*) was used in dressing wounds. The Omaha name for the root was *pei'gatushi*. This was one of the roots employed by the Buffalo doctors as described on page 488.

The root of the cat-tail (*Typha*), called *ça'hi^n*, was used for dressing scalds. The root was pulverized and spread in a paste over the burn. The ripe blossom of the cat-tail was then used for a covering, the injured part being bound so as to keep the dressing in place. The blossom of the cat-tail was called *waha'baigaçko^{n}the*. This word, meaning "to try the corn," is said to have originated in the following manner. The boys used to gather the cat-tail blossoms and try to break them up so as to scatter the seeds. If they were successful they shouted "The corn is ripe," as the cat-tail blossom shed its seeds about the time that corn was ripe enough to eat.

The root of the hop vine (*Humulus lupulus*) was used for healing wounds; this was called *mo^{n}ko^n'basho^{n}sho^n*, "crooked root."

From the root of the wild rose was made a wash for inflamed eyes, known as *wazhi'de*.

The root of the vine *Cucurbita perennis* (*ni'kashigamo*^{n}*ko*^{n}, "human medicine," so called because the root was said to resemble the human form) was used medicinally. The root, pulverized and mixed with water, was taken for pains. Only that part of the root which corresponded to the seat of the pain was used; that is, if the pain was in the head, body, or leg, that portion of the root resembling the particular part affected was taken, etc. This root was used also in protracted labor.

There were many other plants and roots known to the Omaha as having medicinal qualities which were used by men and women of the tribe when attending the sick, but it has been impossible to obtain full knowledge of them. It can be safely said that, on the whole, medicinal remedies were more frequently resorted to in the case of sickness than magical practices. In almost every instance, however, the remedy was accompanied by its appropriate formula of song or ritual.

Fees were always expected by the doctor called to attend the sick or the injured.[a]

The pleasure taken in swimming has been mentioned; this, however, was apart from bathing. In summer the bath was taken in a stream, and afterward the body was rubbed and dried with sprays of artemisia. In winter both men and women erected small tents in which they bathed in warm water. This was not the sweat bath. That kind of bath was always more or less ceremonial, indulged in for the purpose of healing, to avert disaster, or to prepare one's self for some ceremony or duty. A framework of slender poles was bent so as to make a small dome-shaped frame; this was covered tight with skins. Stones were heated over a fire and then placed in the center of the tent. Sweat baths were not usually taken alone, although this was done occasionally. The bathers entered, carrying with them a vessel of water. The coverings were then made fast and the inmates, with ritual or with song, sprinkled the water on the heated stones and sat in the steam. After a sufficient sweat had been experienced they emerged and plunged into cold water, after which they rubbed themselves dry with artemisia or grass. Both men and women took sweat baths but not together; these were employed to relieve headache, rheumatism, weariness, snow-blindness, or any bodily ailment. If a person had been the subject of dreams betokening his approaching death, a priest was summoned. The

---

[a] The word meaning payment for services, as when one hires another to do a certain thing, is *wawe'shi*, such payment being contingent on the service being actually performed. The word employed to designate fees paid a doctor is *waon'the* (*on'tha*, "to throw away), "things thrown away;" the fees paid a doctor are to remunerate services that may or may not bring about the desired result and therefore the fees are as things that may be counted lost. The term *waon'the* is applied to fees paid for admission to membership in the secret societies and also to the payment made for knowledge of medicinal roots, etc.

latter prepared a sweat lodge, and, taking within the person threatened, chanted his special ritual and gave him a strenuous sweat bath, which effectually averted the approach of death. Children were not given baths of this kind except in the case of sickness.

The following ritual was recited while the sweat lodge was being prepared for medicinal purposes:

He! I^{n}shage! eçka
He! Nikashiga petho^{n}ba
Uthe'wi^n kitha i kizhi
I^{n}shage, eçka
Thi wepetho^{n}ba shni ama
Thi wepetho^{n}ba thagthi^n' ego^n
Thi I^{n}da'do^n ke i'shpaho^n ama
I^{n}shage, eçka
Eçko^{n}no^n i^{n}da'do^n ithanibtha te do^n ethe'go^n igkizhi eçka
Uzhu^{n}ge uki'gthixida i do^n, eçka
Thagthi^n abito^{n}thethe xti thagthi^n ego^n
Tade' ui'the duba te, uthuti^n xti thagthi^n ego^n
Thino^n xti 'dado^n ihuthe wathe 'go^n thagthi^n abado^n, eçka
I^{n}shage! eçka
A'wate i te 'do^n
Awate no^{n}de tho^n edo^n
Awate çi te 'do^n ethe'wathe xti thagthi^n tho^{n}zha
Thi no^n xti i^{n}dado^n ihuthe wathe 'go^n thagthi^n abado^n, eçka
I^{n}shage! eçka
Eçko^{n}no^n zhi^{n}ga eçko^{n}no^n
Gudiha ego^n zhuawagigthe bthe ado^n
Nie' thi^{n}ge' xti zhuawagigthe ado^n, eçka
Um'ba no^{n}ba, um'ba tha'bthi^n, um'ba du'ba etho^{n}be pi ko^{n}bthego^n
I^{n}shage! eçka
Go^n wi'bthaho^n, thano^n'o^n e'zha mi
I^{n}shage! eçka
Wa'gaçu shti wo^n iteatha mo^{n}zhi tho^{n}zha, go^n wi'ka
I^{n}shage! eçka

Free translation

Ho! Aged One, eçka,
At a time when there were gathered together seven persons,
You sat in the seventh place, it is said,
And of the Seven you alone possessed knowledge of all things,
    Aged One, eçka.
When in their longing for protection and guidance,
The people sought in their minds for a way,
They beheld you sitting with assured permanency and enduranc[e]
In the center where converged the paths,
There, exposed to the violence of the four winds, you sat,
Possessed with power to receive supplications,
    Aged One, eçka.
Where is his mouth, by which there may be utterance of speech?
Where is his heart, to which there may come knowledge and understanding?
Where are his feet, whereby he may move from place to place?
We question in wonder,

Yet verily it is said you alone have power to receive supplications,
Aged One, eçka.
I have desired to go yet farther in the path of life with my little ones,
Without pain, without sickness,
Beyond the second, third, and fourth period of life's pathway,
Aged One, eçka.
O hear! This is my prayer,
Although uttered in words poorly put together,
Aged One, eçka.

This ritual shows with unusual clearness the symbolic character of the stone as well as the native anthropomorphic habit of mind. In the ritual the stones are addressed, generically and anthropomorphically, as "Aged One," a title of highest respect. The "Aged One" is spoken of as having persisted through all time since the gathering of the primal seven, to have sat at the center where the paths converge, and endured the shock of the four winds, those mighty forces which bring life and can destroy it. Because of this enduring quality, abiding throughout all stress and change, the stone symbolized the steadfast power of Wako^{n}'da, the permeating life of all nature, and so was possessed with "power to receive supplications"—this despite the fact that reference is made in the ritual to the lack of means on the part of the stone of man's ability to express his volitions (as organs of speech, feeling, and motion). Therefore to it man turned for protection and help when beset by distress of body or mind. It will be recalled that the Omaha used the sweat lodge not only for curative purposes but to avert disaster, as impending death, and also as a preparatory rite. Here is set forth the recognition of the contradiction between the inertia of the actual stone and the vitality of the stone as a symbol. The mental attitude of the Omaha when he addresses the stone can be discerned—his thought is not centered on the apparent stone, but passes on to the quality or power which the stone typifies. What is true of the stone applies to the animals, the thunder and lightning, and the cosmic forces to which the Omaha addressed himself. All were symbols of qualities he recognized in man and projected upon natural objects and phenomena.

XIII

DEATH AND BURIAL CUSTOMS

Death was looked on as one of the inevitable things in life. The old men have said: "We see death everywhere. Plants, trees, animals die, and man dies. No one can escape death and no one should fear death, since it can not be avoided." While this view tended to remove from the thought of death any supernatural terrors, it did not foster the wish to hasten its approach. Length of days was desired by all and the rites attendant on the introduction of the child to the teeming life of nature (see p. 115) and those connected with the entrance of the child into its place in the tribe (see p. 117) all voice a prayer for long life, "to reach the fourth hill." Although not unknown, suicide was rare, and its rarity was owing perhaps to the belief that the spirit as well as the body perished in self-destruction. Generally speaking, no matter how hard the conditions under which he was living, the Omaha clung tenaciously to life.

The belief in the continuation of the natural relationships after death necessarily led to the fixing of a locality where the dead dwell. The mystery of death in some way seems to have become associated with the mystery of night and the stars. The Milky Way was regarded as a path made by the spirits of men as they passed to the realm of the dead. While the mystery of dissolution seems to have demanded that the abode of the dead should be removed from the earth, there were other thoughts and feelings that inclined the Omaha to conceive of its being possible for the dead to come near and act as helpers of the people. In the attempts of the Omaha to give concrete form to vague ideas concerning life and death we come upon the mythic stage of thought and observe how closely all their thoughts on these subjects were interwoven with their conception of a common and interrelated life, a living force that permeates, and is continuous in, all forms and appearances. By virtue of this bond of a continuous life the dead, though dwelling in a distant, undiscernible region, are able to come near their kindred on the earth and to lend their assistance in the avocations with which they have been familiar. This belief of the Omaha in the unification and the continuity of life assists toward the understanding of his point of view in reference to his appeals for help to the animals and the natural forces.

All of these symbolized to him certain faculties and powers individualized, so to speak, in the eagle, the wolf, the elk, the earth, the rock, the water, the tree, the thunder, the lightning, and the winds. All these forms, he believed, exist in the realm of the dead as well as in that of the living and the life which informs them, like that which informs man, is continuous and unbroken, emanating from the great mystery, Wako^{n}'da.

The Omaha believed also that under certain conditions the realm of the dead is accessible to the living. For instance, a person in a swoon was thought to have died for the time and to have entered the region of death. It was said of one who had fainted and recovered that "he died [fainted] and went to his departed kindred, but no one would speak to him, so he was obliged to return to life" [recovered consciousness]. It was further explained: "If his relatives had spoken to him he would never have come back but would have had to stay with the dead." It seems probable that the stories told by certain persons who had swooned as to what they saw in visions have had much to do in forming the Omaha imagery of the other world. It will be recalled that the sign of the tabu was put on the dead in order that they might be recognized by their relatives, as on the feet of a dead member of the We'zhi^{n}shte gens, moccasins made from the skin of the male elk to whom before his death the animal was tabu.[a] These and like customs confirm the general statement that life and its environment beyond the grave were thought to be conditioned much as on the earth, except that the future state was generally regarded as being happier and freer from sickness and want. It was said that there are seven spirit worlds, each higher than the one next preceding, and that after people have lived for a time in one world they die to that world and pass on to the one next above. When asked if death in the next world does not cause the same sorrow that it does here, the reply was: "It is not the same as here, for the people, having once passed through death and rejoined their kindred, recognize that the parting is only temporary and so they do not grieve as we do here."

There was no belief among the Omaha in a multiplicity of souls—"man has but one spirit" the old men declared—nor has any trace of belief in metempsychosis or in metamorphosis been discovered among this people.

---

[a] The statement has been made (*11th Ann. Rep. Bur. Ethnol.*, 542), "In two of the buffalo gentes of the Omaha (the Iñke-sabĕ and Hañga) there is a belief that the spirits of deceased members of those gentes return to the buffaloes," and the buffalo is spoken of as "the eponymic ancestor." The writer here cited fell into the error of regarding the animal which furnished the peculiar symbol in the rites of these kinship groups as the progenitor of the members of the groups. No such confusion seems to have existed in the Omaha mind. Men were not believed to be descended from animals. If the expressions "Buffalo people," "Elk people," "Deer people," or "Thunder people," were used, these descriptive terms were not employed in a literal sense but as tropes.

As the environment in the spirit world is similar to that on the earth, the avocations seem to be the same and it would appear as though interest in the affairs of this world never wholly ceases. The warriors attended the Thunder and it was said that sometimes during a thunderstorm the voices of certain brave men not living could be recognized. The chiefs seemed to consort together for, according to one explanation, the aurora borealis is caused by the chiefs holding a dance. Another explanation accounted in a more prosaic manner for this phenomenon, declaring it to be the light of the sun as it makes its way from the west back to the east.

There does not seem to have been any conception among the Omaha of supernatural rewards or punishments after death. The same conditions which make for good conduct here were believed to exist in the realm of the dead. It was said that at the forks of the path of the dead (the Milky Way) there "sat an old man wrapped in a buffalo robe, and when the spirits of the dead passed along he turned the steps of the good and peaceable people toward the short path which led directly to the abode of their relatives, but allowed the contumacious to take the long path, over which they wearily wandered." It is probable that the difference in the treatment believed to be accorded the good and the bad indicates white influence as does also the story that there is a log across a chasm over which the dead must pass; the good experience no difficulty, but the bad in crossing find the log so unstable that they sometimes fall off and are lost. The simple and ancient belief seems to have been that the Milky Way is the path of the dead. It was said also that the spirit of a murderer "never found his way to his relatives, but kept on, endlessly searching but never finding rest." The restless ghosts were supposed to whistle and for this reason children were easily frightened by whistling.

Many tales are told concerning ghosts. Those who have camped on old battlefields have heard the sounds of fighting, and persons becoming separated on hunting expeditions have told of hearing the coming of strange people, who made camp, set up their tents, and went about their usual avocations. A narrator of one of these stories declared that all the members of his family heard these sounds—even the dogs barked; but on looking out of the tent nothing was to be seen. These ghostly visitants did not always come at night; sometimes they stayed during the day and continued talking and moving about their unseen camp. Similar stories have been told by persons who had been left behind in the village when the tribe moved off on the annual hunt, tales of how the ghosts came and took possession of the earth lodges and held dances and feasts. In only one instance was it claimed that these visitors became partially visible. In that case the narrator said: "Only the feet and the legs as high as the knees could be seen;" and then added: "If I had been alone a little while longer I think I should have finally been able to see the entire figure and recognize the people, for at first I could see only their feet." Ghosts bent on mischief, as tampering with food after it was prepared for eating, could be thwarted by placing a knife across the open vessel containing the food. A ghost would not meddle with a knife. Nor would ghosts ever cross a stream; so, if a person was followed or chased by a ghost, he would make for a stream, wade it, or even jump across it. No matter how small the stream, it made an impassable barrier between himself and his ghostly pursuer.

The following dreams were thought to betoken death:

To have the Wa′waⁿ pipes presented to one ceremonially.

To have snakes enter one's body; but if the dreamer shuts his eyes, stops up his nose and ears, and clenches his hands so as to prevent the snakes forcing their heads between his fingers, and thus succeeds in keeping out the snakes, he will escape death.

To dream of lice.

If a horse shies at a person, it is because the animal sees blood on him, indicating that the man will soon die.

Whatever restraint the Omaha was trained to put on himself during the ordinary experiences of life was abandoned when death entered the family circle. No one, man or woman, was ashamed to weep at such a time. Mourners seem to have found relief from the mental pain of sorrow by inflicting physical pain—slashing their arms and legs. To cut locks of hair and throw them on the body was a customary expression of grief, as was wailing. At times the cries of the mourners could be heard on the hills in the early morning and during the night watches. Sad as was the sound of this active expression of grief, it was not so pathetic as the silent form of sorrow, which sometimes terminated in death. The mourner would draw his blanket over his head and with fixed downward gaze sit motionless, refusing to eat or to speak, deaf to all words of comfort and sympathy, until at last he fell senseless.

Abandonment of all that otherwise would be prized seems to have been characteristic of the Omaha expression of grief. Manifestations of this kind were not confined to the time immediately following bereavement but whenever a person was reminded of his sorrow there was a fresh expression of grief. At the He′dewachi, which was a festival of joy (see p. 251), those who since the last celebration had lost children or other near relatives were wont to wail over the remembrance while others were shouting exultantly their anticipations of pleasure at the coming festival. Or, it might happen while the tribe was on the annual hunt that a woman who had left the camp to gather wild potatoes would suddenly remember the fondness of a lost child for these roots; on her return she would take the store she had gathered to the center of the tribal circle and there throw down the product of her digging and return empty-handed to her tent. Her act was recognized by all the people as that of a person in sorrow whose thought was fixed on the dead and whose grief made her careless of present physical wants.

Very soon after death the body was prepared for burial, which took place within a short time. Rarely more than a day elapsed between death and burial. The best clothing was put on the dead and regalia was sometimes added, as well as a man's weapons and shield. The tent cover was sometimes lifted at the bottom so that persons from the outside could look on the dead as he lay prepared for burial.

In olden times the body was borne on a rude litter and placed in the grave in a sitting posture, facing the east. Graves were usually made on a hilltop. A shallow hole was dug and the body placed in it, and poles were arranged over the opening upon which earth was heaped into a mound. Mound burial was the common practice of the Omaha. After the acquisition of horses, one of these animals was sometimes strangled at the grave but it was never buried with the man. The personal belongings of men, women, and children were usually deposited in the grave.

Some time after the death and burial of a young man or woman the parents gave a feast, and invited to it the companions of the deceased. After the feast races were run and property contributed by relatives was divided among the winners. Young women took part in the contest if the dead was a girl, and young men raced if one of their own number had died.

The placing of food on the grave has been explained as an act of remembrance and has been likened to the offering of food when a bit was dropped ceremonially into the fire in token of the remembrance of Wako^{n}'da's gift of food to man. Other similar acts of offering food, all of which partook of the character of remembrance, were instanced in explanation, none of which were done because of a belief that the dead needed or partook of the food.

A fire was kept burning on the grave for four nights that its light might cheer the dead as he traveled; after that time he was supposed to have reached his journey's end.

When a man or woman greatly respected died, the following ceremony sometimes took place: The young men in the prime of life met at a lodge near that of the deceased and divested themselves of all clothing except the breechcloth; each person made two incisions in the upper left arm, and under the loop of flesh thus made thrust a small willow twig having on its end a spray of leaves. With the blood dripping on the leaves of the sprays that hung from their arms, the men moved in single file to the lodge where the dead lay. There, ranging themselves in a line shoulder to shoulder facing the tent, and marking the rhythm of the music with the willow sprigs they sang in unison the funeral song—the only one of its kind in the tribe. The contrast between the bleeding singers and the blithe major cadences of the song, suggestive of birds, sunshine, and the delights of the upper air, throws light on the Omaha belief relative to death and to song. "Music," it was explained, "can reach the unseen world and carry thither man's thought and aspiration. The song is for the spirit of the dead; it is to cheer him as he goes from his dear ones left behind on the earth; so, as he hears the voices of his friends, their glad tones help him to go forward on his inevitable journey." The song was therefore addressed directly to the spirit of the dead. Of the ceremonial it was further explained that "the shedding of the blood was for the mourners; they were to see in it an expression of sorrow and sympathy for the loss that had come to them." The cutting of the flesh, as has been already stated, was a common method of indicating grief. There was a custom that obtained among the Omaha which also referred to the belief that sound could reach the dead; hence wailing had to cease after a time, for the reason that "the departing one must not be distressed as he leaves his earthly home behind him, since he is obliged to go forward on his journey." This custom is consonant with the meaning of the music of the funeral song, which has no words, only vocables.

FUNERAL SONG

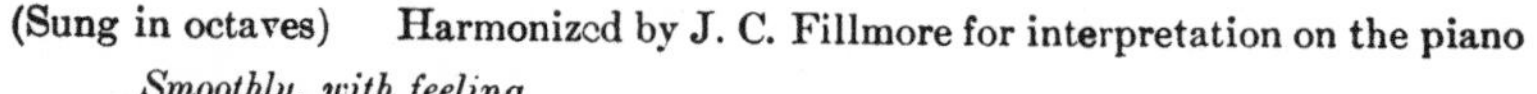

At the close of the song a near relative of the dead advanced toward the singers and, raising a hand in the attitude of thanks, withdrew the willow twigs from their arms and threw them on the ground. This ceremony, with its bleeding singers and its song of blythe, happy strains, at first glance might appear as a savage rite, devoid of human feeling; but when studied it is found to be an unselfish expression and to emphasize the Omaha belief in the continuity of life and of human relationships.

Among men relief from the stress of grief was generally sought in some stirring occupation, as a war party would afford. Consequently a bereaved father was apt to join the first party that proposed to "go upon the warpath;" if he had lost a little child he would tuck its small moccasins in his belt. On slaying an enemy he laid the moccasins beside the slain in the belief that the dead man would recognize and befriend the little child as it slowly made its way toward its relatives in the other world.

XIV

RELIGION AND ETHICS

There was no class or group among the Omaha whose distinctive duty was to teach either religion or ethics. Religious and ethical teachings were embedded in the rites of the gentes and of the tribe, but there were no succinct, practical commandments as to beliefs or actions expressed in them. The duty of explanation and instruction to the laity, concerning the meaning and teaching of these rites, devolved on the thoughtful elders of the tribe, who generally belonged to those eligible to the office of keeper, and formed a kind of hereditary priesthood.

The Keeper

In every gens or subgens there was a particular family to which belonged the hereditary right to furnish the keeper, who had charge of the sacred object of the gens together with its rituals and rites. This man held no title apart from the name of the object or rite of which he had charge; he was the keeper (*athi^n*, "to possess" or "keep") of the White Buffalo Hide or of the Sacred Pole, or of the rite of Turning the Child, etc. He alone possessed the authority to perform the ceremony, recite the rituals, and conduct the rites committed to his care; it was also his duty to instruct his son and successor, and to transmit this knowledge and right to him. In the event of the death of all the male members of the family of a keeper, the Seven Chiefs were required to select another family in the same subgens to take up the duties of keeper. The compensation given to the keepers for their services has been spoken of (p. 212). A keeper's mode of life did not differ from that of other men; he did not ordinarily wear any part of his ceremonial dress or adopt a peculiar garb to distinguish his calling, nor did the keepers dwell apart from other members of the tribe. They were held in respect and generally conformed their lives to the sacredness of their official duties. Keepers sometimes became chiefs; this was true of the last keeper of the Sacred Pole, he who transferred this ancient object to the writers for safe-keeping (p. 223) and narrated the Sacred Legend of the tribe.

WE'WAÇPE

This name was applied to tribal religious rites and is significant of their object. The definition of this term can not be given in a word; *we'waçpe* means "something to bring the people into order and into a thoughtful composure." The term bears testimony to the thoughtful character of the people, for while the institution of some of the rites of this class was credited to "old men," this should not be taken too literally, for several of the ceremonies show evidence of a growth that may have extended through a long period. The word indicates, however, a discriminating observation of the social value of religious rites not only as a power to hold the people together by the bond of a common belief and the enjoyment of its ceremonial expression, but as a means to augment in the popular mind the importance of self-control, of composure, and of submission to authority.

The rites termed We'waçpe partook of the nature of prayer and were believed to open a way between the people and the mysterious Wako^n'da (p. 597); therefore they had to be accurately given in order that the path might be straight for the return of the desired benefit. A mistake in rendering a ritual had to be atoned in some cases by a ceremony of contrition in order to avert trouble from the entire people, as the interruption of the prescribed order in a religious ceremony was believed to be a subject for supernatural punishment.

We'waçpe rites were institutional in character and were so regarded by the tribe. They were distinct from individual rites, as, for example, the rite wherein the youth sought to come into relation with the supernatural. The latter experience was strictly personal nor was its character changed if the peculiar type of the vision or dream gave the youth the right of entrance into one of the secret societies.

The rites and ceremonies, both public and private, of the secret societies, except those of the Ho^n'hewachi, do not belong to the We'waçpe class. This society partook somewhat of the character of an order of chieftainship; its ceremonies related to the cosmic forces and therefore touched on religious conceptions.

The following rites belonged to the We'waçpe class:

Those connected with the maize.

Those pertaining to the annual buffalo hunt and the White Buffalo Hide; these rites were closely related to the securing of the food supply.

The rites and rituals belonging to the two Sacred Tribal Pipes and those of the Sacred Pole; both of these pertained to the governing power of the tribe and the authority vested in the chiefs. While dependence on Wako^n'da was recognized in all of these rites, they were so directly concerned with the temporal welfare of the people that the religious element was somewhat overlaid by the material benefits sought through the ceremonials.

The introduction of the child to the cosmos.

Turning the Child.

The consecration of the boy to Thunder.

The He′dewachi, the only ceremony in which all the people—men, women, and children—took part and were led by the two Sacred Pipes, borne by their hereditary keepers, in the rhythmic advance by gentes toward the symbolically decorated pole standing in the center of the large circle made by the assembled tribe. The teaching of this joyous and picturesque ceremony, it may be recalled, was that the tribe must be a living unit, even as the tree and its branches are one (p. 251).

The Wa′wa^n ceremony; this was classed with the We′waçpe because it was a means of bringing about peaceful relations within and without the tribe.

Wako^N′da

Wako^n′da is not a modern term and does not lend itself to verbal analysis. The word *wano^n′xe* means "spirit." The ideas expressed in the words *wako^n′da* and *wano^n′xe* are distinct and have nothing in common. There is therefore no propriety in speaking of Wako^n′da as "the great spirit." Equally improper would it be to regard the term as a synonym of nature, or of an objective god, a being apart from nature. It is difficult to formulate the native idea expressed in this word. The European mind demands a kind of intellectual crystalization of conceptions, which is not essential to the Omaha, and which when attempted is apt to modify the original meaning. Wako^n′da stands for the mysterious life power permeating all natural forms and forces and all phases of man's conscious life. The idea of Wako^n′da is therefore fundamental to the Omaha in his relations to nature, including man and all other living forms. As has been said by a thoughtful member of the tribe, "No matter how far an Omaha may wander in his superstitious beliefs and attribute godlike power to natural objects, he invariably returns to Wako^n′da, the source of all things, when he falls into deep and sober thought on religious conceptions."

Visible nature seems to have mirrored to the Omaha mind the ever-present activities of the invisible and mysterious Wako^n′da and to have been an instructor both in religion and in ethics. The rites pertaining to the individual (p. 115) reveal clearly the teaching of the integrity of the universe, of which man is a part; the various We′waçpe rites emphasize man's dependence on a power greater than himself and the idea that supernatural punishments will follow disobedience to constituted authority. Natural phenomena served to enforce ethics. Old men have said: "Wako^{n}'da causes day to follow night without variation and summer to follow winter; we can depend on these regular changes and can order our lives by them. In this way Wako^{n}'da teaches us that our words and our acts must be truthful, so that we may live in peace and happiness with one another. Our fathers thought about these things and observed the acts of Wako^{n}'da and their words have come down to us." Truthfulness in word and in action was fundamental to the scheme of ethics taught among the Omaha. As applied to action, it involved the idea of honesty and of faithfulness to a duty laid upon a person, whatever its nature, whether of a scout (p. 425), a runner in search of a herd of buffalo (p. 279), or the performance of a rite by its proper custodian. No untruthful report or evasion of responsibility was permitted to go unpunished, the penalty it was believed being inflicted supernaturally. The instances related concerning the fate of the keepers of the Sacred Tent of War who shirked their responsibilty and met their death by the lightning stroke were cited as proof of the watchfulness of Wako^{n}'da over truthfulness as applied to acts. For like reason, all vows had to be kept. Sometimes a man when praying for success in hunting vowed to give the first deer or other game secured to Wako^{n}'da, and no man having made such a vow would break it, even though he and his family had to go hungry. (Such offerings were always handed to a keeper.)

While the conception of Wako^{n}'da may appear somewhat vague certain anthropomorphic attributes were ascribed to it, approximating to a kind of personality. Besides the insistence on truthfulness in word and deed already mentioned, there were other qualities involving pity and compassion, as shown in the account given in the Sacred Legend concerning the institution of the rite of No^{n}'zhi^{n}zho^{n} (p. 128) and in the rite itself and its accompanying prayer (p. 130). All experiences in life were believed to be directed by Wako^{n}'da, a belief that gave rise to a kind of fatalism. In the face of calamity, the thought, "This is ordered by Wako^{n}'da," put a stop to any form of rebellion against the trouble and often to any effort to overcome it.

Not only were the events in a person's life decreed and controlled by Wako^{n}'da, but man's emotions were attributed to the same source. An old man said: "Tears were made by Wako^{n}'da as a relief to our human nature; Wako^{n}'da made joy and he also made tears!" An aged man, standing in the presence of death, said: "From my earliest years I remember the sound of weeping; I have heard it all my long life and shall hear it until I die. There will be partings as long as man lives on the earth; Wako^{n}'da has willed it to be so!"

The use of the term *Wako^{n}'da* in the songs of the Washis'ka athi^{n}, or Shell society, and the I^{n}'gthu^{n}, or Thunder society, needs a word of explanation, as it has led to misunderstandings of Omaha belief.

This use has been frequently explained to the writers, who have been urged not to fall into error as to what is meant by *Wako^{n}'da*. These explanations have come from members of the societies to which the songs belonged wherein the word occurs, as well as from men who did not belong to these secret societies, so that the writers feel sure that there is a distinction in the Omaha mind between varying meanings of the word *wako^{n}'da*. The Wako^{n}'da addressed in the tribal prayer and in the tribal religious ceremonies which pertain to the welfare of all the people is the Wako^{n}'da that is the permeating life of visible nature—an invisible life and power that reaches everywhere and everything, and can be appealed to by man to send him help. From this central idea of a permeating life comes, on the one hand, the application of the word *wako^{n}'da* to anything mysterious or inexplicable, be it an object or an occurrence; and on the other hand, the belief that the peculiar gifts of an animate or inanimate form can be transferred to man. The means by which this transference takes place is mysterious and pertains to Wako^{n}'da but is not Wako^{n}'da. So the media—the shell, the pebble, the thunder, the animal, the mythic monster—may be spoken of as wako^{n}'das, but they are not regarded as *the* Wako^{n}'da.

Personal prayers were addressed directly to Wako^{n}'da. A man would take a pipe and go alone to the hills; there he would silently offer smoke and utter the call, *Wako^{n}'da ho!*, while the moving cause, the purport of his prayer, would remain unexpressed in words. If his stress of feeling was great, he would leave the pipe on the ground where his appeal had been made. This form of prayer (made only by men) was called *Niniba-ha* (*niniba*, "pipe"), "addressing with the pipe."

Women did not use the pipe when praying; their appeals were made directly, without any intermediary. Few, if any, words were used; generally the sorrowful or burdened woman simply called on the mysterious power she believed to have control of all things, to know all desires, all needs, and able to send the required help.

Interrelation of Men and Animals

The relation of animals to the various rites of the gentes is difficult to explain for the reason that the outlook on nature and all living creatures, of the white race is so different from that of the Indian. Accustomed as we are to classify animals as domesticated or wild and to regard them as beneath man and subservient to him, it requires an effort to bring the mind to the position in which, when contemplating nature, man is viewed as no longer the master but as one of many manifestations of life, all of which are endowed with kindred powers, physical and psychical, and animated by a life force emanating from the mysterious Wako^{n}'da.

An old Indian explained: "All forms mark where Wako^n'da has stopped and brought them into existence." The belief that the power of Wako^n'da is akin to the directive force of which man is conscious within himself is implied in the old man's remark; each "form" was the result of a "stop," where there had been a distinct exercise of the will power, an act of the creative force of Wako^n'da performed. Looking on nature from this standpoint, men, animals, the earth, the sky, and all natural phenomena are not only animated, but they bear a relation to one another different from that which we are accustomed to consider as existing among them; man does not stand apart from, he becomes literally a part of nature, connected with it physically and related to it psychically. As has been said by the old men, "Man lives on the fruits of the earth; this is true when he feeds on the animals, for all draw their nourishment from mother earth; our bodies are strengthened by animal food and our powers can be strengthened by the animals giving us of their peculiar gifts, for each animal has received from Wako^n'da some special gift. If a man asks help of Wako^n'da, Wako^n'da will send the asker the animal that has the gift that will help the man in his need." This view of the interrelation of men and animals, whereby in some mysterious manner, similar to the assimilation of food, man's faculties and powers can be reinforced from the animals, may assist in explaining why animals play so large a part in Omaha rites.

This belief concerning the interrelation of men and animals may furnish the key to a better understanding of the myths of the Omaha and their cognates, some of which appear to be survivals of a time when this belief was in an active and formative stage, a time when man was trying to explain to himself the mystery of his conscious life and of his environment. Many thoughts arising from this mental effort, while intrinsically abstract, became concrete through an imaginative, dramatic story, serious in character, with a burden that could not be shifted from symbolic to matter-of-fact speech. In some such way and at a period far back in the history of the people the myth may have had its rise. Viewed by the light of Omaha tribal rites and rituals, it seems probable that some of the myths may be survivals of very ancient ceremonies, skeletons, so to speak, from which the original ceremonial covering has disappeared.

Many of the mythic stories found among this group of cognate tribes are in some of their details obscene, a characteristic for which no adequate explanation is to be found in the daily life and customs of the people or in the rites as practised during recent centuries. Offensive as some of these stories are, they often exhibit a titanic audacity that gives to them a kind of grotesque dignity. Even mythic stories of this class may also be survivals, which have suffered not only from the wear and tear of ages but from accretions of minds not of the highest type. Natural functions have demanded explanation, and in the absence of teaching based on knowledge of physical laws, man's fancy here as in the world around has run riot. Among all peoples there is an undercurrent of indecent stories that show a strange kinship and that may have a common psychical origin.

Although, according to the Omaha view, man is so closely connected with the animals, he was not born of them; no trace has been found showing any confusion or mixture of forms; no Omaha believes that his ancestors ever were elk, or buffalo, or deer, or turtle, any more than that they were the wind, the thunder, or the sky. Myths which speak of the union of the earth and the sky appear to be an attempt to express in concrete form the idea that a dual force represented in the masculine and feminine forms is fundamental to all creative processes and was ordained by Wako^{n}'da. The recognition of this dual force in nature seems to have been common to all races, but it has been variously emphasized by different peoples. The idea was a vital one to the Omaha, as has been shown in their tribal organization (p. 134), but it did not assume the strongly anthropomorphic aspect into which it crystalized among Eastern races. The Omaha did not project this dual force into gods and goddesses, their imagination did not so incline to express itself; it was occupied in seeking psychical counterparts to man among birds and animals, in drawing ethical teachings from the natural phenomena of night and day, and in finding lessons in tribal unity and strength from the branching tree.

Veneration for the Ancients

The belief in the continuity of life made natural the thought that the venerable men who had been instrumental in establishing the ceremonies of the tribe did not abandon interest in the affairs of the people because of their death. (See Ponca Feast of Soldiers, p. 309.) While the worship of ancestors did not exist among the Omaha, reverence was paid to the memory of the Ancient Ones whose thoughts on the relation of man to Wako^{n}'da embodied in rituals and ceremonies became the medium of religious teaching for the people. The symbolic figure *uzhi^{n}'eti* (p. 241) represented this belief and reverent feeling toward the Ancients.

Position of Chiefs

Chiefs were respected not only because of their authority, but as having been favored by the unseen powers, who had granted them help and had strengthened their ability to be steadfast in purpose during the years wherein they struggled to perform the acts required (p. 202) to enter the rank of chief. Because of this relation to the unseen powers, a chief had to be deliberate in speech and in movement, for all his words and acts were more or less connected with the welfare of the people, and by the authority vested in his office the chief was allied to the all-ruling and mysterious Wako^n'da. As the rites connected with the Sacred Tribal Pipes were the medium between the chiefs and Wako^n'da, there was no means by which to atone for, or condone, any mistake or mishap occurring during the ceremonial filling and smoking of these Pipes. Instances have been related in which such an act of sacrilege was followed by death.

Totems

The so-called "personal totem" was not an object of worship, and only in a very limited sense could it properly be termed a fetish. It was a token or kind of credential of the vision granted the youth during his fast; he did not appeal to the thing itself, but to that which it represented, the form sent by Wako^n'da, which could reach him personally, "have compassion" on him, and therefore bring to him the help he required in his hour of need. A reverent attitude was maintained toward all rites and ceremonies that dealt with man's relation to the unseen and tolerance was shown to usages that differed from their own.

Magic

Magic formed no part of the Omaha religion in either faith or practice. All the rites and ceremonies classed as We'waçpe were religious in character and singularly free from anything that could properly be called magical. The supernatural punishments that have been referred to can hardly be considered as connected with magic. Certain other beliefs and acts, as that help or punishment could be brought about through the exercise of will power, in the *wazhi^n'thethe* (p. 583) or the *wazhi^n'agthe* (p. 497), were not regarded as magical practices, nor were the means employed by the Ghost and Thunder societies to look into the future; these were thought to be different from the usages of the Shell and Pebble societies. Only the members of the two societies last named claimed to be endowed with the ability to exercise powerful magic, and their operations were confined in the main to their own membership.

Witchcraft, such as is said to have existed in other tribes, was not found among the Omaha. There was general fear and dread of magic, but no one who practised it was persecuted or punished for his acts; he might be avoided, but he would remain unmolested.

Warfare and Ethics

The influence on warfare of the higher ethics has never been pronounced in the history of any race or people and the Omaha were no exception to the rule. As has been stated, when in battle an Omaha found escape impossible he fought until he died. He aimed to kill his enemy, not to take him captive, for there was no custom of adoption among the Omaha as with the Osage; therefore neither men, women, nor children were made prisoners. War meant devastation and probable death to those who engaged in it. While it was not waged along humane lines, sometimes women were allowed to escape. The story is told of a war captain who, when a woman was fleeing, said to his men, "Let your sister go!" The term for aggressive warfare (p. 403) implies that such warfare meant fighting with *men*, a contest between warriors. In view of what has just been said, it was natural that the Omaha should have regarded capture as equivalent to death. With reference to the treatment accorded their enemies it may be added that no authentic account has been obtained of the torture of anyone by the Omaha during the last century or more.[a]

Terms for Good Traits and Good Conduct

It may assist toward making clearer Omaha ethics as applied to social life to give some of the terms that denote excellence of character and desirable social qualities.

U'piçka, a very old term, meaning that a person is unselfish.

Wazhi^{n}'çabe, applied to one who holds himself in control, who avoids all words and deeds that might lead to unpleasantness.

Wa'gaçu, one who is straightforward, whose word can be depended on.

Wawe'no^{n}hi^{n}, one who is willing to help and to serve others.

Waho^{n}'e shto^{n}, one who never forgets to acknowledge a favor, no matter how small; a courteous person.

Watha'ethatha, a sympathetic person.

Wazhi^{n}' çabe, hospitable (*çabe*, cautious, prudent).

Debi'go^{n}tha, one who can be persuaded, who will yield; also, a generous and hospitable person.

Wapiu^{n}', applied to a bright child who said clever things. Such a child, it was generally thought, would die young.

Wa'bagthagtha, diffidence.

---

[a] The term *wa'nagthe* implies ownership and the right of the owner to exercise his pleasure with impunity. This word was applied to the birds or animals captured by the Omaha and kept near their lodges, as raccoons and crows. Later the term was transferred to the domestic animals introduced by the white race, since these animals were owned and used as their owners pleased. *Na'gthe*, as a verb, signified "to abuse," "to torment," and could be used to characterize conduct; as a noun, it meant "captive." The song sung by a warrior when going to face death in battle (p. 427) was called *na'gthe waan*, "captive song;" the name probably referred to the custom in other tribes of torturing captives, and indicated, as above explained, the Omaha view of the fate of the captive in war.

Terms for Bad Traits and Bad Conduct

Almost equally helpful in understanding a people is to note the phases of character and conduct for which they have terms implying disapproval or contempt. The following belong to this class:

I'uçi shto^{n}, a liar.

Wamo^{n}*'tho*^{n} *shto*^{n}, a thieving person.

Nio^{n}*'shto*^{n} and *nage'shto*^{n}, applied to a quarrelsome person.

U'sh'athi^{n}*ga*, an impudent, forward person.

U'shige, one who seeks opportunities to take liberties with women.

Wano^{n}*'bthe tu*^{n}*ga*, a glutton.

Wathito^{n}*to*^{n}, a meddler in other people's things or affairs.

Wathi'hideshto^{n}, one who interferes with, or meddles with, another's affairs or business.

Mo^{n}*'ça*, a boastful person.

I'uthatha, a tale bearer.

Ie'go^{n}*ç shto*^{n} describes one who invents speeches and declares that others have made them.

De'geuthishi, an obstinate person.

Wani'te, a stingy person.

We'githe shto^{n}, one who "sponges" on others.

Wana' shto^{n}, a beggar.

U'zhi^{n} *shto*^{n}, one who begs with the eyes.

Wado^{n}*'beçnede*, one who stares.

Wazhethi^{n}*ge*, an impolite person who forgets to mention terms of relationship in order to thank and be courteous.

Mishke'da, lewd woman.

Proverbs

The following are a few Omaha sayings or proverbs:

"Stolen food never satisfies hunger."

"A poor man is a hard rider."

"All persons dislike a borrower."

"No one mourns the thriftless."

"The path of the lazy leads to disgrace."

"A man must make his own arrows."

"A handsome face does not make a good husband."

Religion and ethics, closely interwoven, pervaded the life of the tribe, and in judging the evidences of constructive thought on these topics one should not consider them apart from the natural and social environment of the people.

XV

LANGUAGE

An analysis of the Omaha language or a presentation of its vocabulary, grammar, and syntax would demand a fullness of treatment that is not possible at this time. A few words, however, as to the medium by which the people expressed their thoughts are fitting in order to make more complete the present account of the tribe.

The Omaha belong to the large linguistic group known as the Siouan.[a] The numerous tribes which form this group may be classified in subgroups by placing together those whose speech shows comparatively slight dialectic differences. This classification has been accomplished by the United States Bureau of American Ethnology, the Siouan family being divided into seven groups.[b] Group II, designated by the arbitrary term *Dhe'giha* or *The'giha* (see p. 37) is composed of five cognate tribes: The Omaha, Ponca, Quapaw, Osage, and Kansa.

Omaha grammar is complex rather than simple, the complexity being increased by the use of particles as prefixes and suffixes and by the incorporation of pronouns. By these means a word is modified in form and its meaning is enhanced, made more definite, more circumstantial, in a manner impossible in any European language. Such a modified word may require a sentence for translation into English.

Naturally verbs are the most susceptible to modification, but nouns are not exempt; the particles joined to the latter are generally adjectival in character so that the listener always learns something of the character, appearance, or location of the object spoken of. A few simple examples may make clearer the above statement:

Shi^{n}'nuda	to^{n}	Shi^{n}'nuda	ke	Xthabe'	te	Xthabe'	ke
Dog (the)	standing	dog (the)	lying	tree (the)	standing	tree (the)	lying

Zho^{n}'hide	tho^{n}
stump (the)	round

[a] This term bears evidence as to the early method by which the names of Indian tribes were generally obtained. The question, "Who lives beyond you?" put to a tribe was apt to elicit the answer, "Our enemies!" In this fashion the Chippewa replied through their French interpreter, who corrupted the native word into *Nadowissioux*, "snake-like," metaphorically meaning "enemies." The final syllable, *sioux*, caught the ear of the French and became fastened as a common name on the neighboring Dakota tribes. It was finally transferred to the great linguistic group to which the Dakota belong by Albert Gallatin in his monumental work, A Synopsis of the Indian Tribes in North America (*Trans. Am. Antiq. Soc., Archæologia Americana*, II, Worcester, Mass., 1836).

[b] See Handbook of American Indians, *Bull.* 30, *Bur. Am. Ethnol.*, pt. 2, 579.

Mo^n'ke bthi'xo^n ha, "I broke the arrow with my hands" (man speaking): *mo^n*, arrow (the); *ke,* long; *b,* I; *thi,* action with the hand or hands; *xo^n*, broke; *ha,* masculine termination of a sentence.

Mo^n'ke ano^n xo^n ha, "I broke the arrow with my feet" (man speaking)—*no^n*, action by or with the feet.

Mo^n'ke bpixo^n ha, "I broke the arrow by the weight of my body" (man speaking): *bpi,* action by the weight of the body, lying or sitting; here the pronoun "I" is implied; *ga* implies action by striking; *tha,* action by biting; *ba,* action by pushing or thrusting.

While there are definite meanings for the particles attached to nouns, idiomatic usage changes the meanings and applications. For example: *Pa'heke tu ithe ha* may be literally rendered thus—

Pahe'	ke	tu	ithe	ha
Hills (the)	long	blue	came	masc. termination of sentence

But in this case the literal translation fails to give the meaning of the sentence, namely: "The sight of the long range of hills that lay far in the distance came to our vision as merged in blue." Such an example (many similar ones could be given) indicates how much of the real meaning of a myth, a story, or a native conversation can easily elude the foreigner, or one who obtains these only from a literal translation.

In an unwritten language like the Omaha it is difficult for one of another race to master all the verbal details and grammatical complexities of form and usage, a difficulty augumented by the care that must be exercised in training the ear and the vocal organs in the phonetics of the speech and the observation of the accents. A mistake in either sometimes changes the direct or the implied meaning of a word.

There seem to be five sounds each of the vowels *a* and *u;* four of *e;* three of *i;* and two of *o.* The vowels *i* and *o* are frequently followed by the nasal *n.* All vowels are sometimes "exploded" as are also at times the consonants *k, p,* and *t.* The following consonant sounds correspond to those of English: *b, d, g, m, n, p, s, t, y, z.* There is a consonant kindred to *d* and *t,* but distinct from either, and another similarly related to *b* and *p.* Other sounds, particularly the few gutturals of the language, must be indicated by combinations of two or more letters. *Th* has two sounds, one as in "the," the other as in "thin;" *f* and *l* sounds do not occur. The phonetics of the language has never yet been scientifically investigated.

While Omaha speech is not unmusical it is forceful and virile rather than liquid and flowing.

Accents are important; there are cases in which the shifting of an accent completely changes the meaning of a word. In certain forms of address the position of the accent denotes the sex of the person speaking. The determinative particle at the end of a sentence changes according to the sex of the speaker.

The Omaha language lends itself to picturesque and graphic detail more than to generalized statements of facts and experiences, yet it would be a mistake to regard it as not adapted to the expression of abstract thought.

In the preceding chapters there is evidence going to show that the Omaha were inclined to depend on the powers of thought and reflection for ability to bring about beneficial changes in governmental forms, tribal rites, and ceremonies. A notable instance of this trait is the coinage of the word *we'waçpe* (see p. 596) to denote those ceremonials instituted "to bring the people into order and thoughtful composure," a condition favorable to the reception of an appeal to reason and to securing the recognition of authority. The idea embodied in this word must have been the outcome of long and careful observation of social actions and of thoughtful reflection on such observation. The word affords also evidence of the adaptability of the language to the expression of abstract ideas. Another example of the expression in a single word of a complex idea derived from social observation and experience is found in the term *ni'kie* (see p. 136). Many similar examples could be given.

Although the tribe was without written records, it was not without a traditional wealth of thought expressed in rituals and rites that corresponded, in a sense, to literature. These exercised an educative influence and left an impress on the mind of the people that never was wholly obliterated. Those whose position gave them free access to these storehouses of the thoughts and aspirations of the sages of the tribe, came under a masterful control. Not only the thoughts embodied in the rituals and rites, but the language with which they were clothed dwelt in the minds of these men and acted as a refining and uplifting power that was reflected in their choice of words and their manner of expression, and resulted in a quality of attainment somewhat equivalent to our term "scholarly." When discoursing on serious subjects, such men did not express themselves in colloquial terms used in every day pursuits, but selected their words and constructed their sentences appropriately to convey the thoughts that transcended the ordinary affairs of life. Dignified converse of this character was beyond the full comprehension of those not versed in the sources whence these thoughtful "old men" drew their inspiration.

Correlation of the influences bred of environment, avocations, customs, traditions, beliefs, and ideals is essential to the understanding of the life and of the speech of an American Indian tribe.

XVI

CONCLUSIONS

Looking back over thirty years of acquaintance with and study of the Omaha tribe, certain characteristics of the people become apparent.

The traditions of the Omaha indicate that the physiographic conditions of their environment have always been marked by the absence of extremes, as of climate—long seasons of heat and dryness or protracted periods of benumbing cold; nor do they appear to have experienced the shocks and calamities that are met with in a volcanic region; nor have they dwelt amid strikingly impressive features of the landscape, as lofty mountains and deep canyons. On the contrary, they seem to have lived in an hospitable country, where summer and winter without unusual intensity have followed each other in orderly progression. So, too, the days and nights were without the sharp contrasts found in many regions. This equable movement of the seasons and of the days seems profoundly to have impressed the Omaha mind and to have led to a conception of stability and the attribution to it of a high ethical quality, one which came to be regarded as desirable for man, which he should strive to reproduce in his own life and in his relations to others. This quality he allied to the idea of truthfulness. The orderly progression of the seasons and of day and night he regarded as one method by which Wako^{n}'da taught man to be truthful, so that his words and acts could be depended on. From the emphasis put on truthfulness and the relegation of the punishment of falsehood to Wako^{n}'da, through such natural agencies as the storm and the lightning, which broke the ordinary calm and stable order of the heavens, we discern how fundamental had become the idea of the necessity of truth to the stability of all forms of life, natural and social.

It may be that because of this manner of viewing nature the Omaha mythologies are less complicated and ornate (if that term may be allowed) than are those of some other tribes. The Omaha seem to have been given more to a practical than a fanciful view of nature and of human life. While this peculiarity may have tended to make them somewhat prosaic along given lines, it led to a certain sturdiness of character that caused them to place a higher value on faculties of the mind than on emotional attributes.

The Omaha estimate of the value of thought is strongly brought out in their Sacred Legend, which briefly recounts their experiences from the time when they "opened their eyes and beheld the day" down to the adoption of the Sacred Pole as an emblem of governmental authority. Every acquisition that bettered the condition of the people was the result of the exercise of the mind. "And the people thought" is the preamble to every change; every new acquirement, every arrangement devised to foster tribal unity and to promote tribal strength, was the outcome of thought. The regulation of the annual tribal hunt, wherein the individual was forced to give way for the good of the whole people; the punishment of murder as a social offense; the efforts to curb the disintegrating war spirit, to bring it under control, to make it conserve rather than disrupt the unity of the tribe—all were the result of "thought." So, too, was the tribal organization itself, which was based on certain ideas evolved from thinking over natural processes that were ever before their observation. The Sacred Legend speaks truly when it says "And the people thought."

While the Omaha were a thoughtful and a practical people, they were not without poetic feeling, as their ceremonies and rituals indicate—those, for instance, which heralded to the universe the birth of a child, which introduced the child to its place and duties as a member of the tribe, and which in the presence of death gave sympathy to the mourners and at the same time cheered the departing one as he entered on his journey to the realm of spirits.

Like all other tribes, the Omaha was strongly anthropomorphic in its outlook on nature. Everything lived and partook of man's qualities. This is clearly shown in the ritual of the corn (p. 261), in the address to the stone in the sweat-lodge ritual (p. 577), and in other rites and rituals given in the preceding pages. The idea of personality is dominant in the language and in the religious beliefs and practices. The force within this personality was recognized as that of the will, that power which directs one's actions so as to bring about desired results.[a] By its iteration of the phrase "and the people thought,"

[a] This moving force, or will, is called *wazhin'*, a word used in compounding many words which indicate the use of this dominant force in man. Thus, *wie'wazhin* means to do something of one's own free will unbiased by another (*wi*, "I;" *e*, sign of the objective; *wazhin*, "will power"). When the Omaha first saw a railroad train moving along without visible aid from man or animal, a name was given it derived from the foregoing word: *E'wazhin nonge* (*nonge*, "to run"), "it runs of its own will." Anger is called *wazhin piazhi* (*piazhi*, "bad," "evil"). *Wazhin piazhi* therefore signifies that in anger the will power is charged with evil and the man becomes dangerous to himself and to others. Kindness is termed *wazhin' çabe* (*çabe*, "to be guarded, circumspect in word or behavior"). The word indicates the Omaha conception of what constitutes kindness—it is to use one's will to guard one's speech and conduct so as not to injure anyone. The word for "patience" (*wazhin' çnede*) presents another aspect of self-control: *çnede* means "long;" to be patient demands that a man's will be kept for a considerable length of time to a given course.

One more example, because it bears directly on this power to think, to discriminate, to draw conclusions, and so influence action: *wazhin' çka* means "intelligence," "discernment," "wisdom" (*çka*, "white" or "clear"). *Wazhin' çka* is the application to mental processes of the natural experience of seeing. When the atmosphere is clear, objects can be distinctly discerned, their peculiarities noted, and also their relation to one another; so, when the mind is clear, discrimination is possible as are reasonable conclusions—it is the white, unclouded mind that can perceive what is conducive to the best in words and in deeds, to the attainment of wisdom. These compounded words, which could be multiplied, all go to confirm the statement that the people thought on conduct and its consequences when framing words to describe lines of behavior.

the Sacred Legend, which preserved the experiences of the years, emphasized the vital fact that better conditions are always attained by the exercise of thought, not by magical interferences.

Thus it would appear that the Omaha tribe was a group of native Americans sturdy in mind and in body; more given to industrial than to artistic expression, gifted with an elemental statesmanship and the ability to discover the power of a religious motive for the preservation of social order and the maintenance of peace. While the people were good fighters, they came to recognize that fighting is not the only arena for achievement, and (as their name for tribe indicates) that it is best employed in the defense of the home and the integrity of the tribe.

APPENDIX

RECENT HISTORY OF THE OMAHA TRIBE

CONTACT WITH THE WHITE RACE

The time when the Omaha tribe first came into contact with the white race can not be fixed with exactness but it is probable that the meeting did not take place until about the middle of the seventeenth century, when the French were encountered. Intercourse between the Omaha and the French was never close or prolonged, nor marked by any attempt on the part of Frenchmen to disturb Indian customs or to become possessed of Indian lands. The spirit of adventure or desire to enter into trade actuated those who first strayed into the Indian country. During their stay they mixed with the people on friendly terms and were chiefly concerned in an endeavor to introduce articles of white manufacture among the natives and to establish permanent trading relations. The English, on the contrary, were colonists from the first and aimed to become possessed of land. This they sought to obtain through some form of purchase, always expecting the Indians to vacate the territory acquired and find homes elsewhere, an expectation which frequently gave rise to trouble and involved hardship on the natives. The difference in the relations between the Omaha and the French and the Omaha and the English is reflected in the names given to these two nations. The French were called Wa'xe ukethi^{n}; the probable derivation of *wa'xe* has already been given (p. 82); *ukethi^{n}*, "usual," "not strange" or "uncommon"—the term implying that these white men mingled with the people and did not consider themselves strangers. The English were called Mo^{n}hi^{n} to^{n}ga (*mo^{n}hi^{n}*, "knife;" *to^{n}ga*, "big"); the name Big Knife, given the English, old Omaha men said, did not originate in the tribe but was borrowed by the Omaha from some other tribe. The English were known by this name to the Winnebago, the Iowa, the Oto, the Osage, and the Ponca, all members of the same linguistic family as the Omaha. It is not improbable that the Dakota name for American, Long Knife, is a modified form of the old term for Englishman. The name Big Knife is said to have come into use because of the swords worn by the English. The present Omaha word for sword, *mo*^{n}*çe weti*^{n} (*mo*^{n}*çe*, "metal;" *weti*^{n}, "war club"), was given to the sword when the Omaha learned its special use.

The French and the English were the only white nationalities with which the Omaha had direct relations. They learned of the Spaniards also, whom they called by a corruption of that name, Hespayu'na. The Omaha classed the Germans, Swedes, Italians, and Irish as one people, calling them Ie'thashathu (*ie'*, "speech;" *thashathu*, "rattled" or "confused")—"they of the rattled or confused speech." The Negro is called Wa'xeçabe (*waxe*, "white man;" *çabe*, "black")—"the black white man."

EARLY TRADERS

By the middle of the seventeenth century Frenchmen had pushed westward beyond the Great Lakes and trading posts had sprung up along the adventurers' trails. The French held the trade of the Omaha and were not supplanted by the English and Americans until the latter part of the eighteenth century. Old men of the last century remembered the stories their fathers told of going on a long journey to trade at a post "on a great lake far to the north." This was probably the post spoken of by Carver as "Fort La Reine" on Lake Winnipeg. "To this place," he writes, "the Mahahs who inhabit a country two hundred and fifty miles southwest come to trade."[a] It is not improbable that the Omaha knew of the first trading post on the Missouri river, about 250 miles above its mouth, erected in 1722, and known as Fort Orleans; this fort presaged the coming of the white trader into the Omaha country. During the contention between the French and the English in the middle of the eighteenth century, into which so many Indian tribes were drawn as partisans, the Omaha were fortunate in being sufficiently removed from the sphere of activities to escape entanglement. In fact not only during the wars between the French and English but during those between the English and the Colonists the Omaha took no part, so that the tribe has never taken up arms against any of the white race. While the Omaha kept clear of these difficulties, they were not able to elude the evil influences incident to white contact, many of which were accentuated through the rivalries that sprang up between the fur-trading companies.

At the close of the French and Indian War, in 1763, the English were left in control of all the country to the east of the Mississippi and English traders gradually made their way westward into the territory

[a] Three Years' Travels through the Interior Parts of North America, etc., by Jonathan Carver, 69, Philadelphia, 1796.

previously occupied exclusively by the French. This nearer approach of the English to the Omaha country soon began to make itself felt along lines that developed rapidly after the Louisiana Purchase had brought their country under the control of the United States—a change that had the effect of relieving American traders from international embarrassments—and as a result, trading posts quickly spread along the Mississippi and Missouri rivers, with St. Louis as headquarters.

No important post was built in the immediate vicinity of the Omaha villages but during the last decade of the eighteenth century men in the employ of the fur companies visited the people and instituted trading relations with them. The story of Blackbird, mentioned on page 82, is a memorial of this contact. During the first quarter of the nineteenth century a small post was established near the Omaha village and maintained there for a time. The usual custom among the traders before the establishment of a United States Indian agency among a tribe was to erect a small log cabin and to time the trader's visit so that he would be present with his goods when the tribe returned from its annual hunt, or when special hunting parties which went out exclusively for pelts came back with the product of the chase. At no other time was anyone connected with the trading company present among the Omaha. The trader's arrival was signaled by the firing of guns to draw the people together for business.

Introduction of Metal Implements

From the first the native industries were affected by the advent of the traders, who introduced articles of white manufacture. It was not long before the metal knife replaced the native implement of chipped stone. It is said that when metal knives were first brought by the early traders they cost the Omaha the value of one dollar apiece. An interesting example of the conservation, in ceremonies, of early types of useful articles is found in the requirement that one of the gifts essential in the rite of tattooing (p. 503) was a number of the strong, red-handled knives of the kind first known to the tribe. The metal knife soon became the constant companion of men and women, serving all domestic purposes, but it never supplanted the ancient flint knife in tribal rites. The lock of hair taken from the head of the male child when he was consecrated to Thunder (p. 122) was cut by a flint knife; only a flint knife could be used when bleeding for curative purposes. The ancient name (*mo^{n}hi^n*) was transferred without change from the flint to the metal knife. The name for the stone ax, *mo^n'çepe,* was similarly transferred to the metal ax; that for "hoe," *we'e,* was afterward given to the plow. Sooner or later all stone implements yielded to those of iron and the chipping of stone became a lost art. One survival held well into the last century, namely, the making and the use of stone disks, (*i^{n}'thapa*), between which the kernels of corn were pounded to make meal for porridge. These disks were portable and served as a "hand mill" when the people were traveling. Bone awls gave way to awls of iron, which the Indians always fitted into handles of bone; the old name, *wa'ku,* was retained. An iron blade was bound to the edge of the elk-horn scraper to facilitate its use in preparing hides for tanning. Iron hoes supplanted the ancient implement made from the shoulder blade of the elk. The stone implements connected with the daily needs of the people were the first to be displaced by iron ones.

Decline of Old Avocations and the Effect on the People

With the coming of the trader and the introduction of iron implements and other articles for daily use new conditions confronted the Indians; they were no longer obliged to make all the articles required for use and the time formerly occupied by the long and wearisome process of chipping and rubbing stone was now left free. Furthermore, the stimulus for acquiring skill in the old-time industries was withdrawn. The new iron implements which had brought about this change in conditions had been acquired by bartering pelts. Barter was not new to the people. It had long been practised between various tribes; minerals, seeds, shells, and other articles had found their way by this means into regions remote from their natural environment, but it is safe to say that up to the time of the coming of the white trader no Omaha had slain animals for merely commercial purposes. The barter in pelts established by the traders was therefore different in character from any barter that had been practised between tribes and was destined to give rise to a new industry among the Indians—that of hunting for gain. Heretofore hunting had been carried on in order to secure food and other necessities—clothing, shelter, and bone with which to make implements; moreover it had been conducted with more or less religious ceremony, which had directed the Omaha thought toward Wako^{n}'da, as the giver of the means by which to sustain life, as shown in the rites connected with the annual buffalo hunt (see p. 275) and planting the maize (see p. 262). The quest of game for profit introduced new motives for hunting and also of cultivating the soil, motives not consonant with the old religious ideas and customs; consequently under their influence such customs slowly but inevitably fell into disuse. The effect on the Omaha mind of their obliteration was to weaken the power of ancient beliefs and to introduce new standards, commercial in character; as a result the Omaha became less strong to resist the inroads of new and adverse influences which came with his closer contact with the white race.

The new character given to hunting produced permanent effects not only on the thought of the people but on their ancient mode of life. The stimulation of hunting as an avocation weakened the influence of the old village life, created different standards of wealth, enhanced the importance of the hunter, and greatly increased the labors of the women in preparing pelts and skins for the market. There is good reason to ascribe to the last-named condition an impetus to the practice of polygamy among the Omaha. There was no special working class in the tribe nor could labor be hired. In the old time one woman could scarcely give proper attention to all the skins secured by a good hunter; still less could she do the additional work occasioned by the pressure of trade.

Changes in Ornaments and Decoration

The traders' wares were not confined to tools. Many novelties were brought which appealed to the people and soon created new wants. Glass beads of gay colors lent themselves to decoration as the more cumbersome shell beads could not, but bead decoration did not replace at once porcupine quill work. The latter demanded training, skill, and patience, whereas beads were easily used and made with little effort a garment effective in ornament and coloring, so that in time their use became popular. The old name for the shell bead (*hi^{n}çka'*) was transferred to the new glass bead. Silver or brass bangles and finger rings were never as much liked by the Omaha as by some other tribes. The silver "ear bob" introduced by the traders was called *pe'ugashke* (*pe*, modified for euphony from *pa*, meaning "nose;" *ugashke*, "to attach"). This name may refer to the ceremonial piercing of the nose during the tattooing ceremony (see p. 503) for there is no tradition that the Omaha ever wore nose rings. The name for "earring" is *u'wi^n*, an old term that strange to say was never applied to the silver "ear bob" brought by the traders. These "ear bobs" were much liked as earrings; sometimes they adorned the entire lobe of the ear.

Another saving of labor in comparison with old methods was involved in buying paints from the traders. The paint was sold in small packages not much larger than a paper of darning needles and the price of one of these packages in the last century was the value of twenty-five cents. The old term for "red paint," *waçezhide* (*waçe*, "clay;" *zhide*, "red") was applied to the trader's article as was the old name for "green paint" (*waçe'tu*). Blue paint was called *mo^{n}thi^{n}katu* (*mo^{n}thi^{n}ka*, "earth;" *tu*, "blue"); yellow paint, *mo^{n}thi^{n}ka çi*, "yellow earth"—both old names. Great quantities of paint were sold, this article alone yielding a large profit to the trader.

Introduction of Cloth

The heavy woolen cloth called strouding was probably introduced by the English traders during the latter part of the eighteenth century. In the middle of the last century it cost the Omaha from four to six dollars per yard. Broadcloth cost from eight to twelve dollars per yard. When the Omaha first saw strouding he had no idea of cloth, so when it was spread before him he gave to it the name of the largest stretch of a given surface for clothing with which he was acquainted, the skin robe, calling this cloth *wai^n'*, "robe." When, however, he wished to speak of cloth he added the word denoting the color; thus, *wai^n'tu*, "blue cloth," or *wai^n'zhide*, "red cloth," while the simple word *wai^n'* still designated the skin robe. Broadcloth was called *wai^n'shnaha* (*wai^n'*, "robe;" *shnaha*, "smooth,") because of the difference between its surface and that of strouding.

Strouding was used by the men for leggings, breechcloths, and sometimes for robes. Women made of it skirts, sacks, and leggings extending only to the knees. Broadcloth was not employed by the men; this material was bought by the richer members of the tribe for women's skirts and leggings. Sometimes a woman possessed a robe made of broadcloth. With the introduction of strouding and broadcloth needles and thread became known. Needles were called *wa'kuzhi^{n}gau'ude* (*waku*, "awl;" *zhi^n'ga*, "little;" *u'de*, "with a hole"). Thread was named *waho^n'*, meaning "something spun." Pins were not known until well into the last century. It was about the middle of the nineteenth century when calico was introduced by American traders; owing to its cheapness, it speedily became the material commonly used by the people. It was called *waxi^{n}ha*, "thin skin." The commercial value attached to dressed skins made them too valuable for common wear, a fact which aided in promoting the substitution of strouding for clothing; later, the high price of the strouding increased the sale of calico.

Steel traps, used to facilitate the catching of beavers, were early introduced by the traders; these were called *mo^n'çe*, "metal." The unqualified word *mo^n'çe* came to signify "trap," and the act of trapping was called *mo^n'çeuzhi*, "to put or place in metal." The principal furs supplied by the Omaha were buffalo, bear, beaver, mink, raccoon, and deer skins. The people were good hunters and trappers and were regarded as a desirable tribe to deal with. Canvas as a substitute for the buffalo-skin tent cover became common about the middle of the last century and took the old name of the tent cover, *ti'ha*, "tent skin."

Introduction of Guns

Guns were introduced toward the close of the first quarter of the nineteenth century, receiving the name *wahu'to^{n}the*, "to make a noise with." The bullet was called *mo^n'çemo^n*, "metal arrow;" gunpowder was called *mo^{n}xu'de*, "ashes." The first guns received by the Omaha were flintlocks; rifles did not reach them until the third or fourth decade of the last century. The use of guns destroyed another native industry, arrow making, and made pointless some of the old teachings to the young (see p. 331). Copper kettles and tin and iron utensils took the place of the native pottery, consequently the pottery industry was abandoned. Wooden bowls and cups gradually disappeared from family use but the former were retained in the sacred tribal ceremonies and other rites of a serious character.

Introduction of Money; Pelt Values

Before the Omaha had dealings with the United States Government little, if any, coin had been seen by the tribe. The smallest unit of value among the skins used in barter with the traders was the raccoon skin, rated at twenty-five cents. *Mika'ha ithawa* (*mika'ha*, "raccoon skin;" *ithawa*, "to count with") became the established name of a quarter of a dollar. A dollar was called *wi^n'bthuga* (*wi^n*, "one;" *bthu'ga*, "whole" or "unit"); a fifty-cent piece, *mo^{n}ço^n'thi^{n}ha*, "half;" a dime, *shuga'zhi^{n}ga* (*shuga*, "thick;" *zhi^{n}ga*, "little"—"little thick"). A silver half dime was called *bthe'kazhi^{n}ga* (*bthe'ḳa*, "thin;" *zhi^n'ga*, "little"—"little thin"); a nickel (5 cents), *we'thawaça'to^n* (*wethawa*, "counters;" *ça'to^n*, "five"); a copper cent, *we'thawazhide*, "red counter;" seventy-five cents, *mika'haithawa tha'bthi^n* (*tha'bthi^n*, "three"), the value of three raccoon skins. A thousand dollars was called *ku'ge wi^n* (*ku'ge*, "box;" *wi^n*, "one"), the name originating from the custom of packing this number of silver dollars in a small box for convenience of transportation. In the case of payments to Indian tribes by government agents the term for the number 1,000 was *gthe'bo^{n}hiwi^{n}to^{n}ga* (*gthe'bo^n*, "ten;" *hiwi^n*, "progressing toward one;" *wi^{n}to^{n}ga*, "big").

The following prices were obtained for the skins named, in the middle of the last century: Buffalo, $15 to $20; otter, $12 to $15; mink, $2 to $5; beaver, $4 to $6. As beavers were plentiful and the use of traps facilitated catching them good trappers sometimes gave up the more laborious pursuit of large game and confined their efforts to securing beavers, in this way being able to secure good pay for their skins and at the same time to keep their families supplied with meat. Comparatively little trading in furs was done for cash. Trading on a barter basis continued until the destruction of the fur-bearing animals brought the old-time trader's career to an end.

Introduction of Intoxicants

The competition among the rival fur companies led to the introduction of intoxicating liquors among the tribes for the purpose of securing skins and trade. So great was the trouble experienced by the tribes, and so earnest were the appeals from the old chiefs and other leading men, that as early as 1802 President Jefferson made this traffic the subject of a message to Congress, which resulted in the passage of an act forbidding the sale of liquor to Indians, under penalty. Knowledge of congressional action traveled slowly in those days and laws were difficult to enforce in the sparsely settled country; consequently the fur trade continued to be stimulated and the natives demoralized by intoxicants offered by the trader. The harm done by this unlawful procedure has not yet passed away from the tribes in the United States. It is singular that "fire water" should be a common term for intoxicants in widely different languages. The Omaha word is *pede'ni*, literally "fire water" (*pede*, "fire;" *ni*, "water").

The Omaha tribe did not escape the baneful influence of liquor. The traders plied the people with rum; it was cheaper than goods to use in barter and although the traffic was illegal, the gain to the companies was so great that their agents were instructed to take the chances of detection; they did so and unfortunately generally succeeded in eluding discovery.

DRUNKENNESS AND ITS PUNISHMENT

In the third decade of the last century an incident occurred in the Omaha tribe which is still spoken of; this took place in the hut erected to accommodate the visiting trader and his wares.

The agent of a trading company had arrived with his half-breed son, then a lad about seventeen years old, who acted as clerk. The Indians had gathered with their pelts and had received goods and liquor in payment. Late one afternoon, when the clerk was alone in the hut, two men, more or less intoxicated, came in and began to quarrel. A third with his little son entered the hut to trade but, being afraid of the quarreling men, he kept back from them. A fourth man entered who had had liquor and was disposed to be troublesome and the quarreling men seemed to excite him still more, when, catching sight of the quiet man and his boy, he drew his knife, rushed at him and buried the weapon in his throat. As his victim fell dead the drunken man realized his deed and became suddenly sober. The two men ceased to quarrel and stole away, leaving the murderer alone with the dead man and the young half-breed clerk. Meanwhile the boy had run off to spread the news of his father's death. The clerk counseled the guilty man to remain in the hut, as it was his only place of safety, and for a time he heeded this advice; but at last he exclaimed: "I have forfeited my life. I may as well meet my death now!" and went out into the night. He had gone only a few steps when he was shot with an arrow and shortly died.

The horror of this murder and the realization it brought to the young clerk that liquor was robbing the people of their manhood and morality so impressed him that he then and there registered a vow that if he ever rose to a position of power in the tribe he would use his authority to break up the habit of drinking. Years passed, and this young clerk, who was Joseph La Flesche, became one of the principal chiefs of the tribe. True to his vow, he issued an order that men who drank were to be flogged.[a] During the time that Chief La Flesche remained in power drunkenness was practically checked in the tribe. Unfortunately cabals arose. The right of the chief to inflict such severe penalties was questioned by men who were not interested in the moral welfare of the people. Other authorities were invoked and in the end liquor found its way surreptitiously among the people. But the drastic measures of the chief were not soon forgotten and years elapsed before their effect was wholly lost.

Government Control of Traders

In accordance with the English policy, by which the Crown had the right to regulate trade and to license traders, the Articles of Confederation reserved that right to Congress. An act of 1786 required Indian traders to be citizens of the United States. An act of 1790 vested the power to appoint traders in the President or an officer appointed by him. When, by virtue of the Louisiana Purchase, the Omaha country became part of the domain of the United States trading with the tribe came under the restrictions of the laws mentioned. After the tribe passed under the control of the "Agency system" resident traders were licensed by the Indian Bureau. These traders opened stores on the reservation and absorbed the trade of the tribe. The destruction of the buffalo herds in the seventh decade of the last century, the rapid increase of white settlements, and finally the opening of the country by railroads, all produced marked and lasting effects on the life and avocations of the people, bringing the industry of hunting to a close and diminishing greatly the influence and the business of the trader.

---

[a] It happened that a prominent man, whose reputation for bravery was second to none, yielded to temptation and became drunk. He was a very close friend of the chief and everyone thought that the chief would not order this friend, a man honored by the tribe, to be flogged like a common offender. But the order was given and the "soldiers" who were commanded to execute the punishment advanced to the warrior's tent, not without serious questionings as to whether they might not have to fight the offender, who had never been defeated in battle. The warrior was in his tent; he heard the "soldiers" approaching and knew their errand. He stepped out to meet them. As he appeared, the "soldiers" halted; looking at them he said: "Do your duty. I broke the order of the chief and must take my punishment." He was duly flogged; no one of the "soldiers" dared to abate his strokes. As a result of this warrior's act, he not only rose higher in the esteem of the tribe because of his manly recognition of his fault but his action strengthened the chief in his effort to put a stop to drinking. Until his death, which took place toward the close of the last century, this warrior was one of the most respected and influential men in the Omaha tribe.

INTRODUCTION OF NEW FOODS, GAMES, AND DISEASES

Besides the numerous changes in tools, weapons, and clothing brought about by the traders, new foods were introduced, which eventually became common among the people. Wheat became known in the second decade of the last century, receiving the name *wamu'çke*. This name was applied also to bread made from wheat. Coffee was known earlier and was called *mo^{n}ko^{n}çabe*, "black medicine." Sugar was termed *zho^{n}ni* (*zho^{n}*, "wood;" *ni*, "water"), evidently a transfer of the name for "maple sugar." To the large white potato was given the name of the native potato, *nu*. Beef and all other fresh meats were called by the old term *tanu'ka*, "wet meat."

Two new games were received from the white people—playing cards and checkers. Cards were called *wathi'baba*, "something spread out repeatedly with the hands," the name referring to the act of shuffling and dealing the cards. The suits were called as follows: Diamonds, *ke'pa* ("turtle head"); hearts, *ni'deawi^{n}* ("buttock"); spades, *mo^{n}'-hiçi* ("arrow-head"); clubs, *t'a'zhi* (literally, "never dies"), referring, it is said, to the flower immortelle. Checkers were spoken of as *wako^{n}'pamo^{n}gthe* (*wako^{n}*, "to gamble;" *pa*, "head;" *mo^{n}gthe* "bowed"—"to play with bowed head").

New diseases found their way among the people. Smallpox (*di'xe*) wrought great havoc just before 1800, reducing "the once powerful tribe to a few hundreds." Measles (*di'xebtho^{n}çe*, "little smallpox") was almost as fatal and is still dreaded. Malaria (*wa'xewakega*, "white man's sickness") would seem from the name to have come from contact with the white race and changed environment.

INTRODUCTION OF NEW WORDS

Many new words were coined to meet the changed conditions. The following are in common use:

Store, u'thiwi^{n}ti, to trade in.
Window glass, we'ugo^{n}ba, to make light with.
Chimney, tihuko^{n} (*ti*, tent; *hukon*, old name of the smoke vent).
Table, wa'thate, to eat on.
Chair, a'gthi^{n}, to sit on.
Rocking-chair, a'gthi^{n}kipiaçaça, to rock one's self in.
Scales, we'thiho^{n}, to lift with.
Stove, mo^{n}'çeunethe, iron to make fire in.
Shovel, pe'deithiçe, to take fire with.
Bottle, pe'xeha, gourd skin.
Brick, i^{n}e'nazhide, stone burned red.
Wagon, zho^{n}mo^{n}thi^{n}, walking wood.
Horse, sho^{n}ge.
Cattle, te'çka, white buffalo.
Chickens, wazhi^{n}'gazhide, red birds.
Pigs, ku'kuçi.

Shoes, zho^{n}hi^{n}be, wooden moccasins.

Stocking, hi^{n}begawi^{n}xe (*hi^{n}be*, moccasins; *gawi^{n}xe*, to wind around the foot). Formerly matted grass was wound about the foot under the moccasin.

Button, mo^{n}geithagashka (*mo^{n}ge*, breast; *ithagashka*, to fasten with).

Ring, nombeuthixtha (*nombe*, hand or finger; *uthixtha*, to tnrust in).

Spade, to^n′deino^{n}çe, to cut the ground with.

Pitchfork, xa′deithiçe, to rake grass with.

Reaper, wamu′çkeino^{n}çe, to cut wheat with.

Mower, xa′deino^{n}çe, to cut grass with.

Saw, we′magixe, to cut with.

Grist mill, u′no^{n}tube, to grind in.

Silver, mo^n′çeçka, white metal (used also for "money").

Gold, mo^n′çeçkaçi, yellow white metal.

Sailboat, mo^{n}de′gio^n, flying boat.

Watch, or clock, mi′ido^{n}be, to look at the sun.

Rubber, haçi′çige, elastic skin.

Telegraph, mo^n′çeiuçishto^n, lying metal (referring to the incredulity with which the telegraph was received).

Postage stamp, i^{n}dewathaçkabe (*i^{n}de′*, face; *wathaçkabe*, to stick on).

Railroad train, e′wazhi^{n}no^{n}ga, self runner.

Harness, sho^n′gewei^n, for horses to carry.

Bridle, mo^n′çethahe, metal to bite.

President of the United States, Itigo^{n}thaiuzhu (*itigo^{n}thai*, grandfather; *uzhu*, principal).

Commissioner of Indian Affairs, Itigo^{n}thaizhi^{n}ga (*thai*, to whom; *zhi^{n}ga*, little).

General, Nudo^{n}ho^{n}gauzhu (*nudo^{n}ho^{n}ga*, war leader; *uzhu*, principal).

Colonel or Captain, Nudo^{n}ho^{n}gazhi^{n}ga (*zhi^{n}ga*, little).

Private, thei^n, kettle carrier.

Bayonet, mo^{n}dehi, spear.

Flag, haçka (*ha*, skin; *çka*, white); the name arose from the use of the flag of truce.

Paper, waba′gtheçe, to make stripes on.

To read, we′thadi (*we*, the act; *thade*, to speak).

Teacher, waba′gtheçewethade, one who reads paper.

To write, waba′xu, to make marks.

Pen or pencil, we′baxu, to write with.

School, waba′gtheçeathaditi, paper, to read, house—the house where paper is read.

Minister or clergyman, wago^n′çe, one who instructs.

Newspaper, waba′gtheçegawa, paper open, opened paper.

Photograph, i^{n}de′ugaxe, face picture.

Milk, te′çka mo^{n}çeni (*te′çka*, cow; *mo^{n}çe*, udder; *ni*, water).

Flapjack, wamu′çke btheka (*wamu′çke*, bread; *btheka*, thin).

Cake, wamu′çke çkithi (*çkithi*, sweet).

Peaches, she hi^n shkube (*she*, apple; *hi^n*, hair; *shkube*, deep or thick).

Chinaware, waçe′ço^{n}uxpe, clay dishes.

Tumbler (glass), ni′ithato^{n}no^n′xeego^n, water, to drink, spirit-like—to drink water from that which is like to a spirit, translucent.

Spoon, mo^n′çetehe, metal buffalo horn (referring to the old spoons of buffalo horn, *tehe*).

Fork, wa′kuwethate (*wa′ku*, awl; *wethate*, to eat—awl to eat with).

Pin, wa′kuzhi^{n}ga, little awl.

Coal, no^{n}xthe, charcoal.

Kerosene, no^{n}xthe wegthi (*wegthi*, grease).

Marbles, i^{n}ezhi^{n}ga (*i^{n}e*, stones; *zhi^{n}ga*, little).

A few old terms survive and are applied to modern conditions, as the phrase, *Tiupe*, "I am going to make a visit," (*ti*, tent; *upe*, to creep into); the word refers to the stooping posture necessary in entering the low opening of the tent. Even if going into a large dwelling the Omaha would say *Tiupe*, as did his forefathers.

TREATIES WITH THE UNITED STATES

The first treaty between the United States and the Omaha was made at Portage de Sioux in July, 1815 (U. S. Stat. at Large, vol. VII, p. 129). Similar treaties were made at that time with a number of tribes that during the War of 1812 had been more or less under the influence of English traders. The purpose of this treaty was to "place all things in every respect on the same footing as before the late war between the United States and Great Britain." Injuries were to be "mutually forgiven," "peace maintained," and the United States acknowledged by the tribe as its protecting power.

It was about the time of making this treaty that the Government took the first measures against the smallpox. The Omaha were persuaded to submit to vaccination and this treatment may have been instrumental in saving the tribe from the inroads of the disease, when, in 1837, some of the tribes to the northward were almost exterminated by it.

The second treaty was made at Council Bluffs in 1825 (U. S. Stat. at Large, vol. VII, p. 282); this related mainly to granting supremacy to the United States in punishing those who committed offenses and to the protection of traders. The Omaha agreed not to furnish ammunition to hostile Indians. In both these treaties the Omaha were dealt with under the name "Maha," this form arising from misunderstanding on the part of the whites of the native speaker, who lightly sounded as *u* the initial letter of Omaha, at the same time placing the emphasis on the second syllable.

In the treaty of July, 1830 (U. S. Stat. at Large, vol. VII, p. 328), made at Prairie du Chien, the Omaha, together with the Sauk and Foxes, Bands of the Sioux, the Iowa, Oto, and Missouri tribes, ceded to the United States their claim to lands within the present State of Iowa. The Omaha, Iowa, Oto, Yankton, and Santee Sioux agreed that a reservation in the present Nemaha county, Nebraska, should be given their half-breed kindred, 640 acres to be allotted to each individual. The half-breeds among the Omaha all received their quota of lands on this reservation. Some of them left the tribe and went to live on their newly acquired allotments; others accepted land the but disposed of it and never left the tribe. Under this treaty the Omaha received their first payment from the United States for ceded land and were promised a blacksmith and farming implements—a promise that was not fulfilled until several years later. The headquarters of the Western Superintendent of Indian tribes was at St.

Louis. To him reported subordinate officers, called Agents, who were placed in charge of the several tribes that were being assigned about this time to tracts reserved for their use, some of which covered the region in which their villages were situated.

At the time of this treaty (1830) the Omaha had left their village on Omaha creek, near the site of the present town of Homer, Dakota county, Nebraska. They had been driven thence by the continued warlike incursions of the Sioux and were living to the southwest in the vicinity of the Elkhorn river.

In a treaty made at Bellevue during October, 1836 (U. S. Stat. at Large, vol. VII, p. 524), the Omaha, together with the Oto, Missouri, Yankton, and Santee Sioux, ceded to the United States their claim to land lying between the State of Missouri and the Missouri river, and received payment therefor. The Omaha agreed to build their village near the agency that had been recently established at Bellevue, the Government promising to break and fence 100 acres for the use of the tribe.

Between 1836 and 1854 the Omaha villages were not far from Bellevue. This United States Indian agency had control over the affairs of several tribes besides the Omaha, some of which had been reduced in numbers by disease and other mishaps. During this period the Omaha made two attempts to return and live on their old village site near Homer but each was frustrated by Sioux war parties threatening their families, crops, and ponies.

In 1854 the Omaha made a treaty with the Government at Washington (U. S. Stat. at Large, vol. X, p. 1043) by which they ceded their hunting grounds in Nebraska, keeping for their own use a tract of 300,000 acres bordering the Missouri river a few miles south of the place where their old village, near Homer, had stood. A provision was introduced into the treaty, which was repeated in most of the treaties of that date made with Indian tribes, namely, to survey a portion of the reservation and apportion a certain amount of land to those individuals who desired to possess permanent homes (sec. 6). A sawmill and a gristmill were to be erected and maintained out of tribal funds, on the new Omaha reservation; also a blacksmith and a farmer were to be provided. The moneys received for the land ceded by this treaty were to be held by the United States and the payments were arranged to extend through forty years.

By a treaty of March, 1865, made at Washington (U. S. Stat. at Large, vol. XIV, p. 667) the Omaha sold to the United States a strip from the northern part of their reservation, for the occupancy of the Winnebago tribe, which had been removed from their old home in Minnesota. A portion of the payment for this land was to be expended for stock, implements, breaking of lands, etc. The provision for allotting the Omaha individual holdings, contained in section 6 of the treaty of 1854, was repeated and the stipulation made that their half-breed relatives then residing with them should be included in the promised allotment.

By an act of March 3, 1871, the mode of government negotiations with Indian tribes was changed; treaties were no longer to be made but legislation was to be enacted, the execution of any act to be "with the consent of the tribe."

By the act of June, 1872 (U. S. Stat. at Large, vol. XVII, p. 391), the Omaha sold to the Government 50,000 acres from the western part of their reservation. A portion of the proceeds of this sale was to be expended for fencing farms, building houses, purchasing implements and live stock, and establishing and maintaining schools.

Under an act of June, 1874 (U. S. Stat. at Large, vol. XVIII, p. 170), 20 additional sections in the northern part of the reservation were sold for the use of the Winnebago tribe.

By an act of August 7, 1882 (U. S. Stat. at Large, vol. XXII, p. 341), the Omaha were given their lands in severalty, each man, woman, and child receiving a portion of the tribal land, which was secured by a patent, the United States holding the patent in trust for twenty-five years, during which time the land was not taxable and could not be encumbered or sold; at the end of the trust period patents in fee were to be given to the original allottees or their heirs, according to the laws of the State of Nebraska. The act placed the Omaha under the laws of the State, civil and criminal. The unallotted land in the southwestern township of the reservation and west of the railroad running between Sioux City, Iowa, and Omaha, Nebraska, was thrown open to purchase by white settlers.

By a clause in the "severalty act" of February 7, 1887, the Omaha as allotted Indians became citizens of the United States.

A right of way was granted to a railroad through the reservation in 1894 (U. S. Stat. at Large, vol. XXVIII, p. 95). The right was extended and new rights were granted in 1896 (U. S. Stat. at Large, vol. XXX, pp. 344, 912). The survey of the Sioux City and Western Railroad was approved by the Secretary of the Interior May 2, 1905. The road was completed and was running through the reservation in April, 1907. Two towns were located on this railroad, the land being negotiated for with Indians who had inherited the tracts and were permitted by an act of Congress to sell the lands. The town site of Rosalie was approved by the Secretary of the Interior January 18, 1906, and the first lot was sold in the summer of 1907; the town was named for the late Rosalie La Flesche Farley, a daughter of Joseph La Flesche. Its population in 1910 was 147. The town site of Walthill was approved by the Secretary of the Interior at the same time as that of Rosalie and the first lots were sold on May 22, 1907. The town was named for Walter Hill (son of J. J. Hill), who had had charge of the construction of a portion of the railroad on which the town lies. The deeds for the lands sold by the Indians for these town sites were withheld for a time through the influence of Susan La Flesche Picotte, M. D., and other members of her family, until the provision was made that—

No malt or spiritous or vinous liquors shall be kept or disposed of on the premises conveyed, and that any violation of this condition, either by the grantee or any other person claiming rights under said party of the second part, shall render the conveyance void and cause the premises to revert to the party of the first part, his heirs or assigns.

With the sanction of the Secretary of the Interior this clause was inserted in all town-site deeds on the Omaha and Winnebago reservations. In the town of Walthill the Townsite Company restricted

FIG. 126. Graded school at Walthill, Nebraska.

the material of buildings on the main street to brick and stone; while this action temporarily retarded the erection of structures, it has added greatly to the appearance and permanency of the town. The population (1910) of Walthill is 810. In less than a year after its organization the town expended $14,000 for a commodious brick and stone building (fig. 126) for a graded school, in which both white and Indian children receive instruction.

WORK OF MISSIONARIES

It would be difficult to trace the tribe or even the direction whence the first missionary influence came to the Omaha. In the last decade of the eighteenth century individuals of the tribe had descended the Missouri to St. Louis to carry their pelts for barter. While there they saw something of civilized modes of living and noted the religious customs of the residents of the town. Through intercourse with tribes among which missions had been established came a vague knowledge concerning Christianity. In the early part of the nineteenth century a few Frenchmen employed with the trading companies had taken Omaha women as wives but these men had not shown a proselyting spirit nor had they made any change in the mode of native life or in the native beliefs. Sometimes the sons of these men were taken to St. Louis on their fathers' trading trips; here they acquired some knowledge of the French language and of business methods, the possession of which enabled them to assist their fathers in the duties connected with trading. In some instances these sons were sent to school and learned to speak English and in two cases, those of Logan Fontenelle and Louis Sansouci, they were able to serve as official interpreters. It was not until the third decade of the nineteenth century that the Omaha came into direct contact with missionaries and then the contact was occasional rather than constant. In 1845 the first permanent mission was established by the Presbyterian denomination at Bellevue, Nebraska. At that time the Omaha had been induced by the Government to settle near Bellevue, partly for the sake of protection from their enemies, the Sioux, and partly to bring them under the supervision of the newly established Indian agency. A school was built for the mission on land claimed by the Omaha tribe and several Omaha children were brought under the influence of the teachers. In the gardens and fields attached to this school the Omaha had their first opportunity to observe the practical use of the plow and other agricultural implements. When the iron hoe introduced by the traders superseded the shoulder blade of the elk no change was made in the old method of planting and cultivating corn. Until the Omaha beheld the fields of the mission they had never seen the earth turned over in furrows and corn planted in long straight rows. At this mission school some of the Omaha children received their first instruction, scanty as it was, in avocations that were to help them to meet the changed conditions of living so soon to come upon their people. Already Missouri was a State; homes were being erected within sight of the Missouri river; the Mormons had already crossed that stream and had passed on farther to the westward. Nebraska was soon to become a territory and the new settlers were casting hungry eyes on the Indians' land. In 1853 a United States commission arrived at Bellevue to take the preliminary steps looking to the extinguishment of the Omaha right of occupancy of the broad fertile lands lying on the Missouri north of the Platte river. The following year a group of chiefs and other leading men went to Washington, passing down the Missouri and up the Ohio in boats, crossing the Alleghany mountains by slow stages, and so making their way to the capital, where the treaty of 1854 was executed. Within the next three years the Omaha left Bellevue and turned their faces northward toward their reservation but before leaving they donated a square mile of land to the Presbyterian Mission, on which Bellevue College stands today.

The Mission

In 1857 the Presbyterian Mission followed the tribe and the next year a large stone structure erected for its use was completed. The mission house (fig. 127) stood on a bench overlooking the Missouri river. Behind it rose the bluffs; below it stretched a broad bottom heavily timbered in some parts and opening out here and there into wide savannahs. In this ample building a boarding and day school was

Fig. 127. The old "Mission," now fallen to decay.

maintained. The assembly hall served as a chapel. The missionaries and their families dwelt in the house, and the Omaha children were thus brought under their immediate care. The children were all given English names, most of which remain until the present time, having become the accepted names of families and appearing on the land patents. For nearly thirty years this mission school was kept up, being in general faithfully and effectively managed. The children were taught to speak, read, and write English. The boys were instructed in farming and the care of stock, the girls (see fig. 128) in cooking and the making of garments. The work accomplished by these missionaries has been of lasting benefit to the people and the teachers and workers who so assiduously labored to prepare the Omaha to live among their rapidly increasing white neighbors are today held in grateful and affectionate remembrance.[a] The church, which held its meetings in the school assembly room, numbered among its membership many native men and women. The industrious and orderly lives of these Christian Omaha reflected the earnestness with which they sought to apply to their daily lives the Christian precepts taught them at the mission and its school during the closing decades of the last century. In 1885–6 another mission building was erected by the same denomination in the southern part of the reservation, but after a few years it was abandoned. About this time a church (fig. 129) was built near the agency, not far from the blockhouse erected in 1864 to protect the government employees from Sioux war parties, and services conducted by the regular pastor are still held in this edifice.

FIG. 128. An Omaha girl, a "Mission" scholar.

One great difficulty beset the efforts of the missionary teachers; this was the influence exerted on the native mind by the contradiction between the principles taught as belonging to Christianity and the conduct of most of the white people with whom the Indian came into contact. Regarding all white persons as Christians, he naturally looked to their lives for the exemplification of their beliefs. The Indian's old religion taught that the man who spoke or acted falsely was in danger of supernatural punishment; instances were known to the people in which the lightning stroke had cut short the life of the unfaithful person. The Indian was now brought into con-

[a] For the names and record of the men and women who devoted themselves to missionary work among the Omaha tribe, the reader is referred to the Annual Reports on the Foreign and Home Missions of the Presbyterian Church, which alone has ministered to this tribe.

tact with persons who could speak untruthfully and yet seemingly suffer no evil consequences and it is not surprising that the Omaha found it difficult to reconcile the precepts taught by the missionaries with the conduct of many of the white people whom he met. As a result, he could not give hearty acceptance to a religion which seemed to have so little power over the lives of those who professed it. The teaching of his fathers he still reverenced and he was slow to change his native point of view of justice and of truth. Yet there were here and there men and women to whom the life of Jesus Christ appealed,

FIG. 129. The Omaha church.

The "blockhouse" which formerly stood on the right has been removed. The church has now (1911) been enlarged at an expense of more than a thousand dollars, raised by the Indians.

who recognized in it a high ideal difficult of attainment, and perceived that failure to realize it in the life of a person is to be attributed to the weakness of the individual rather than to the ideal itself.

NEW RESERVATION AND AGENCY

The agency buildings on the new reservation were placed about three miles west of the Missouri river on the only road in that region which ran from the trading posts on the south to those that were near the Missouri farther to the north; this was known as "the military road." In the course of a year or two the Omaha divided and settled in three villages: one in the southeastern part of the reservation; another (the largest) near the agency; the third to the northeast not far from the banks of the Missouri. This division of the people had no tribal significance. When the tribe moved out on its annual buffalo hunt, the people camped as one body, forming the *hu'thuga* (see p. 138); the old tribal organization was not affected in any way. The Middle village, as the one near the agency was called, was on the stream now known as Blackbird creek. The picture of the earth lodge shown in plate 19, taken more than twenty-seven years ago, represents the last of these lodges, erected at the time the Middle village was built.

Agency Buildings

At the time when the Omaha reservation was established the Missouri river was the highway of travel. The steamers from St. Louis brought the supplies needed for the agency and the mission. The landing place was on the bottomland below the mission buildings. Here the agency shops were first erected and in these the boys from the mission school were permitted to work and learn something of the carpenter's and the blacksmith's trade. Later a boarding school was established at the agency, to which the shops were removed, and a saw mill and a grist mill were built. All these were given up before the close of the last century. Public day schools were established and the agency shops were supplanted by private enterprises of the native population.

In 1878 Congress provided for the establishment of Indian police, who were to be directly under the authority of the United States Indian agent: they were to maintain order; to arrest offenders, including those engaged in the illegal liquor traffic; to return truant children to school; to protect government property; and to perform various other services. A few years subsequent to this a number of "police" were appointed at the Omaha agency; some of the best men of the tribe were included in the force. Their duties gave them and through them the people practical lessons in some of the methods employed in white communities to promote social welfare and order—a lesson that was timely, as settlements were rapidly springing up around the reservation and contact with the white race was increasing daily.[a]

PRESSURE OF TRADERS ON TRIBAL AFFAIRS

The changes in the avocations and life of the Omaha brought about through the influence of the traders have been spoken of; but there were other ways in which the traders had made themselves felt. Trading companies made gifts to chiefs and other leading men whom

[a] For the details of the United States Indian Service and of the efforts made by the Government to assist the tribe to a knowledge of civilized life, see the Annual Reports of the Commissioners of Indian Affairs.

they found pliant and government officials through the influence of traders sometimes made "paper chiefs" by giving certificates to such men. Medals were hung about their necks, flags were presented to them, and efforts were made to keep them loyal to the trading companies. English traders succeeded the French and the American the English, consequently the medals, flags, and certificates of one nation had to be relinquished when another nation came into power; finally the United States authorities had to see that American badges were substituted for foreign gifts. This outside pressure on tribal affairs complicated the life and thought of the people and disturbed the ancient forms and authority of the chiefs. The people could no longer pursue the path their fathers had trod—changes were on every hand. The steady stream of immigrants brought added trouble and perplexity. Indian garden patches were often treated as though maize grew wild and few rights of the natives were respected in the onward rush of white men. All this was more or less bewildering to the mass of the tribe. Sometimes, however, a man was able to lift himself above the turmoil and discern the trend of events. Such a man was Big Elk, the last chief of his name; his apprehension of coming events and his counsel, embodied in a sort of allegory, have been given on page 84. Big Elk impressed his own outlook on the changeful future on a half-breed youth toward whom he was drawn in friendship and whom he afterward adopted. This young man, Joseph La Flesche, later became so powerful a factor in the welfare of the tribe that it is proper to give a few details of his career. The facts here presented were obtained from Waje′pa (Wa′thishnade, pl. 29) during his last visit to the writers in Washington, shortly before his death.

JOSEPH LA FLESCHE

In the early part of the last century an Omaha boy was taken captive by the Sioux. He grew up among his captors and became a man of influence among that people. One of his sisters became the wife of Joseph La Flesche, a French trader in the employ of one of the fur companies. A son was born of this union, probably about 1818, in the old village To^{n}′wo^{n}to^{n}ga, on Omaha creek. The long absences of her husband, made necessary by trading business, were irksome to the young Omaha wife and she finally left her French husband and married one of her own tribe. Little Joseph was about six years old when his mother married again. He was taken by his aunt to visit her brother, who was living with the Sioux, and remained three years or more. While there he learned to speak the Dakota language, which he never forgot. At the time he returned to the Omaha with his aunt his father was there trading with the tribe. He pleaded with the aunt to give him his son but she refused. A few years later she consented and La Flesche took his son to St. Louis, where the lad learned to speak French; later he accompanied his father on trading expeditions. Young Joseph was a favorite with the old Omaha chiefs, especially with Big Elk, and used to talk with them and learn from them the qualifications requisite for chieftainship. The tribe was then living in the vicinity of Bellevue. La Flesche became impatient with his son and reproved him for lingering with the chiefs but the youth was becoming versed in tribal customs and lore and already had determined in his mind to become a chief. Joseph continued, however, to accompany his father on trips and learned to speak the Iowa, Pawnee, and Oto languages. He was a good hunter and planned to enter into trade on his own account; this he did later on and was quite successful. It was while living in the vicinity of Bellevue that he finally concluded to settle down and cast his lot with his mother's people and he soon became identified with them. He had seen enough of the world to recognize that the white race were in the country to stay and that the Indian would have to conform more or less to white ways and customs. The problem how to meet the new conditions that were already looming on the horizon of tribal life occupied much of his thought as well as the mind of Big Elk. One summer about this time (probably between 1845 and 1850), when the tribe were preparing to go on the annual buffalo hunt, Big Elk asked Joseph to join the preliminary council (see p. 276). No objection was raised and he was given a seat next to Big Elk. This was a marked step forward in the young man's proposed career. He had already begun to make the gifts necessary toward chieftainship (see p. 202) as well as to count his hundred (see p. 495). At this time Big Elk's son was living and it was the wish of the chief that this son should succeed him. But the young man died and after that event Joseph became recognized as the son of Big Elk and was counted as belonging to the We'zhi^{n}shte gens; this was contrary to usage, for, as his mother belonged to the I^{n}ke'çabe gens and as his father was white, he should have been considered as belonging to her gens. Meanwhile the tide of settlers increased and while Joseph La Flesche (fig. 49) was carrying forward plans to rise to the place occupied by Big Elk he was also engaged in thoughts and projects for helping the people forward to the best advantage in the new path he saw opening before them, which they must take. He watched the mission school established at Bellevue and talked with the missionaries. He was active in the negotiations which resulted in the selection of the present reservation when the Omaha disposed of their hunting lands to the United States. On the death of Big Elk in 1853 Joseph La Flesche had fully complied with the old requirements for chieftainship; he took Big Elk's place and became one of the two Ni′kagahi u′zhu, or principal chiefs. He was with the Omaha delegation that went to Washington to complete the treaty of 1854. La Flesche argued with the officials against payments being made in goods. He demanded that the tribe receive money for their land, declaring that with money the people could buy what they needed—tools, food, clothing. The silver dime he used to illustrate his contention was long cherished in memory of the victory which gave to the Omaha cash payments instead of merchandise but which won for him the enmity of certain trader factions. He had gathered about him at Bellevue the young, active men of progressive spirit, who formed the nucleus of what afterward became known in the tribe as the "young men's party." When the tribe occupied their new reservation and were settling in villages Joseph La Flesche selected a site slightly south of that on which "The Mission" was about to be built and there he formed a village which he planned should be somewhat similar to a white settlement.

"The Village of the 'Make-believe' White Men"

For this new enterprise the followers of Joseph La Flesche cut logs and hauled them to a sawmill, where they were prepared for use. Joseph hired white carpenters to construct his own house and under the direction of these mechanics the men of the village erected small frame houses for themselves out of the lumber secured from the logs. The shingles had to be purchased. Joseph's house was a large building two stories high with rooms on both sides of the hall; here he had a store and for several years carried on considerable trade. He laid out roads, one leading to the agency, one to the steamboat landing and Mission, and one through the center of the village. On this last road and branch roads stood some of the houses. He fenced a tract of 100 acres or more in the bottom and furnished the oxen and plow to break this land. It was divided into separate fields so that each man in the village could have a tract of his own for cultivation. A few families started other little fields not far from the village. It was on this bottom that the first wheat raised on the reservation was planted. Sorghum and large crops of corn were also harvested and in the winter the men hauled their produce on the ice to Sioux City, then a newly formed settlement on the Iowa side of the river to the north. All the children of this village were sent by their parents to the Mission School. The conservatives of the tribe called this village by the derisive name, "the village of the 'make-believe' white men."

The enterprise shown by the people of this village had a marked influence on the tribe in general. La Flesche's action in reference to drunkenness has been told (p. 621). Of course this man did not escape criticism and he had to endure persecution because of his championship of what he thought were the rights of the people. Through all the changes that came about he remained until his death, in 1888, a leader of the tribe. Throughout his eventful life he bore well his part in all the rites and requirements of chieftainship and lived to cast his vote as a citizen of the United States. The following incident is characteristic of the man: Although he could "count" more than needed to entitle him to place the "mark of honor" (see p. 505) on his daughters, he would not have them tattooed nor would he permit the ears of his sons to be pierced. When questioned why he, who had fulfilled so many of the ancient requirements, should have refused so to distinguish himself and his children, he replied: "I was always sure that my sons and daughters would live to see the time when they would have to mingle with the white people, and I determined that they should not have any mark put upon them that might be detrimental in their future surroundings."

SURVEY OF THE RESERVATION

The promise made in the treaty of 1854 and repeated in 1865, that the land should be surveyed in order that the people might enter on tracts and possess their individual homes was not fulfilled until 1872. It was the influence of the village of "the 'make-believe' white men" that stimulated the people of the other villages and finally secured the delayed governmental action. The eastern portion of the reservation, from the Missouri to the Omaha Creek region, was surveyed into townships and the usual subdivisions. Oxen and breaking plows were bought with tribal money and prairie was broken on the selections that were made by many of the people, their right to the land selected being secured to them by certificates issued by the Government. The people spent all the winter after the survey was made in cutting timber and hauling it to the agency mill. Only a few reaped benefit of their labor by having their logs made into lumber and the houses built. The bulk of the material gathered was never used; like many other promises, the fulfillment was deferred until the people lost hope and ambition.

EXTERMINATION OF THE BUFFALO

About this time the slaughter of the buffalo herds had seriously affected the supply of the game, so that after 1876 there were no more annual buffalo hunts and a new dilemma confronted the people. Unused to depend solely on a diet of grain and not accustomed to the taste of beef, they suffered from the change. It was during this distress that the tribe sought to make their appeal to Wako^{n}'da through the old ceremonies connected with the anointing of the Sacred Pole (see p. 230) by purchasing beef as a substitute for buffalo meat (see p. 244). A few of these costly experiments brought a new sorrow—the realization that the food on which their fathers had depended and which through past centuries had never failed, had been destroyed although they had been taught that the buffalo had been sent "from every quarter" for man's use, by Wako^{n}'da (see ritual, p. 294). Distress of mind accompanied their distress of body. The maize remained to them and its cultivation increased, as did the raising of wheat. These articles they sold to the white settlements and with the proceeds bought food. Pigs, chickens, and cattle were raised in moderate numbers. The once thrifty Omaha had become poor; they never received rations from the Government, however, but struggled on by themselves, the older people supported by the hopefulness and efforts of the younger generation.

During the period of the Civil War the Omaha were loyal to the United States Government and served as scouts and guards during the construction of the Union Pacific Railroad.

ESTABLISHMENT OF "THE COUNCIL"

The enforced abandonment of the annual hunt and the changes taking place in the life and habits of the tribe led to a modification in tribal government, one favored by the United States agency officials. Questions frequently arose the determination of which required cooperation between the tribe and the Agent. Tribal meetings were cumbersome and difficult to manage, so it came about that a "council" was formed of a small number of chiefs and other leading men, who could be easily called together by the Agent. Chieftainship in the old meaning of the term thereby lapsed. The council represented the people but all governing power had become centered in the United States Indian Agent.

Nothing belonging to the past now seemed stable to the Omaha; only the familiar landscape remained to remind them that they were still in the land of their fathers.

THE PONCA TRAGEDY

Suddenly, in 1877, like a bolt out of the blue sky, came the distressing removal of their kindred, the Ponca, from their home on the Niobrara river to the Indian Territory. The pathetic return in the spring of 1879 of Standing Bear and his followers, bearing the bones of that chief's dearly loved son for burial, and the coming of United States soldiers to carry them back to the dreaded "hot country," brought terror to every Omaha family. Thinking that their own homes might be in danger, some of the men took the certificates for their individual lands and houses to the larger white settlements and consulted lawyers in order to find out the legal value of these papers. When they were told that the certificates carried no patent rights to the land the fear and sorrow this knowledge brought passed description. It seemed that the very ground was cut from under their feet, that they were forsaken by all in whom they had ever put trust, and that even the Government which they had always respected had betrayed them.

APPEAL FOR LAND PATENTS

Such were the practical conditions when one of the writers entered the tribe for ethnological study. She knew little of political affairs but firmly believed that were the truth known to the United States Government its officials would give the Omaha a legal right to their homes and to the land hallowed by the graves of their fathers. Actuated by this belief, much time was spent in gathering data concerning the efforts of those among the people who had striven to gain their livelihood on the lands for which they held certificates or on tracts selected since the issuance. These men were invited to join in a petition to Congress, here given as an historical document[a] that proved of importance to the Omaha tribe and was the forerunner of the Severalty Act of 1887, which marked a change in the policy of the Government toward the Indian tribes of the United States.

MEMORIAL OF THE MEMBERS OF THE OMAHA TRIBE OF INDIANS FOR A GRANT OF LAND IN SEVERALTY

To the Senate of the United States:

We, the undersigned, members of the Omaha tribe of Indians, have taken our certificates of allotment of land or entered upon claims within the limits of the Omaha reserve. We have worked upon our respective lands from three to ten years; each farm has from five to fifty acres under cultivation; many of us have built houses on these lands and all have endeavored to make permanent homes for ourselves and our children.

We therefore petition your honorable body to grant to each one a clear and full title to the land on which he has worked.

We earnestly pray that this petition may receive your favorable consideration, for we now labor with discouragement of heart, knowing that our farms are not our own and that any day we may be forced to leave the lands on which we have worked. We desire to live and work on these farms where we have made homes that our children may advance in the life we have adopted. To this end and that we may go forward with hope and confidence in a better future for our tribe, we ask of you titles to our lands.

Respectfully submitted.

---

[a] Sen. Misc. Doc. No. 31, 47th Cong., 1st sess.

Then follow the signatures of 55 men. The statistics for each signer, as to the amount of land he cultivated, the stock he owned, and the number of persons dependent on him for support, were appended, together with such remarks as he desired to make in his behalf.

The following "remarks" quoted from this petition are typical of the burden that was voiced by each man.

Xitha'gaxe said:

I have worked hard on my land so that I should not go round begging. I thought the land was my own, so I went to work and cultivated it. Now I have found out it is not my own, and this makes me stop. I am afraid if I should build a house and spend money on it I would lose it if the Government should move the Indians from this land. Three times I have cut wood to build a house. Each time the agent told me the Government wished to build me a house. Every time my wood has lain and rotted, and now I feel ashamed when I hear an agent telling me such things. * * * I want a title to my land; I want a house that is my own.

Hon'donmonthin:

When I was a boy I saw much game and buffalo and the animals my forefathers used to live upon, but now all are gone. Where I once saw the animals I now see houses and white men cultivating the land. * * * I want a title for my land. I am troubled about it. * * * In the morning I get up and look at my fields, and I wish that God may help me to do better with my land and let it be my own.

Mawa'donthin:

I have taken hold of the plow. I did not know how, but I put in my ponies and my wife held the reins. * * * There is a party among us in favor of titles. When it first started I was one of them. * * * I want a title to my land. I may never know all the good it will bring but my children will know. * * * If I were a young man I would say more; but I am too old to speak much. The reason I have worked so hard is that I wished to set an example to others that they might see how an old man could work because he wanted to.

Wa'thishnade:

Before I began to farm I was just a wild Indian doing as I pleased, going round the country looking for death. * * * We have no government on the reserve. We have trouble which we would not have if we had government and law. We want these. We are right among the white people, and as we have no law we can't get along very well. There are persons living on the reserve who have certificates of allotment; they believe that the land is theirs and that they can always keep it. I know differently. * * * I went on my farm with my certificate. I believed the land was mine. I have found out the land is not mine; that the Government can take it away. We are going to ask for our titles. As long as the Government does not give them, we will ask until the Government gets tired. We won't stop asking until we get our titles.

Du'bamonthin:

* * * The road our fathers walked in is gone, the game is gone, the white people are all about us. There is no use in any Indian thinking of the old ways; he must now go to work as the white man does. We want titles to our lands that the land may be secure to our children. When we die we shall feel easy in our minds if we

know the land will belong to our children and that they will have the benefit of our work. There are some Omahas who do not yet care for titles. We desire the Government to give titles to those who ask for them. * * * We are willing the others should do as they please but we are not willing that they should keep us from getting titles to our lands. Our children would suffer even a greater wrong than would befall us. Give us who ask titles to our lands. * * * Do not let us be held back and our children be sufferers because of the inaction of those who do not seem to care for the future.

Om'pato^{n}ga:

When we look at a person we are apt to know what that person is thinking of. All who look at me must know I am thinking of a title to my land. * * * I wish I could speak English, then I could tell you directly from my heart of the way in which I wish to go. * * * We want titles to our lands. We are thinking of little else. We shall think of little else until we get our titles. We are afraid of losing our lands. When we receive titles to our farms then we shall be treated as men.

Joseph La Flesche:

* * * I was born in this country, in Nebraska, and I have always lived among the Indians. There was a time when I used to look only at the Indians and think they were the only people. The Indians must have been long in this country before the white man came here. * * * In the spring they would take their seed and farm their 1 or 2 acres. There were no idlers, all worked in the spring. Those who had no hoes worked with pieces of sticks. When they had their seed in, they went on the hunt. They had nothing to worry them; all they thought of was their little garden they had left behind. In the middle of the summer they came back with the skins for their tent cloths, the meat for their food, and the skins for their clothing. They made use of all animals. When they got home they gathered their corn, dried it, buried a part of it, and taking enough to serve them started out on the winter hunt to get furs. Then it was I used to see white men, those who were going around buying furs. Sometimes for two or three years I would not see any white men. At that time the country was empty, only animals were to be seen. Then after a while the white men came, just as the blackbirds do, and spread over the country. Some settled down, others scattered on the land. The Indians never thought that any such thing could be, but it matters not where one looks now one sees white people. These things I have been speaking about are in the past and are all gone. We Indians see you now and want to take our steps your way. * * * It seems as though the Government pushes us back. It makes us think that the Government regards us as unfit to be as white men. The white man looks into the future and sees what is good. That is what the Indian is doing. He looks into the future and sees his only chance is to become as the white man. When a person lives in a place a long time he loves the place. We love our lands and want titles for them. When one has anything he likes to feel it is his own and belongs to no one else, so we want titles; then we can leave our land to our children. You know, and so do we, that some of us will not live very long; we will soon be gone into the other world. We ask for titles for our children's sakes. For some years we have been trying to get titles but we have never heard from the Government. * * * We are not strong enough to help ourselves in this matter, so we ask you to help us. In the past we only lived on the animals. We see that it is from the ground that you get all that you possess. The reason you do not look upon us as men is because we have not law, because we are not citizens. We are strangers in the land where we were born. We want the law that we may be regarded as men. When we are in trouble we want to have courts to appeal to. The law will teach wrongdoers. It will prevent trouble as well as punish those who commit offenses.

We know that in asking for titles we are asking for that which will bring responsibility. We are ready to accept it and to strive to fulfill its requirements. It seems as though in the past the Government had not listened to the words of the Indians. We know our own needs, and now we speak to you directly.

The petition was presented by the Hon. John T. Morgan, of Alabama, in the United States Senate, was ordered printed—and there the matter rested. All that winter the writer and the Indians waited for a response. Almost every day some Indian would ride over the snowy hills and ask: "Any news from Washington?" and every day the same answer had to be given: "None." It was a heartrending wait for all who knew of the little missive that had gone to the

FIG. 130. A modern Indian home, not far from site of the old "Mission."

country's capital, but particularly for the sender. On her one hand stood the trusting Indians, feeling that their homes were in danger from forces they could not face, could not even speak to and be understood by, and, on her other hand, stood the Government, great and strange, almost unapproachable, but which alone held the power to avert the feared disaster.

With the spring came a firm resolve to follow that petition and make it heard by those who had the power to act on it. A long, and for a time a single-handed, campaign followed. Addresses were made by Miss Fletcher in Washington before congressional committees, before churches, in the parlors of leading citizens, until the story of the Omaha people bore results in the passage of the act of August 7, 1882 (see p. 624). The following year the provisions of the act were carried out by the writers, and every man, woman, and child of the tribe received a share of the land inherited from their ancestors.

On March 3, 1893 (27 Stat., 612), Congress amended the act of August 7, 1882, and granted to wives 80 acres of land in their own right and the same amount to children. The provisions of this act were carried out in 1900.

The twenty-five-year "period of trust" has been fraught with many experiences, not all of which have been happy. The untaxable character of the land has made improvements in roads and bridges slow and the increasing value of farms in that vicinity has brought pressure on the Omaha to lease their allotments. Many have done so; the

FIG. 131. An Omaha farmer's home.

act has not been altogether evil nor has it been wholly good for the people. It has brought the Indian into closer contact with white neighbors and established business relations between them. While the Omaha have learned much from this relationship, in some instances, as was natural, they have come to depend on the income derived from leasing their property rather than on their own labors, to secure the full product and profit from their lands, a condition not altogether favorable to a healthful social growth. When one of the writers was last among the tribe (during the summer of 1910) and recalled the conditions that obtained thirty years ago, the present state showed how much, during the intervening years, had been thought out and accomplished by the people. (See figs. 130–132.) Although she missed the presence of the old men who were formerly the leaders in progress, she saw the results of their leadership manifested in the comfortable homes on farms tilled by the Indians, in the increasing ability of the people to manage their own affairs, in the attendance of the children at school, in the growing appreciation of the value of temperate habits, and in the capacity the Omaha are showing for maintaining themselves under the new conditions imposed on them by the white race.

Here and there quaint survivals of old customs under a new guise could be noted, as in reference to marriage. Men and women still observe the old rule of exogamy and when a man dies, his widow feels that she honors her husband's memory by remaining in the family, a

FIG. 132. A well-to-do Omaha farmer and his family.

feeling shared by any unmarried brother of the deceased, who, even if much younger than the widow, promptly becomes her husband.

During the recent years of stress there have been noble men and women in the tribe who have stood steadily for virtuous, industrious living, and their example has exerted an influence all the stronger because coming from within, not from without, the tribe, and this influence is a vital and a growing power.

PRESENT CONDITION

The "period of trust" technically expired during the year 1910. Realizing the unwisdom of throwing at once indiscriminately on the people so large a property burden and the necessity of protecting the interests of the old and the backward, the Indian Bureau has appointed a commission to determine what individuals among the Omaha are prepared to be released absolutely from the care of the Government.

The following is the latest official statement[a] concerning the tribe:

The population according to the last census was 1,270. Ninety per cent of those under forty years speak English to some extent; many of them speak quite well. All except a few of the very old understand English and most of the men between forty and sixty can speak it a little.

All live in houses, none in tents except as a change in the summer time. With the exception of about twenty, the men dress in citizens' clothes. Most of the women dress after a fashion of their own, which is partly like that of a white woman. Several of the younger women dress in all respects as white women do. None of the very old women and very few of the old men ride horseback. The young men often ride. A few of the young women ride but they always dress for the purpose with divided skirts, using men's saddles. About 95 per cent of the people own carriages and buggies and most of them have good teams and take fairly good care of them.

About 90 per cent of the children of school age and in proper health are in school a reasonable portion of the year. I do not recall but one healthy child between the ages of ten and twenty who has never attended school and he speaks English quite well. There are fourteen public schools on the reservation besides the graded school at Walthill. There have been 110 or 115 Omaha children in the public schools the past year. They are given the same recognition as the white children and show about the same ability.

Two members of the tribe are merchants, two are attorneys, one is manager of the athletic teams of Wabash College, one is a physician, three or four are extensively engaged in real estate and stock business, a few are in the government service, and a great number are making good homes for themselves as farmers.

Fourteen Omaha families live in the town of Walthill and more than sixty lots are owned by Omaha. Several families reside in the town of Rosalie.

---

[a] Extract from a letter by Supt. John M. Commons, dated September 10, 1909.

INDEX

NOTE.—Throughout this index references are to the Omaha tribe unless otherwise indicated.

Page

ACORUS CALAMUS S., medicinal use........ 584
ADMINISTRATIVE REPORT.................... 7–14
ADOPTION, custom of—
  Omaha.................................... 603
  Osage.............................. 61–62, 603
ADORNMENT, PERSONAL................... 349–354
A'GAHAMO^{n}THI^{n}, story of.................. 480
AGENCY, OMAHA, description............ 629–630
AGRICULTURE—
  general account............ 95, 269, 275, 339, 635
  white influence on................... 614, 626
ALBION COUNTY, NEBR., reference.......... 99
ALLOTMENT. *See* Lands.
AMERICAN ANTIQUITIES, preservation........ 10
AMERICAN MUSEUM OF NATURAL HISTORY, permit granted........................... 11
AMUSEMENTS, account of................ 363–370
  See also Games.
ANCESTORS, Omaha attitude toward........ 601
ANCIENTS. *See* Ancestors.
ANIMALS—
  chief food animals...................... 271
  in Osage legend.......................... 63
  known to Omaha..................... 103–104
  place in nature...................... 357–358, 511–516, 518, 533, 588–589, 599–601
  See also names of animals.
ANNUAL BUFFALO HUNT. *See* Buffalo hunt, annual.
ANTELOPE, hunting..................... 271, 275
"ANTELOPE," STEAMER, reference............ 87
ANTIQUITY of human remains, Florida...... 10–11
APPALACHIAN MOUNTAINS, ancient home of Omaha..................................... 35
ARAPAHO, Omaha name for................. 102
ARCHÆOLOGICAL INSTITUTE OF AMERICA, reference................................. 11
ARCHEOLOGICAL COLLECTIONS, character..... 12
ARCHEOLOGICAL EXPLORATIONS, permits for. 11
ARCHEOLOGICAL SITES, catalogue........... 10
ARIKARA—
  early contact with Omaha............ 74, 75–78
  influence on Omaha.................. 102, 112
  Omaha name for......................... 102
  party to peace conference.......... 74, 218, 376
  source of Wa'wa^{n} pipes.................... 47
ARIZONA, reference.......................... 8
ARKANSAS RIVER, references............... 57, 67
ARKANSAS (STATE), references............. 57, 74
ARMOR, used by Padouca..................... 79
ARROWS—
  connected with Sacred Pole....... 228, 242, 247
  in Shell Society ceremony........... 562, 564

ARROWS—Continued. Page
  manufacture.......................... 449–452
  marking of......................... 42, 43, 452
  origin..................................... 70
  used by Padouca........................... 79
ATHAPASCAN STOCK, unknown to Omaha.... 102
AVOCATIONS. *See* Occupations.

BAD VILLAGE, account of............... 85–86, 99
BALL GAME, description.............. 169, 197–198
BANNOCK, Omaha name for................. 102
BARTEL, WILLIAM P., service of............ 13
BATHING, reference........................ 585
  See also Sweat baths.
BEAR—
  association with Tha'tada gens.......... 42
  connection with Mo^{n}chu' ithaethe..... 486–487
  hunting................................... 275
  See also Black bear.
BEAVER CREEK, references.............. 100, 101
BELLEVUE COLLEGE, reference.............. 627
BELLEVUE, NEBR., references...... 100. 626, 632, 633
BELLEVUE, TREATY OF...................... 623
BIÇE'WAA^{n}. *See* Love songs.
BIG COOK. *See* U'ho^{n}to^{n}ga.
BIG ELK, name of three Omaha chiefs....... 83–84
BIG ELK, Omaha chief—
  account of...................... 83–84, 631, 632
  keeper of pack................. 554–555, 558–559
  references..................... 205, 405, 518, 562
BIG HEART—
  acknowledgment to........................ 58
  on groups of Osage........................ 62
BIG KNIFE, name applied to English...... 611–612
BIG SIOUX RIVER, references............ 73, 74, 80
BIRDS—
  associated with powers of air............ 404
  associated with Thunder.............. 415–416, 426, 434, 437, 441
  in Sacred War Pack.................... 411, 412
  names................................ 104–105
  sayings about............................ 335
  See also Thunder birds.
BIRTH CUSTOMS (Omaha cognates)...... 115, 116
BLACK BEAR—
  special connection with man.......... 512, 518
  symbolized in Shell society.............. 559
BLACKBIRD CREEKS, references............ 91, 630
BLACKBIRD HILLS, reference................. 83
BLACKBIRD, Indian chief, account of......... 82
BLACK DOG—
  on visions among Osage............... 132–133
  Osage legends told by..................... 62

Page

Blackfeet—
- Omaha name for........................ 102
- White Buffalo Hide among.............. 284

Black Hills, S. Dak., reference............ 102
Blue Earth river, references............. 73, 80
Boas, Dr. Franz, work of................. 9
Boat. *See* Bull-boat.
Boone county, Nebr., references........ 100, 101
Bourgmont, de, reference................. 81
Bow creek, Nebr., reference.............. 85
Bows—
- in Ponca legend......................... 49
- in Shell Society ceremony............... 562, 564
- manufacture............................. 448–451
- origin.................................. 70
- used by Padouca......................... 79

Buffalo—
- albino sacred........................... 284
- as tabu animal.......................... 47
- connection with origin of maize.......... 76–78
- connection with Te'ithaethe............. 487–488
- disappearance........... 29, 33, 244, 619, 634–635
- origin................................. 71, 147, 239
- represented in Shell Society figure....... 559
- special connection with man.............. 512

Buffalo hunt, annual—
- control of Council of Seven............. 209–210
- dispatch of scouts.................... 142, 423–426
- general account 137, 270–271, 275–283
- leadership in I^{n}ke'çabe gens............ 146–147
- preservation of order..................... 215
- references............................ 45, 46, 357–358
- religious element in...................... 309
- rites connected with..................... 200, 596

Buffalo hunt (Ponca), ritual connected with.................................. 442, 446
Buffalo hunt, winter, account of.......... 271
Bull-boat, description..................... 36, 37
Burden strap, description................ 339–340
Bureau of American Ethnology, linguistic classification of Siouan tribes.............. 605
See also Administrative report.
Burial customs. *See* Funeral customs.
Burt county, Nebr., reference............. 100

Caches, description...................... 98–99, 275
Caddo—
- Omaha name for......................... 102
- reference............................... 112
- Wa'wa^{n} ceremony among................... 74

Calendar, terms used in.................. 111
California, Southern, explorations in..... 11
Calumet pipes, reference.................. 207
Canoes, references........................ 72, 81
Captive songs—
- examples................................ 427–431
- reference............................... 603

Captives, treatment....................... 603
Carver, Jonathan, on early trade of Omaha. 80–81, 612
Catlin, on value of white buffalo hide...... 284
Cat-tail, medicinal use.................... 584
Cedar, associated with thunder rites........ 42
Cedar county, Nebr., reference............ 99
Cedar creek, reference.................... 99
Cedar Pole—
- account of........................ 229, 457–458
- references............... 194, 200, 217, 219, 494

Ceremonies. *See* Rites and Rituals.
Character of Omaha, summary.......... 112–114
Cherokee—
- lands purchased from.................... 57
- Ponca name for.......................... 103

Cheyenne—
- hunting ground.......................... 89
- Omaha attack on......................... 87
- Omaha contact with...................... 73
- Omaha name for.......................... 102
- party to peace treaty................ 74, 218, 376
- *See also* Southern Cheyenne.

Chiefs—
- clothing................................ 355, 356
- effect of traders' influence on.......... 630–631
- one for each grand division.............. 135
- part in ritual of White Buffalo Hide..... 289
- position................................ 601–602
- *See also* Chieftainship, Council of Seven Chiefs.

Chieftainship—
- early history............................ 202
- emoluments of chiefs and keepers..... 212–213
- lapsing................................. 635
- offenses and punishments................ 213–216
- orders of chiefs........................ 202–206
- *See also* Chiefs, Council of Seven Chiefs.

Childbirth, references.................... 584, 585
Children—
- amusements................... 362–366, 369–370
- baby names abandoned.................... 117
- care and training........................ 327–333
- consecration of boy to Thunder........ 122–128
- exempt from sweat baths.................. 585
- introduction into tribe................... 117
- introduction to Cosmos.................. 115–116
- in Wa'wa^{n} ceremony....................... 379–380
- property of.............................. 362
- puberty ceremony........................ 128–133
- rites connected with...................... 597
- Sacred Shell intrusted to................ 455, 457
- treatment in war........................ 403, 426
- *See also* Etiquette.

Chippewa, relations with Omaha............ 102
Christianity. *See* Missionaries.
Çi^{n}'dexo^{n}xo^{n}, group under, account of 178, 179–180
Civil War, Omaha in the.................... 635
Clan, reference............................ 195
Clark creek, reference..................... 100
Clark, Miss May S., work of................ 13
Clay on the head, significance 129
Clayton, J. B., work of.................... 13
Cloth. *See* Weaving.
Clothing—
- affected by advent of trader............. 616
- at meetings of Hethu'shka................ 461
- general description..................... 354–356
- materials........................ 272, 347–348
- of members of Pebble society............ 565
- of members of Shell society.............. 519
- of warriors............................. 409–411
- origin.................................. 71
- rites for obtaining...................... 195
- robes........................... 354, 356–362
- storage in caches........................ 98–99

Club, description.......................... 448

Page
COLORADO, field work in ... 7, 10
COLORS, Omaha terms for ... 111
COLUMBUS, Omaha name for ... 101
COMANCHE—
meeting with Ponca ... 79–80
Omaha name for ... 102
Spanish influence transmitted through ... 114
See also Padouca.
COMMISSIONER OF INDIAN AFFAIRS, acknowledgment to ... 8
See also Office of Indian Affairs.
COMMONS, SUPT. JOHN M., acknowledgment to ... 642
COMPASS, POINTS OF, references ... 111, 113
CORN—
cultivation ... 252, 626
in Ponca legend ... 49
place in Wa'waⁿ ceremony ... 379
ritual ... 609
See also Maize.
COUGAR, special connection with man ... 512
COUNCIL BLUFFS, treaty of ... 622
COUNCIL GOVERNING TRIBAL—
modern form ... 635
on annual buffalo hunt ... 276, 277–278, 280, 302–304
COUNCIL OF SEVEN CHIEFS—
at Watha'wa ... 497–500
authority as to keepers ... 595
general account ... 206–212
gens represented in ... 172
origin ... 74
part in anointing Sacred Pole ... 230–233
part in authorizing war ... 142
part in buffalo hunt ... 276, 280, 281, 283, 423, 425
punishment of offenders ... 213
references ... 196, 203, 236
use of kinship terms in ... 314
COURTSHIP, account of ... 318–324, 361
CRADLE-BOARD, description ... 327
CREATION MYTHS—
in Pebble Society ritual ... 570–571
Osage ... 63
reference ... 171–172
rites connected with ... 177–178, 195
CROW—
as helper of man (Omaha, Ponca) ... 445–446
connection with warfare ... 441, 442
in Omaha mythology ... 175
Omaha name for ... 102
Ponca name for ... 103
reference ... 204
"CROW, THE"—
description ... 441–446
references ... 279, 282
CUCURBITA PERENNIS, medicinal use ... 585
CULIN, STEWART, work of ... 9

DAKOTA COUNTY, NEBR., references ... 99, 100, 623
DAKOTA (TRIBES)—
albino buffalo sacred among ... 284
attacks on Iowa and Omaha ... 86
hunting ground ... 89
name applied by, to Americans ... 611
societies introduced from ... 486
DANCING— Page
at Hethu'shka meeting ... 466, 468
grass (or Omaha) dance ... 461
in He'dewachi ceremony ... 259
in Hoⁿ'hewachi ceremony ... 502, 507
in Moⁿwa'dathiⁿ and Toka'lo societies ... 486
DAY—
in Omaha conception ... 128, 494
in Ponca conception ... 507
symbolism of ... 254, 517
See also Sky.
DEATH—
foretelling of ... 489–490
general conception ... 489–490, 588–591
Hethu'shka teaching as to ... 475
in story of Shell society ... 514–515
Sacred Shell associated with ... 457
See also Funeral customs, Thunder.
DEER—
connection with Shell society ... 518, 559
hunting of ... 270, 271–272, 274–275
among Ponca ... 44
DEERSKIN, tabu to Ponca gens ... 44
DE L'ISLE, MAP OF, reference ... 80
DESCENT among the Omaha ... 38
DES MOINES RIVER, references ... 36, 72, 88, 94
DHE'GIHA, application of term ... 605
DICTIONARIES, INDIAN, in preparation ... 9
DISEASE AND TREATMENT—
bathing ... 585–587
case cited ... 487–488
doctors ... 487–489
general account ... 582–584
pain in head (Ponca cure) ... 43
treatment by Pebble society ... 567
See also Magic; Plants, curative; Wounds; and specific names of diseases.
DISMAL RIVER, references ... 88, 91
DIVORCE, status ... 326
DOCTORS, treatment by ... 487–489
DODGE COUNTY, NEBR., reference ... 100
DOGS—
among Ponca ... 49, 79
discovery of ... 72
DRAMA, absence of ... 369
DREAMS. *See* Visions.
DRUM—
description ... 371
in Feast of Hoⁿ'hewachi ... 500–501, 507
in Hethu'shka Society ceremonies ... 461, 466
in Pebble Society ceremonies ... 566
in Shell Society ceremonies ... 520, 523, 533
in treatment of disease ... 582–583
DRUNKENNESS, account of ... 618–619
DU'BAMOⁿTHIⁿ, remarks of ... 637–638
DUNDY, JUDGE, on legal status of Indians ... 51
DWELLINGS—
bark houses ... 74, 78
earth lodge ... 75–76
general description ... 95–99
interior arrangements ... 334, 337, 362
origin ... 71
property of the women ... 326
tipi ... 76
DYES, preparation ... 346

Eagle— Page
  associated with Tha'tada gens, 42
  connection with pipe, 162
  connection with Shell society, 512, 559
  in Ponca tradition, 47
  part in rites, 159
  reference, 204
  represented in Pebble society, 566
Eagle feathers—
  as war honor decorations, 438–439, 441
    Ponca, 440
  in Wa'wa^n ceremony, 376–377, 397–398
  on heads of heralds, 500
  on war bonnet, 446–448
  on washa'be (staff), 276
Earth—
  in Creation legend, 570–571
  in Omaha conception, 117, 134, 600
  symbolized in Shell society, 513–514, 517, 559–560
Earth lodge—
  adopted from Arikara, 75–76, 112
  building of, 339
  description, 95, 97–98
Earth people, place in Omaha organization, 135–139
  See also Ho^n'gashenu.
East Bow creek, reference, 99
Eçka, meaning of expression, 445, 572, 578
Editorial work, 12
Elk—
  as man's helper (Osage), 63, 571
  hunting of, 271, 274
  rites associated with war (Osage), 194
  special connection with man, 512
Elk gens. See We'zhi^{n}shte gens.
Elkhorn river, references, 88, 89, 100, 408, 623
Elk people (Osage), reference, 63
English, influence on Omaha, 114, 611–612
  See also Missionaries, Traders.
Environment, ceremonials affected by, 261
Environment of Omaha. See Habitat.
Eskimo language, sketch of, 9
Ethics—
  fundamental principles, 134
  influenced by environment, 608
  influenced by natural phenomena, 597–598
  in Hethu'shka songs, 470
  in warfare, 602–603
  moral equality of sexes, 324
  See also Religion and ethics.
Ethnological collections, character, 12
Ethnological researches, permits for, 11
Etiquette, description, 334–337
Exogamy, among Omaha and cognates, 33, 38, 135, 140, 325, 641
Explorations on public lands, permits for, 11
Ezhno^n'zhuwagthe, Omaha warrior, 100
Ezhno^n'zhuwagthe shko^{n}thaitho^n, battle at, 100

Family, authority in, 325–326
Farley, Rosalie La Flesche, reference, 624
Fasting, in puberty ceremony, 129, 131
Fauna known to Omaha, 103
Feast of Soldiers (Ponca), account of, 44, 500
Feast of the Count, account of, 497–500
Feast of the Ho^n'hewachi— Page
  general description, 500–503
  tattooing, 503–509
Fewkes, Dr. J. Walter, researches, 8
Field Museum of Natural History, researches, 8
Fillmore, Prof. John Comfort—
  acknowledgments to, 31
  on song in Wa'wa^n ceremony, 388
Fire, references, 70, 117
Fishing, account of, 312
Fish known to Omaha, names of, 106
Flageolet. See Flute.
Fletcher, Miss Alice C.—
  efforts in behalf of Omaha, 639–640
  monograph by, 14
Flora known to Omaha, 106–107
Florida, field work in, 7
Flute, description, 371–372
Fontenelle, Logan—
  death, 100–101
  reference, 626
Food—
  effect of extermination of buffalo, 634–635
  fishing, 312
  new foods introduced, 620
  offerings of—
    at feast in Shell society, 537–538
    in Ho^n'hewachi ceremony, 500
    on graves, 592
  Ponca, 45, 309–311
  preparation, 70–71, 340–342
  property in, 363
  rites for obtaining, 195
  storage in caches, 98
  wild turnips, 277
  See also Hunting, Maize, Wheat.
Forest Service, permits granted by, 11
Fort La Reine, references, 80, 612
Fort Orleans, references, 81, 612
Fox, silver, special connection with woman, 512
Fremont, Omaha name for, 101
French—
  contact with Quapaw, 67
  influence on Omaha, 81, 114, 611–612, 626
  See also Traders.
Friendship in Omaha life, 318–319
Funeral customs—
  articles buried with dead, 363
  foot racing, 369
  general description, 591–594
  gifts to chief's family, 205
  in Shell society, 553–554
  moccasins on dead (Omaha, Osage, Ponca), 144, 358
  painting the dead, 397
  strangling of horses, 83
  See also Mourning customs.
Fur trade—
  account of, 614–615
  references, 613, 616, 617, 618, 625, 626

Gahi'ge To^{n}ga, meaning of term, 559
Gallatin, Albert, as an authority, 605
Gambling, account of, 366, 367–368, 451

GAMES— Page
ball game 197–198
general description 363–369
legend of hoop-and-buffalo game 148–149
new games introduced 620
GATI'DEMO^n^THI^n^, a Ponca magician 491, 492
GENTES—
general discussion (Omaha and cognates) 38, 135, 137, 195–196, 211
indicated by cut of hair 198
See also names of tribes and of gentes.
GERMANS, Omaha name for 612
GHOSTS, in Omaha conception 215–216, 489–490, 590–591
GHOST SOCIETY, account of 489–490, 602
GILA (UPPER) VALLEY, antiquities 11
GILL, DE LANCEY, work of 12
GIU^n^'HABI, War Pack of 406, 434
GOVERNMENT. *See* Tribal government.
GRAND MEDICINE (Chippewa), reference 102
GRASS DANCE, application of term 461
GREAT HO^n^'GA, gens of Kansa and Quapaw 40
See also Ho^n^'gato^n^ga.
GREAT LAKES, reference 81
GRO'NI^n^, kinship group (Osage) 58, 60–61
GROUND CHERRY, large-bladder, medicinal use 584
GUNS, introduction of 617
GURLEY, JOSEPH G., work of 12
GYMNOCLADUS CANADENSIS, medicinal use 584

HABITAT of Omaha—
general description 33, 70–72, 85–94, 608
influence on political unity 199
summary as to 112–114
HAIR, HUMAN—
ceremony of cutting 122–128
connection with life of individual 123, 124
in thunder ceremony 143
lock from boy's head 613
manner of wearing 350, 352
Osage, Ponca, Sioux 132
symbolic cutting 42–46, 198
used with pipe of Sacred Pole 227
See also Scalp lock, Scalps.
HAIRY BEAR, on part of Wa'wa^n^ ceremony 401
HAKO (PAWNEE) CEREMONY, reference 74, 380
HANDBOOK OF LANGUAGES, work on 9
HANDBOOK OF THE INDIANS, progress of 7, 8, 9, 12, 13
HE'DEWACHI CEREMONY—
classed with We'waçpe 597
description 251–260, 591
part taken by Wathi'gizhe subgens 149
references 148, 200, 217, 243, 496
HE'DEWACHI POLE—
painting 148
part in He'dewachi ceremony 252, 253
reference 218, 229
selection 251
symbolism 255
HERALD, TRIBAL—
in election of chief 205
in Ho^n^'hewachi ceremony 498–500
in "mark of honor" ceremony 503, 506
office among Ponca 46
of Hethu'shka society 460
scouts summoned by 424

Page
HERBS, medicinal use 582–583
See also Plants (curative).
HETHU'SHKA SOCIETY—
general description 459–462
meeting 462–469
references 50, 169, 439, 481
songs 460, 465, 466, 469–480, 482
HEWETT, EDGAR L., work of 10, 12
HEWITT, J. N. B., work of 9
HI'ÇADA, subgens of Waça'be (Ponca) 42, 48, 52–53
HIDES, uses 272, 342, 345
HILL, J. J., reference 624
HILL, WALTER, reference 624
HODGE, F. W., work of 7, 12
HOLMES, W. H., CHIEF—
report 7–14
work 7
HOMER, NEBR., reference 99, 623
HO^n^, gens of Kansa 67
HO^n^'DO^n^MO^n^THI^n^, remarks of 637
HO^n^'GA, application of name 40–41
HO^n^'GA, gens (Omaha)—
Council of Seven convened by 196
general account 40–41, 153–159, 194–195
in anointing Sacred Pole 231, 232, 237
in He'dewachi 252, 259
names in 70
part in establishing Nini'bato^n^ divisions 201
references 45, 147, 160, 203, 589
See also names of subgentes and of other divisions.
HO^n^'GA (Osage)—
division of 40, 41, 61, 64
kinship group 58, 60, 61, 62, 63
HO^n^'GA SUBGENS—
connection with sacred corn 262
watho^n^' appointed by 276
HO^n^'GASHENU DIVISION—
place in tribal organization 40, 135, 138, 195, 196–198
reference 208
represented by Sacred Tent 154
See also Earth people and names of gentes.
HO^n^'GASHI^n^GA, gens (Kansa) 67
HO^n^'GATO^n^GA—
gens (Kansa) 40, 67
group (Quapaw) 40, 68
HO^n^'GA UTANATSI—
gens (Kansa) 40
kinship group (Osage) 40, 58–59, 62, 63, 199
HO^n^'GAXTI, division of Washa'beto^n^ subgens (Ho^n^'ga) 147–148, 155, 159
HO^n^'GAZHI^n^GA, group (Quapaw) 68
See also Small Ho^n^'ga.

HO^n^'HEWACHI SOCIETY—
admission 211, 212, 378
among Oto 501
feast of the Ho^n^'hewachi 500–509
general description 493–495, 507–508
one hundred wathi^n^'ethe, the 495–497
part in authorizing war party 416
punishment inflicted by 583–584
references 253, 285
rites 596

Ho^n'hewachi society—Continued. Page
  songs ... 502–503, 508
  Watha'wa ... 497–500
Hop vine, medicinal use ... 584
Horses—
  as gifts ... 496
  decoration ... 352–353
  discovery ... 79–80
  ownership ... 363
  strangled in funeral ceremonies ... 83, 592
Hough, Dr. Walter, work of ... 11
Hrdlička, Dr. Aleš, work of ... 10–11, 12
Hubtho^n', Ponca village ... 51
Hudson Bay Company, reference ... 81
Hu'inikashiha, group (Quapaw) ... 68
Human body as known to Omaha ... 107–109
Humulus lupulus, medicinal use ... 584
Hu^n'ga—
  blessing of ... 400
  painting of ... 397
  significance of name ... 379–380, 384, 389–390, 393
Hunting—
  affected by trade conditions ... 614–615
  butchering ... 307
  Indian attitude in ... 309
  relation to religious rites ... 155
  See also Buffalo hunt.
Hu'thuga—
  application of name by Ponca ... 42
  arrangement of ... 122, 141, 153–154, 160
  compared with tsi'huthuga ... 58
  general discussion ... 137–141, 196–198
  references ... 194, 195, 207, 208
  See also Ho^n'gashenu, I^{n}shta'çu^{n}da division.

I'bashabe, explanation of term ... 219–220
Ice gens. *See* Nu'xe.
I'ekithe, subdivision of Nini'bato^n subgens. 148, 149, 153, 154
Illustration work of Bureau ... 12
Implements—
  brooms ... 98
  for domestic work ... 340–341
  for skin dressing ... 342–344, 345
  manufacture ... 338–339
  metal ... 613–614, 616, 617
  mortars and pestles ... 99
  paint brush ... 228
  stone ... 613–614
Indian delegations, study of ... 12
Indian games, monograph on ... 9–10
  See also Games.
Indian languages. *See* Handbook of Languages; Language.
Indian Office, U. S. *See* Office of Indian Affairs.
Indian Police, reference ... 630
Indians, legal status ... 51
Indian Territory—
  field work ... 7
  references ... 51, 57
Indian tribes, technology and art ... 7
I^{n}gthe'zhide gens, account of ... 183–185, 201
I^{n}gtho^n'çi^{n}çnedeweti, subgens of Thi'xida (Ponca) ... 43
I^{n}gtho^n'ushko^n, Osage name for Hethu'shka society ... 459
I^{n}gthu^n' ithaethe society, description ... 490–493
  See also Thunder society.
I^{n}ke'çabe gens—
  connection with sacred corn ... 262
  custodian of Sacred Tribal Pipes .. 196, 207, 209
  general account ... 146–151
  names in ... 147
  on annual buffalo hunt ... 271, 277
  part in establishing Nini'bato^n divisions. 201
  part in He'dewachi ... 252, 257, 258
  references ... 154, 261, 379, 589
  War Pack from ... 434
  See also names of subgentes and of other divisions.
I^n'kugthi athi^n. *See* Pebble society.
Insects known to Omaha ... 106
I^{n}shta'çu^{n}da division—
  place in hu'thuga ... 138, 196–198
  references ... 61, 208, 355
  rites in charge of ... 195
  See also names of gentes included; Sky people.
I^{n}shta'çu^{n}da gens—
  birth customs ... 115
  connection with Turning the Child ... 118
  general account ... 185–194
  in He'dewachi ... 258
  position in hu'thuga ... 122
  rites belonging to ... 196–197
  Sacred Tribal Pipes prepared by .. 196, 207, 209
  See also Nini'bato^n, Washe'to^n.
I^{n}shta'maza. *See* La Flesche, Joseph.
I^{n}shta'thabi, account of ... 147
Iowa (State), reference ... 622
Iowa (tribe)—
  association with Omaha ... 35
  attacked by Dakota ... 86
  early relations with French ... 81
  Hethu'shka society among ... 459
  mentioned by Le Sueur ... 80
  name applied to English by ... 611
  Omaha name for ... 36, 102
  party to treaties ... 73, 74, 218, 622
Irish, Omaha name for ... 612
Iroquoian stock, unknown to Omaha ... 102
Iroquois language, sketch of ... 9
Italians, Omaha name for ... 612

Jefferson, President, on liquor traffic among Indians ... 618
Jeffery, map of, reference ... 80
Jemez Plateau region, survey of ... 10
Jerking meat, process of ... 344

Kansa, gens in several tribes ... 38, 66, 67
Kansa (tribe)—
  general account ... 40, 66–67
  linguistic classification ... 605
  meaning of term lost ... 40
  reference ... 169
  relation to other tribes ... 35, 37–38
  tribal organization ... 141

KANSA (TRIBE)—Continued. Page
See also Kansas (tribe), Kaw, and names of gentes and of other divisions.
KANSAS RIVER, reference........ 81
KANSAS (STATE), origin of name........ 169
KANSAS (TRIBE), Omaha name for........ 101
See also Kansa, Kaw.
KAW, Omaha name for........ 101
See also Kansa, Kansas (tribe).
KAXE'NOⁿBA—
in battle with Sioux........ 100–101
references........ 99, 496
KEEFE, H. L., acknowledgment to........ 642
KEEPERS—
account of........ 595
emoluments........ 212–213
reference........ 205, 598
KE'Iⁿ, subgens (Tha'tada)—
account of........ 161, 165–167
reference........ 162
rites........ 159
See also Turtle subgens.
KE'NIKASHIHA, group (Quapaw)........ 68
KENTUCKY COFFEE TREE, medicinal use........ 584
KICKAPOO, Omaha name for........ 102
KI'KUNETHE SOCIETY, description........ 485–486
KINSHIP GROUPS (Osage)........ 58–61
KINSHIP TERMS........ 313–318
KIOWA—
Omaha name for........ 102
researches among........ 8
KOⁿ'ÇE GENS—
custodian of Sacred Pipes........ 459, 461
general account........ 169–171
part in ball game........ 366
See also names of subdivisions.

LA FLESCHE, FRANCIS—
as joint author........ 14, 30
researches among Osage........ 69
LA FLESCHE, JOSEPH—
account of........ 619, 631–634
death........ 224
references........ 30, 118, 624
remarks of........ 638
tribal relics saved by........ 222
LAKE ANDES, S. DAK., reference........ 73
LAKE MICHIGAN, reference........ 72
LAKE WINNIPEG, references........ 80, 81, 612
LANCE, description........ 448
LANDS—
allotment........ 33, 247–248, 636–640
to Ponca........ 41
cessions to United States........ 72, 75, 89, 100, 624
Pawnee........ 89
Quapaw........ 67
original allottees........ 642–654
See also Reservations, Severalty act, Treaties.
LANGUAGE—
discussion........ 605–607
new words introduced........ 620–622
LARGE VILLAGE, location........ 86, 99
LEARY, MISS ELLA, work of........ 13
LEAVENWORTH, Omaha name for........ 101
LEGAL STATUS of Indian........ 51
LEGGINGS, description........ 354–355
LE SUEUR, on location of Omaha........ 80

LEWIS AND CLARK— Page
meeting with Omaha........ 87
reference........ 99
story of Blackbird........ 82
LIBRARY, work of........ 13
LIFE, in Omaha conception........ 357, 415–416
LIGHTNING—
connection with Shell society........ 512, 519, 562
in Omaha conception........ 188, 457
rites connected with........ 177–178, 185
symbolized in Omaha ceremony........ 127
LINCOLN, NEBR.—
Omaha name for........ 101
reference........ 342
LIQUORS, INTOXICATING—
introduction........ 618–619
prohibition........ 625
LITTLE BEAR (Ponca), story of........ 50
LITTLE CHIEF (Ponca). See Zhiⁿga'gahige.
LITTLE COLORADO VALLEY, ARIZONA, antiquities........ 8
LITTLE VILLAGE, location........ 100
LODGE used in Sacred Pole ceremony........ 231
See also Earth lodge.
LONG, cited as authority........ 184
LONG KNIFE, Dakota name for American........ 611
LOUISIANA—
linguistic stocks........ 8–9
reference........ 74
LOUISIANA PURCHASE, references........ 613, 619
LOUP COUNTY, NEBR., reference........ 100
LOUP RIVER, reference........ 90
LOVE SONGS, description........ 319–321, 375
LOWER BRULE', Ponca name for........ 103

MAGIC—
association with sickness........ 582, 583
in Pebble society........ 565–567, 580
in Shell society........ 547, 550, 551, 553, 554–565
Omaha attitude toward........ 602
"shooting" in ceremonies........ 530–531, 532, 537
See also Occult powers, Sleight-of-hand.
MAHA, MAHAHS, variants of *Omaha*........ 80–81, 622
MAIZE—
cultivation........ 112, 269, 635
origin........ 71, 76–78, 147
parts and preparation........ 269–270
red ears tabu........ 147–148
rites connected with........ 155, 159, 200, 261–269, 596
Ponca........ 45
See also Corn.
MAKOⁿ', gens (Ponca), reference........ 309
MALARIA, reference........ 620
MANDAN—
Omaha name for........ 102, 486
White Buffalo Hide among........ 284
MAPLE CREEK, reference........ 408
MAPS, use of, by Indians........ 88
"MARK OF HONOR"—
account of (Omaha, Osage)........ 219–221
in Hoⁿ'hewachi ceremony........ 502
references........ 154, 252, 285, 325
significance........ 494
MARQUETTE, Wa'waⁿ ceremony found by........ 74
MARRIAGE—
determined by relationship........ 313

MARRIAGE—Continued. Page
forbidden within gens.................... 137
general account..................... 318, 327, 641
See also Divorce, Exogamy, Polygamy.
MARSHALS. *See* "Soldiers."
MA'THETEUNE. *See* Buffalo hunt, winter.
MAWA'DOⁿTHIⁿ, remarks of.................. 637
MEASLES, references........................ 582, 620
MEDICINES, known to secret societies........ 459, 522, 559, 560
See also Plants, curative.
MESA VERDE PARK, establishment......... 10
MESA VERDE REGION, COLORADO, ruins of.. 10
METAMORPHOSIS, absence of belief in......... 589
METEMPSYCHOSIS, absence of belief in........ 589
MEXICAN ANTIQUITIES, publication on....... 9
MEXICO, EASTERN, researches....... 8
MIGRATIONS of Omaha....................... 72, 75
MIHA'KE NIKASHIHA, group (Quapaw)...... 68
MI'INIKASHIHA, group (Quapaw)............ 68
MI'KAÇI, group of Moⁿ'thiⁿkagaxe gens 172
MI'KAÇI SONGS............................. 416–420
MIKA'TOⁿKE RIVER. *See* Des Moines river.
MIKE'NITHA, group under, account of.. 178, 179–181
MILKY WAY, the, in Omaha conception... 588, 590
MINK, special connection with woman....... 512
MINNESOTA RIVER, reference................. 73
MINNESOTA (STATE), references 72, 623
MISSIONARIES, work of.................. 625–629, 633
MISSISSIPPI RIVER, references....... 36, 57, 72, 73, 74
MISSOURI RIVER—
in Omaha history........ 72, 73, 74, 75, 78, 80, 100
in Ponca legend.......................... 49
Omaha villages on........................ 85–89
references................ 57, 91, 626, 627, 629, 630
trading post on.......................... 81, 612
MISSOURI (STATE), references................ 57, 72
MISSOURI (TRIBE)—
Omaha name for.......................... 102
party to treaties........................ 622, 623
MIXA'ÇKA (Ponca), story told of............. 446
MI'XAÇOⁿ, group of Moⁿ'thiⁿkagaxe gens..... 172
MOCCASINS—
description.............................. 355
in birth ceremonies...................... 117
in ceremony of Turning the Child...... 118, 121
material for............................ 272, 345
significance 144, 358–359, 594
use by members of Shell society.......... 519
use by war parties....................... 409
use on the dead.......................... 408
MONCHU' INIKASHIHA, group (Quapaw)..... 68
MOⁿCHU' ITHAETHE SOCIETY, description.. 486–487
MOⁿCHU'NOⁿBE. *See* Shu'denaçi.
MONEY, introduction of..................... 617
MOⁿ'HIⁿÇI, keeper of Sacred Pipe ritual...... 187
MOⁿ'HIⁿTHIⁿGE, keeper of Tent of War..... 452–454
MOⁿIⁿ'KA, gens of Kansa.................... 67
MOⁿKOⁿ', gens of Ponca................. 44, 48, 439
MOⁿSO'TSEMOⁿIⁿ, an Osage gens............ 39
MOⁿ'THIⁿKAGAXE GENS, account of 38, 171–175
See also names of subdivisions.
MONTHS, names of.......................... 111, 113
MOⁿWA'DATHIⁿ SOCIETY, description......... 486
MOⁿXE'WATHE, on White Buffalo Hides..... 284
MOON—
in Creation legend....................... 570
in Osage legends......................... 63

MOON—Continued. Page
peculiar influence of (Omaha, Osage).... 132
symbolized in Shell society. 512, 513, 517, 559, 562
symbolized in tattooing.................. 506
MOONEY, JAMES, work of.................... 8, 12
MORGAN, HON. JOHN T., petition presented by.................................... 639
MORMONS, reference......................... 626
MOURNING CUSTOMS—
general account......................... 495–496
in He'dewachi............................ 253
throwing locks of hair on the dead...... 124
See also Funeral customs.
MUSIC—
characteristics........................... 323
songs, singing, rhythm............ 126, 373–375
Wa'waⁿ ceremony 376–400
Ponca................................ 400–401
See also Songs.
MUSICAL INSTRUMENTS—
general description.................... 371–372
in He'dewachi ceremony.................. 256
See also Drum, Flute, etc.
MUSKHOGEAN STOCK, unknown by Omaha .. 102
MYTHOLOGY, character................ 600–601, 608

NA'GTHE WAAⁿ. *See* Captive songs.
NAMES—
baby names—
abandonment of...................... 121
in use among Omaha................. 314
of children (Ponca)....................... 45
of women............................. 145, 200
personal—
distribution.......................... 137
etiquette of........................ 334–335
evidence of former union of tribes.... 39
Osage................................ 64–67
reference to rites.................... 255
symbolism............................. 38, 39
For personal names, *see also* names of tribes and of gentes; Ni'kie.
NAⁿ'PANTA, group (Quapaw) 68
NATCHEZ DICTIONARY, preparation 9
NATURAL PHENOMENA, Omaha names for... 110
NEBRASKA—
jurisdiction over Omaha................. 624
Omaha lands in......................... 623
NEGRO, Omaha name for..................... 612
NEILL, on trade of Omaha.................. 80–81
NEMAHA COUNTY, NEBR., reference......... 622
NEW MEXICO, field work in............... 7, 10, 11
NEZ PERCÉS, Omaha name for................ 102
NICHOLS, MRS. FRANCES S., work of........ 13
NIDA, application of term.................. 194
NIGHT—
associated with death.................. 588
in Omaha conception.............. 128, 494, 505
in Ponca conception.................... 507
symbolism........................ 254, 513, 517
NI'KAGAHI SHA'BE, account of............ 202–204, 205, 206, 208
NI'KAGAHI U'ZHU, account of 208, 498–500
NI'KAGAHI XU'DE, account of......202–204, 206, 210
NI'KAPASHNA, gens (Ponca)—
account of 44
funeral custom.......................... 358

Ni'kapashna, gens (Ponca)—Continued. Page
personal names 54
references 41, 42, 48
See also names of subgentes.
Ni'ka wakondagi, kinship group (Osage) 58, 60–61
Ni'kie, explanation of term 136, 607
Ni'kie names, taking of 117, 121, 144–145
Ponca 140
Ni'kie rites, distribution 137
Ponca 140
Nini'baton subdivisions—
Inke'çabe gens 147–151, 252, 257, 397
Inshta'çunda gens 185–186, 187–190
Kon'çe gens 169, 170–171
Mon'thinkagaxe gens 174–175
origin 201–202
reference 207
Tapa' gens 178, 182–183
Teçin'de gens 175, 176–177
See also Nonxthe'bitube.
Niobrara river, references 41, 49, 51, 85, 89, 93
Nonxthe'bitube, subdivision of Nini'baton subgens 148, 149, 151–152, 254
Non'zhinzhon rite, account of 128–133
North Dakota, former habitat of Omaha 72
Nu'donhonga, head of lodge, Shell society 516
Nuga'xti, significance of name 144
Nuge'teune. *See* Buffalo hunt, annual.
Numbers, symbolism—
four 121, 129, 131, 171, 218, 231, 242, 253, 255, 258, 259, 277, 278, 287, 309–310, 380, 381, 400, 420, 489, 497, 499, 509, 510, 511, 513, 514, 515, 516, 518, 520, 521, 522, 523, 526, 562, 563, 565
multiples used in rituals 242
seven 207, 242, 277, 512, 513, 515, 516, 518
three 221, 242
Nu'xe gens—
Osage 46–47
Ponca 38, 41, 42, 46–47, 48, 57, 61, 355
reference 355
Nu'xe, subgens of Kansa, Osage, Quapaw 38

Occult powers, possession of 490–491
See also Magic.
Occupations—
affected by advent of traders 614–615
men 203, 338–339
See also names of occupations; Women.
Offenses, general account 213–216
Office of Indian Affairs—
action toward Omaha 642
permits granted by 11
See also Commissioner of Indian Affairs.
Oglala—
battle with Omaha 100, 101
Omaha name for 102
Ponca name for 103
Ohio river, references 36, 72, 94
Oklahoma—
field work in 7
home of portion of Ponca 41
present home of Kansa 66
present home of Osage 57, 67
"Old Men, the," in Omaha legend 201, 207
Omaha City, Omaha name for 101
Omaha creek, references 86, 87, 91, 99, 100

Page
Omaha dance, application of term 461
Om'patonga, remarks of 638
On'pon inikashiha, group (Quapaw) 68
O'pxon, group (Osage) 63
O'pxon inikashikithe, gens (Kansa) 67
Oregon, field work in 7
Orientation—
of dwellings 97
of He'dewachi tree 253
of hu'thuga 137, 138, 196
Ornamentation, affected by advent of traders 615
See also Adornment.
"Orphans," Omaha name for Ponca 41
Osage—
birth ceremonies 116
ceremony similar to He'dewachi 260
custom of Adoption among 61–62, 603
early relations with French 81
elk rites 194
funeral customs 358
general account 57–58
Hethu'shka society among 459
kinship groups 58–61
linguistic classification 605
manner of wearing hair 132
"mark of honor" among 219–221
myths 457, 571
name applied to English by 611
Omaha name for 45, 101
organization 57–58, 140
party to peace with Cheyenne 73
personal names 64–67
relation to other tribes 35, 37–38
separation from Ponca 38
traditions 38, 40, 47, 62–64
visions among 132–133
we'ton waan among 423
See also names of gentes and of other divisions.
Osprey, Fla., researches at 10–11
Oto—
dress of members of Shell society 519
drum in Hon'hewachi ceremony 501
early relations with French 81
Hethu'shka society among 459
moccasins in birth ceremonies 117
name applied to English by 611
Omaha name for 102
party to treaties 73, 74, 623
reference 43
war with Omaha 87
Otter, special connection with woman 512
Owl—
in Ponca legend 47
special connection with woman 512
Ozark mountains, reference 57

Packs of War, Sacred—
account of 404–408
Ponca 439–441
authority for war parties 415, 416
part in dispatching scouts 424
part in Wate'giçtu ceremony 434–437
See also Wain'waxube.

Padouca— Page
meeting with Ponca 79–80
party to peace treaty 81
reference 49
village on Dismal river 88
See also Comanche.
Pahu'thoⁿdathoⁿ, location 100
Painting—
adornment in Shell society 519, 522–523
decoration of horses 352–353
in Pebble society 565–566
in Wa'waⁿ ceremony 397
paint brushes 239, 354
references 350, 615–616
"Paper chiefs," account of 85, 212, 631
Papilion creek, references 91, 100
Pa'thiⁿgahige, group under 178, 181
Pawnee—
defeated by Ponca 446
early relations with French 81
habitat 88–89
Hethu'shka society among 460
hunting ground 89
name for Ponca 43
Omaha name for 102
Spanish influence through 114
Wa'baçka's defeat of 406–408
warfare with Omaha 87
Wa'waⁿ ceremony 377, 379–381, 400
Peabody Museum report, on "White Buffalo Ceremony" 284
Peace—
calumet symbol of 207
importance attached to 211–212
in control of Council of Seven 209
Nini'batoⁿ divisions associated with 201
rites for preservation of 195
Pebble society—
explanation of teachings 570–571
general account 565–567
magic in 565, 580–581, 583, 602
opening ritual 568–571
references 171, 172
relation to Shell society 529, 581
rituals for sweat lodge 571–578
"shooting" of members 530, 537
songs 566–567, 579
Pe'degahi, information from 558–559
Pennsylvania, field work in 7
Personal names. *See* Names.
Pe'toⁿ inikashiha, group (Quapaw) 68
Phonograph, in connection with Omaha music 373
Physalis viscora, medicinal use 584
Picotte, Dr. Susan La Flesche, reference. 625
Pine Ridge Sioux, reference 101
Pipes—
belonging to Sacred Pole .. 226–227, 230–233, 238
belonging to Te'pa itazhi 161–162
belonging to White Buffalo Hide 283, 284, 286–289, 290
custodianship (Ponca) 44
from Sacred War Pack 415
in Adoption ceremony (Osage) 62
in Hethu'shka society 459, 460, 461, 462, 464, 465–466
in Hoⁿ'hewachi ceremony 496, 498, 499
Pipes—Continued. Page
in "mark of honor" (Osage) 220
in Shell society 520, 521, 562–563
of Tent of War 142, 424–425
peace pipes—
calumet 207
in charge of Wazha'zhe gens (Ponca). 46
in Osage legend 46, 62
in Ponca legend 47, 48
in Wa'waⁿ ceremony 43
Sacred Tribal—
bearers 149, 162
custody 148
description 135, 207
in annual buffalo hunt 276, 277
in connection with Council of Seven 196, 207–209
in election of chief 204
in establishment of Nini'batoⁿ divisions 201
in He'dewachi 251, 253, 255, 257, 258
in preservation of peace 205–206, 215
keeper 208
reference 217
rites 261, 596, 602
ritual for filling 187–188, 195, 208–209
significance 207
Te'pa subgens associated with 159
significance 201
use in prayer 599
war pipes (Ponca) 44
Wa'waⁿ pipes 43, 47, 162, 375, 376–378, 380
Pipestem, in annual buffalo hunt .. 276, 280, 281, 282
Pipestone quarry, reference 36
Plants—
curative—
description 584–585
in story of Shell society 516
reference 487
edible, description 341–342
See also Herbs.
Platte river, references 49, 80, 86, 88–89
Pleiades, reference 177
Points of the compass 111
Point Village (Ponca), reference 51
Poison—
in punishment of offenders 213
in Shell society 559, 560, 561, 564
Polygamy, references 326, 615
Ponca City, Iowa, reference 86
Ponca, gens of several tribes 47, 67, 217
Ponca, meaning of term lost 40
Ponca river, reference 92
Ponca (tribe)—
arrow-marking among 42, 43, 452
belief as to ghosts 216
ceremony of conferring war honors 439–441
conception of Day and Night 507
customs in 18th century 50
Feast of Soldiers 309, 500
food supply 45
general account 41–42, 452
hunting ground 89
legends 47–50, 446
linguistic classification 605
manner of wearing hair 132
"mark of honor" among 506, 507

PONCA (TRIBE)—Continued. Page
murder among... 216
name applied to English by... 611
Omaha name for... 101
party to treaties... 73, 74, 218, 376
personal names... 51–57
population and villages... 51
punishment of offenders... 48
recent history... 51
references... 29, 67, 73, 194, 217
relation to other tribes... 35, 37–38, 39
removal... 635–636
rites and customs of gentes... 42–47
ritual connected with tribal hunt... 442–446
separation from Omaha... 78–80
separation from Osage... 38
Thunder society... 490–491
traditions... 38, 40, 41
tribal circle... 42
tribal organization... 48, 61, 140
warfare with Omaha... 87
Wa'waⁿ ceremony... 400–401
We'toⁿ waaⁿ among... 423
See also names of gentes and of other divisions.
POⁿ'CAXTI, gens of Ponca—
account of... 44–45
personal names... 54–55
references... 41, 42, 48
POPULATION—
Kansa... 66
Omaha... 33–34, 642
Ponca... 51
Quapaw... 67
PORTAGE DE SIOUX, treaty of... 622
PORTO RICO, researches in... 8
POTAWATOMI, Omaha name for... 102
POTTERY—
abandonment... 617
description... 340, 341
manufacture... 71
PRAIRIE DU CHIEN, treaty of... 72, 622
PRAYER—
addressed directly to Wakoⁿ'da... 599
in decoration of horses... 353
in Pebble Society ritual... 573
Omaha conception of... 128–129, 130, 188
on annual buffalo hunt... 278, 281
pipe associated with... 201
uzhiⁿ'eti as symbol of... 241–242
PRESBYTERIAN CHURCH, work of... 626–629
PROPERTY among Omaha—
discussion of... 362–363
in songs... 373
PROPERTY OF BUREAU, description... 14
PROSTITUTION, absence of... 325
PROVERBS, examples of... 604
PUBERTY CEREMONY, account of... 128–133
PUBLICATIONS OF BUREAU... 12, 13
PUBLIC LANDS, permits for explorations on... 11
PU'GTHOⁿ SOCIETY, account of... 481–485
PUNISHMENTS, account of... 213–216
See also Wazhiⁿ'agthe.
PUTNAM, PROF. FREDERIC WARD, acknowledgments to... 29
QUAPAW— Page
general account... 67–69
linguistic classification... 605
Omaha name for... 36, 101
Omaha parting from... 72
relation to other tribes... 35, 37–38
tribal organization... 141
See also names of gentes.
QUILL WORK, description... 203, 345–347
QUIVER, description... 452

RACCOON, special connection with woman... 512
RACCOON RIVER, reference... 88
RACING, FOOT, reference... 592
RAILROADS, development... 624
RATTLES—
description... 372
in Feast of Hoⁿ'hewachi... 500
in He'dewachi... 256
in Wa'waⁿ ceremony... 377
used by Shell society... 520
RATTLESNAKE, reference to... 213
RELATIONSHIP, terms of... 313–318
RELIGION AND ETHICS—
affected by advent of traders... 614–615
conception of cosmic order... 134–135
conception of life... 357–358
interrelation of men and animals... 599–601
keeper... 595
position of chiefs... 601–602
proverbs... 604
relation to warfare... 402–403, 602–603
religion and political unity... 196, 199–200
terms for bad traits and bad conduct... 604
terms for good traits and conduct... 603
totems... 602
veneration for the Ancients... 601
We'waçpe... 596–597
See also Death, Ethics, Magic, Wakoⁿ'da.
REPUBLICAN RIVER, reference... 94
RESEARCH WORK... 7–11
RESERVATIONS—
Kansa... 66
Omaha—
account of... 623, 624, 625, 629–630
original allottees... 642–654
survey of... 634
Ponca... 41
Quapaw... 67
RHYTHM in Indian music... 375
RITES AND RITUALS—
general character... 194–198, 607, 609–610
introduction of child to Cosmos... 115–117
introduction of child into tribe... 117–128
See also names of rites and rituals, and under names of societies and tribes.
RIVERS known to Omaha... 89–94
ROBE, the, discussion of... 356–362
ROCKY MOUNTAINS—
in Ponca tradition... 79
known to Omaha... 102
ROPE, GRAPEVINE, in Omaha tradition... 36
ROSALIE, account of... 624–625, 642
ROSEBUD BRULE', Ponca name for... 103
RUNNERS, in annual buffalo hunt. 279–280, 300–302

Sacred Legend— Page
character 113
on acquisition of Wa'waⁿ ceremony 376
on early habitat and conditions 70–72
on meeting with whites 81–82
on origin of Noⁿ'zhiⁿzhoⁿ rite 128–129
on political unity 199, 201
on primitive clothing 356–357
on Sacred Pole 218–219
on the maize 261
on tribal character 608–609, 610
references 251, 255
Sacred Packs, description 226–228
Sacred Packs of War. *See* Packs of War.
Sacred Pipes. *See* Pipes.
Sacred Pole—
anointing ceremony 213, 230–233, 244, 273, 363
ceremonies 243–251, 596
description 224–225
gifts to 205
in annual buffalo hunt 280
in He'dewachi ceremony 251–260
keeper 208
legend of 44, 223–224
"mark of honor" 219–221
origin 44, 73, 74, 217–219
references 70, 160, 279, 458, 494, 609
ritual songs 233–242
symbolism 236, 243
tent of 154, 195
See also Sacred Packs, Sacred Tents.
Sacred Shell—
account of 200, 454–458, 494
reference 194
Sacred Tents—
account of 221–222
contents 278–279
custody 154
in Turning the Child 118
on annual buffalo hunt 278–279
references 155, 194–195, 277, 487
See also Tent of War, White Buffalo Hide.
Sacred tree, origin 49
Sacred tribal pipes. *See* Pipes.
Sacred White Buffalo Hide. *See* White Buffalo Hide.
Salt, source 342
Salt creek, reference 342
Sanborn, John P., Jr., service of 12
Sansouci, Louis, reference 626
Santee—
attack on Omaha 100
Omaha name for 102
Ponca name for 103
See also Santee Sioux.
Santee Sioux, party to treaties 622, 623
See also Santee.
Sapir, Edward, work of 9
Sarasota Bay, Fla., researches at 10–11
Sauk, Omaha name for 102
Sauk and Foxes, party to treaty 622
Scalp lock—
care bestowed on 128
description 350
in Sacred War Pack 412
Scalp lock—Continued. Page
in war honor decorations 438–439, 440
significance 124
specimen in Sacred Shell 457
Scalps—
connection with Sacred Pole 225, 226
taking of, a war honor 437
use in victory dance 432
See also Scalp lock.
Schools, account of 625, 626, 627–630, 642
Scouts, on buffalo hunt 142, 423–426
Scout song, example of 420–421
Separate Hoⁿ'ga, gens of Kansa 40
Serpents. *See* Snakes.
Seven Chiefs. *See* Council of Seven Chiefs.
Severalty act, references 33, 41, 624, 636
Sex conception—
in cosmic order (Omaha) 134–135, 502
in tribal organization—
Omaha 138–140, 196–198
Osage 141
Ponca 140, 507
See also Hu'thuga.
Sha'be. *See* Ni'kagahi sha'be.
Shell creek, references 89, 90
Shells, sacred, description 520
See also Sacred Shell.
Shell society—
adornment of members 519
ceremonies on death of member 553–554
magic practised in 547, 550, 551, 553, 554–565, 583, 602
organization 516–520
origin 509–516
punishment of offenders 554–565
reference 457
regular meetings—
general account 520–521
opening ceremony 521–533
public ceremony 533–553
relation to Pebble society 529, 565, 566, 581
"shooting" of members 530–532, 533, 553
similar to Grand Medicine of Chippewa 102
songs 31, 533, 537, 543, 546, 598–599
Shell, symbolism 187
Shield, description 452
Sho'ka, application of term 58
Shoⁿ'geçabe, keeper of pack (Ponca) 439
Shoⁿ'toⁿçabe, acknowledgment to 58
"Shooting" of members—
in Pebble society 566
in Shell society 530–532, 533, 537
Shoshonean stock, unknown to Omaha 102
Shu'degaxe (Ponca)—
keeper of pack 43, 439
story told of 446
Shu'denaçi—
account of 248
legends told by 70, 223–224
on site of old Omaha villages 72
Singing. *See* Songs.
Siouan family, stock, tribes. *See* Sioux.
Sioux—
distribution of He'thushka among 460
general organization 141
linguistic classification 605
manner of wearing hair 132

SIOUX—Continued. Page
origin of name 605
Ponca name for 103
reference 50
reservation 51
warfare with Omaha 100, 623
See also Dakota, Oglala, Santee.
SIOUX, BANDS OF THE, party to treaty 622
SIOUX CITY, references 101, 633
SKIN DRESSING, account of 71, 342, 345
SKUNK, special connection with man 512
SKY—
in Omaha conception 134, 600
night, rites relating to 177
symbolism in Shell society 513
SKY PEOPLE, THE—
place in Omaha organization 135, 138, 139
represented by Sacred Tent 154
See also Iⁿshta'çuⁿda division.
SLEIGHT OF HAND, in Moⁿchu' ithaethe 486
SMALL HOⁿ'GA, gens (Kansa, Quapaw) 40
See also Hoⁿ'gazhiⁿga.
SMALLPOX—
account of 86–87, 620, 622
references 582
SMEDES, MISS EMILIE R., work of 13
SMITHSONIAN INSTITUTION, researches of 8
SMOKED YELLOW. *See* Shu'denaçi.
SNAKES, references 45, 46, 213, 506
SOCIAL LIFE—
amusements 363–370
care and training of children 327–333
clothing 354–362
courtship and marriage 318–327
etiquette 334–337
friendship 318–319
kinship terms 313–318
personal adornment 349–354
property 362–363
SOCIETIES—
based on similarity of visions 133
dress 359
entrance fees 212–213
magic in 583, 602
property 363
reference 33
secret—
admission 585
Hoⁿ'hewachi 493–509
Iⁿgthuⁿ' ithaethe 490–492
Moⁿchu' ithaethe 486–487
Pebble society 529, 565–581
rites 596
Shell society 509–565, 566, 581
Te' ithaethe 487–489
Wanoⁿ'xe ithaethe 489–490
social—
Hethu'shka 459–480
Ki'kuⁿethe 485–486
Moⁿwa'dathiⁿ 486
Pu'gthoⁿ 481–485
T'e ga'xe 486
Toka'lo 486
See also names of societies, as above.
"SOLDIERS"—
account of 210, 442
in buffalo hunt 215, 279, 281, 282
SONGS— Page
bear song 487
captive songs 427–431, 603
connected with societies or rites 502–503
funeral song 593
general description 373–375
in treatment of disease 582–583, 585
love songs 319–321, 375
property in 363
Thunder songs 491–493, 598–599
wolf songs 410–411
woman's songs 320–323, 421
See also names of societies.
SOUTH DAKOTA, references 72, 73, 85, 102
SOUTHERN CHEYENNE, researches among 8
SOUTHWEST SOCIETY of Archæological Institute of America, permit granted 11
SPANIARDS, Omaha name for 612
SPANISH INFLUENCE, references 67, 81, 114
SPEAR, description 448
SPECK, FRANK J., work of 9
SQUIRREL, special connection with woman 512
STANDING BEAR, account of 51, 635
STANDING BUFFALO, Ponca legend told by 49
STARS—
associated with death 588
in Osage legend 63
rites relating to 177, 195
symbolized in Shell society 513–514, 517, 559, 560
symbolized in tattooing 504–505
STEVENSON, MRS. M. C., work of 7–8
ST. JAMES, NEBR., reference 85
ST. LOUIS—
Omaha name for 101
reference 136, 625–626
site of trading post 82
STONES, symbolism of 45, 171–172, 587
STONE-WORKING—
methods 338
origin 70
STREAMS known to Omaha 89–94
SUBGENTES, discussion of 136, 137
SUICIDE, rare among Omaha 588
SUN—
in Creation legend 570
in Osage legends 63
symbolized in Shell society 512, 513, 559, 562
symbolized in tattooing 504
woodpecker associated with 207
SWAN—
in story of Shell society 514
special connection with woman 512
SWANTON, DR. JOHN R., work of 8–9
SWEAT BATHS, description 585–587
SWEAT LODGE, rituals for 571–578, 609
SWEDES, Omaha name for 612
SWEET FLAG, medicinal use 584
SWIMMING, as an Omaha amusement 369–370

TABUS—
bear (black) 160
birds 42, 161, 365
buffalo—
head 149, 159, 162
tongue 155, 283
buffalo-horn spoons 339
buffalo (male) 47

Tabus—Continued. Page
- charcoal 148, 178, 254
- children instructed as to 122
- clay 172
- corn (red ear) 147, 252, 254, 261
- crane 154
- creeping insects, bugs, worms, etc 186, 188
- deer 358
- distribution 137
- elk 143, 144, 145, 194, 358, 589
- fetus of animals 175, 176, 184
- meaning of term *tabu* 136
- paint (green or blue) 43
- punishment for violation 144
- snakes 45, 46, 506
- soot 45, 172
- swan 172
- tezhu' 154, 273
- turtle 161
- verdigris 169, 178

Tade'ata, subdivision (Ko^{n}'çe), account of. 169, 170, 197–198

Taha'to^{n} itazhi, subdivision of Ni'kapashna (Ponca) 44

Ta'ikawahu, keeper of pack (Ponca) 439

Tanning, process 342, 345

Taos, N. Mex., field work at 7–8, 11

Tapa' gens—
- account of 177–183
- funeral custom 358
- War Pack from 434
- *See also* names of the several groups.

Tapa'xti, account of 178, 179–180

Taste, terms of 110–111

Tattooing—
- among Omaha and Osage 219–221
- "mark of honor" 503–509
- references 613, 615
- significance 494

Teçi^{n}'de gens—
- account of 175–177
- birth customs 115
- *See also* names of the several divisions.

Teço^{n}'ha. *See* White Buffalo Hide.

T'e ga'xe society, description 486

Te inikashikithe, gens (Kansa) 67

Te' ithaethe society, description 487–489

Te'nikashiha, group (Quapaw) 68

Tent covers—
- decoration 353–354
- material 272, 345, 616
- reference 275

Tent of War, Sacred—
- account of 142, 423
- connection with Thunder 403
- contents 213, 221–222, 411, 452–458
- custody of 194
- in dispatch of scouts 424, 425
- keeper 208, 211
- references 200, 229, 554

Tent Sacred to War. *See* Tent of War.

Tents, the property of women 362
- *See also* Tent covers, Tipi.

Tenu'ga, Omaha priest 249

Tenu'gano^{n}pewathe, Omaha warrior 99

Tenu'gano^{n}pewathe shko^{n}thaitho^{n}, location 99

Page

Te'pa itazhi, subgens (Tha'tada), account of 159, 161–162, 167–168, 169, 209

Te'une. *See* Buffalo hunt, annual.

Texas, references 8–9, 74

Tezhu'—
- meaning of term 233, 273
- preparation 342
- references 154, 213, 236, 238

Tha'tada gens—
- bear and eagle associated with 42
- general account 159–168
- in annual buffalo hunt 277
- *See also* names of subgentes and of other divisions.

Thaw fellowship, reference 29

The'giha, application of term 37, 605

Thiku'wi^{n}xe. *See* Turning the Child.

Thi'xida, gens (Ponca)—
- general account 43
- personal names 53
- references 41, 42, 48, 439
- *See also* names of subgentes and of other divisions.

Thi'xida, Pawnee name for Ponca 43

Thomas, Dr. Cyrus, work of 9

Thugina. *See* Fontenelle, Logan.

Thugina gaxthiitho^{n}, location 100–101

Thunder—
- as god of war 200, 402–403, 404, 415–416, 435, 441, 464, 477
  - Ponca 439, 440
- Cedar Pole related to 219, 229, 458
- consecration of boy to 122–128
- in beliefs of Ponca 42
- in He'dewachi ceremony 253–254, 260
- rites connected with 142–143, 160, 177–178, 185
  - Osage, Ponca 47
- Sacred Pole allied to 154
- Sacred Shell associated with 457
- significance in Turning the Child 117, 119–121
- tutelar god of Hethu'shka 459

Thunder birds—
- connection with Sacred Pole 229
- in Omaha mythology 218, 457

Thunder group (Osage) reference 61

Thunder society—
- account of 490, 493
- free from magic 602
- songs 598–599
- *See also* I^{n}gthu^{n}' ithaethe.

Ti, lodges of Shell society 516

Time, divisions 111

Tipi, description 76, 95–97

Tlingit, material relating to 8

Tobacco—
- connection with waba'ho^{n} 206
- in thunder ceremony 143
- *See also* Pipes.

Toka'lo society, account of 486

To^{n}'deamo^{n}thi^{n}, keeper of Ponca War Honor Pack 43

Tonkawa, Ponca name for 103

To^{n}'wo^{n}gaxe, Omaha chief 100, 171–172

To^{n}'wo^{n}gaxe shko^{n}thaitho^{n}, location 100

To^{n}'wo^{n}ni creek, reference 86

To^n'wo^{n}pezhi. *See* "Bad Village." Page
To^n'wo^{n}to^{n}ga, Omaha village.......... 86, 631
To^n'wo^{n}to^{n}gatho^n, location.......... 99
See also Large Village.
To^n'wo^{n}zhi^{n}ga, location.......... 100
Totems, account of.......... 195, 602
Tracy, Edwin S., acknowledgments to.......... 31
Traders—
general account.......... 612–613
Government control.......... 619
influence.......... 82–84, 114, 212, 614–616
introduction by—
cloth.......... 616
guns.......... 617
intoxicants.......... 618
metal implements.......... 613–614
money.......... 617
Traditions—
Dakota.......... 73
Kansa.......... 38
Omaha—
environmental conditions.......... 608
gentes.......... 199
origin of Shell society.......... 509–516
Sacred Pole.......... 218
tribal migrations.......... 36, 38, 72–75
See also Sacred Legend.
Osage.......... 38, 40, 47, 62–64
Ponca.......... 38, 40, 41, 47–50, 485
Arikara.......... 75
crow and wolf.......... 446
meeting with Padouca.......... 79–80
Sacred Pole.......... 218
Quapaw.......... 38
See also Creation myths.
Travoix, use of.......... 275
Treaties with the United States—
account of.......... 89, 622–625
Pawnee.......... 89
Ponca.......... 41
See also Lands.
Trees—
known to Omaha.......... 106
sacred to He'dewachi ceremony.......... 255
Tribal circle—
Omaha. *See* Hu'thuga.
Osage.......... 58–61
Ponca.......... 42
Tribal government, development.......... 199–202
See also Chieftainship.
Tribal organization—
Kansa.......... 141
Omaha—
basic principles.......... 134–141, 194–198, 402
disintegrating tendencies.. 199–201, 402–403
Osage.......... 57–58, 62–64, 140–141
Ponca, Quapaw.......... 140–141
reference.......... 74
See also Tribal government.
Tribal Pipes. *See* Pipes.
Tsedu'ga, gens (Kansa).......... 67
Tsi'uthuga, Osage tribal circle.......... 58–61
Tsi'zhu—
gens (Kansa).......... 67
kinship group (Osage).... 58, 60, 61, 62, 63, 64–65
Tunica dictionary, preparation.......... 9
Turning the Child, ceremony of— Page
Omaha.......... 117–122, 199–200, 401
Ponca.......... 44–45
Turtle, connection with rites.......... 506
Turtle, subgens of several tribes.......... 38
Turtle bearers. *See* Ke'i^n subgens.
Twenty-sixth Annual Report, material for. 8
Two bulls (Ponca), reference.......... 50
"Two Old Men, The." *See* Old Men.
Typha, medicinal use.......... 584

U'ho^{n}to^{n}ga, Omaha warrior.......... 100
U'ho^{n}to^{n}ga t'ethaitho^n, location.......... 100
United States Indian Office. *See* Office of Indian Affairs.
Uno^n'baha, keeper of Pack (Ponca).......... 439
Uzhi^n'eti, symbolic figure—
description.......... 234, 241–242, 254
reference.......... 601
U'zhu—
explanation of term.......... 208
officer in Shell society.......... 516, 522–523, 537–538, 559

Vaughan, Dr. T. Wayland, work of.......... 10–11
Verdigris river, references.......... 57, 92
Victory dance, description.......... 432
Victory song, example.......... 432–433
Village creek, reference.......... 86
Village-maker, Omaha chief.......... 100, 171–172
"Village of the 'Make-Believe' White Men," reference.......... 633–634
Villages—
general description.......... 95–99
historic.......... 99–101
identification of sites.......... 72–73
location.......... 629–630
reference.......... 623
situated on Missouri.......... 85–89
term for "village".......... 135–136
Village sites (Arikara).......... 75
Visions—
connected with societies.......... 459, 489–490, 565
representation of.......... 353
significance.......... 130–133, 486, 487, 488, 591
Vocabularies.......... 103–112, 113

Wa'baçka—
story of.......... 211, 406–408
War Pack of.......... 434
Waba'ho^n, meaning of term.......... 206
Waça'be—
gens (Osage).......... 47
gens (Ponca).......... 41, 42, 47, 48, 52–53
See also names of subgentes.
Waça'be itazhi, subdivision (Tha'tada)—
account.......... 141, 160, 161, 162–164, 486–487
rites.......... 142–143, 159
Waça'bezhi^{n}ga, story of.......... 50
Wae'gaxtho^n. *See* Buffalo hunt, annual.
Waha'xi, story of.......... 495, 496
Wai^n'. *See* Robe.
Wai^n'waxube, account of.......... 213, 404–405
See also Packs of War, Sacred.
Waje'pa, acknowledgment to.......... 631
See also Wa'thisnade.

WAKI'DEZHIⁿGA— Page
information from 567
ritual used by 571

WAKOⁿ'DA—
assurance as to buffalo 286, 295, 296
food offerings to 335–336
general account 597–599
in Hethu'shka 465, 466
in origin of Noⁿ'zhiⁿzhoⁿ rite 128–129
in Pebble Society ritual 570, 571
in Ponca legend 49
Omaha conception of 128–129, 130, 133, 134, 589
prayer to, on annual buffalo hunt 281
references 143, 160, 208, 209, 212, 239, 240, 241, 278, 415, 445, 486, 560–561, 582, 608, 634–635

WAKOⁿ'MOⁿTHIⁿ—
account of 283–284
songs obtained from 249–250

WAKOⁿ'TA INIKASHIHA, group (Quapaw) 68
WALTHER, HENRY, work of 12
WALTHILL, account of 624–625, 642
WANOⁿ'ÇE, meaning of term 271
WANOⁿ'KUGE, Omaha warrior 101
WANOⁿ'KUGE SHKONTHA I THOⁿ, battle at 101
WANOⁿ'SHE. *See* "Soldiers."
WANOⁿ'XE, significance of term 597
WANOⁿ'XE ITHAETHE SOCIETY, description 489–490
WAR BONNET, description 359, 446–448

WARFARE—
aggressive—
as a relief from grief 594
authorization of war party 405–408
departure of war party 415–421
organization of war party 408–409
return of war party 431–434
significance 211, 402–403
waiⁿ'waxube 404–405
authorization 142, 200
clouded sky emblematic of war 392
contents of Tent of War 452–458
defensive—
authority for 415
departure of war party 426–431
in tribal estimation 211, 431
return of war party 432
significance 402
under We'zhiⁿshte gens 423, 454
dispatch of scouts 423–426
dress of warriors 409–411
elk rites associated with (Osage) 194
ethics 602–603
influence on tribal development 402–403
method of fighting 427, 441
Ponca war honors ceremony 439–441
relation to marriage 325
Sacred War Packs 411–415
secondary to peace 211
war ritual (lost) 424
Wate'giçtu 434–448
weapons 448–452
we'toⁿ waaⁿ 421–423
See also Tent of War; Thunder; War honors; Wars.

WAR HONOR PACKS, property of Thi'xida gens (Ponca) 43

WAR HONORS— Page
awarded at Wate'giçtu ceremony 431
conferring ceremony (Ponca) 43, 439–441
counting 447–448
decorations 255, 358, 446–448
in He'dewachi society 252
in He'thushka society 461
in Wa'waⁿ ceremony 398, 399–400
reference 351
See also Wate'giçtu, Wathiⁿ'ethe.

WARRIOR, position of, in tribe 122–123

WARS (OMAHA)—
intratribal 99
with Cheyenne and Oto 87
with Oglala 100, 101
with Pawnee 87, 88
with Ponca 87
with Santee and Yankton 100
with Sioux 100, 623
with unknown tribe 99

WA'SA INIKASHIHA, group (Quapaw) 68
WASHA'BE, meaning of term 154–155

WASHA'BE, gens (Ponca)—
account of 45
references 41, 42, 48, 55, 439

WASHA'BE (STAFF)—
care of 278
description 204–205, 275, 276
on annual buffalo hunt 280, 281, 282
references 206, 304

WASHA'BE, subgens (Hoⁿ'ga)—
in annual buffalo hunt 277, 279, 283
in charge of Sacred Tent 155
washa'be (staff) made by 276

WASHA'BETOⁿ, subgens (Hoⁿ'ga), account of. 154–155, 158–159, 205, 283
See also Hoⁿ'gaxti division.

WASHE'TOⁿ, subgens (Iⁿshta'çuⁿda)—
account of 186–187, 190–194
ceremony in charge of 115
connection with Turning the Child 118
position in hu'thuga 122
reference 39

WASHINGTON, D. C.—
reference 136
treaty of (1854) 623, 626–627, 633
treaty of (1865) 623–624

WASHIⁿ'HA, acknowledgment to 58
WASHIS'KA ATHIⁿ. *See* Shell society.

WATE'GIÇTU CEREMONY—
general description 434–437
in charge of We'zhiⁿshte gens 142
Ponca war honors ceremony 439–441
reference 43
"The Crow" 441–446
war honor decorations 438–439

WATHA'WA, description 497–500
WATHE'XE, application of term 219, 458, 494
WATHI'GIZHE SUBGENS, account of. 148–149, 151–153

WATHIⁿ'ETHE—
count of, in Hoⁿ'hewachi 498–499
description 202–206, 212, 213, 495–497
in connection with Wa'waⁿ party 378
reference 208

WA'THISHNADE—
acknowledgment to 631
remarks of 637

Page
WATHI'TOⁿ, subdivision (Hoⁿ'ga), account of 154, 157–158
WATHOⁿ', office of 147, 149, 275–283
WATOⁿ'THE, meaning of term 342
WAU'WAAⁿ, description 320–323
WA'WAⁿ CEREMONY—
adopted from Arikara 112
among Ponca 400–401
beginning among Omaha 376
character of songs 382, 386–388, 390–395, 400
classed with We'waçpe 597
description 376–400
distribution 74–75
Omaha and Pawnee versions compared 377, 379–381, 400
party in charge of 378
pipes 47, 162, 375, 376–378, 380
references 43, 211, 363, 496
with another tribe 381–400
WAXTHE'XETOⁿ, meaning of term 221
WAXTHE'XETOⁿ, subgens (Hoⁿ'ga)—
account of 154, 156–158
connection with Sacred Pole 205, 221, 230, 273
WAXTHE'XE XIGITHE ceremony—
meaning of term 230
reference 219
WAZHA'ZHE, as a name 38, 40
WAZHA'ZHE—
gens (Kansa) 67
gens (Ponca) 41, 42, 45–46, 47, 49, 56, 309
kinship group (Osage) 58, 59, 62, 63
See also names of subgentes.
WAZHA'ZHE (TRIBE). *See* Osage.
WAZHA'ZHEWADAIⁿGA, acknowledgment to 58
WAZHIⁿ'AGTHE, a form of punishment 216, 497, 583–584, 602
WAZHIⁿ'GA, story of 477, 478
WAZHIⁿ'GA INIKASHIHA, group (Quapaw) 68
WAZHIⁿ'GA INIKASHIKITHE, gens (Kansa) 67
WAZHIⁿ'GA ITAZHI, subgens (Tha'tada)—
account of 159, 160–161, 164–165
reference 161, 365
WAZHIⁿ'THETHE, help through will power 497, 583–584, 602
WEAPONS—
description 448–452
introduction of guns 617
manufacture 338
Padouca 79
property in 363
See also Arrows, Bows, etc.
WEATHER SIGNS, examples 112
WEAVING, description 347–348
WE'BASHNA, account of 122–128
WE'GAÇAPI, account of 50, 439
WE'KU feast, account of 496
WESTERN SUPERINTENDENT of Indian Tribes, reference 622–623
WE'TOⁿ WAAⁿ—
description 421–423
reference 583
WE'WAÇPE RITES, account of 596–597, 602, 607
WE'ZHIⁿSHTE GENS—
funeral customs 144, 358, 589
general account 142–145
in charge of Cedar Pole 457
WE'ZHIⁿSHTE GENS—Continued. Page
in charge of war rites 122, 196, 200–201, 423, 454
in He'dewachi 258
part in dispatch of scouts 425
part in establishing Nini'batoⁿ divisions 201
personal names 145–146
position in hu'thuga 122, 141
recapitulation 194
references 42, 160
tabu 194
WHEAT—
cultivation 635
introduction 620
reference 633
WHISTLE, description 371, 377
WHITE BUFFALO HIDE, SACRED—
account of 283–286
associated with Sacred Pole 229
gifts to 205
keeper 208
on annual buffalo hunt 278, 280, 281, 283
references 155, 160, 262, 509
rites 596
ritual 232, 249, 286–309
tent 154, 194–195, 282, 283, 284–286
WHITE EAGLE (Ponca)—
account of 49–50
narrative by 49, 216
WHITE RIVER, S. DAK., reference 85
WHITES, THE—
contact with 81–82, 114, 611–612
influence 29–30, 519, 620–622
work of missionaries 625–629
See also names of nationalities (English, French, etc.); Traders.
WICHITA, Omaha name for 102
WILD ROSE, medicinal use 584
WIND PEOPLE. *See* Kansa.
WIND SUBGENS. *See* Tade'ata.
WINDS—
life-giving power of 45, 198, 578, 587
in ceremony of Turning the Child 117, 119–121
in Osage legend 63
reference 199
rites connected with 66, 169
WINNEBAGO—
augury by 415
name applied to English by 611
Omaha name for 102
references 78, 581
reservation for 623–624, 625
WISSLER, DR. CLARK, permit requested by 11
WITCHCRAFT, absent from Omaha 583, 602
WOLF—
as helper of man (Omaha, Ponca) 445–446
in war honor decorations 441, 442
special connection with man 512
symbolism of 171
WOLFSKIN, in Sacred War Pack 413–415
WOLF SONGS, in war parties 410–411
WOMAN'S SONGS, description 320–323
WOMEN—
amusements 366–367, 369–370
animals specially connected with 512
as u'zhus in Shell society 516
bearers of "mark of honor" 325, 327, 509
clothing 355–356, 360, 519, 616

WOMEN—Continued. Page
friendship among ... 318
hair dressing ... 352
Hethu'shka protectors of ... 474
in buffalo hunt ... 274, 277
in He'dewachi ceremony ... 252, 253, 254, 259, 502, 507
in Sacred Pole ceremony ... 241–243, 247
in war ... 403, 409, 411, 426, 603
membership in societies ... 459
moral standard ... 323
names ... 145, 200
Nonzhinzhon rite optional with ... 129
occupations ... 203–204, 326, 339–340, 353, 615
care and training of children ... 327–333
cooking and foods ... 340–342
preparing skins ... 342–345
quillwork ... 345–347
weaving ... 347–348
work on dwellings ... 96, 97, 98
position in tribe ... 313–314, 326–327, 337
prayers ... 599
presence injurious to wounded ... 582
property rights ... 362–363
singing ... 374
sitting posture ... 329
songs ... 320–323, 421

WOODPECKER— Page
in Ponca legend ... 47
used on tribal pipes ... 135, 207
WOODWORKING, methods of ... 338–339
WORD LISTS. See Vocabularies.
WOUNDS, treatment of ... 487, 582

XITHA'GAXE, remarks of ... 637
XTHEXE', meaning of term ... 219, 494
XU'BE, group of Mon'thinkagaxe gens. 172, 173–174
XU'DE. See Ni'kagahi xu'de.
XU'KA, subdivision (Tha'tada)—
account of ... 160, 163–164
in anointing Sacred Pole ... 231–232

YAKIMA INDIANS, researches among ... 9
YANKTON—
fights with Omaha ... 100, 480
Omaha name for ... 102
party to treaties ... 622, 623
Ponca name for ... 103
YUCHI INDIANS, researches among ... 9

ZHINGA'GAHIGE (Ponca)—
group under ... 178, 181
references ... 50, 409
ZUÑI INDIANS, monograph on ... 7

O

Lightning Source UK Ltd.
Milton Keynes UK
UKHW042105021218
333359UK00001B/135/P